CONTEMPORARY LEADERSHIP *and* INTERCULTURAL COMPETENCE

To my mother, Phyllis Moodian, and my father, Armand Moodian.
Thank you for your love and support.

To Margaret Minnis.
Thank you for your inspiration and encouragement.

CONTEMPORARY LEADERSHIP *and* INTERCULTURAL COMPETENCE

Exploring the Cross-Cultural Dynamics Within Organizations

Michael A. Moodian
Chapman University
EDITOR

Los Angeles • London • New Delhi • Singapore • Washington DC

For information:

SAGE Publications, Inc.
2455 Teller Road
Thousand Oaks, California 91320
E-mail: order@sagepub.com

SAGE Publications India Pvt. Ltd.
B 1/I 1 Mohan Cooperative
  Industrial Area
Mathura Road, New Delhi 110 044
India

SAGE Publications Ltd.
1 Oliver's Yard
55 City Road
London EC1Y 1SP
United Kingdom

SAGE Publications Asia-Pacific
  Pte. Ltd.
33 Pekin Street #02-01
Far East Square
Singapore 048763

Printed in the United States of America

Library of Congress Cataloging-in-Publication Data

Contemporary leadership and intercultural competence: exploring the cross-cultural dynamics within organizations/editor, Michael A. Moodian.
    p. cm.
Includes bibliographical references and index.
ISBN 978-1-4129-5452-5 (cloth)
ISBN 978-1-4129-5453-2 (pbk.)

   1. Leadership—Cross-cultural studies. 2. Organizational behavior—Cross-cultural studies. 3. Intercultural communication. I. Moodian, Michael A.

HD57.7.C6665 2009
658.4′092—dc22   2008022450

This book is printed on acid-free paper.

15 16 17 18 19 20   9 8 7 6 5

Acquisitions Editor:	Al Bruckner
Editorial Assistant:	MaryAnn Vail
Production Editor:	Laureen A. Gleason
Copy Editor:	Tony Moore
Typesetter:	C&M Digitals (P) Ltd.
Proofreader:	Marleis Roberts
Indexer:	Diggs Publication Services
Cover Designer:	Candice Harman
Marketing Manager:	Jennifer Reed Banando

CONTENTS

ACKNOWLEDGMENTS

"Happiness lies in the joy of achievement and the thrill of creative effort."

—Franklin D. Roosevelt

This book would not have been possible without the assistance of Dr. Charles Fischer. Thank you, Chuck, for your mentorship throughout this process. I am fortunate to have you as a friend.

It is an honor to work with a brilliant group of contributing authors. Thank you to the incredible scholars whose chapters are featured in the pages that follow. Special thanks to Al Bruckner, MaryAnn Vail, Laureen Shea, Diane Foster, Tony Moore, and the entire staff of Sage Publications.

Thank you to the faculty and staff of the organizational leadership doctoral program at Pepperdine University, led by Dr. June Schmieder-Ramirez, associate dean, and Dr. Farzin Madjidi, program director. At California State University, Fullerton, thank you to Dr. Anthony Fellow of the Department of Communications and Dr. Myron Orleans and Dr. Michael Perez of the Department of Sociology.

Special thanks to my family, including my aunt, Loretta Leilani Miyashiro; my uncles, James Miyashiro (in loving memory, 1939–2007) and Daniel Ladeira; my brother, Stephen Keith Carvalho; my cousins, Michele Compton and James Miyashiro; my nieces and nephew, Kasie, Kepano, Stephenie, and Kaili Carvalho; Nicole Miyashiro; and all of the members of my family throughout the world. I would also like to thank my close friends and extended family for their support over the years—notably, the Beckman family, the Almeida family, and Teresa Shapley.

Finally, thank you to the fellow faculty, students, and staff members at the Irvine campus of Chapman University.

—Dr. Michael A. Moodian
Rancho Santa Margarita, CA, USA

INTRODUCTORY COMMENTARY

Valuing the Diversity of a Nation

◆ Michael S. Dukakis

In this day and age, leadership, particularly in the public sector, must include both a deep respect for and a real understanding of the extraordinary and growing range of cultures and backgrounds that increasingly confront an American politician or policymaker.

For those of us who are first- or second-generation Americans, that respect and understanding should come naturally. After all, we or our parents came here as immigrants. We often found ourselves facing hostile or indifferent receptions from people who had been here for many generations. One would assume that we would have an almost instinctive understanding of the importance of diversity and a sense of how one genuinely involves people and institutions from across the ethnic and racial spectrum in what we do. Unfortunately, that is not always the case. In fact, some of the worst racial and ethnic prejudice in the United States often comes from people whose families arrived here not that long ago. We made it, but we often have difficulty getting used to the fact that we must learn to live with the newest generation of immigrants, who often have skin darker than ours and speak languages we don't understand.

I was reminded of that a few years ago when Kitty and I had breakfast with two professionally successful Greek Americans who were complaining about the waves of Mexican immigrants that were arriving in Southern California. I had to point out to them that our parents had faced similarly hostile feelings as they brought a different culture and the Eastern Orthodox religion to America, and that if anyone should understand the hopes, aspirations, and fears of newly arrived Mexicans, it was us!

For a political leader that means not only understanding and respecting the kind of diversity that is today's America but genuinely involving ethnic and racial leaders and constituencies in what one does, particularly if it affects them directly. It means reaching out and recruiting staff members who represent a variety of races and ethnic backgrounds and working hard to make sure one understands them and appreciates the contributions they can make to their adopted country and to the developing of policies that benefit everybody, including newly arrived Americans.

These new Americans have much to offer. They come here with energy and hope. They have high aspirations for their children. They work hard, often at two or three jobs. They have often left totalitarian societies because they want the freedom and opportunity that democracy offers them, and they want to be full partners in our great American experiment.

Any American political leader worth his or her salt should take them seriously. If one can speak a few words or more of their language, so much the better. It is another reflection of the respect in which you hold them.

I was lucky. I had a scholarship to study one semester in Peru, and since the Greek and Spanish accents are identical, the fact that I had been brought up bilingual in Greek and English made learning decent Spanish a lot easier for me. But I also had the chance to study Korean when I was in the army there in the mid-1950s; to study a good deal of French in both high school and college, which my Haitian constituents could understand; and since Greeks and Italians can't talk without using their hands, I could do a pretty good imitation of an almost-Italian when I arrived at the Sons of Italy with my standard greeting: "*Oggi, siamo tutti figli d'Italia.*" ("Today we are all sons of Italy.")

But it wasn't just an act. I loved the opportunity it gave me to connect with a lot of people who had shared the same experience my parents had had in coming to this country as immigrants and living the American Dream.

So my advice to aspiring political leaders in this country, no matter what their background, is not only to understand their immigrant experience but to appreciate the extraordinary richness it has given to America. And by all means reach out to these communities of new Americans and make them part of what you do.

It will pay dividends—both personally and politically.

PART I

INTRODUCTION

1

JOURNEYS THROUGH THE ECOLOGICAL NICHE

An Introduction to and
Overview of the Textbook

◆ Michael A. Moodian

In the 21st century, leadership success may be unattainable without intercultural competence. Concurrently, in today's global environment, contemporary leaders must display a keen ability to interact effectively with individuals of different cultures. This book specifically focuses on two principal aspects of leadership and cross-cultural competence. First, the text will focus on the understanding of the role of cultural diversity and intercultural issues in the modern workplace. Second, the text will build on this understanding to demonstrate how cultural diversity can be used as a tool to build successful organizations. Too often it seems as if issues of diversity are viewed as a liability within organizations. However, as stated so eloquently in the introductory commentary, an ability to embrace and adapt to diversity is one that will pay dividends for the leaders of today.

In recent times, there have been tremendous advancements in both societal and managerial responses to cultural diversity. For example, in *Managing Diversity*, Gardenswartz and Rowe (1998) explain that affirmative action alone is not an adequate management philosophy. Instead, there is now a three-part approach that includes affirmative action, the valuing of differences, and the managing of diversity. In *Basic Concepts of Intercultural Communication*, Bennett (1998) counters the Golden Rule of treating another as one would want to be treated with the intercultural philosophy in which differences are not minimized and one who is truly interculturally competent is able to practice mutual adaptation and integration within various cultural settings.

To apply this to organizational studies, take an example such as the process of employee engagement. Perhaps the most critical element of the success of a high-performing organization is the level of engagement among the organization's employees. It goes without saying that a leadership commitment to empowerment and an embracing of concepts such as equifinality will result in an increase in individual motivation on a micro level and an engaged workforce on a macro level, ultimately positively affecting bottom-line results (Tubbs, 2006). Those organizations that are highly political and ridden with fear and distrust will ultimately receive apathetic conformity among the employee base, similar to what Freire (1970/2003) refers to in *Pedagogy of the Oppressed* as the result of the "banking concept of education." An oppressive environment results in a lack of passion and accountability for the purpose and vision of the organization.

However, there is one particular area of emphasis that is growing rapidly in its importance—an organization's response to a culturally diverse employee base. Today only 10% of the countries in the world are racially or ethnically homogeneous (Harris, Moran, & Moran, 2004). This means that in an increasingly global environment, the cross-cultural dynamics of an organization can no longer be approached as a liability. Ultimately, to create a high-performing organization with an engaged employee force, a total commitment to diversity and inclusion must be prevalent throughout all levels—from senior management to hourly labor.

This contrasts with the historical response to issues of diversity, which has focused on assimilating individuals into the ideological philosophy of the majority. This response transitioned to a structural/system imbalance approach in the 1980s, in which diversity was stressed, but at a superficial level. Today we realize that the optimal management of a diverse workforce is achieved through an intercultural approach or through one of mutual adaptation between leadership and employees (Hammer, 2002). Employee engagement may be unattainable without a focus among leadership on incorporating cross-cultural competence training.

How much is lost in major organizations owing to a lack of cross-cultural competence among leaders? In the United States, for example, concepts such as "thinking outside of the box" and risk taking are valued and considered vital to success (Hofstede, 1980). However, maintaining an ethnocentric leadership philosophy among a diverse workforce will offer negative consequences when trying to engage employees and will ultimately downgrade the performance of the organization. If leadership is a primary effect on behavioral engagement, a complete commitment to diversity and continued training related to intercultural competence development will play a vital role in engaging employees and aligning them toward the organization's goals.

In many chapters, this book will utilize specific definitions for the concepts of leadership and intercultural competence. Northouse (2004) defines leadership as "a process whereby an individual influences a group of individuals to achieve a common goal" (p. 3). Meanwhile, Bennett and Bennett (2004) define intercultural competence as "the ability to communicate effectively in cross-cultural situations and to relate appropriately in a variety of cultural contexts" (p. 149). Developing intercultural competence is not something that can easily be accomplished simply through exposure to an international assignment (Moodian, 2007); there are various factors that must be implemented for this to occur. The point at which the two concepts intersect is the focus of this book.

◆ *Evolution of the Textbook*

The idea for this text was first spawned after I participated in the Intercultural Development Inventory workshop (presented by the Intercultural Communication Institute) in Portland, Oregon, in 2005. Originally, the vision of the text was one in which there would be a compilation of chapters that related specifically to instruments used in intercultural training (an expansion of Paige's [2004] chapter in the *Handbook of Intercultural Training*). However, after further conceptualization, it was determined that the instrumentation component was one piece of a much larger puzzle. Thus, the instrument chapters evolved into Part IV: Measuring Intercultural Competence. Parts on understanding cultural diversity's evolving role and applying cultural comprehension to organizations were added to provide an all-encompassing overview of topics.

PHILOSOPHY, APPROACH, AND USE

Many chapters are presented from the view of an organizational leader in the United States; however, the goal of this text is not to be centered on an American perspective only. There are components of multiple chapters that focus on effective leadership from a global perspective. The principal approach of the book is to blend theory with practical applications. The intended audience includes graduate-level MBA, international business, human resource management, organizational behavior, educational leadership, public administration, and organizational leadership students, as well as senior corporate managers, human resource practitioners, and government leaders.

The textbook is organized into five separate parts—Part I contains the introductory chapters, Part II focuses on understanding the evolving role of cultural diversity in the workplace, and Part III focuses on applying cultural comprehension to organizations. The focus of the book will shift in Part IV, where various chapters that detail specific tools to measure intercultural competence are presented. Part V contains the final chapter and a concluding commentary.

CLOSING THOUGHTS

In a world embedded in ethnocentrism and androcentricity, this book is intended to contribute to the growing body of literature related to the understanding and development of intercultural competence. The growing importance of fostering such competence within the world's leaders is vital at a micro level and will help advance the leadership process at a macro level for many years to come. A noted philosopher once said, "Three things make the superman [or superwoman] and they are the greatest gifts of divine generosity: a fertile mind, a deep understanding, and a cultivated taste" (Gracian, 1637/1993, p. 173). The theories, insights, and philosophies of the accomplished contributors to this text are intended to help nurture such a fertile mind, promoting this deep understanding and cultivated taste among both emerging and experienced leaders.

◆ References

Bennett, J. M., & Bennett, M. J. (2004). Developing intercultural sensitivity: An integrative approach to global and domestic diversity. In D. Landis, J. M. Bennett, & M. J. Bennett (Eds.), *Handbook of intercultural training* (3rd ed., pp. 147–165). Thousand Oaks, CA: Sage.

Bennett, M. J. (1998). Overcoming the Golden Rule: Sympathy and empathy. In M. J. Bennett (Ed.), *Basic concepts of intercultural communication: Selected readings* (pp. 191–214). Yarmouth, ME: Intercultural Press.

Freire, P. (2003). *Pedagogy of the oppressed.* New York: Continuum. (Original work published in 1970)

Gardenswartz, L., & Rowe, A. (1998). *Managing diversity: A complete desk reference and planning guide* (Rev. ed.). New York: McGraw-Hill.

Gracian, B. (1993). *The art of worldly wisdom: A collection of aphorisms from the works of Baltasar Gracian* (M. Fischer, Trans.). New York: Barnes & Noble. (Original work published in 1637)

Hammer, M. R. (2002). *The Intercultural Conflict Style Inventory: Increasing competence across the cultural divide.* Ocean Pines, MD: Hammer Consulting.

Harris, P. R., Moran, R. T., & Moran, S. V. (2004). *Managing cultural differences: Global leadership for the twenty-first century* (6th ed.). Oxford, UK: Elsevier-Butterworth-Heinemann.

Hofstede, G. (1980). *Culture's consequences: International differences in work-related values.* Newbury Park, CA: Sage.

Moodian, M. A. (2007). *An analysis of intercultural competence levels of organizational leadership doctoral students.* Unpublished doctoral dissertation, Pepperdine University, Malibu, CA.

Northouse, P. (2004). *Leadership theory and practice* (3rd ed.). Thousand Oaks, CA: Sage.

Paige, R. M. (2004). Instrumentation in intercultural training. In D. Landis, J. M. Bennett, & M. J. Bennett (Eds.), *Handbook of intercultural training* (3rd ed., pp. 85–128). Thousand Oaks, CA: Sage.

Tubbs, S. L. (2006). *A systems approach to small group interaction.* Boston: McGraw Hill.

UNDERSTANDING THE BASICS OF CULTURE

◆ Dharm P. S. Bhawuk, Dan Landis, and Vijayan P. Munusamy

Learning about cultural differences is important for international managers, because behavioral mistakes and misattribution can lead to dysfunctional relationships and can be a cause of poor organizational performance. There are many definitions of culture, and our goal here is to present some ideas that business practitioners may find useful when thinking about culture. We present seven perspectives that may help practitioners deal with cultural differences effectively.

1. Culture often entails a knee-jerk response to behavioral settings.

A teacher walks into a class in South Asia (India, Bangladesh, Pakistan, Nepal, Sri Lanka), and students stand up. This is unlikely in Western societies. The behavior of South Asian students is automatic, and the meaning—that students are showing respect to the teacher—is to be deciphered in further thinking about why this behavior occurred. Another example that Westerners often find amusing is the spontaneous behavior in Eastern cultures of one taking the full responsibility of paying the lunch or dinner bill. The meaning here is that Easterners nurture relationships and view them as long term where reciprocity is founded in unequal exchange. In short, we may not find the same behavior in every culture, given the same behavioral setting. Thus, culture shapes human behavior. Behaviors are the visible part of cultural practices, and the reasons behind behaviors, which constitute the underlying values and belief systems, are the invisible part of cultures. What people do in a culture can be observed; why they do it needs to be learned by further reflection and often asking questions of people of that culture. Behaviors often offer concrete instances of cultural differences that can be observed and studied, and it is a good place to start the examination of culture.

Generally, people act in a certain way or perform a task in a certain way in a culture because it is often efficient to do so. Cultural practices are backed up by years of experience in a given ecology. The type of clothes people wear (cotton versus wool), the food people eat (often directed by what is grown in a certain area), the way houses are constructed (facing south in cold climates, having steep roofs in areas where there is snowfall, etc.), and so forth are guided by environmental conditions and are inherently efficient for the most part. Cultural practices are effective in solving environmental problems and thus help reduce anxiety. Simply put, cultural practices capture years of experience of what works. Thus, people find behaviors that are different as odd and surprising and often disapprove of such behaviors, leading to cross-cultural misunderstanding and conflicts. What works leads people to believe that their way is the best way, and thus all cultures socialize people to become ethnocentric. Accepting that we are ethnocentric makes it easy to learn new behaviors when we visit another culture. The emotional attachment to one's own cultural behavior can be attenuated by accepting that all cultures are workable systems in their own ecosystem.

2. Culture constitutes a distribution of behaviors.

The mean of any behavior can be viewed as the cultural norm (Triandis, 1994), and cultural differences can be examined by comparing the means (see Figure 2.1). Thus, in one culture the mean of a particular behavior—say, starting a meeting, when men or women get married, when adult children leave their parents' home to start their own home, and so forth—may be higher than what is found in another culture. Not only the mean, but the variance for a particular behavior could also be different across cultures. In some cultures, a particular behavior may have a small dispersion compared to another culture. For example, in some culture most young men may get married around the age of 24 (say 60%), whereas in another culture there may be much more dispersion in when young men get married (say only 20% get married around the mean age of 35). When there is a little dispersion, the culture is called tight, but when there is a lot of dispersion, the culture is said to be loose.

Viewing cultures as having a distribution of behaviors allows us to accommodate for individual differences. For example, even in a country where most people are late, there are a few people who are meticulously punctual, and an international manager would do well by starting with the norm of a culture but then refine his or her understanding by incorporating individual differences in behaviors. It should be noted that it is plausible that a behavior has a skewed distribution in a culture, as also it is possible that a

Figure 2.1   Culture as a Distribution of Behaviors

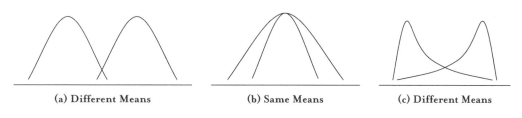

| (a) Different Means | (b) Same Means | (c) Different Means |

behavior has right skew in one culture and left skew in another culture. Interestingly, even in such a situation, it is possible to find some people in either culture who act the same way, allowing for both finding individual differences in behavior within a culture and finding similarity among some people between cultures. This, however, does not minimize the fact that the cultures are quite different in the distribution of such a behavior.

3. Culture is the antecedent to all human behaviors.

Building on the culture and social behavior model presented by Triandis (1994), Bhawuk (2003) presented a general model of creative behavior that can be easily adapted to a general model of culture and behavior (see Figure 2.2). According to this model, culture is shaped by ecology and history. For example, the geographic vastness of the United States (an ecological factor) has led to the development of freeways and the auto industry, with little emphasis on public transportation. The mountainous nature of many countries (e.g., Nepal) has led them to develop air transportation to connect the remote areas since building highways is simply not possible. In the Netherlands, people have developed a complex system of canals to take advantage of their ecology, as the country is below sea level.

Similarly, history shapes culture. For example, people developed a culture of the melting pot in the first half of the 20th century in the United States. This made sense because the immigrants were Europeans who could all become alike by simply accepting English as the means of communication. However, with the immigration of Hispanics, Chinese, Japanese, and others, the melting pot model did not work as well, and the nation has slowly moved away from the melting pot model to include the growing diversity of people. It is plausible to think of the U.S. government adopting a policy of more than one national language in the future like many other countries, which would change the national culture significantly. History of colonization similarly shapes the culture of many countries in Asia and Africa, traces of which can be found in their art, music, literature, food, way of life, and thinking. Thus, ecology and history shape culture, which in turn shapes how people behave in that culture.

Clearly, culture is important in determining behavior, but it also interacts with the zeitgeist (or spirit of a particular time) and leadership to shape people's behaviors. The ecologically and historically shaped culture is often the powerful traditional culture, hidden deep in the heart and mind of culture. However, the zeitgeist is an equally important part of culture, and it has a reciprocal relationship with the traditional

Figure 2.2   A General Model of Culture and Human Behavior

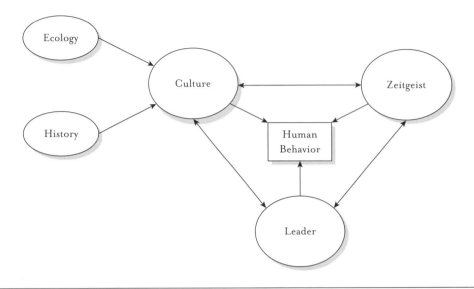

culture. With economic development, we see growth of urbanization in most parts of the world. Urban culture would constitute a part of the zeitgeist of these cultures. The cultural differences between cities in different countries speak for the interaction between the zeitgeist and the traditional culture. For example, in many cultures people stop at a stop light even at midnight when nobody is on the street, whereas in some cultures people do not do so even during the day if there is no traffic coming from the other direction.

How leaders act in a culture is quite compatible with the culture, and at the same time leaders also create new cultures to bring about change in society. The leadership in Singapore has created a culture of meritocracy and strict discipline, which stands in stark contrast to the culture of its neighboring countries, emphasizing the role of leadership in shaping culture. Gandhi started the culture of *Satyagraha*, or civil disobedience, which did not exist before him and has become a standard tool for protesting by unions and students in

South Asia and many other parts of the world. Thus, leaders go on to shape the zeitgeist and culture in the long term in a significant way. Therefore, it makes intuitive sense that whereas ecology and history serve as the antecedents of culture, culture, zeitgeist, and leaders have reciprocal relationships in shaping human behaviors.

This is particularly important for business managers to keep in mind, because they often have to deal with organizational culture and need to differentiate organizational culture from national culture. Organizations are shaped by the national environment and by the imperatives of the industries in which they operate. For example, when organizations face international competition, they develop procedures, tools, and routines that are different from organizations that do not face international pressure. Organizations that face a turbulent environment are likely to be effective if they are less bureaucratic and allow people who interact with customers to make decisions as needed, whereas organizations that operate in a stable environment can often afford to be guided by rigid policies. Airlines are likely to be similar in their operation across cultures—in loading cargo, handling passengers, scheduling planes, planning routes, and so forth. However, their human resource practices are often shaped by the national culture of the country in which they are incorporated. Superior–subordinate relationships, leadership practices, hiring practices, and so forth are likely to be influenced by national cultures and laws. Thus, leadership in a particular culture may have commonality across different industries but may be different from leadership practices in other cultures.

It is often useful to think about organizational culture as a microculture, or a third culture, especially when multinationals operate beyond their own cultural boundaries. An example of how microculture operates in real business environment is illustrated in the following example. Federal Express (FedEx) pursued a strategy of global expansion in the 1980s when the U.S. market did not offer the annual growth that the organization desired. As FedEx is in the business of delivering packages to different parts of the world on time, they are meticulous about pickup and delivery times. In the United States, their standard package pickup deadline in most locations is 5 p.m. However, their standard package pickup deadline times did not go over well in countries that do not follow an 8–5 work schedule. In Spain, for example, most businesses close at 8 p.m. As a result, simply following their U.S. schedule led Federal Express to incur heavy financial losses. The lesson here is that culturally blind business strategies and imposing a microculture that is different from the macro culture (e.g. imposing work processes that are successful in the American culture on other cultures) can result in serious business consequences (Herbig, 1997).

In other instances, a multinational may create a hybrid culture that takes elements from more than one culture and is then viewed as a third culture. For example, a company may not fuss about people arriving at a certain time in the morning but may not tolerate late delivery of goods and services to customers, thus synthesizing two opposite values in different behavioral settings, rather than having one value for all behavioral settings. This would be an example of creating a third culture.

4. Culture provides complex cognitive and affective frameworks that are used to support the behavioral system.

As noted above, behaviors are visible, but the cognitive and affective systems are not transparent (see Figure 2.3). So when an American manager moves from Los Angeles to Hong Kong, though the person is far removed from his or her native culture, this native culture is right there in the head of the person. If the person has a meeting at 9 a.m., he or she will show up at the venue at that time even though the local managers may come 15 or more minutes late. Can the American manager simply switch to the new practice of coming late to meetings? That is unlikely because the person is hard-wired with certain meetings protocols—arrive a few minutes before time, greet everybody, present an agenda, go through each of the items on the agenda, and finish the meeting on time. The script of the meeting is a part of the larger cognitive framework that is present in the manager's mind (biologically housed in the brain!).

In some cultures, people pay special attention to their relationship with others, and we call these collectivist cultures. In other cultures, people pay attention to themselves without paying much attention to others, and we call these individualistic cultures. In individualistic cultures, people employ rational cost–benefit analysis and the principle of equal exchange in their social interactions, whereas in collectivist cultures, social interactions are marked by unequal exchange over a long period. In individualistic cultures, people do their own thing and their behavior is guided by attitudes, values, and beliefs. On the other hand, in collectivist cultures people pursue group goals and follow norms. In collectivist cultures people pay much attention to context, but this is not so in individualist cultures. For this reason, collectivist cultures are also referred to as high-context cultures. On the other hand, individualist cultures are referred to as low-context cultures (Hall, 1976). Thus, we can examine and understand the difference in the cognitive schema of people in different cultures by using the theory of individualism and collectivism (Triandis, 1995; Bhawuk, 2001) or other such theoretical constructs.

Similarly, cultures provide us with affective frameworks. We know when to get happy, sad, upset, or angry and how to express our emotion. In some cultures, it is acceptable to express one's anger publicly, but not so in other cultures. Similarly, in some cultures, it is acceptable to show affection in public, but not so in other cultures. Thus, in different cultures people are socialized to carry different cognitive and affective frameworks. To be effective across cultures we have to learn different frameworks and be comfortable in applying them when we are in another culture. Like all behavioral skills, such skills come through hard work and practice.

4 major characteristics of culture

Text 5. Culture is characterized by
Essay people, space, time, and language.
1. →7

At the core of any culture lies a group of people, a populace. Culture deals with people in an ecological context, or people living in a geographical area or space (see Figure 2.4). The space or geography defines the people and their behavior because people have to interact with the environment for sustenance and survival. When people occupy some space or live in a geographic area for a long time, they develop ways of dealing with the environment, and they pass it on to their

Figure 2.3   Culture as a System of Cognition, Affect, and Behaviors

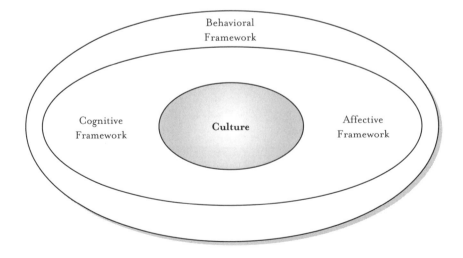

children, generation after generation. Such knowledge changes with time and space, as the environmental factors change over time—resources are depleted, natural conditions shift rivers and basins, and so forth. Thus, culture does change over time, but rather slowly, as a function of geographic changes. When knowledge is created to be passed on from one generation to another, often specialized languages evolve. Language is one of the most crucial aspects of cultures, so much so that often language becomes the most significant representative of a culture. Thus, culture is what is passed on from generation to generation by people living in a certain geographic area of the world in a certain time period through a common language (Triandis, 1994).

The importance of these elements in the construal of culture can be seen in the destruction of culture. When people are eliminated, either by natural forces or by other people, their culture goes away with them. When people are dispersed from their natural environment, their culture changes, slowly but definitely, because culture is a collective human response to environment.

People in different cultures view land or space differently. For example, in some cultures, land is collectively owned and cannot be bought or sold, but not so in other cultures. When people are forced through legislation to adopt individual ownership of land, which happened during the colonization of many traditional cultures by Western countries, often the original cultures go through major crises.

Time captures many aspects, and one of them is generations of people. If cultural practices are not transmitted from one generation to another, cultures change, often seen in third and fourth generations of migrants. And finally, when people are not allowed to use their language, as happened with colonial powers restricting many native cultures, then people lose much of their cultural knowledge and practices. Loss of culture in marginalized groups of people clearly shows that these elements and their loss lead to the destruction of cultures (Bhawuk & Anbe, 2007).

Language is a crucial component of culture (Hall, 1976), and it makes cultures resilient. When people migrate, they leave

Figure 2.4   Essential Elements of Culture: People, Time, Space, and Language

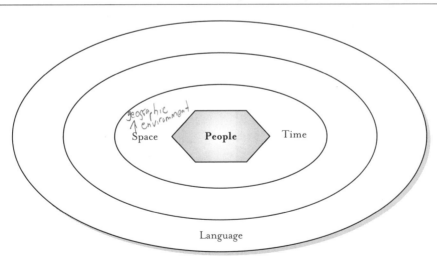

their space, but they take their language with them, and with it their cultures get transmitted over time through generations. Language also becomes a bridge across cultures, because people who share a language can communicate effectively. Thus, travel becomes easier for tourists when hosts speak multiple languages and communicate with the tourists in the tourists' native tongue. The French-speaking people across the globe are able to communicate with each other, as are the English-speaking people. Communication gaps or misunderstanding between people who speak the same language—e.g., English, but are from different cultures, such as the United States and the UK, or United States and India—demonstrates that language is an important part of culture, but culture is more than language.

6. Culture is not the same as nation.

Most nations have several cultures within their borders, even when all citizens speak the same language (House, Hanges, Javidan, Dorfman, & Gupta, 2004). For example, even before there was heavy immigration from the commonwealth nations, Britain contained many different cultures. The norms and values of Yorkshire were quiet different from that of Londoners. Now, of course, Britain has a large population of Southeast Asians who, while they speak English, are not Christian and are arguably very different in their values and beliefs from most other English people. The borders of nations will be particularly subject to culture change as mixing from neighboring countries occurs. Viewing culture as a composite of subcultures helps us to better understand the subcultures of different social groups (e.g., gender, ethnicity, language, age). For example, the behavioral distribution of minority cultures can be compared with the

behavioral distribution of a majority culture. Recognizing the distinction among various subcultures is important, as what is considered normal behavior may be largely based on norms of the dominant culture. Managers should recognize the heterogeneity in culture within a national boundary and not accept facile generalizations. They should also strive to be aware of the local culture when they are assigned to manage a facility in another country.

7. Culture is ever changing and dynamic.

Culture is not a static phenomenon. It changes as people from other areas come into contact with different norms, beliefs, and values. It can also change as a result of governmental policies. For example, moral beliefs in China changed as a result of the "opening up" of the country to the rest of the world in 1978. Another example has to do with beliefs of racial superiority, which in the United States have radically changed in the past five decades and in South Africa in the last 20 or so years. However, culture often changes rather slowly and can be viewed as superorganic (Kroeber, 1917). In other words, there may not be significant changes in human behavior in a particular culture in one's lifetime. This is the case in many traditional cultures that have managed to keep away from the economic and technological development found in the West. It is important that managers recognize how cultures change and seek the most current cultural information in the area to which they are assigned. If they remain at their posts for any length of time, they may find significant cultural changes occurring.

We find discussion of the above ideas useful in communicating with others about culture and also in learning about other cultures. We hope that the reader will be able to build on these basic ideas their understanding of what culture is by organizing their experiences in a complex cognitive, affective, and behavioral systems of framework.

◆ Discussion Questions

1. How is culture shaped by ecology and history?

2. What does it mean when one is said to be "culturally programmed" to act in a certain way?

3. Describe your culture and how it differs from other cultures in your neighborhood.

4. How is culture ever changing and dynamic?

◆ References

Bhawuk, D. P. S. (2001). Evolution of culture assimilators: Toward theory-based assimilators. *International Journal of Intercultural Relations, 25*(2), 141–163.

Bhawuk, D. P. S. (2003). Culture's influence on creativity: The case of Indian spirituality. *International Journal of Intercultural Relations, 27*(1), 1–22.

Bhawuk, D. P. S., & Anbe, K. (2007). *The importance of historical analysis in the study of culturally marginalized people: The case of native Hawaiians.* Paper presented at the 11th Biennial Conference of Society for Community Research and Action, Pasadena, California, June 7–10.

Hall, E. T. (1976). *Beyond culture.* York: Doubleday.

Herbig, P. A. (1997). *Handbook of cross-cultural marketing.* New York: Haworth Press.

House, R. J., Hanges, P. J., Javidan, M. J., Dorfman, P. W., & Gupta, V. (Eds.). (2004). *Culture, leadership, and organizations: The GLOBE study of 62 societies.* Thousand Oaks, CA: Sage.

Kroeber, A. L. (1917). *Zuni kin and clan.* New York: Trustees.

Triandis, H. C. (1994). *Culture and social behavior.* New York: McGraw-Hill.

Triandis, H. C. (1995). *Individualism and collectivism.* Boulder, CO: Westview.

3

DEVELOPING AND IMPLEMENTING A MULTICULTURAL VISION

◆ Carlos E. Cortés
and Louise C. Wilkinson

"You cannot step into the same river twice."

—Heracleitus

"I always skate to where the puck is going, not to where it's been."

—Wayne Gretzky

"In time of change, learners inherit the earth, while the learned find themselves beautifully equipped to deal with a world that no longer exists."

—Eric Hoffer

"Everything good has to be done over again, forever."

—E. L. Woodward

"All things are possible until they are proved impossible—and even the impossible may only be so as of now."

—Pearl Buck

Multicultural envisioning—the continuous creation and refinement of vision in order to develop personally, act more empathetically, and lead more effectively amid diversity. This idea has taken form through our course Developing and Implementing a Multicultural Vision, which has been taught annually since 1995 at the Summer Institute for Intercultural Communication.

We focus on envisioning because creating visions for our multicultural future can help synthesize what we know and to what we aspire. When visions vividly describe a desired future, they have the magnetic power to draw us toward them and galvanize action. By making envisioning a continuous part of their way of life, people can transcend many of the restraints that prevent them from empathetic participation in a multicultural world.

Multicultural envisioning can help individuals and organizations deal with the realities, inevitabilities, opportunities, and challenges of living and working in a world of striking differences and often unrecognized human commonalities. It can help individuals clarify their own thinking about diversity, shape their diversity-related actions, and draw others to their diversity-related goals and dreams. It can also help organizations and institutions discover new diversity-related opportunities, address current and future diversity-related challenges, and become better contributors to a constructive multicultural future.

On a micro level, multicultural envisioning might be used by individuals coming to grips with their own cultural influences and personal development in order to function more effectively in a world of diversity. On a macro level, it might be a major international organization attempting to envision the global future, assess the implications for its own operation, and develop ideas for both organizational success and for acting more responsibly in a multicultural world.

Between the micro and macro, multicultural envisioning can take many forms: a local organization reaching out to multiple groups in the quest for better intergroup relations; a company developing products and providing services that respond to the changing nature of their consumers or even help create better intercultural understanding; a community attempting to foster greater inclusion for residents with different cultural identities and experiences; or a university or school system trying to create a more welcoming and equitable climate for students, faculty, and staff of all backgrounds as well as build programs that prepare students for constructive participation in a diverse world.

What makes envisioning different from merely creating a vision? Three principal factors: (1) continuity: constantly recreating one's personal or organizational vision; (2) enrichment: continuously expanding the goals of becoming a more complete multicultural person or a more diversity-responsive organization, rather than relying on a static plan with fixed, measurable, quantifiable targets; and (3) action: not simply dreaming or musing but stimulating action directed toward a vision, even as that vision is being rethought and expanded.

Not based on a set of *attainable* nouns and adjectives, multicultural envisioning is premised on diversity-related life as a present participle, a series of "ings" that connote the ongoing, evolving nature of a healthy, constructive engagement with a changing world of diversity. While envisioning can contribute to multiple diversity endeavors, such as the development of intercultural competencies and the fulfillment of diversity strategies, it can also carry individuals and organizations much further. Because of multicultural envisioning's potential power and value, we invite you to consider some of its possibilities and complexities in the hope that you, too, may decide to pursue the path of envisioning.

◆ *Individual Envisioning*

All people are multicultural beings. That is, we are all influenced (not determined) by the multiple cultural groups to which we belong, even though we may not recognize all of those influences. In addressing multiculturalism, we use the term *culture* in a capacious way to include not only geographic, national, transnational, racial, and ethnic groups but also groups based on such categories as age, gender, religion, sexual orientation, language, and differential abilities. This reflects our focus on how multiple groups influence individual thinking and behavior.

Cultures contribute to personal belief systems and worldviews. They contribute to group-based tendencies to perceive, interpret, and act. They help foster values, create common bonds, and influence perceptions of and behavior toward others. Moreover, because of their complexities—often involving group-based organizations, institutions, media, rituals, and intricate patterns of belief and action—such groups may also be thought of as "cultural systems."

Yet we are not fully aware of the cultural influences that so deeply affect our views of the world. As Edward Hall (1990) pointed out, "Culture hides more than it reveals, but strangely enough what it hides, it hides most effectively from its own participants" (p. 29). Personal multicultural development involves an increasing understanding of the impact of cultural influences on oneself and others.

◆ *Developmental Models*

To provide conceptual grounding for personal multicultural envisioning, it is useful to compare developmental models posited by a number of theorists. Each theorist hypothesized a set of linear developmental stages and suggested a conception of an ideal, evolved individual state. However, despite the differences between these models, most theorists concur on one basic idea: To continue to make progress (however defined), at some point the individual must undergo a major shift in consciousness. We will look briefly at consciousness shifts within six developmental theories.

Abraham Maslow (1943, 1970) proposed a hierarchy of needs. The lower, or "deficiency," needs (comfort, security, love, belonging, status, and self-esteem) provide primary personal motivation. Once these are mostly fulfilled, people are then motivated toward self-actualization—becoming the most that they can be. This includes honestly facing realities, internalizing a system of morality less dependent on external authority, and judging others with less prejudice. Initially, Maslow saw self-transcendence—being driven by greater purpose outside of self—as the apex of his hierarchy, but he later speculated that moments of self-transcendence could occur at any stage.

Stephen Covey (1989) posited a human progression with two consciousness shifts, from "dependent" to "independent" and "independent" to "interdependent." Dependent people live reactively according to scripts provided by others. The consciousness shift to independence involves becoming more proactive, examining those given scripts, making independent choices, and taking greater responsibility for one's own thoughts and actions. In Covey's second consciousness shift, the recognition of interdependence of all people leads one to choose principles for living that support both better interpersonal relations and the common good.

Brian Hall (1994) developed his model based on shifting values priorities. In his first two consciousness phases, people tend to accept others' conceptions of truth, reality, and morality. His major "mind shift" occurs when people move from being outer directed to inner directed. This independence makes possible the further development of a commitment to the larger world and to empowering others.

Where Hall addressed values, Lawrence Kohlberg (1958, 1981) focused on the development of moral judgment. His major consciousness shift involves movement beyond conventional into postconventional morality. To reach that level, people learn to step outside of societal definitions of morality and try to determine the moral guidelines that they believe should serve as foundations for action. In doing so, they seek universal principles for moral action, including respect for all. Kohlberg posited empathy as a way to achieve the principle of impartiality.

Kieran Egan (1997) focused on yet another basic idea: understanding. In his fourth "philosophic" stage, the quest for certainty drives people to construct mental schemata that they believe represent absolute truth. Some people move on to a fifth "ironic" stage, a major consciousness shift in which they conclude that all "truths" are constructed and that no conceptual constructs actually represent the complexity of the multivocal world. The reflexiveness of this stage can lead to greater conceptual flexibility and a belief that all perspectives have certain validity.

In his Developmental Model of Intercultural Sensitivity, Milton Bennett (1998) posited a major shift from an "ethnocentric" to an "ethnorelative" worldview. In the ethnocentric phase, people assume that their own cultural worldviews equate with reality, and, as a result, they only see and judge other cultures by using their own culture's lens. Those in the ethnorelative phase become aware that their own culture's worldview is

only one of many ways of seeing and being in the world. They learn about different cultural norms, values, and behaviors and develop an ability to shift their perspectives to more successfully view the world through other cultures' perceptual lenses.

While each theorist framed the world in his own way, all of the models posit at least one major shift in consciousness required for further development, shifts that generally include five characteristics:

1. Reducing dependence on others to guide one's thoughts and actions

2. Recognizing that there are myriad, potentially valid concepts of truth constructed by people and cultures to make sense of a complex, uncertain world

3. Deciding that it is still necessary to construct one's own way of understanding the world and to determine principles for ethical action in order to function in a complex world

4. Considering and even empathizing with multiple perspectives while integrating the principle of respect for difference

5. Acknowledging interdependence in committing to a higher good

◆ Conceptualizing the Great Divide

When applied to diversity, we have labeled this developmental consciousness shift the Multicultural Great Divide. On the one side reside those whom we conceive as "culturally constrained." Those who decide to embark on the never-ending journey across the Divide can be thought of as "cultural transcenders."

Who are the "culturally constrained"? They are people who have not moved beyond the limits of their own cultural moorings and lenses. In fact, they may not even be aware of those lenses, let alone have thoughts of moving beyond them.

Such constraint impedes their understanding of how cultural forces influence their own beliefs and actions, as well as the values and behavior of those who come from other backgrounds. They may fear venturing into the realm of uncertainty that comes with a serious engagement with alternative cultural perspectives, instead cleaving to the "clear" answers provided by tradition and established belief patterns.

Certainly there are advantages to pursuing a life of cultural constraint. It provides a sense of security, with unambiguous answers for even complex culturally influenced issues. It encourages dependence on others—such as societal and cultural authorities—to establish values, behavioral norms, ethical guidelines, and moral codes. Because culturally constrained people generally do not realize how thoroughly they are locked into their cultural worldviews, they feel little pressure to try to perceive the world through the eyes of others or attempt to understand their culturally driven perspectives.

As a result, they rigidly apply their own culture's values, norms, and restrictions when making judgments about the beliefs and actions of others. When they do seek to connect with those from other cultures—and culturally constrained people do have the capacity for selfless and compassionate action—they nonetheless fail to recognize that others may be experiencing the world differently.

In contrast are "cultural transcenders," those who have committed to making the passage across the Multicultural Great Divide. In this consciousness shift to "transcending," the security of "constraint" is left behind as they embark on their multicultural journey (Cortés, 2002).

Cultural transcenders are characterized by their curiosity and willingness to explore the complexities of diversity. They seek not only to *recognize* the existence of cultural differences but also to *understand how* those differences have influenced values and beliefs. Not only to recognize culturally varying experiences but also to try to understand how those differing experiences have influenced ways of viewing the world. Not only to recognize that, in the words of the old Chinese proverb, "We see what is behind our eyes," but also to open up their cognitive structures to try to see as others see.

Transcenders recognize the challenges inherent in the multicultural journey. They know that better understanding of the multiplicity of cultural perspectives may well influence, maybe unsettle, their own personal perspectives; that they will need to treat knowledge as contingent upon time, place, and cultural context; that what you know today may need to be modified by what you learn tomorrow. In short, that cultural transcending involves a commitment to living with uncertainty. Transcenders might well be those who, in the words of CBS TV commentator Eric Sevareid, "have the courage of one's doubts as well as one's convictions in this world of all too passionate certainties."

♦ *Crossing the Great Divide*

Individual level

The consciousness shift from "cultural constraint" to "cultural transcending" involves approaching the Multicultural Great Divide not as a chasm to be breached in search of a defined destination but rather as the beginning of a never-completed journey through a land of constant change and continuous learning. It is the consciousness shift into a world of constant consciousness shifting (Wilkinson, 2007).

By clarifying the dimensions of that difficult shift, multicultural envisioning can help in this continuous intellectual and emotional challenge. It can foster intercultural growth, ethical contemplation, empathetic action, and engagement with a rapidly changing world. Following are seven examples of individual multicultural envisioning that should be included in that journey.

1. *Envisioning group membership and individuality*—How do you conceive of people as individuals while still recognizing them as members of groups? All people belong to numerous cultural cohorts, clustered around such factors as race, ethnicity, gender, religion, age, or languages spoken. For each individual, those multigroup influences intersect in unique ways. As Confucius pointed out, "Men are, by nature, pretty much alike; it is learning and their behavior that makes them different from each other." The more you learn about any cultural group, the greater insight you are likely to gain about the possible beliefs, perceptions, and actions of individual group members. But group generalizations can easily harden into stereotypes. Therefore, transcenders need to consciously resist that seductive certainty, remain open to new group knowledge, and hone their ability to draw constructively and flexibly on that knowledge as clues to, not as stereotypical assumptions about, individuals (Cortés, 2000).

2. *Envisioning cultural perspectives*—As transcenders become increasingly aware of how other people are influenced by the cultures to which they belong and as they learn more about individual cultures themselves, they should also try to view the world through the eyes of those cultures. While transcenders may still operate primarily by using their own cultures' perceptual lenses, they should also strive for the flexibility to transcend them—set them aside while attempting to better understand the perspectives of others. Moreover, such understanding can lead to empathy—an imaginative participation in how others may view and react to the world around them.

3. *Envisioning cultural moorings*—Rudyard Kipling cautioned, "What should they know of England who only England know?" Even as transcenders learn more about other cultures, they are also likely to become more analytical about how their own multiple cultures have influenced the way they view the world. However, the movement from constraint to transcending does not require a rejection of one's cultures. Rather the envisioning process should lead to viewing one's own cultural influences from a more detached, multi-perspectival vantage point. This may result in consciously restraining, maybe even reconsidering, one's cultural influences while thinking about or interacting with those of other backgrounds. It may also actually deepen an appreciation of and commitment to one's basic cultural tenets.

4. *Envisioning intercultural judgment*—In this engagement with otherness, transcenders will inevitably confront differing values, norms, ethical systems, and moral codes. It is not enough, like Polonius in *Hamlet*, to be in favor of the good things and opposed to the bad things. There are conflicting perceptions of such concepts as equity, fairness, responsibility, and justice. Disagreements will arise about how these ideas play out

when applied to concrete dilemmas of personal living and organizational functioning. Transcenders should try to comprehend different culturally based moral imperatives and the ethical foundations of the beliefs and practices of other cultures. In the process, they should try to enlarge their own repertoire of possible moral principles and assume greater responsibility for developing their own diversity-related belief systems rather than relying on cultural conditioning for making intercultural judgments.

5. *Envisioning limits*—Such intercultural judgment inevitably forces transcenders to confront the complex issue of "limits." How far are you personally willing to go in respecting different cultural expressions? Where (and why) do you establish your own personal limits to accepting other cultural practices? In the abstract, a commitment to multicultural understanding involves trying to become flexible in dealing with others on their own terms. However, even if transcenders succeed in understanding beliefs or actions from the perspectives of their practitioners, they will ultimately hit the limits wall, encountering culturally driven beliefs and actions that they find so abhorrent as to fall beyond the pale of tolerance, acceptance, and certainly respect. Such limits may arise from one's cultural conditioning or from one's new, still-developing individual belief system. While multicultural envisioning does not embrace anything-goes moral relativism, it does impel transcenders to try to understand other cultural systems and reflectively analyze their own critical reactions to others' beliefs and practices.

6. *Envisioning empathetic action*—But the envisioning process is not merely an engagement with the heart and mind. It also propels and influences action. What then, distinguishes culturally transcending from culturally constrained action? Both forms of action may seek to improve the lives of others. However, transcenders (as contrasted with the culturally constrained) place a premium on cross-cultural understanding and empathy. When making action-oriented decisions, they try to understand how others from different backgrounds might view their actions and how those actions might even undermine other cultural ways of being.

7. *Envisioning and re-envisioning one's worldview*—T. S. Eliot once lamented, "We had the experience but missed the meaning." While engaging in these other six multicultural envisioning processes, transcenders will almost inevitably find that their journey raises challenges about—in fact, may even shatter some of—their own culturally based personal beliefs, values, and perceptions. To avoid a descent into a state of endless confusion brought about by mounting complexity, the envisioning journey should also involve continuous resynthesis—constantly re-creating structure out of potential chaos. Even while contemplating differing perspectives and moral imperatives, transcenders should try to forge a new, personal (albeit transitory) synthesis of their own thinking about diversity and continually test that renewed personal belief system in their decisions and actions. However, since the envisioning process is ongoing, this resynthesis should not harden into a new set of rigid constraints. Rather it should serve as an invitation for further expansion of awareness and engagement with the richness of multicultural complexities.

◆ *Organizational Envisioning*

To this point we have focused on envisioning as a personal process. However, the engagement with diversity often occurs with or within organizations and institutions. As with personal envisioning, it is useful to consider existing models to provide a conceptual base for organizational envisioning. David Thomas and Robin Ely (1996) suggested three such models, which they labeled paradigms of how organizations address diversity.

DISCRIMINATION AND FAIRNESS PARADIGM

According to Thomas and Ely, this type of organization emphasizes such basic issues as recruitment, retention, advancement, mentoring, and compliance with diversity-related laws and regulations. The driving force of those organizations is assimilation. They recruit diverse people and then integrate them with little regard to the inherent value they bring to the organization *because* of their cultural backgrounds, experiences, and perspectives.

ACCESS AND LEGITIMACY PARADIGM

In contrast, some organizations attempt to build strength from diversity by matching organizational demographics to the demographics of their constituent groups. Diverse employees are sometimes assigned to operate within niches based on assumed group knowledge, demonstrated linguistic ability, or perceived group compatibilities—for example, to communicate with, develop products for, market to, or serve specific populations.

Yet while such organizations recognize and benefit from a conscious use of diversity in targeted niches, they do not consider how a broader approach to diversity could improve the overall operation of the organization. Moreover, those members who are employed to deal with cultural niches may end up being pigeonholed as "niche specialists" and denied opportunities for advancement within the central structure of the organization.

LEARNING AND EFFECTIVENESS PARADIGM

Organizations that operate according to Thomas and Ely's third paradigm incorporate some of the practices of the first two types but also go beyond. They value the personal and cultural experiences of their members and the resulting group-based perspectives they can bring to the organization, but rather than viewing group members merely in terms of their niche function, these organizations seek to enhance their core institutional culture, structure, and operation by inviting contributions based on members' special group knowledge and perspectives.

Thomas and Ely's third paradigm suggests the enormous possibilities of a broader approach to diversity, although such an openness to change can threaten staunchly held beliefs about organizations. Depending on their ability to shed culturally constrained adherence to old values, beliefs, and approaches to organizational structure and operations, some third-paradigm organizations may well become transcendent—moving across the Multicultural Great Divide.

Organizational level Test ?

ENVISIONING AND TRANSCENDING PARADIGM

Thomas and Ely's three paradigms provide a useful way of viewing diversity and organizations. However, we would like to propose yet one additional framing, which we call the Envisioning and Transcending Paradigm. It incorporates the strengths of Thomas and Ely's three paradigms but also involves a full consciousness shift into organizational cultural transcendence.

As with individuals, organizations moving across the Multicultural Great Divide commit themselves to the envisioning process. They continually seek new ways of dealing with diversity—to draw upon multiple cultural perspectives for analyzing issues, to attract and retain diverse members, and to revisit and revise policies, procedures, and structures. In doing so they also continually re-envision the very nature of the organization. Following are six examples of organizational multicultural envisioning.

Quiz ?

1. *Envisioning diversity as a potential strength*—An Envisioning and Transcending organization views cultural diversity as a strength upon which it can build, not a problem that must be resolved. While it does not deny that diversity sometimes creates challenges, the organization develops a culture in which diversity questions are initially framed as opportunities for discovering new ways of seeing or operating that provide greater potential value. If the organization deems the strength-from-diversity frame to be inappropriate in a particular instance, it would still address the dilemma by considering diverse perspectives in an attempt to envision the best outcome for all involved. Envisioning and Transcending organizations avoid the artificial framing of diversity issues as a simplistic battle between irreconcilable opposites—differences versus commonalities, cultural expression versus assimilation, or special interests versus common goals. Rather, the presence of diversity

affords an opportunity to foster a creative, expanding, re-envisioned conception of unity.

2. *Envisioning a culturally inclusive climate*— But building strength from diversity is merely cheerleading if it stops with slogans. How, in fact, does an organization move from constraint to transcending when dealing with diversity? This question raises basic issues that must be addressed. What current organizational diversity-related beliefs and values no longer serve the growing vision of an inclusive organization? What policies and practices favor those of certain backgrounds or create obstacles (even if unintended) to the full participation of members of other groups? What actions can be taken to foster a more inclusive climate in which members of the organization feel welcome—in fact, encouraged—to draw upon their diverse cultures, experiences, and experience-based knowledge to contribute to greater organizational effectiveness and an expanding vision?

3. *Envisioning the role of diverse groups*—Beyond fostering a better climate of inclusion for culturally diverse members as individuals, in what ways should the organization support them as members of groups? For example, organizations have varied in their willingness to support official "affinity groups"— groups based on such identities as race, ethnicity, gender, and sexual orientation. Some have declined this tack, wary of potential group balkanization. Others have found that the support of such groups fosters greater dedication to the organization and generates innovative ideas. Organizations need to envision the possible benefits of supporting such initiatives while at the same time considering and planning for possible unintended consequences.

4. *Envisioning organizational equity*—Culturally transcending organizations envision diversity-related equity as a basic value and as central to their operations, both internally and externally. They develop policies and practices based on the idea that an emphasis on equity and human dignity can contribute to organizational effectiveness by providing greater opportunities for full participation. Yet tensions often arise because of differing views of what constitutes equity. Consider the passionately differing views about such equity-related issues as immigration, affirmative action, speech codes, inter-gender behavior, workplace language use, and accommodation to personal religious beliefs.

A pervasive contributor to polarizing arguments is the false assumption that equity always means treating everybody alike. In fact, where difference is involved, sameness of treatment may be inequitable.

Take the example of "potty parity." Recognizing that inequities occur when high-impact facilities like theaters and sports complexes have the *same* number of men's and women's bathroom stalls, a growing number of states have legislated differential gender ratios in all new high-impact venues. As they build and revisit their policies and practices, transcending organizations need to recognize the possible disparate impact of applying the same policy to all people, despite their differences, and to look at equity from as many perspectives as possible.

5. *Envisioning cultural accommodation*—The pursuit of equity raises yet another fundamental question. To what extent, and at what cost, should the organization accommodate diversity by treating certain groups of people differently? That issue was addressed, for example, by the 1990 Americans With Disabilities Act. To provide for more equitable access and opportunities, it established a useful although challenging guideline—"reasonable accommodation." Organizations must accommodate to disabilities, yet those accommodations only need to be reasonable—a useful, yet hardly clear-cut, rule of thumb for envisioning many diversity-related organizational issues.

6. *Envisioning organizational culture*—Because of the very continuity of envisioning, transcending organizations face the inevitable challenge of creating a culture that thrives on constant change. To do so, members should be made integral to organizational envisioning and, in the process, should be encouraged to move beyond cultural constraint and become transcenders themselves. Steps include creating an equitable climate that encourages individuals to share diverse envisioning perspectives and providing training opportunities that foster cultural transcending.

ENVISIONING DIVERSITY AS AN ADAPTIVE CHALLENGE

Many diversity-related organizational issues are currently being addressed by using traditional problem-solving strategies. Although at times this may be appropriate, when applied to the wrong issues, a narrow problem-solving approach not only fails but often creates greater complications. As H. L. Mencken opined, "There is always a well-known solution to every human problem—neat, plausible, and wrong."

Unintended consequences resulting from applying misguided "solutions" may actually exacerbate diversity-related conditions, situations, or dilemmas. Two insightful essays—"The Work of Leadership" by Ronald Heifetz and Donald Laurie (1997) and "Dilemmas in a General Theory of Planning" by Horst Rittel and Melvin Webber (1973)—emphasize the importance of assessing the inherent nature of situations rather than automatically moving into a problem-solving mode.

A problem-solving approach may be appropriate for "tame" (Rittel & Webber) or "technical" problems (Heifetz & Laurie). With tame/technical problems, the goal is clear, uncontroversial, and perceived similarly by all (or nearly all) involved. Three conditions exist: There is one major cause that can be dealt with in isolation from other possible contributing factors; there is one best solution that can be technically determined; and there are clear guidelines or precise measures for determining if and when a solution has been achieved.

By and large, such tame/technical problems tend to exist within closed systems, disconnected from other systems (including group cultural systems). Therefore, they can be acted on without significant reverberations or unintended consequences for other systems. Since there are no collateral consequences if the solution "fails," another solution can be tried without penalty.

Such a uni-causal, technical problem-solving approach appeals to culturally constrained people who have a deep attachment to certainty and authority. However, cultural transcenders—those willing to admit, confront, and even embrace complexity and uncertainty—are better able to recognize when there are different, more complex types of issues, referred to as "wicked problems" (Rittel & Webber) or as "adaptive challenges" (Heifetz & Laurie).

Such wicked problems/adaptive challenges do not have clear solutions and are perceived differently by those involved. In fact, they may be controversial precisely because people often approach them with strong, conflicting, sometimes emotionally laden values. These challenges exist particularly in open systems—that is, when many systems intersect, including cultural systems. They have multiple causes, some of which are rooted in systems outside of the organization itself. There are no clear or precise measures for determining if and when solutions have been achieved. Yet some people may still be determined to characterize such challenges as tame or technical problems (although they may not use that language) and continue to insist on the vain search for a single best "solution."

Many complex diversity-related challenges are debated endlessly in search of rational, technical, measurable problem-solving solutions. Some of the issues raised earlier—such as affirmative action, speech codes, and the quest for equity—spawn often-passionate conflicts about the "real" problem or the single "correct" solution. For example, people search for definitive answers to the recruitment and retention of diverse (sometimes global) employees and how to "solve" systemic discrimination, complicated by the fact that some of those involved may benefit from inequities even without recognizing it.

Closely aligned with the tendency to view each issue as a problem to be solved is the propensity to see dilemmas as "either/or" situations. In this either/or approach, one of the two options must be selected and the other rejected.

In contrast, in their book, *21 Leaders for the 21st Century: How Innovative Leaders Manage in the Digital Age* (2002), Fons Trompenaars and Charles Hampden-Turner posited an alternative view—that successful intercultural leadership requires the creative resolution of key dilemmas. Focusing on the differing values of national cultures, they addressed a series of dilemmas that they find central to most transcultural organizational work.

In their analysis, they posited a set of key dilemmas that most often surface in cross-cultural organizational work. These dilemmas encompass basic values differences they see operating between national cultures and yet often play out in very concrete ways in organizational life.

Those whom we have categorized as culturally constrained are likely to see the worth of only one pole of a values dilemma. For example, they are apt to choose universalism (rule making) or particularism (exception finding); they may choose individualism (self-interest and personal fulfillment) or communitarianism (group interest and social concern). However, those whom we have called transcenders are more likely to see the possibilities inherent in drawing on both poles.

Trompenaars and Hampden-Turner suggested that successful organizational strategies are built on integrating the two poles in a "virtuous circle" in which the strengths of each pole are actually fed by the other pole. Organizational issues, including those related to diversity, are fraught with dilemmas. Approaching diversity-related dilemmas as adaptive challenges, which can be addressed with such strategies as the "virtuous circle," can help an organization function more effectively within our Envisioning and Transcending Paradigm.

These complexities raise serious multicultural envisioning issues for organizations: How to envision the intricate nature of different diversity-related challenges and the dilemmas involved. How to envision the factors to be weighed in creating strategies and making decisions. How to envision an effective approach to those challenges by building on and synthesizing differing values. How to envision and deal with the potential consequences of the selected actions. In short, how to use envisioning to provide transcending leadership.

◆ *Visionist Multicultural Leadership*

There are many kinds of effective leadership, sometimes involving people without formal power or position. A final element of multicultural envisioning involves contemplating the elements of visionist diversity-related leadership.

Even in regard to diversity, there can be effective leaders who are not cultural transcenders. Without transcending, they may make decisions and take actions that bring benefits to certain diverse groups. Moreover, even cultural transcenders may adopt leadership styles that do not involve envisioning.

In contrast, "visionist multicultural leaders" are transcending leaders who make envisioning a central part of their leadership style. Following are seven examples of the multicultural envisioning capacities of visionist leaders.

1. *Continuity*—For visionist leaders, "staying the course" does not mean coming up with a vision and sticking to it, whatever the consequences. In fact, it means staying the course of continual re-envisioning. For a visionist, learning is an endless process that necessitates a constant rethinking of worldview and multicultural vision.

2. *Collaboration*—Visionist leaders create and model a culture of openness and exploration. In the words of Nobel Prize winner Naguib Mahfouz, "You can tell whether a man is clever by his answers. You can tell whether a man is wise by his questions." Visionist leaders ask probing, strategic questions and listen carefully to the answers, no matter how challenging. They create a climate that encourages others to participate in envisioning by contributing ideas, including perspectives drawn from their diverse group cultures and experiences. Visionist leaders are comfortable amid conflicting voices, the expression of pent-up frustrations, and the surfacing of competing values—a

situation that may provide clues to deeper diversity-related complexities. In the words of the old Jewish proverb, "A wise man hears one word and understands two."

3. *Capaciousness*—Heifetz and Laurie (1997) suggested that leaders should "go to the balcony" to try to get an overview of the myriad interacting causal chains and active forces, including cultural systems. By following their advice in addressing diversity-related questions, visionist leaders can develop a greater understanding of the dynamic interlocking forces involved in the issues and challenges of the organization. They will also be better able to envision the complex nature of interdependence, including with those who are culturally different, even in distant locations.

4. *Framing*—Whether coming forth with a decision, elucidating common ground, or providing new envisioning directions, visionist leaders need to hone the ability to reframe rapidly (Bolman & Deal, 2003). This includes reframing pseudo-tame/technical problems into adaptive challenges so that inappropriate efforts are not made at misdirected problem solving. The mental flexibility necessary for rapid reframing is enhanced by the transcender's ability to recognize and understand multiple perspectives.

5. *Resynthesis*—Eric Hoffer concluded, "In products of the human mind, simplicity marks the end of a process of refining, while complexity marks a primitive stage." Faced with what could easily become information overload and multi-perspectived chaos, visionist leaders draw upon their powers of creativity to clarify misunderstandings, integrate ideas, and provide visionary syntheses that advance, not merely summarize, the envisioning

dialogue (Gardner, 2007). Such ongoing resynthesis is critical to the envisioning process and to preventing organizations from losing their ability to focus and act even while envisioning continues.

6. *Principled decision making*—Even as multi-perspectived collaboration and envisioning proceed, visionist leaders must make decisions. In deciding on specific issues, they should draw upon the insights derived from multicultural envisioning, from "going to the balcony" to understand complex dynamics, and from creative resynthesis of polarizing dilemmas and multiple perspectives. What is *reasonable* accommodation? What principles of ethics, morality, and justice should be considered in action decisions? How can the pursuit of equity be made more inclusive? Visionist leaders are willing and able to ponder these complexities without surrendering the decisiveness necessary to help their organizations stay focused on their evolving goals.

7. *Empowering action*—"I am he as you are he as you are me and we are altogether," wrote John Lennon in "I Am the Walrus." In making decisions and taking action, visionist leaders accept the obligations that come with a heightened sense of interdependence. They empower organizational members by involving them in the envisioning process, encouraging them to become transcenders, and fostering their capacity for visionist multicultural leadership. Visionist leaders also feel responsibility to the world outside of their organizational boundaries. They guide the organization to act empathetically in that larger world in ways that further justice and equity, embody a respect for human dignity, and reflect an increasing understanding of diverse cultural perspectives.

◆ *Conclusion*

As Queen Victoria intoned, "Change must be accepted . . . when it can no longer be resisted." The world around us is changing rapidly. The globe is shrinking (Friedman, 2005). Diversity-related issues are increasing in nations around the world. Such changes require not only new but also constantly renewed thinking.

Multicultural envisioning provides an avenue for addressing the complexities inherent in a world of diversity. At the personal level, envisioning can help individuals embark on a lifelong journey as cultural transcenders and perhaps visionist multicultural leaders. At the organizational level, envisioning can help an organization strengthen its capacity to deal with multicultural challenges, build strength from diversity, enrich the capabilities of its members, and contribute to the world around it. Multicultural leaders can draw on envisioning to help individuals and organizations cross the Multicultural Great Divide and take effective diversity-related action.

Nehru of India summed up the human dilemma as follows: "Life is like a game of cards. The hand that is dealt you is determinism; the way you play it is free will." Cultural diversity is a core element of that determinism. Multicultural envisioning is an empowering way of using that free will to work toward the best that is in us and the best that can be accomplished for and with the diverse people of the world.

◆ *Discussion Questions*

1. What is one reason that might cause you to embark on a culturally transcending journey and one reason you might hesitate to do so?

2. What is one individual challenge you would need to address should you decide to embark on the journey across the Multicultural Great Divide?

3. In your environment or organization, how might you encourage others to cross the Multicultural Great Divide?

4. What is one major challenge your current organization might face should it attempt to become an Envisioning-and-Transcending organization?

5. Name someone you might consider to be a visionist multicultural leader and explain why. In what ways did this leader engage others in an envisioning process?

6. Specify one additional quality beyond those listed in the chapter that you believe would be essential for a visionist multicultural leader.

7. What previous experiences have you had with vision building? After reading this chapter, how might you suggest changing the vision-building processes in which you were involved?

◆ *References*

Bennett, M. J. (1998). Intercultural communication: A current perspective. In M. J. Bennett (Ed.), *Basic concepts of intercultural communications: Selected readings* (pp. 1–34). Yarmouth, ME: Intercultural Press.

Bolman, L. G. & Deal, T. E. (2003). *Reframing organizations: Artistry, choice, and leadership* (3rd ed.). New York: Wiley.

Cortés, C. E. (2000). *The children are watching: How the media teach about diversity.* New York: Teachers College Press.

Cortés, C. E. (2002). *The making—and remaking—of a multiculturalist.* New York: Teachers College Press.

Covey, S. R. (1989). *The 7 habits of highly effective people: Powerful lessons in personal change.* New York: Simon & Schuster.

Egan, K. (1997). *The educated mind: How cognitive tools shape our understanding.* Chicago: University of Chicago Press.

Friedman. T. L. (2005). *The world is flat: A brief history of the twenty-first century.* New York: Farrar, Straus and Giroux.

Gardner, H. (2007). *Five minds for the future.* Cambridge, MA: Harvard Business School Press.

Hall, B. P. (1984). *Values shift: A guide to personal & organizational transformation.* Rockport, MA: Twin Lights Publishers.

Hall, E.T. (1990). *The silent language.* New York: Doubleday.

Heifetz, R. A., & Laurie, D. L. (1997, January/February). The work of leadership. *Harvard Business Review,* 124–134.

Kohlberg, L. (1958). *The development of modes of thinking and choices in years 10–16.* Unpublished doctoral dissertation, University of Chicago.

Kohlberg, L. (1981). *The philosophy of moral development.* San Francisco: Harper & Row.

Maslow, A. H. (1943). A theory of human motivation. *Psychological Review, 50,* 370–396.

Maslow, A. H. (1970). *Motivation and personality* (2nd ed.). New York: Harper & Row.

Rittel, H. W. J., & Webber, M. M. (1973). Dilemmas in a general theory of planning. *Policy Sciences 4,* 155–169.

Thomas, D. A., & Ely, R. J. (1996, September/October). Making differences matter: A new paradigm for managing diversity. *Harvard Business Review,* 79–90.

Trompenaars, A., & Hampden-Turner, C. (2002). *21 leaders for the 21st century: How innovative leaders manage in the digital age.* New York: McGraw-Hill.

Wilkinson, L. C. (2007). A developmental approach to uses of moving pictures in intercultural education. *International Journal of Intercultural Relations, 31,* 1–27.

PART II

UNDERSTANDING THE EVOLVING ROLE OF CULTURAL DIVERSITY IN THE WORKPLACE

THE EFFECTIVE MANAGEMENT OF CULTURAL DIVERSITY

◆ Lee Gardenswartz and Anita Rowe

Long before the now famous Hudson Report sent shock waves through corporate America in 1987 with its predictions about demographic changes affecting the workforce, diversity was on the radar screens of forward-thinking business leaders across the country. EEO laws of the 1960s and 1970s and affirmative action requirements were already putting attention on equity in the workplace, and immigration was bringing a wider range of cultures and languages to both the workforce and marketplace. Finally, global business realities were highlighting the need for increased cultural understanding and flexibility. Because of vision and necessity, companies began to understand that diversity was a business issue and managing it effectively was a strategic imperative for growth and survival.

◆ *Laying the Foundation With an Inclusive Definition of Diversity*

Diversity is not a liberal ideological movement, to be supported or resisted. Rather, it is a reality in today's business environment. Managed well, diversity provides benefits that increase success.

However, when ignored or mismanaged, it brings challenges and obstacles that can hinder the organization's ability to succeed. The right question then is not, do we have to deal with diversity, but rather, how do we manage it to reap its potential benefits? At its core, diversity is about inclusion and exclusion. The foundation for effectively leveraging diversity lies in defining it in a broad and inclusive way. Organizations that define it broadly, involving all dimensions of similarity and difference around which there are inclusions and exclusions that affect the business, find that there is greater buy-in and strategic relevance. There is also a stronger business case and less resistance when all in the organization can see themselves reflected in the definition and can identify inclusions and exclusions that play out in the organization every day through us-versus-them attitudes, stereotypes, assumptions, preconceived expectations, and differences in treatment.

Our model, the Four Layers of Diversity (Figure 4.1), is used in many organizations across the country to frame the issue and encourage discussion and involvement in managing diversity. The multiple dimensions of diversity around which there is inclusion and exclusion are depicted in four concentric circles. Personality, relating to individual style and characteristics, is in the center. Whether a person is an introvert or extrovert, reflective or expressive, quick paced or methodical, a thinker or a doer, for example, all influence how the individual will be treated, get along with others, and progress in the organization. The second layer, the Internal Dimensions, comprises the six aspects of ourselves over which we have little control. Our gender, age, sexual orientation, race, ethnicity, and physical ability are for the most part not choices, yet they influence our treatment in organizations, the roles we play in life, and the expectations of us,

both our own and others. The third layer, External Dimensions, comprises those that are the result of life experiences and choices. Aspects such as religion, education, marital status, work experience, and recreational habits are areas around which employees can connect or disconnect, be valued or disrespected, depending on how these dimensions are seen and used.

The last layer, Organizational Dimensions, contains those aspects of similarity and differences that are part of work in the organization. What difference might it make if someone is the CEO or an entry-level employee, in marketing, manufacturing, human resources, or customer service, a manager or a union shop steward? These dimensions also affect both treatment of employees and productivity of the organization.

All these aspects represent areas in which there may be similarity and common ground as well as differences. When well managed, these differences have the potential to bring new perspectives, ideas, and viewpoints needed by the organization. However, if mismanaged, they can sow the seeds of conflict and misunderstanding that sabotage teamwork and productivity and hinder effectiveness. To maximize the ability to manage this complex set of differences, organizations need to have a framework and strategy. The following three areas of focus offer a framework.

◆ A Framework for Managing Diversity as Organizational Change

Over the years, we have witnessed and been part of many diversity initiatives and strategies. Some worked effectively, some only in part, but few accomplished all of their original objectives. Those that came out of a

Figure 4.1   The Four Layers of Diversity

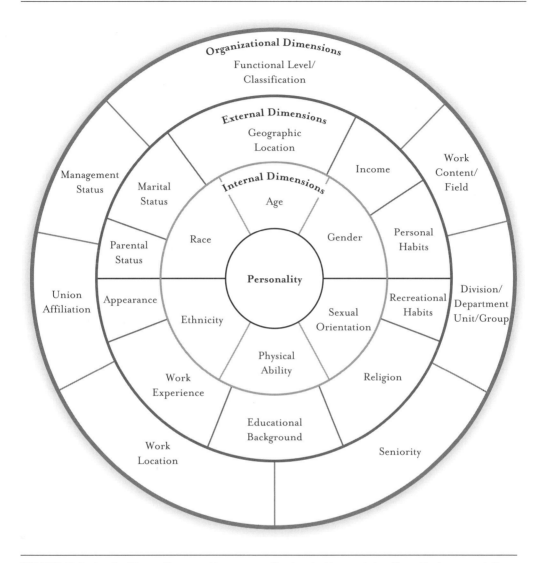

SOURCE: © Society for Human Resource Management. Reprinted with permission. From Gardenswartz & Rowe (2003); Internal Dimensions and External Dimensions, adapted from Loden & Rosener (1991).

"check off the box" mentality or were looking for a quick fix never had traction and had little impact. The efforts that had longevity did so because they were thorough and affected the structure at an operational level.

Diversity benefits are leveraged successfully when an initiative is looked at as a culture change intervention with both people and systems interlocked and working for the benefit of the whole. This kind of change is almost always an unwieldy process that takes time, tenacity, and determination to see it through. The following framework creates a manageable structure for getting through the process and yielding results.

For an organization to get its arms around the complexity of diversity culture change, it needs to focus on three arenas: (1) individual attitudes and behaviors, (2) managerial skills and practices, and (3) organizational values and policies. The individual attitudes and behaviors component asks employees to do some intrapersonal work that involves identifying their attitudes and beliefs on a wide range of topics such as how they feel about multiple languages spoken in the workplace; attitudes toward whether coworkers can be openly gay in the workplace; conflicting union and management positions on any number of policies; and the hottest diversity topic of the early 2000s—generational differences, or how 20-somethings and 60-somethings vary in their view of the world of work. Change in this arena requires identifying and acknowledging the feelings that come from these differences and the behaviors that result as well. For example, if my attitude toward 20-somethings is that they are shallow and uncommitted, my behavior is likely to be standoffish, uncollaborative, and unresponsive in helping them acculturate to the organization. These behaviors will ultimately affect organizational culture, outreach, and openness to fellow employees as well as services delivered to customers. Training to affect individual attitudes and behaviors has probably yielded the most success in diversity initiatives over the last 25 years. There are many remarkable and impressive examples of change that we have seen. They are a necessary first step but insufficient to change the culture of the organization.

The second arena in which change needs to takes place is that of managerial skills and practices. The essence of this change is the recognition that one style of management does not fit all. Managerial practices must be tailored to suit a wide range of employees.

Depending on one's culture, for example, feedback about performance may be delivered very directly, or it may also be given in a much more indirect and subtle way, sometimes with the help of an intermediary or cultural interpreter. Another example of the wide range of practices needed has to do with norms involving meeting participation and giving feedback to bosses. In hierarchical cultures, direct questions or feedback to a boss would be unthinkable, yet it is expected in most parts of the United States. Another cultural difference is how pats on the back or other positive reinforcements are given. Properly acknowledging exemplary performance requires cultural knowledge and sensitivity. In many cultures, public acknowledgment is totally humiliating. In such cases, acknowledging good work, perhaps with a very private and quiet thank you or a note in the employee's file, works wonders, instead of public acknowledgment, which could be mortifying. Managers need to know these differences among their employees because they affect conflict resolution, accountability, team cohesion, commitment, and ultimately work performance.

The last arena of change that is required to successfully leverage diversity involves changes in organizational values and policies. This area is the most complex in which to make progress, and we have seen the least success here. Adjusting the promotional system, for example, or how people are hired and recruited to create a broader talent pool and a more equitable organization, requires complex work that has many steps. For example, how do you begin the process of selecting recruiters who themselves are diverse? And if they are diverse by the internal dimensions, that does not necessarily mean they are open to differences and are themselves objective about others. Sometimes they push for people who look or act like them.

Sensitizing recruiters is only one step in a longer process. How do you then make sure you have broad hiring panels? What are the policies and practices around creating an equitable posting system? Where in the feedback-gathering process do you get feedback from employees about how the system works? How do you hold managers accountable for the diversity changes you are trying to achieve? And once an organization gets the feedback, who is charged with the follow-through of using input and implementing the changes? It's methodical and can be tedious, but it is very important. Organizations that stick with the detailed process can reap just rewards, but these changes don't happen without absolute commitment and follow-through. Our caveat here is this: Be mindful of the law of unintended consequences. When one system is fixed, undoubtedly other glitches crop up elsewhere. One university medical center worked very hard to create relief for employees with young children. They did so, but the burden then fell to those who had no children or whose children were no longer at home, and a new problem resulted. That was the end result, but certainly not the initial intent. Thinking strategically and cleverly about all possible outcomes is absolutely critical.

To make culture change happen, we suggest the following seven-step process. While the steps are presented here in a linear fashion for conceptual purposes, often many steps may be going on at the same time.

STEP 1: GENERATING EXECUTIVE COMMITMENT

Where the leadership of an organization goes, the rest of the organization will follow. In all our years of doing this work, on only one occasion have we seen a grassroots effort lead to success. For the most part, executives have to lead the way. It is, however, fallacious to assume that leadership is only at the executive level. Employees at *every* level of the organization need to demonstrate leadership on this topic if diversity is really to permeate culture. The question is, how do you make the case for it so that everyone buys in?

The business case is about capturing talent, understanding markets, utilizing diverse perspectives for innovation, knowing how and how not to pitch products, and, ultimately, how to generate employee commitment. Executive leaders need to be role models and advocates for this strategic focus. They can do this by using their bully pulpit and talking about it. They can demonstrate support by talking about how important it is in newsletters, online, or by introducing training classes and attending them as well. We had one CEO chair the companywide diversity council, and at every meeting, business unit leaders knew they would be held accountable for reporting their progress. Another division leader wanted to have diversity integrated into the organization through a leadership and team-building lens and had classes to teach this. Because the sites were far-flung, he made a video that was shown at the beginning and end of every session. No one mistook the importance of this work. On the other hand, we have had people tell us that in their organizations, diversity is the last thing mentioned and the first they eliminated when time and money was in short supply. The message about the priority placed on diversity always gets out. This reminds us of what Ralph Waldo Emerson said about 150 years ago: "I can't hear what you're saying because who you are rings so loudly in my ears." People cannot and will not be fooled. Real commitment is transparent . . . so is the lack of it.

STEP II: ASSESSMENT

Experts agree, and experience in organizations validates, that effective diversity management is data driven. Setting off to create a strategy without having accurate data is like starting on a journey into a new territory blindfolded and without a map. The essential task of assessment is twofold. First, assessment helps the organization understand its current state regarding diversity. It provides data to see where there are exclusions that are hindering the organization's effectiveness or ability to achieve its goals and where there might be additional inclusions that could help. These data help the organization identify needs and then set priorities, goals, and objectives for its diversity strategic plan. Second, assessment provides data that serve as a benchmark to measure against once the strategy is implemented.

Four methods can be used to collect assessment data. A review of existing data is often the first step. Employee opinion survey results; customer satisfaction information; demographic data about the workforce, labor force, and marketplace; turnover statistics; and grievances and complaints are examples of the wealth of information that organizations can find in their store of already existing data. Another method is through interviews with leaders, which can provide information about goals and expectations for diversity and perceptions of challenges and obstacles. A third method, convening focus groups with managers, supervisors, and employees, can give the organization critical information about employees' perceptions of treatment and inclusions and exclusions that affect the organization. Finally, survey questionnaires can give statistical information about employees' perceptions of the organization's diversity management. All these sources of data provide key information

needed to clarify the business case for the diversity initiative and to identify areas of focus for plans and changes. A tangential benefit of assessment is that the process also serves to communicate and educate about diversity and involves staff in the process at an early stage.

STEP III: DIVERSITY COUNCIL

Questions are frequently asked about the purpose and use of diversity councils. A culture change process needs some infrastructure in the organization to guide the process, and diversity councils are a common vehicle to use. Their purposes are several. They can be a two-way communication vehicle, getting feedback from employees and giving it to executives as the beginning of dialogue, and in the other direction, explaining diversity and the initiative to employees. They can keep diversity on the radar screen and field answers to the questions of what and why regarding diversity. They can also be a visible structure, signaling that diversity is relevant. The council should be a body that reflects the whole organization. In other words, when people see diversity council members, at least one person on the council should reflect them by work unit, location, gender, age, race, and other diversity dimensions.

The primary task of most councils is to define obstacles and opportunities for increasing organizational effectiveness, then make recommendations that can be considered at the highest levels of the organization and given to the appropriate structures to be acted on. They also monitor change process and evaluate results. Diversity councils rarely do the long-term change work themselves because council members all have full-time jobs.

For the council to function effectively, in our experience, it needs 2 days of training prior to its initial work. Day 1 focuses on diversity content training so members can more fully understand themselves, their own reactions to differences, what diversity is and how it affects the organization. Day 2 is a planning day when the council sets up its own norms and determines how to get data so it can do its work. It defines its mission and begins the discussion of goal setting and measures of success. To help them be effective after the initial session, there needs to be consistency in meeting times with meetings no longer than a month apart. Ongoing training and team development is a critical factor in effective councils. The best chance for success takes place when there is adequate and ongoing training, work on relevant issues, adherence to agreed-upon norms, and accountability by all involved.

STEP IV: SYSTEMS CHANGES

For diversity management to be effective, more than awareness and sensitivity is required. Organizational systems and operational practices need to be aligned with diversity goals. Systems such as recruitment, hiring, promotion/career development, and compensation/benefits, which affect how the organization treats employees and uses diversity, need to be examined and often modified. Organizations sometimes find they need to conduct pay equity reviews, adjust scheduling and benefits, and revamp promotional processes to ensure fairness and equal access. Setting diversity performance objectives for staff, using diverse hiring panels, and requiring managers to look at a diverse slate of candidates before making a hiring decision are other examples of systems changes that are often made. Others include the establishment of affinity groups or employee associations and mentoring processes,

making promotional criteria and processes more transparent, and expanding outreach efforts in recruiting. All of these changes are aimed at enhancing the organization's ability to recruit and retain top talent and leverage the differences they bring.

STEP V: TRAINING

Training frequently gets a bum rap for not changing organizations. It is not designed to do that. Training can create awareness and help people develop knowledge and skills, and the awareness, knowledge, and skills gained through training can ultimately result in behavior change throughout the organization at individual and team levels. However, it cannot carry the weight of culture change.

The primary initial content areas for diversity training start with what it is and why it matters.

Each organization needs its own definition of diversity and business case. The other two essential components of basic training center on understanding culture at organizational, team, national, and personal levels and how it influences interactions and behavior on the job, and also understanding and managing the phenomena of stereotypes, prejudice, and assumptions. Human beings have always engaged in this prejudgment and labeling process; however, there are ways to manage our immediate unconscious assumptions better, and helping employees learn those ways is part of the content. Beyond basic diversity training, there can also be management training on topics such as building diverse teams, giving performance reviews effectively across different cultures, and handling anger and conflict successfully in diverse groups. Regardless of what content one focuses on, our suggestion is to integrate diversity into already existing training. For example, weaving it into the current supervisorial training is an effective way to leverage diversity. That way it becomes integrated more effectively into all training, appears more relevant and application oriented, and faces less resistance when it does not stand alone. In addition, measurement and accountability are essential. What is expected from people as a result of the training effort? Tying the application to daily work gets people's attention, commands respect, and leads to results.

STEP VI: MEASUREMENT AND EVALUATION

One of our best teachers, Dr. John E. Jones, used to say, "What gets measured gets done, and what gets rewarded gets repeated." Measuring the effects of diversity change efforts and evaluating the results is critical. Measurement gives credibility by providing data that show results, and it also uncovers information that can serve as feedback for continual improvement.

Two kinds of questions need to be answered. The first has to do with the process, and the second has to do with results. Both process and results need to be monitored to gain the most from evaluation. Process measures assess how we did, what went well, what didn't, and why. For example, how many employees participated in the mentoring program, and what was their feedback on the experience? Results measure what difference it made for the organization.

For example, what was the percentage of decrease in turnover, and how much did that save the organization?

Measurement is inherently a comparative process, so it needs to be planned from the beginning. Specific criteria and measures need to be set at the beginning of the plan—for example, an increase in the demographic representation of underrepresented groups, an increase in sales in particular markets, a decrease in turnover, or a reduction of disparity between groups in employee satisfaction results. Then, data relative to criteria are collected as the plan is implemented. Assessment data gathered at the beginning can serve as a baseline to measure against, and both hard and soft measures can be used. Hard measures such as sales, productivity, turnover, customer retention, and demographic representation statistics are critical. However, soft measures such as customer and employee survey scores and hotline calls also give valuable information about the impact and results of diversity strategy implementation.

STEP VII: INTEGRATION

An organization knows it is successful at its change process when it no longer has to make diversity a stand-alone topic because it has become part of all operations. Creating a feedback loop so that procedures continue to be improved and refined and new areas for inclusion are pinpointed is key. This continuous loop keeps both the systems and the outcomes viable and significant while also ensuring both relevance and results. Managing diversity is a continually evolving process aimed at ongoing improvement for the success of the organization.

◆ Discussion Questions

1. How is diversity a strategic business imperative for organizations?

2. What are the reasons for using a broad and inclusive definition of diversity in creating a strategy for leveraging it?

3. How might the different dimensions of diversity affect operations, teamwork, productivity, and effectiveness? Which have had the most impact in your experience in organizations? Give some examples.

4. Why is executive-level support important, and what are some keys to gaining leadership commitment?

5. What expectations exist for the diversity council? Who might they report to, and how much clout should this person have?

6. What roadblocks might exist to releasing people for diversity council work, and how can these obstacles be eliminated?

7. What are some examples of systems changes that can increase inclusion to help achieve organizational goals?

8. What are some essential elements of effective diversity training?

9. Into what current training curriculum could elements of diversity be folded?

10. Why is assessment and measurement important in managing diversity effectively?

11. Where is there obvious need and opportunity within the organization, and with consumers, to leverage diversity?

12. What parts of an organization's past history might affect attitudes toward embarking on this change?

13. What pre-work can be done to minimize the cynicism resulting from past experiences that were unproductive?

◆ *References*

Gardenswartz, L., & Rowe, A. (2003). *Diverse teams at work: Capitalizing on the power of diversity.* Alexandria, VA: Society of Human Resource Management.

Loden, M., & Rosener, J. (1991). *Workforce America! Managing employee diversity as a vital resource.* Homewood, IL: Business One Irwin.

5

RELIGIOUS AND SPIRITUAL DIVERSITY IN THE WORKPLACE

◆ Martin F. Bennett

During a breakout workshop at a major international conference for human resource professionals, a woman from a midsized corporation's HR department shared a complicated encounter. During the final stages of an argumentative salary negotiation, the employee finally expressed her dissatisfaction with a proposed pay raise that she believed to be lower then her male counterpart. After a frank discussion, the employee prepared to leave her manager's office, turned, and respectfully stated her hope that "God would guide the final resolution."

As the conference participants heard the employee's exit line, a ripple of laughter moved through the room. Perhaps the response was triggered by the narrator's tone of voice or even the assumed humor in thinking that God's guidance should enter corporate salary negotiations. The facilitators acknowledged the inherent gender issue but seemed to dismiss God's intervention in the business process as mere humor. Had the laughter been related to race, gender, or sexual identity, the reaction would have been processed. In talking with the workshop presenters later about why they let the God comment slip by, they said in a rather surprised but genuine manner, "I never thought of it. You should have spoken up." I didn't.

What was behind this corporate moment? Was this reaction just an idiosyncratic declaration of a devout employee? Was this an expression of an entrenched organizational culture whose Muslim or Evangelical

Christian heritage really believes in a God that does intervene at work? Or was this assertion just an expression of a stressed-out employee whose spiritual affinity enabled her to confront the nastiness of gender discrimination by bringing in her biggest ally—God? We don't know. Nor do we know what was behind the laughter.

Individuals bring their religion and spirituality, or the lack thereof, with them to work. It's real. It exists. It is unlikely that religious and spiritual diversity will have the same acceptance that other aspects of diversity have unless our social environment drastically changes or unless an organization's dysfunctional behaviors force it to the surface. Perhaps this is due to the sense of privacy many individuals have about their religious and spiritual identities, or an apprehension about being labeled as some sort of zealot, or even the lack of positive media attention or scrutinizing watchdog agencies that monitor organizations—and unfortunately, the few agencies who do are in danger of being dismissed as being too sectarian and having a self-serving point of reference.[1]

Religious and spiritual workplace diversity is the acknowledgment of the commonalities and differences that arise from an employee's religious or spiritual identity that when brought forth in the workplace enhances personal and professional growth and organizational development. An alternative definition might choose the less upbeat explanation that religious and spiritual workplace diversity is the process of addressing destructive behaviors—between individuals and within organizational systems—that legitimizes exclusion based on religious and spiritual-based values and beliefs.

Unlike other diversity characteristics that are observable and transparent, religious and spiritual workplace markers are not easily identified. They have to be drawn out. How an organization chooses to manage this aspect of diversity is vital. The first definition focuses on an employee's potential

and builds on positive strengths. The second definition is reactive and rarely taps the values and full possibility that religious and spiritual workplace diversity can bring.

◆ Trends Forcing a New Understanding

Rapidly changing political contexts; globalizing markets; and shifts in social, economic, and cultural patterns within in and across nations have highlighted the need for a fresh analysis of religious and spiritual diversity. South Korea has the largest number of international headquartered companies, although the greatest global wealth still remains in the United States, Europe, and Japan. How then does the mixture of the religious traditions of South Korea—Christianity, Buddhism, Shamanism, Confucianism, and Chondogyo—influence the structure and strategies of these companies as they undergo their globalization process. An increasingly global business environment inevitably leads to an exchange of traditions that are religion based.

Contemporary managers and leaders need to appraise the impact that the following trends have on their organizations and evaluate their long- and short-term cultural implications:

- Rising immigration and use of international workers—both domestically and globally—who bring different religious and spiritual traditions regarding the meaning of work and how they should be managed

- Increased civil right violations based on religious conflict, deteriorating interpersonal relationships, and corporate morale while incurring financial loss and depreciated reputational capital

- Changed definitions that describe diversity as an "individual difference" rather than "a classification," such as "old white men"

- Raised personal and organizational interest in spirituality and its application to life/work balance

- Expanded insight into religious and spiritual ideologies through global technology exposing adherents and skeptics to immediate information, exploration, and dialogue

- Broadened interest in spirituality in general and in evangelism amongst Christians and Muslims

- Intensified domestic and international culture wars degenerating into religious name calling and spiritual cynicism

These are the trends that local, national, and global organizations face in the 21st century. Evaluating your organization in light of these trends will provide the information necessary to build a business case for developing your religious and spiritual workplace diversity program.

◆ *Religious and Spiritual Workplace—Part of Organizational Success*

As religious and spiritual workplace diversity consolidates its position as a constitutive part of an organization's diversity program, leaders and managers can choose from a wide range of interventions to create change. There are traditionally four levels of organizational engagement—namely, the stages of compliance, normalization, utilization, and maximization.[2]

COMPLIANCE

Compliance strategies answer the question, "How are worker's religious and spiritual diversity rights protected in my organization?" This approach complies with state and federal laws that secure employee rights and confronts discrimination, prejudice, and workplace hostility. Compliance is frequently the first and may unfortunately be the only stage that an organization undertakes. Compliance-based interventions are managed by human resource specialists and legal professionals. Often small or moderate-sized companies with limited budgets manage religious and spiritual workplace diversity in this manner. Their responses do not proceed beyond paying fines, training managers on employees' rights, or organizing mandated awareness seminars for staff. Organizations are obliged to comply with regulations; if they don't, unintended consequences will occur. Red Robin Gourmet Burgers settled a case with the EEOC by agreeing to make substantial policy changes as well as pay $150,000 to a Bellevue, Washington, employee. He was wrongfully dismissed because he refused to cover the Egyptian-designed tattoos on his wrists because they were part of his initiation into the Kemetic Orthodox faith, which prohibited him from ever covering those sacred scriptural texts.[3] In general, compliance interventions focus on what should not have happened and rarely explore the potential of what can happen in using the value that this dimension of diversity brings an organization.

NORMALIZATION

A normalization strategy asks, "How has the expression of religious and spiritual diversity become a familiar dimension within my organization's culture?" Normalization moves beyond case law and mandated corrective programming toward a robust acceptance of each employee's religious and spiritual identity, understood as a contributing asset for the development of the organization.

John Tyson, chairman and CEO of Tyson Foods, Inc., put it another way: "If you can talk about the football game on Monday, then you can talk about your faith on Monday."[4] Organizations that are employee focused use religious and spiritual workplace diversity as part of their people-management and motivational systems. They create interventions such as the American Stock Exchange's recognition of Judaism with its Torah study groups; Boeing's support of Christians, Jews, and Muslims through their identity-specific prayer groups; and Microsoft's use of an online prayer service. Taco Bell, Pizza Hut, and Wal-Mart hire chaplains who visit employees in hospitals and offer counseling to deal with stress and depression.[5]

During this stage, religious and spiritual workplace behaviors gradually become observable. Employees may openly express their belief in God's power in the workplace by pausing for a moment of silence or prayer before a meeting or meal. Members freely join religious- or spiritual-oriented affinity groups similar to those that have been established for other aspects of diversity—race, gender ethnicity, and sexual identity. Tom Muccio, president of Procter & Gamble's Global Customer teams, estimates that 80% of his group's employees participate in religious affinity groups.[6]

Many organizations have embraced normalizing religion and spirituality in their organization's culture. In its study titled "The Spiritual State of the Union: The Role of Spiritual Commitment in the United States," the Gallup Organization reported that 64% of employees surveyed said that their current organization either encourages (32%) or tolerates (32%) the open expression of religion.[7] In light of this information, an important distinction is required. While organizations support their employees in openly expressing

their beliefs—a right guaranteed by the first amendment of the Constitution—they are not open to behaviors that exclude or segregate coworkers based on religious bias or prejudice. Such behaviors are in violation of the law.

Although the United States is acknowledged as one of the most religious and spiritually diverse countries in the world, nevertheless it is recognizably monocultural and historically biased to Christianity.[8] Organizations must monitor the pace of their normalization tactics, forestalling inadvertent exclusion of other equally diverse and conceptually legitimate perspectives. They need to manage inclusion of intra-religious workplace dialogue among sectarian Christians, of inter-religious dialogue among Christians, Muslims, Jews, Hindus, and Buddhist coworker's, and appreciative inquiry and acceptance of coworkers who do not espouse any religious or spiritual tradition. Organizations cannot avoid religious and spiritual diversity by claiming to be solely a monocultural environment. If an organization does not have such diversity within its employee population, it will have that range in its customer base, as the marketplace is religiously and spiritually diverse.

UTILIZATION

Organizations that are committed to a utilization strategy ask, "How are religious- and spiritual-influenced ideals, values, and beliefs used in the workplace?" Larger and more global organizations have greater opportunities to use such interventions—some more positively and, unfortunately, some negatively.

Kohler, Inc., a global group providing kitchen and bath fixtures, furniture, power systems, engines, real estate, and hospitality, could have avoided affronting Hindus in

Nepal, Indonesia, Malaysia, Singapore, the UK, and the United States if someone would have recognized the offensiveness of a brass figure of a scantily dressed woman that was used to advertise a designer upscale shower suite. The figure was the Lord Nataraja—a form of Lord Shiva—and the water streaming from its hands was the blessed waters of the Ganges, a far cry from a shower head.[9] Understanding the impact of religious icons, symbols, and texts would have been invaluable to Kohler. Organizations cannot use such ideas without full assessment of their influence on believers as well as nonbelievers. Managers, manufacturing staff, creative people, marketing professionals, and corporate leaders need to constantly evaluate the impact such usage has on their organization's reputational capital. That type of insight occurs when employees' opinions and insights are openly exchanged and where sufficient religious and spiritual cultural literacy exist at a managerial level to facilitate a comprehensive analysis and discussion.

Three areas surface where diversity can be best utilized—employee management, alliance partnerships, and customer service. Approximately four out of every five persons studied in *The Spiritual State of the Union* stated they would like to see open expressions of religion encouraged and tolerated within their organization.[10] If that is true, employees have an increasing expectation that their organizations will create appropriate systems to facilitate that openness. Companies who want to maintain workers as well as become an employer of choice need to create corporate cultures that respects this type of expression. Since many religious and spiritual traditions have different viewpoints of how work fits within their beliefs, managers are required to understand the expectations of subordinates and not just assume that "we are all the same." It is basic to human resource management that

when workers feel a gap between their values and the organization's value they will be stressed, alienated, demotivated, and experience conflict of interests all of which affect performance.[11] Equally true, when alliance partners and customers perceive an organization is respectful of their religious and spiritual traditions, such organizations will be positively sought as business partners. Managers and supervisors are pivotal in handling this level of religious and spiritual diversity engagement since they know the employees who bring consistent organizational value as well as those who for a variety of personal reasons create misunderstandings.

MAXIMIZATION

The final question is, "What remains to be done to harness the value that religious and spiritual workplace diversity can bring to strategic growth and development?" The greatest value that religion and spiritual diversity offers organizations, both large and small, is an intrinsic mindset that provides insight into people's lives and their attitudes to work. Some corporate leaders have projected their religious identities deep within their organizations. For example, ServiceMaster, a conglomeration that includes Termini, TruGreen, ChemLawn, and Merry Maids, was built on the values of its founder and chairman, Bill Pollard, who, after escaping a sudden fire, brought his understanding of God into his business process. His interventions stimulated new human resources practices including stock ownership for all employees and a cap on the wage differential between top and bottom.[12] Truett Cathy, founder of Chick-Fil-A, a chain of fast-food restaurants, and John Tyson, the chairman and CEO of Tyson Foods, have also applied their religious tradition in the management of their organizations, although each of their applications was primarily driven by a specific religious tradition. Few organizations have maximized the cross-religious and multi-spiritual opportunity.

At this level of engagement, a religious and spiritual cultural analysis should be included in the strategic scanning process, especially as organizations search for new products and markets. Several financial institutions, such as AMRO, PNP Paribas, Standard Charter, and Goldman Sachs, have embraced "*Sharia*-compliant" financial products to engage its emerging Muslim markets. Islam demands that wealth cannot be generated from immoral means such as alcohol, gambling, or tobacco. Also, those investments must not earn interest.[13] Christian tradition allows for interest but counsels that the rates should be just. By acknowledging Christian and Islamic workplace traditions and using sound financial acumen these institutions successfully developed new religious and culturally infused business products and found a reconciling strategy that respects each tradition but still allows their institutions to meet their shareholders' expectations.

To accomplish maximization, CEO's, senior corporate executives, and board members need to develop an inclusive religious and spiritual cultural acumen and the aptitude to apply it for the best interests of their organizations. Of all the levels of development, maximization is the least seen. Perhaps this is a reflection of the newness of religion and spirituality as a legitimate aspect of diversity or a lack of understanding of its role in strategic planning. Possibly it is also because of the demoralizing global clash of religious and spiritual ideologies and increasing politicization of religious belief. Time will tell us more.

Each level of engagement has distinctive tasks, as demonstrated in Table 5.1.

While managers and leaders have the responsibility to assist their organizations in developing religious and spiritual workplace diversity, they function at different levels.

◆ Managing for Religious and Spiritual Diversity

Managers are trained to approach here-and-now problems and administer solutions. They supervise all "nut and bolts" interventions. Using their positional power they guide teams in the organization's corporate culture, policies, and procedures. Ideally, managers have the competencies to maximize their employees' idiosyncratic attributes for the benefit of the organization's shareholders and stakeholders.

Contemporary managers need to be knowledgeable about Title VII of the Civil Rights Act of 1964.[14] It obliges all organizations to accommodate employees' religious beliefs unless doing so creates an undue hardship for their organization. Due to the lack of legal clarity, and the confusion as to what Title VII actually considered a "religion," Congress amended Title VII in 1973 and extended legal protection to what is understood today as "spirituality." Religious practices are broadly understood to

> include moral or ethical beliefs as to what is right and wrong and which are sincerely held with the strength of traditional religious views. . . . The fact that no religious organization espouses such beliefs or the fact that the religious groups to which the individual professes to belong may not accept such beliefs will not determine whether the belief is a religious belief of the employee or prospective employee. (Title 29, §1605.1)

This statute also protects individuals who self-identify as humanitarians, atheists, and agnostics. It is a manager's responsibility

Table 5.1   Levels of Engagement

Levels of Engagement	Engagement Tasks
Compliance	• Facilitate the spirit as well as the letter of the law of the United States Civil Rights Act of 1964 and United Nation's Declaration on Religion. • Reconcile dilemmas when employees' religious and spiritual requirements are in conflict with their work responsibilities. • Create cross-functional teams of human resource and legal staff for rapid response. • Include religious and spiritual workplace diversity basics in new hire orientation and monitor compliance. • Design targeted training events to address specific employee or functional needs. • Communicate success stories to demonstrate the organizational value for the inclusion of religious and spiritual workplace diversity.
Normalization	• Create opportunities, both formal and informal, for intra- and inter-religious and spiritual workplace diversity dialogues. • Support an inclusive and tolerant corporate culture with religious and spiritual diversity fully aligned with other diversity initiatives. • Acknowledge religious and spiritual diversity conversations as a component of building an inclusive employee culture and morale. • Check employee acceptance of other's religion- and spirituality-based workplace behaviors in performance-management protocols, team appraisals, and organizational culture studies. • Provide training programs on religious and spiritual workplace diversity as part of required professional development.
Utilization	• Seek religious and spiritual perspective supporting product development, sales initiatives, and market expansion. • Communicate the organization's diversity commitments to external clients and vendors to improve reputation capital. • Develop capacity for faith-based alliance management. • Coach high-potential employees on how to position their religious and spiritual diversity tradition for the best benefit in the organization. • Analyze interpersonal and organizational dilemmas for religious and spiritual implications that have a positive or negative impact on operations.
Maximization	• Support a robust global strategy by appreciative reference to other religion- and spirituality-influenced workplace models. • Endorse corporate social responsibility initiatives inclusive but not limited to religion- and spirituality-based organization. • Provide insight and potential solutions to organizational dilemmas, especially in markets and work environments where religion- and spirituality-based behaviors have created conflict or polarity. • Share the organization's inclusive structure and strategic model in communities where religious and spiritual traditions alienate their broader civic society.

not only to resolve difficult problems but also to create inclusive opportunities that support the employees and the organization's goals.

Since managers hire, train, supervise, and evaluate employees they are the first responders to situations of harassment, discrimination, and workplace hostility. The U.S. Equal Employment Opportunity Commission (EEOC) reported that although the number of charges of religious discrimination in 2005 (3,878) was 9% lower than the post-9/11 record set in 2002, it is one-third more than the number 10 years earlier. Such complaints are lodged by people of many different faiths. Of these complaints in 2005, 20% were made by Muslims, 18% by Christians, 12% by Jews, and 50% by other religions.[15] Unfortunately, many of these cases illustrate the ineptness of managers who exacerbated resolvable situations that ultimately ended in the court.

There are numerous cases that illustrate dilemmas where managers have failed (Table 5.2). They occurred due to the lack of preemptive policy, inept execution by managers and supervisors, insufficient knowledge related to the congruency of prescribed religious behaviors with the organization's requirements, the clash of idiosyncratic religion- and spirituality-based values that are not supported by the enveloping organizational culture, unabated proselytizing, rigid people-management policies, as well as core human and interpersonal communication breakdowns fueled by religion-inspired biases and prejudice.[16]

◆ Practical Steps Managers Have Taken

Managers in both the public and private sectors tactically shape their workplace environment. It is important to remember that not all faith-based requests for accommodations must be met, but many can and should be. Managers have the power to create change—if not a culture of inclusion—by instituting some of the following interventions:

- Allow faith-based groups that are voluntary, open, and non-coercive to meet in the organization's facilities and/or communicate through organizational e-mail.

- Create work schedules that allow for prayer or reflection time—either daily or weekly.

- Support voluntary study of inspirational, spiritual, and sacred books during break time, lunch time, as well as before or after work.

- Authorize flex time and flex vacations to facilitate out-of-office attendance at religious and spiritual gatherings held during normal work hours.

- Create neutral spaces for the sole purpose of personal reflection, medication, or prayer within the organization's facilities.

- Facilitate inclusive, organization-wide celebrations of major religious and spiritual holidays.

- Engage leaders in internal or external training on religious and spiritual workplace traditions to support the continued development of the organization's cultural knowledge.

- Establish religion- and spirituality-based identity groups to provide insight on organizational and personnel issues.

- Monitor all diversity programs and trainers—both in-house as well as external consultants—for consistent inclusion of religious and spiritual diversity themes in case studies, examples, and process analysis.

Table 5.2	Workplace Examples
The Event	*Areas to Reconcile*
• A newly hired Muslim receptionist in a Christian-sponsored healthcare facility was fired for refusing to remove her headscarf and sues her former employer for unlawful dismissal.[1]	• Dress and grooming accommodation • Corporate culture tolerance for diverse values and beliefs • Hiring protocols
• A Catholic worker in a retail store sues after being refused time off to go on a pilgrimage to Yugoslavia during the Christmas shopping season.[2]	• Range of tolerance for exceptions based on personal religious practice • Cultural literacy for distinguishing core religious requirements from personal expression • Flexible leave policy
• A Christian in a large communications firm, who wore an anti-abortion button to work, sued her company when dismissed since coworkers threaten to walk off due to the visual trauma of the pin's graphic.[3]	• Dress, grooming, and religious discrimination and accommodation • Religious expression standards • Unreasonable and hostile imposition of religious belief
• After multiple requests for accommodation were refused, a Jewish professor sues her institution's dean and department head since they consistently rearranged departmental meetings and functions on days that conflicted with her Sabbath preparation.[4]	• Parameters for reasonable accommodation • Equitable work assignment processes • Warning and dismissal policy and procedures
• A manager in a municipal office frequently calls a subordinate a "sinner," demanding that the person repent and attend prayer sessions in order not to go to hell.[5]	• Prescribed management strategies for escalating hostile work environment • Religious expression norms • Unreasonable and hostile imposition of religious belief • Parameters of freedom of speech and hate language • Warning and dismissal policy and procedures

1. Civil Rights Act of 1964, Pub. L. No, 88-352 (Title VII). Available at www.eeoc.gov/policy/vii.html.

2. Office of High Commissioner of Human Rights. (1981). Declaration of the elimination of all forms of intolerance and of discrimination based on religion or belief. (Resolution 36/55 of 25). New York: The United Nations Printing Office. Available at www.unhchr.ch/html/menu3/b/d_intole.htm.

3. EEOC v. Presbyterian Ministries, Inc., 788 F. Supp. 1154 (W.D. Wash. 1992).

4. Arthur, J. S. (1998, June 5). Religious rights not violated, court says. Human Resource Executive, 22.

5. Wilson v. U.S. West Communications, Inc., 860 F Supp. 665 (D. Neb. 1994), aff'd, 58F.3d 1337 (8th Cir. 1995).

6. Andrews v. City of Philadelphia, 895 F.2d 1469 (3d Cir. 1990).

7. Venters v. City of Delphi, 123 F3d 956, 972 (7th Cir 1997).

- Meet annually with human resources and legal teams to review all discrimination, harassment, and hostile environment claims related to religion and spirituality and implement process improvements.

- Identify desired outcome measure and recognizable gaps for religious and spiritual workplace expression.

- Include line-item recognition of religious and spirituality workplace diversity in performance-management tools.

- Measure employee attitudes toward religious and spiritual workplace diversity—both domestic and global—in organizational attitudinal surveys.

A subset of manager competency, known as leadership, displays a different range of competencies. Warren Bennis, a well-known management consultant, succinctly counseled that "A manager does things right, while a leader does the right things."[17]

◆ Leaders Operate Differently in Organizations

Employees and their managers have been the major coordinators of religion and spiritual traditions in the workplace. Dating back to 1985 many American workers recognized that their religious institutions, mainly Christian, were not adequately connecting their core religiosity with their day-to-day reality at work. The resulting Faith-at-Work Movement[18] enabled workers to actively create programs, policies, and practices that to their mind brought "God into the workplace." Today, broader and more inclusive strategic interventions are emerging.

Senior leaders have the broadest responsibilities within organizations and sometimes the greatest distance from the employees. They inspire people to think beyond the restraints of their current accomplishments and embrace the potential of the future. Unlike politicians who personally affirm religiosity but when they see it approaching organizationally run behind the banner of "separation of church and state," private and public sector leaders are more in charge and free to utilize diverse religions and spiritualities as tools to advance the missions and visions of their organizations. How they lead that change is the question.

Tom Chappell, CEO of Tom's of Maine, is a good example. In 1970 he founded a small entrepreneurial company that produced natural personal care products made without artificial and animal ingredients. In March, 2006 Colgate-Palmolive Company purchased the company. Tom Chappell not only increased his company's financial capital but also its spiritual capital. As a leader he stayed mindful of profit but gave away 10% of its pretax profits to charities. Tom's of Maine also gives employees four paid hours a month to volunteer for community service. In its manufacturing process, only ingredients that are good for the environment are used. After studying at Harvard Divinity School, Chappell reengineered his company into a sort of ministry, saying, "I am ministering—and I am doing it in the marketplace, not in the church, because I understand the marketplace better than the church." Understanding that his marketplace also had Muslim and Jewish customers who had stringent requirements for halal and kosher products, Tom's of Maine proudly secured appropriate religious certifications for 90 items within its product line.[19]

While not the only source of ethics, religious and spiritual foundational values and beliefs do have a role in informing business decisions. Studies have identified the positive correlation of religion and ethics, finding that religiosity was a significant predictor of ethical problem recognition.[20]

A group of American businesspersons who self-identified as having a high or moderate level of religious intensity also showed a high level of ethical judgment.[21] It is increasingly evident that economic development cannot be separated from ethical development, which in turn cannot be segregated from the influence of religious and spiritual values.

Unfortunately, the 20th century ended with major ethics scandals such as Enron, Global Crossing, WorldCom, and Cendant. Such scandals make it apparent that corporate culture programs and their statements embossed on laminated cards hung around employee necks do not create ethics or prevent ethics violations. Inclusion of religious and spiritual workplace diversity supports ethical sustainability. Ethical leaders are required to reconcile their organization's actions with the ethical systems of their employees, customers, vendors, and alliance partners.

Corporate ethics require that decisions demonstrate fairness, equity, and impartiality. Diverse religious and spiritual systems will differ on what is considered fair, equal, and impartial. Leaders require good cross-cultural skills to recognize and align those differences. The art of religious and spiritual diversity leadership is the ability to continually evaluate the multitude of perspectives and create an evolving and inclusive dialogue of reconciliation for action.

Another viable expression of religious and spiritual workplace diversity that requires leadership is corporate social responsibility. CSR addresses the responsibility that an organization has to its broader community by conducting its business in an open, ethical, and transparent manner that supports individuals, shareholders, and the external environment. It manifests itself through corporate-sponsored activities ranging from hands-on community development projects, fundraising, matching contribution programs for local and international projects inclusive of religious- and spiritual-based organizations, and the establishment of major foundations that support globalized humanitarian aid. Frequently an employee's religion- and spirituality-based motivations find expression through their organization's CSR program.

◆ **What Leaders Are Challenged to Do**

While managers deal with tactical issues, leaders look at capital development, including employee capital, economic capital, and spiritual capital. Leaders have the ability to uniquely engage their organization when they do the following:

- Conduct yearly religious and spiritual workplace diversity strategy reviews examining how the organization utilizes its innate religious and spiritual capital

- Create an ongoing religious and spiritual workplace diversity advisory board consisting of regional, national, and international representatives who inform leadership of trends, challenges, and opportunities

- Provide virtual and real-time open chat rooms with senior management and board members seeking ideas related to religious and spiritual workplace diversity applications or abuses

- Sponsor internal and external research on organizational success attributed to spirituality- and religion-influenced strategies and systems

- Establish an ethics council to align all organizational behaviors with ethical standards inclusive of those espoused by religious and spiritual traditions

◆ *Key Competencies Managers and Leaders Require*

Managers and leaders require general and specific competencies to go about their work. A competency is a personal characteristic that can predict successful performance and is displayed through consistent behaviors that demonstrate knowledge, a positive attitude in approaching a solution, and a skill to complete the action. Some competencies that managers and leaders master if they are interested in enhancing religious and spiritual cultural literacy are as follows:

AUTHENTICITY

- Understands one's own religious and spiritual orientation and its influence on leadership style, decision making, and ethics

- Maintains transparency in working with coworkers—no personal or spirituality-biased agenda

- Relates well with individuals from a wide range of religious and spiritual backgrounds and acknowledges their innate ethical concerns

INTERPERSONAL AND TEAM SKILLS

- Shows personal and professional respect for coworkers' religious and spiritual workplace perspectives through appreciative inquiry

- Provides effective feedback, corrective direction, and active supervision addressing questionable behaviors related to religious and spiritual bias or prejudice

- Demonstrates inclusion and respect for religious and spirituality workplace traditions by referencing holy day and ritual celebrations, demonstrating culturally appropriate social behaviors, and acknowledging an array of religious and spiritual texts that support the goals of the organization

ORGANIZATIONAL COMMUNICATION CLARITY

- Raises questions and seeks information concerning the underlying religion- and spirituality based values, beliefs, and behaviors observed within the organization

- Documents areas of company/ employee religious and spiritual compatibility and communicates its value to the organization

- Presents the organization's policies that support Title VII for review and process enhancements

CREATIVE PROBLEM SOLVING

- Seeks solutions that comply with federal and state laws that support the company's mission as well as addresses employee's religious and spiritual requirements

- Identifies intra-organizational best-of-class tactics in other departments and implements them in own areas of accountability

- Attends external religion- and spirituality-focused diversity training and applies new insights to the organization's policies and management practices

Cultural exemplars, be they managers, leaders, or employees, exist at all levels in organizations. They demonstrate many of the above competencies and are acknowledged by their peers as consistently displaying the religious and spiritual knowledge, attitude, and skills that effectively support the missions of their organization. Their activities make organizations better. What remains to be determined in many organizations is if these employees will find opportunities to bring these underutilized skills into greater use. Today we would never question the value that race- and gender-based perspectives bring to effective management. Religion and spiritual workplace diversity is still in its infancy and awaits greater recognition.

◆ Conclusion

"Religious and spiritual workplace diversity" has become a catchphrase that is easily acknowledged but rarely instituted until conflict appears. Preemptive policies exist; however, more proactive and strategic change agents are needed in board rooms, in senior and line management positions, and in employee populations.

David Miller, the director of the Yale Center for Faith and Culture, distinguishes organizations as faith-based or faith-friendly. The strength of faith-based organizations is their endorsement of a specific religious or spiritual tradition that is comprehensively integrated into the organization's strategies, structure, and systems. While faith-based organizations honor one religious or spiritual perspective, they leave little room for the acceptance and integration of others' beliefs. The power of faith-friendly organizations is their ability to manage and utilize a fuller array of religious and spiritual workplace traditions for the strategic benefit of their organization and its employees, customers, clients, and alliance partners.

There is urgency for organizations to address religious and spiritual workplace diversity. In examining the relationship between faith and the U.S. economy, the Gallup Poll[22] identified that "almost two-thirds of Americans—churchgoing or not—say the overall health of the nation is heavily dependent on its spiritual health. About seventy seven percent also said that the nation's economy is dependent on its spiritual well-being."[23] If organizations are going to utilize the value of religious and spiritual workplace traditions, they must create strategies and structures to meet the expectations of an increasingly spiritually aware if not alarmed workforce.

Most organizations are currently prepared to address the legal and accommodation issues underlying religious and spiritual workplace diversity. There is a sampling of organizations, such as Tom's of Maine and Tyson Foods, Inc., that demonstrate what faith-based organizations can do when leaders set the strategy and managers implement religion- and spirituality-friendly tactics. It will be up to organizational leaders of the 21st century to effectively develop faith-friendly institutions through their cross-cultural acumen and religious and spiritual literacy to harness the potential that this underutilized and frequently unspoken aspect of diversity offers.

Discussion Questions

1. Is your organization faith-friendly, faith-based, or faithless? How does that designation support or hinder your organization's mission and goal?

2. What major religious and spiritual megatrends are affecting your organization, and what should or can be done about them? What will happen if nothing is done?

3. At what level of religious and spiritual workplace engagement is your organization—compliance, normalization, utilization, or maximization? What needs to be done to move to the next level? Who needs to be involved?

4. How has your organization gained or lost reputational capital due to the way it has managed religious and spiritual workplace diversity? How can that capital be regained?

5. What personal competency or competencies do you need to develop to manage religious and spiritual workplace diversity? What difference could you make in your organization should you exercise those newfound abilities?

◆ *Notes*

1. See Anti-Defamation League (Judaism): www.adl.org; CAIR (Council for American–Islamic Relations): www.cair.com; Catholic League for Religious and Civil Rights: www.catholicleague.org; Sikh American Legal Defense and Education Fund: www.saldef.org; American-Arab Anti-Discrimination Committee: www.adc.org; and American Hindus Against Defamation: www.hindunet.org/anti_defamation.

2. Adapted from Kahn, A., & Gomez, S. (1998). *Challenging diversity: Taking the next step.* Phoenix, AZ: Budshel Press. Available at www.culture-link.com

3. EEOC v. Red Robin Gourmet Burgers, Inc. (W.D. Wash. 2005). No. C04–1291 JLR. Retrieved from www.eeoc.gov/litigation/settlements/settlement09–05.html

4. Walter, M. (2000, February 18). Tyson discusses faith in workplace at business lunch. *Arkansas Democrat-Gazette.* Retrieved from www.nwanews.com/adg/Business/108332/

5. Johnson, H. (2004). Taboo no more. *Training, 41*(4), 22–26.

6. Kinni, T. (2007). *Faith at work: Redrawing the line between religion and business.* New York: The Conference Board.

7. Gallup, G. (2006). *The spiritual state of the union: The role of spiritual commitment in the United States.* Princeton, NJ: The Gallup Organization.

8. According to the CIA World Factbook, the United States is 78% Christian and 10% no religion, while other religions compose 12% of the U.S. population. In descending order, the largest identified religious groups are Protestant (52%), Roman Catholic (24%), Mormon (2%), Buddhist (2%), Jewish (1%), and Muslim (1%).

9. AHAD protests Kohler's use of Nataraja image. Retrieved from www.hindunet.org/anti_defamation/kohler/

10. Gallup, G. (2006). *The spiritual state of the union.*

11. Nadesan, M. H. (1999). The discourses of corporate spiritualism and evangelical capitalism. *Management Communication Quarterly, 13*(1), 3–42.

12. Olian, J. (2003, December 8). Spirituality is finding a place in the workplace. *Seattle Post-Intelligencer.* Retrieved from http://seattlepi.nwsource.com/business/151289_spiritualdivide08.html

13. Islamic finance: Calling the faithful. (2006, December 9). *Economist,* p. 78. Retrieved from www.economist.com/finance/displaystory.cfm?story_id=8382406

14. Civil Rights Act of 1964, Pub. L. No. 88–352 (Title VII). Retrieved from www.eeoc.gov/policy/vii.html

15. Norman, J. (2006, August 28). Worship in the workplace. *Orange County Register.* Retrieved from www.ocregister.com/ocregister/money/small business/article_1255596.php

16. To gather more information on determining religious discrimination cases in your organization or to file a report, contact the U.S. Equal Employment Opportunity Commission at their Web site: www.eeoc.gov/types/religion.html

17. Bennis, W. & Goldsmith, J. (2003). *Learning to lead: A workbook on becoming a leader.* New York: Basic Books.

18. Johnson, A. (2005, March 21). The Faith-at-Work Movement finds a home:

Building a Silicon Valley of the soul in northwest Arkansas. Retrieved from www.msnbc.msn.com/id/7201269/. Eldred. K. (2005) *God at work: Transforming people and nations through business.* Ventura, CA: Regal Books. Miller, D. W. (2007). *God at work: The history and promise of the Faith at Work movement.* New York: Oxford University Press.

19. McLaughlin, C. (2001). *Spirituality in business.* Retrieved from www.visionarylead.org

20. Singhapakdi, A., Marta, J., Rallapalli, K., & Rao, C. P. (2000). Toward an understanding of religiousness and marketing ethics: An empirical study. *Journal of Business Ethics, 2*(4), 305–320.

21. Longenecker, J. G., McKinney, J. A., & Moore, C. W. (2004). Religious intensity, evangelical Christianity, and business ethics: An empirical study. *Journal of Business Ethics, 55,* 373–386.

22. Gallup, G. (2006) *The spiritual state of the union.*

23. Harper, J. (2007, January 31). Spiritual state of union found strong. *Washington Times.* Retrieved from http://pewforum.org/news/display.php?NewsID=12585

THE LEGAL IMPLICATIONS OF CROSS-CULTURAL LEADERSHIP AND TRADE

◆ John C. Tobin

E arlier in this text, Chapter 2 described the basic concepts of culture. We can describe culture as the "shared mental programs that condition individual responses to their environment" (Hofstede, 1980, as cited by Thomas & Inkson, 2003, p. 22). In other words, shared responses to external stimuli are seen as another means of identifying a cultural behavior. Thus, in Japan, when one person listens to another speaking, it is quite common for the listener to utter "hi" from time to time to communicate, "I hear and understand you." Two Westerners in the same example might merely nod frequently or say "uh-huh." Yet, putting the Asian and Westerner together, to translate "hi" as "yes" would be as misleading to the Westerner; as would the habit of nodding to convey "I accept and give honor to you" be confusing to the Asian. Thus, loss of cultural cues can lead to widely different outcomes.

Leaders and businesspersons, those who function across a cultural milieu, must be mindful of the cultural perspective of all players. When focusing on transcultural legal activities, from contracts to litigation, that mindfulness becomes obligatory. As suggested by Early and Ang (2003), cross-cultural players must acquire a broader situational awareness that accounts for what is seen and heard in the mind's eye of both parties across the cultural divide. This chapter borrows from the work of leaders in the fields of organizational behavior and negotiation theory to consider the elements of this situational awareness of culture.[1]

Hofstede (1991) posited various dimensions for distinguishing behaviors between cultures, including individualism/collectivism, power distance (a measure of a culture's hierarchical organization), uncertainty or risk avoidance, and orientation toward goal or environmental concerns (career success versus quality of life). These seemingly simple filters disclosed, for example, the rather remarkable distinction between the United States and Chile for the factor of individualism versus collectivism. Andreas Cruzat (n.d.) noted that conflict, the necessary byproduct of leadership, is viewed as destabilizing and is disfavored in collectivist Chile. Conversely, the individualist United States puts a premium on competitive success through conflict. Legal activities, such as contract formation or formal dispute resolution through litigation, when viewed across these cultural dimensions, lead, unavoidably, to widely divergent results.

◆ Culture and the Law

To better understand the cross-cultural factors of international legal practices, we'll review the key theories underpinning the world's major legal systems. We note that culture, the sharing of common perceptions of outside stimuli by a group, a subset of the value system within a culture, will be its ethics. We note that ethics, a culture or society's rules of acceptable and unacceptable behavior, are transitory over time. We also note that laws are a special subset of ethics, by which the culture or society grants authority to a governing body to enforce transgressions of the rules of acceptable and unacceptable behavior. In contrast, morals,

the black-and-white differential between right and wrong, are typically fixed in time.

SUBSTANTIVE AND PROCEDURAL LAWS

Laws, the codification of a culture's or society's standards of acceptable and unacceptable behavior, are generally formulated, regardless of underpinning legal theory, so as to address two key areas: *substantive laws*, which address conduct between parties (public and private), and *procedural laws*, which address the administration or processing of claims based on the substantive law. Substantive laws are further divided into specific subject matter areas:

- Criminal: laws created by the government that impose duties on persons with respect to the public in general, such as to not kill, steal, or engage in other illegal activities

- Civil: laws created by the government (society) that define the duties owed between private parties

- Regulatory: quasi-criminal duties imposed on organizations on the basis of subject matter, such as occupational, environmental, or land-use regulations

Procedural laws regulate the processing of legal claims or actions through a system that compels compliance with the law. Such laws may specify who or what entity may file a legal claim or initiate litigation; these laws may set time limits within which an action must be initiated or thereafter it is considered abandoned. Such laws often control the staging or processing actions from an initial filing stage, through a fact-finding stage, to a decision-making phase, and, in some systems, to an appellate or reviewing stage. One group of commentators has suggested that the efficiency of a legal system may be inversely proportionate to the complexity or "formalism" of its procedural legal structure (Djankov, La Porta, Lopez-de-Silanes, & Shleifer, 2003).

These two distinctions offer some insight into the manner in which laws come into being within a culture. Let us start with the concept of duty. Generally a duty is an obligation for one party to behave in a specified manner with respect to another. The obligation either stems from a fixed basis, such as a moral system, or a transitory system, such as a community-based code. These distinctions mirror the two major theories of the nature of the law (jurisprudence): natural law and legal positivism. As a working definition, let us consider law as a culture's shared definitions (codification) of duties owed by persons, to one another, within a society.

◆ **Theoretical Basis for World Legal Systems**

NATURAL LAW THEORY

The concept of law's function offered by the theory of natural law arises from St. Thomas Aquinas's observation, "*lex inuista non est lex*" ("unjust law is not law"). Thus, a law that promulgates a duty, which is not grounded in morality, is not a duty at all. Here, the fundamental law is to do good and avoid evil. Since good and evil are objective, or normative, every law must conform to the original imperative. Any deviation from that imperative renders the law unjust. Paraphrasing Sir William Blackstone (1823/1979), the father of the common law of England and a member of the historical lineage of the American legal system, it is forbidden for any valid law to ever conflict with the natural, as the natural law serves as the foundation for all valid laws.

Natural law presumes that man's rational ability, God given, allows humans to rationally determine what is good and what is evil: This is the natural law. In his *Summa Theologiae* (1275/1988), Aquinas asserted that the product of this divinely given rationality was the *eternal law.* Participation in the eternal law by rational creatures is called *natural law.* Ergo, anything ungodly is manifestly evil.

Thus, as the right to govern was given divinely, and in turn, to the kings of the Holy Roman Empire, France, England, Germany, and Spain, opposition to the crown was inherently evil and thus illegal. The key to the validity of a natural law statute was and is inextricable from the nature of good and evil. Paraphrasing Aquinas's statement that an immoral law is not an enforceable law, any statutory provision that does not accord with the unwritten but commonly accepted moral code of a nation is, at the very least, subject to a challenge as to its efficacy.

A leading example of a natural law system is that of shari'a, the legal and judicial system codified in the holy Muslim book, the Qur'an. This system is said to be practiced in its purest form within the Kingdom of Saudi Arabia and in the Islamic Republic of Iran. Brown (1997) has noted that the Islamic shari'a is not an easily identifiable set of rules that can be mechanically applied but rather a long and quite varied intellectual tradition.

Many Middle Eastern countries continue to incorporate some traditional shari'a into their legal codes, especially in the area of personal-status law, which governs marriage, divorce, and inheritance. In other areas of the law, such as the criminal code, most Islamic nations have attempted to limit the application of traditional shari'a, replacing it either with secular legislation or with laws characterized as modern interpretations of shari'a. In general, each nation's legal code tends to reflect a variety of historical and cultural influences. For example, some Middle Eastern legal codes have their roots in the Napoleonic law system and the Ottoman Empire (Brown, 1997).

Likewise, single-party states, such as the (then) Union of Soviet Socialist Republics and the People's Republic of China (at least prior to the economic changes of Chinese Party Secretary Deng Xiaoping in 1982) have utilized Marxism–Leninism, and the theory of social realism served as the moral system underpinning the *natural law* of those countries. Rather than an independent judiciary serving as a neutral third party for the settling disputes between private persons, the party provided bureaucratic agents who served as both fact finders and decision makers within strict ideological guidelines (Grazin, 2000). Finally, tribal law systems, such as those seen in segments of Afghanistan, regions in Africa, and in the northern provinces of Pakistan, also illustrate natural law systems.

Some have commented that theological or ideologically rooted legal systems are "hyper-legalistic" despite their operating without an independent judiciary. Instead, attorneys act as bureaucratic functionaries who measure the acceptability of individual conduct against the tenants of ideology or theology. Thus, all crimes ultimately involve an assessment of the degree to which an individual fails to conform to ideology or theology (Grazin, 2000).

The American legal system, historically rooted in the natural law system of its colonial antecedent, the English Common Law, is somewhat of a variant. Waves of statutory or code-based legislation have made the U.S. system more mixed than a true natural law system. For example, consider the case of *U.S. v. Lynch* (1996; U.S. App. 2d Cir., LEXIS 32729),[2] noted by Himma (1999). In *Lynch*, one litigant sought to validate Aquinas's proposition about immoral law. Mr. Lynch, a member of a pro-life, anti-abortionist organization, was prosecuted by the federal government under the Freedom of Access to Clinic Entrances Act (FACE), which prohibits the threat or use of force to obstruct the entrance to a reproductive health provider. In seeking the invalidation of the statute, the defendant argued that the FACE statute protected the taking of human life, contrary to any natural or moral formulation of law, and hence was null and void. The Court of Appeals for the Second Circuit upheld Lynch's federal district court conviction, citing the trial court judge's ruling on the defendant's natural law argument:

> That seal above my head says . . . this is Caesar's court. This is not a church, this is not a temple, this is not a mosque. And we don't live in a theocracy. This is a court of law. I will look at all the *legal* issues. (emphasis added) (U.S. v. Lynch, at 32734)

This case illustrates the turbulence in the long path of development of the law in the United States, which has waxed and waned between natural law (consider the 19th Amendment establishing prohibition as the law of the land) and legal positivism (illustrated by a United States Supreme Court decision defending the burning of the United States flag as free speech under the 1st Amendment.) The controversy continues today as the several states consider "defense of marriage" amendments to state constitutions, in the shadow of congressional rejection of a defense of marriage amendment to the U.S. Constitution. As will be discussed below, the American legal system is an admixture of natural law and legal positivism that sometimes seems as war with itself (Hart, 1994).

Culture and Natural Law

Not surprisingly, Hofstede's dimensions for the so-called natural law countries emphasize collectivism and risk aversion. These trait are illustrated by the more typical tribal or sectarian collectivism of many of the nations of the Arabian Gulf, the middle ground of Pakistan, to the more extreme examples of the USSR of the past and the People's Republic of China. In all of these nations, the individual is expected to submit to the will of the collective, and change is glacial, at best. This trait seamlessly reinforces the broad differences in power distance or the hierarchical nature of these countries (Hofstede, 1991). Likewise, adherence taken to the path of those who have gone before vitiates against change and supports risk aversion. Thus, as has been noted before, rather than an independent judiciary serving as a neutral third party for settling disputes between private persons, the judiciary of natural law countries provides bureaucratic agents who serve as both fact finders and decision makers within strict theological or ideological guidelines (Grazin, 2000).

However, the seeming harmony dissolves when the United States and Common Law countries (generally, the British Commonwealth), which all have natural law as a historical antecedent to their systems, are included in the category of natural law states. The majority of this subset of countries are remarkably individualistic, risk seeking, and relatively flat in terms of power distance. The explanation, if one is possible, is that, as further discussed below, the adversarial countries tend toward a blend of natural law and legal positivism.

THEORY OF LEGAL POSITIVISM

The polar or conceptual opposite of the natural law system is that of legal positivism. This theory derives from the convergence of the thoughts of two of the great philosophers of the 19th century, Bentham and Hobbes. Jeremy Bentham (1748–1832) was the British philosopher who founded the doctrine of *utilitarianism*. Sir Thomas Hobbes (1588–1679) said, "Law, properly, is the word of him, that by right hath command over others." Key to Hobbes's notion was that there existed a social contact between men, by which each person's original power is yielded to a sovereign who regulates conduct. The concept of a sovereign imposing a system for order combines with Bentham's concept of the greatest good for the greatest number in forming the foundation of legal positivism.

More recently, Harvard law professor H. L. A. Hart, in *Positivism and the Separation of Law and Morals* (1958), laid out a tripartite architecture for explaining positivism. The three key precepts of legal positivism are:

- The *social fact thesis* posits that a law is valid if based upon a social fact—in other words, an authoritative entity within a society formed or promulgated the law. This thesis goes to the source of authority of law.

- The *conventionist thesis* posits that the promulgation of the law, the social fact, occurred according to the prescribed procedure of the authority.

- The *separationist thesis* posits that the validity of the law does not per se depend on any stated system of morality. Note that this is to be distinguished from the fact that a particular law may have a moral component or relationship to a moral. The key is that the positivist theory of law does not rely on the existence of any particular system of morality.

Thus a duty under legal positivism is a law adopted by the authority recognized for the enforcement of laws by the culture or society, as a whole, by which procedures are established to define the standards of acceptable conduct and the consequences, including any penalty for variance from that standard.

A key example of a legal system based on legal positivism is the the original Napoleonic Code, or *Code Napoléon* (originally called the *Code Civil des Francais*, or civil code of the French), the French system of laws established at the behest of Napoleon. It entered into force on March 21, 1804. It was based on Roman law and followed Justinian's *Corpus Juris Civilis* in dividing civil law into (a) personal status, (b) property, and (c) the acquisition of property.

The intention behind the Napoleonic Code was to reform the French legal system in accordance with the principles of the French Revolution. Before the code, France did not have a single set of laws, and the existing ones were rooted in the natural law system that supported the hierarchical, feudal law systems of the day. Premised on the principles of the French Revolution, liberté, equalité, fraternité, the Civil Napoleonic Code rejects the premise of natural law and is decidedly positivist. The law is found solely in the statutes, without reference to an external moral or natural law.

Culture and Legal Positivism

What was said for the natural law states— i.e., that they are largely collectivist, risk averse, and hierarchical—is not mirrored in the countries hewing more toward the theory of legal positivism. Here, according to Hofstede (1991), there is an odd disharmony: Certain of the countries adopting the paragon of legal positivism, France and the Scandinavian countries, rank among the top ten in cultural dimensions of individualism versus collectivism, and careerism versus quality of life, and risk taking versus risk aversion. But the same rankings show several other civil law countries—e.g., much of South America—as being quite collectivist and risk averse.

Here, the point is that even cultures that share the same legal systems may view the formation of legal states, such as a contract, or a breach of a contract, from fundamentally different viewpoints. For example, contract formation in France may be handled on a one-to-one basis without significant reference to hierarchy. But the same process in South America— e.g., Chile—would be much more of a collectivist, hierarchical, and risk-adverse process. One factor does appear to be uniform; states employing civil law systems tend toward a risk-adverse approach (Hofstede, 1991). Thus, in civil law countries, the element of face, or personal embarrassment, may be a key cultural cue.

◆ World Legal Enforcement Systems

One key measure of the effectiveness of a culture's laws is the means or the efficacy of enforcing compliance with the law, whatever its source or authority, by a court or other enforcement system. Enforcement systems may be broken down into those with or without a judicial system (i.e., an independent entity), separate from the law-giving authoritative source, which has co-equal power to interpret and enforce the law. Within systems having a tradition of a judicial system, sometimes called rule of law systems (Miller & Perito, 2004), a further division may be made: common law adversarial system and civil law inquisitorial system.

✓ RULE OF LAW STATES

According to Kessler (2005), the distinction between the inquisitorial and accusatorial/adversarial models encompasses at least seven different aspects of the litigation:

1. Whether the court or the parties determine the litigation's scope and content

2. Whether the court or the parties decide to initiate the litigation and to take the actions needed to move it forward

3. Whether the litigation is composed of discrete stages and whether steps not taken at a particular stage are thereafter precluded

4. Whether the value of the proof is fixed formally, by rule or determined rationally, by free evaluation of the judge

5. Whether proceedings are conducted in writing or orally and whether proof is written or oral

6. Whether the court deals directly with the parties and witnesses or indirectly through some intermediate agency

7. Whether proceedings are conducted in public or in secret

The key distinction is which entity controls the course of the case: the court, the government, the throne, one party, or the litigants?

ADVERSARIAL/ COMMON LAW SYSTEMS

The adversarial system has its roots in the common law developed in Elizabethan England. Based on natural law at its inception, but swept by successive waves of positivism, the adversarial system is based on two pillars: (1) that the judge, an impartial fact finder with broad discretion, sifts and winnows the truth from the competing presentations of the advocates (attorneys) of the contesting parties, and (2) the principle of stare decisis, that the same impartial judge then applies the text of the law to the controlling facts that he or she has found, in a fashion that harmonizes with the published decisions of past cases so as to create an uninterrupted interpretation of the law. Judges in the adversarial system have wide authority to interpret the law but have little control over the initiation or scope of the litigation. Instead, and solely through designated professional functionaries (i.e., attorneys), the parties interact with the judicial officer to jointly exercise control over the progress of the case. Upon the colonization of the New World, which became the United States of America, the adversarial system became the lodestar of the American legal system of jurisprudence (Kessler, 2005). The former and current British Empire (Australia, Egypt, the Hong Kong Special Administrative District of the PRC, Ireland, India, Jordan, New Zealand, and Pakistan) and the British Isles are all adversarial/common law countries.

INQUISITORIAL/ CIVIL LAW SYSTEMS

An illustrative example of the inquisitorial or civil law system is the Napoleonic Code, which was intended to reform the French legal system in accordance with the principles of the French Revolution: liberté, equalité, fraternité. The Napoleonic Code rejected the premise of natural law and is decidedly positivist. The Napoleonic Code, and its derivatives in other countries, is inquisitorial, in that the judge, not the parties, determines the initiation, scope, and extent of the litigation. Each case is unique before the court and will not usually serve as a precedent for other cases.

In civil law systems, the judge's ability to interpret the law is quite limited, the decisions are not published, and the common law concept of stare decisis does not operate. Consistency comes from the limitations placed on the judge's ability to interpret the words of the statute, as opposed to simply applying the statute's words to the facts of the particular legal question at hand. Moreover, the legal professionals serve their clients only in an advisory role, with little direct interaction with the judges.

Following this analysis, shari'a may be seen as a variation from the standard inquisitorial model. Shari'a procedurally follows the inquisitorial model by using a fact-finding judge with the power to define the scope of the investigation. The power of judges in a shari'a system, like that of a civil law system, is limited to application, as opposed to interpretation. However, shari'a varies from the civil law model by being heavily influenced by a natural (moral) law theory.

The distinctions between the rule of law systems are represented in Table 6.1.

NON–RULE OF LAW STATES

The enforcement model for states where the law is both made and enforced by a supreme religious leader, a ruler, or a state entity (such as a party) largely follows the inquisitorial model. Here, an agent of the ruler/cleric/party serving as the fact finder determines the scope of the inquiry and makes the final determination. However, the role of the agent and the limits of his or her decision making are strictly defined by the religious, ideological, or tribal source of the law. Interpretation of the law may be subject to influence or revision by the ruling/ clerical/party political element of the government.

In looking at the People's Republic of China, an evolving pattern may be noted. One writer noted that Imperial China had long had "rule by law." However, the concept of shifting power from the central government to a truly independent judiciary would be a very broad step (Peerenboom, 2000). Peerenboom suggests that the explosive economic expansion in the PRC may shift power but might only facilitate a system of rule of law because cross-cultural trade requires some predictability in enforcement (of laws). Further, as a first step, Peerenboom suggests that China first introduce *procedural* rule of law measures, such as an independent judiciary, rather than substantive measures such as a rule of stare decisis.

RELATIVE ADVANTAGES AND DISADVANTAGES OF THE SYSTEMS

Generally, the goal of any judicial system should be equal access to the adjudicator, as well as more predictable, factually linked,

Table 6.1	The Distinctions Between the Rule of Law Systems
Common Law	*Civil Law*
Based on case law	Based on statutes
Emphasizes supra-statutory or natural legal rights	Positivism—statutes are sources of rights
Principal of stare decisis recognized; case-by-case inclusion and exclusion and analogy	Lawyer and judges work from statutory text
Adversarial	Inquisitorial

SOURCE: "The Success of Judicial Review," by M. Shapiro, 1999, in J. K. Kenney, W. M. Reisinger, and J. C. Reitz (Eds.), *Constitutional Dialogues in Comparative Perspective*, New York: St. Martin's Press.

and rationally transparent results (Miller & Perito, 2004). The adversarial/common law systems should have all these attributes, because the parties largely control the initiation and pace of litigation, and the judicial officers are guided by the concepts of stare decisis. Moreover, the judges of the adversarial systems typically have wide discretion in interpreting the language of the laws.

However, the goals of a transactional quality of fact-based consistency and transparency in decisional logic are not always met by the adversarial model. Djankov et al. (2003), have noted that English-model legal systems (common law) has significant cost due to incidence of litigation because of the ready ability of disputing parties to initiate and pursue lawsuits within the judicial systems as a means of seeking redress to legal disputes. Further, although to lesser degree than in civil law states, the English model states had considerable "formalism," which led to less efficiency. Formalism is described as systems-embedded procedural requirements governing the initiation and prosecution of litigation, as well as requirements for legal professionals to pursue the litigation. Efficiency was reflected by the total time necessary to initiate, pursue, and conclude two sample legal actions: the eviction of nonpaying tenant and the collection of a bad check.

Further, some critics of the American adversarial system, especially those advocating tort reforms, argue about the high cost of litigation, as well as the seeming unpredictability of outcomes of similar actions filed in differing states (e.g., Illinois or California auger for substantial limits on judicial discretion). Indeed, these parties argue that the lack of any cap or ceiling on monetary recovery for products liability and medical negligence liability claims make the system more like a game of chance than a system of justice (AMA, 2005).

Alternately, the inquisitorial system or civil-code-based system has empirical support for perceived greater efficiency due to the civil law's lesser emphasis on litigation (Djankov et al., 2003). Thus, given the substantial limitation to the discretion of judges in civil law systems, coupled with the courts' control over the initiation of and continuation of litigation, data suggest that inquisitorial or civil law systems are slightly more efficient and substantially less costly. Moreover, civil law systems have a degree of predictability not seen in adversarial or common law systems, due to the limitation on discretion of the judges in interpreting the code.

On one level, the model most likely to meet this paradigm would be the religious, inquisitional model, because it is based on a fixed source of law (natural law), which should manifestly give predictable results across variable, factual, and transactional patterns for reasons that are readily apparent. However, one study suggests that at the lack of rigorous and uniform training for the clerics who are designated as the adjudicators has lead to quite differing results within the shari'a courts of at least one country: post-9/11 Afghanistan (Miller & Perito, 2004).

◆ When Parties Engage in Legal Interactions Across Cultural Lines

RULE OF LAW COUNTRIES

Adversarial/Common Law

Within the adversarial system, and the countries adopting that system, risk aversion is low and change is enshrined within the system. Thus entities such the members of the judiciary, the legal professionals who advocate specific interpretations to the judges during litigation, as well as the legislatures that promulgate new laws or changes to existing laws all have the ability to change the interpretation or formulation of the law.

Overlaid on the Hofstede element of risk aversion is the degree of collectivism versus individualism. In these countries, especially the United States, which have a federal system of state governments, judges and legislators are encouraged to act as individual change agents rather than to seek consensus with the larger collective. Finally, given the ready access to legislative representatives in most common law countries, lobbyists, paid or unpaid, may also be viewed as change agents. A note of caution here, for in the United States, a concerted effort by one political party to consolidate its lobbying within the "K Street Project" has had negative effects for that party (Scahill, 2006).

Inquisitorial/Civil Law

Conversely, the actors who function with substantial risk-seeking behavior within the adversarial system are drawn toward more collectivist and risk-averse behavior within the inquisitorial civil law system. Here, both judges and legal professionals are significantly limited in their ability to effect change through broadened interpretations of the law. Moreover, the likelihood of engaging in legal actions such as contracting or litigation is undercut by the more collectivist and risk-averse nature of these cultures. Also, because many civil law countries tend to have stronger central governments and weaker state or provincial governments, the focus on change agents will be on the central government. From the legal actor's point of view, especially one from another culture, the establishment and continuation of relationships with senior members of the partnering organization, as well as the central government, are key elements for success.

NON–RULE OF LAW STATES

Within these countries, effecting change is both simpler and more complicated. As the legal systems of these countries place institutional reliance on the continuing validity of the underlying religion or ideology, change is disfavored. Effecting modifications to interpretations of the law or significant changes to the law requires a delicate distinction between re-interpretation on the one hand and religious or political heresy on the other. That said, economic development has been suggested as a mechanism for change in countries that heretofore have not had an established rule of law. It has been said that the burgeoning economic change in the People's Republic of China cannot help but bring about the advance of the rule of law in that country. One group of scholars (Djankov et al., 2003), however, suggests that the jury may still be out on that question. Blodgett (2005), a former financial and securities analyst writing for *Slate* magazine, suggests that the Chinese leadership may be seeking a form of capitalism without such democratic notions as the rule of law.

◆ Summary

In light of this global analysis, what conclusions may organizational leaders draw about the hazards of operating across differing legal and cultural system?

First and foremost, as noted above, the opportunity to facilitate change within the legal domain is radically different between the domain of rule of law nations (those with independent judiciaries) and non–rule of law nations. Moreover, the location and efficiency of those change agents is significantly different within nations following either of the two rule of law systems. Second, the legal domains within natural law–based systems with adversarial enforcement will differ from legal positivist systems with inquisitorial enforcement. Finally, operation within rule of law nations will differ markedly from those in non–rule of law nations.

Operations in rule of law nations will be markedly more predictable and reliable, whether in an adversarial or inquisitorial system. The operations will also be occasioned by the cost and risk restraints of litigation and formalism, as discussed above. In inquisitorial or civil law countries, more linear predictions may be made for operations based on the limitations on those nations' judges to apply the law rather than interpret it. That said, civil law nations do carry the burden of greater government regulation and the accompanying temporal and financial cost. As with the decentralized judiciary seen in the United States, an adversarial or common law nation brings its unique challenges to organizations. For example, due to the influence of regional customs, judges may interpret laws in differing manners. Witness the regional differences in the decisions testing the validity of "blue laws," a product of the American puritan era, which prohibited the operations of most businesses on the Sabbath ("In the Battle for Sunday," 2003). Where blue laws were the standard until the end of the Second World War, fewer than five states, including Utah, still limit business and alcohol sales on Sunday.

Operations in non–rule of law nations will be at once simpler and more complicated, especially in nations with a theocratic legal system. Given this legal domain's significant reliance on religious text, and the belief in the inerrant nature of that text, an organization's operations will be constrained to the extent that day-to-day operations include activities inconsistent with the theocratic law. For example, consider the Kingdom of Saudi Arabia, considered here as a non–rule of law country due to the lack of an independent judiciary (U.S. Department of State, 2005). Western businesswomen doing business in the kingdom are impaired as business agents because women are treated as a lesser class under that country's law

(U.S. Department of State). Likewise, when operating outside one's home legal system, for good or ill, a thorough working knowledge of the underlying theory supporting the law of a country is essential for effective business.

This is not to say that an organization's operations will always be severely constrained in non–rule of law nations. Witness the People's Republic of China, an avowedly communist, Marxist–Leninist state. The explosive commercial intercourse between the Middle Kingdom and the West in the last 10 years has brought about change in day-to-day business operations in the PRC. That the leadership of the Communist Party of China can embrace capitalism, the anathema of Karl Marx's *Das Kapital*, manifests the potential for significant change in the source for that nation's law, the party's ideology. The lesson for organizational leaders is that situational awareness of cultural cues or perceptions, along the continuum between the fixed site of morals and the transitory site of ethics, is essential for effective transcultural operations.

◆ *Discussion Questions*

1. The author adopts Hofstede's definition of cultural as a shared inventory of interpretations of words, actions, gestures, attitudes, and behaviors. What other definitions explain the operation of a cultural interpretation of communication and conduct?

2. "Cultural cues" are the inflections, gestures, and other verbal and nonverbal signals that serve as a kind of shorthand or code within a society or culture. Provide specific examples of cultural cues for a classroom discussion.

3. The author suggests some linkage between the kind of legal enforcement system (adversarial/inquisitorial) and Hofstede's cultural dimensions of individualism/collectivism, power distance, risk adversity or affiliation, and goal orientation. Suggest examples of this linkage—e.g., theologically based/inquisitorial systems tend toward collectivism, substantial power distance, risk adversity, and careerism (often, subject to gender limitations).

4. What specific areas of cultural research should a potential cross-border leader pursue before engaging in substantial bilateral activities?

5. Prepare suggestions for ways of dealing with conflicting cultural cues for a classroom discussion.

◆ Notes

1. Groundbreaking credit goes to Geert Hofstede; but later inquiries—e.g., Andreas Cruzat for the Center for Arbitration & Mediation, Santiago, Chile—mirrored, in part here, confirm that situational awareness of culture is a global requirement.

2. Levy illustrates the admixture of natural law and legal positivism that is American legal theory. The case is not cited as precedential authority, in accordance with the rules of the United States Court of Appeals for the Second Circuit.

◆ References

American Medical Association (2005, October 19). *Medical liability reform—Now.* Retrieved June 12, 2006, from: www.ama-assn.org/go/mlrnow

Aquinas, T. (1988). *Summa theologiae* [Summary treatise of theology]. *On Law,* *morality and politics.* Indianapolis, Hackett. (Originally published in 1275)

Blackstone, W. (1979). *Commentaries on the law of England. Books 1–4, 1765–1769.* Chicago: University of Chicago Press. (Originally published in 1823, Oxford, UK: Clarendon Press)

Blodgett, H. (2005). China's biggest gamble: Can it have capitalism without democracy? A prediction. *Slate.* Retrieved June 12, 2006, from: www.slate.com/id/2117169/

Brown, N. (1997). *The rule of law in the Arab world: Courts in Egypt and the Arab states of the gulf.* Cambridge, UK: Cambridge University Press.

Cruzat, A. (n.d.) *Cross-cultural negotiation and dispute resolution.* Retrieved May 15, 2007, from: www.camsantiago.com

Djankov, S., La Porta, R., Lopez-de-Silanes, F., Shleifer, A., (2003). Courts. *Quarterly Journal of Economics, 118*(2), 453–517.

Early, P. C., & Ang, S. (2003). *Individual interactions across cultures.* Stanford, CA: Stanford University Press.

Grazin, I. (2000). *On essential traits of the post communist revolution in legal education.* Proceedings of the 2000 International Conference of Legal Educators, Association of American Law Schools. Retrieved May 15, 2007, from www.aals.org/2000international

Hart, H. L. A. (1958). Positivism and the separation of law and morals. *Harvard Law Review, 71*(593). (Later reprinted in Hart, H. L. A. (1983), *Essays in jurisprudence and philosophy.* Oxford, UK: Clarendon Press.)

Hart, H. L. A. (1994). *The concept of law* (2nd ed.). Oxford, UK: Clarendon Press.

Himma, K. E. (1999) Positivism, naturalism, and the obligation to obey the law. *Southern Journal of Philosophy, 36*(2).

Hofstede, G. (1980). *Culture's consequences in work related values.* Beverly Hills, CA: Sage.

Hofstede, G. (1991). *Culture and organizations: Software of the mind.* London: McGraw-Hill

In the battle for Sunday, the "blue laws" are falling. (2003, December 5.) *Christian*

Science Monitor. Retrieved May 3, 2007, from www.csmonitor.com/2003/1205/p01s02-usju.html

Kessler, A. (2005, July). Our inquisitorial tradition: Equity, procedure, due process, and the search for an alternative to the adversarial, *Cornell Law Review,* 90(5), 1181–1275.

Miller, L., & Perito, R. (2004). *Establishing the rule of law in Afghanistan.* U.S. Institute of Peace Special Report No. 117, U.S. Institute of Peace. Retrieved May 26, 2006, from http://www.usip.org/pubs/specialreports/sr117.html

Peerenboom, R., (2000). China and the rule of law: Part I. *Perspectives, 1*(5), Retrieved May 26, 2006, from www.oycf.org/Perspectives/5_043000/china_and_the_rule_of_law.htm. NOTE: This, the first of a two-part essay, excerpts and summarizes some of the main points from "Ruling the country in accordance with law: Reflections on the rule and role of law in contemporary China" *Cultural Dynamics 11*(3), 315–351 (1999), and a revised and expanded version of that article, which is forthcoming in Chinese in *Zhongguo shehui zhuanxing shiqi de falu fazhan: Zhongmei xuezhe lunwenji.* Beijing: Falu Chubanshe, 2000. These two versions of the article, which contain full citations and footnotes, are available by emailing peerenbo@law.ucla.edu.

Scahill, J. (2006, February 20). Exile on K Street. *Nation.* Retrieved June 22, 2006, from www.thenation.com/doc/20060220/scahill

Thomas, D. C., & Inkson, K. (2003). *Cultural intelligence: People skills for global business.* San Francisco: Berrett-Koehler.

United States Department of State. (2005). *Country report for the Kingdom of Saudi Arabia* (pp. 2, 4). Retrieved June 13, 2006, from www.state.gov/g/drl/rls/hrrpt/2004/41731.htm

7

GLOBAL HUMAN RESOURCE MANAGEMENT

◆ Jennifer Palthe

I n an age of unprecedented change, the pace and scope of global mergers, acquisitions, divestitures, and corporate expansion is driving tremendous change in the way organizations source, deploy, and manage people worldwide. It is well recognized that global business success is dependent on the ability of organizations to acquire and develop the best employees from around the world,[1] and the field of global human resource (HR) management is subsequently gaining prominence as a major strategic tool to strengthen the competitive position of global corporations.[2] People are pivotal to a global corporations' competitive success as information, capital, and technology cannot be mobilized effectively in their absence.[3] The purpose of this chapter is to highlight the key distinctions between domestic and global HR, the impact of the globalization age on HR management, and the importance of global HR management. It also aims to clarify how the predominant global trends are influencing each facet of HR, including areas like international assignment management, performance management, global compensation and benefits, strategic global HR, organizational development and change management, global HR leadership, and global staffing, training, and development.

In essence, this chapter aims to provide readers with an appreciation for the tremendous challenges that staffing, training, developing, assessing, and rewarding human resources on a global scale presents.

◆ *Distinctions Between Domestic and Global HR Management*

Domestic HR management involves the activities undertaken by an organization to utilize its human resources effectively within a single national context.[4] The various functions that may be involved in managing this resource include the following:

- Staffing (recruitment and selection)
- Training and development
- Performance management
- Compensation and benefits
- Organizational development

Global HR management is defined as the effective utilization of human resources on a global scale. It encompasses primarily the same areas as domestic HR management but with several key distinctions, including the following:[5]

EXPANDED SCOPE OF HR ACTIVITIES

In a multinational operation, the HR department engages in a number of activities not necessarily present in a typical domestic HR department. These include the provision of language translation services, relocation and socialization activities for expatriates and their families, taxation counseling, housing and education assistance, the establishment of relations with foreign governments, and other expatriate administrative services.

BROADER PERSPECTIVE IS NEEDED

Global HR managers must broaden their competencies to include not only general knowledge about all the nations in which their organization operates but also relevant HR practices, legal systems, and historical, cultural, political, and social issues that are likely to affect their HR decisions and practices.

MORE PERSONAL INVOLVEMENT IN EMPLOYEES' LIVES

Ensuring expatriate success abroad demands that HR departments become more personally involved in their employees' lives. Assistance with travel arrangements for expatriates and their accompanying family members, helping with housing, providing assistance with education alternatives for children, and offering network opportunities for trailing spouses are a few of the additional responsibilities that global HR departments accrue.

MANAGEMENT OF THE WORKFORCE MIX OF PARENT- AND HOST-COUNTRY NATIONALS

As foreign operations progress toward maturity, the emphasis placed on HR activities change. In the early stage of a firm's development, parent-country nationals tend to be used more often and more emphasis is placed on the use of parent country HR activities and programs. As foreign activities increase, host-country nationals tend to be relied upon more heavily and the responsibilities and activities of local HR departments abroad tend to expand.

COPING WITH ADDITIONAL RISKS AND DIFFICULTIES

Often, the consequences of financial and personal failure in the global arena are more substantial than in domestic HR. Direct costs associated with failed international assignments can cost organizations as much as three times the domestic salary of an expatriate. Indirect costs such as interrupted careers, damaged corporate relationships, and expatriate dissatisfaction may be substantial. Terrorism presents another risk to organizations sending people abroad. Global HR departments need to consider political risk and terrorism when planning international activities and when sending expatriates to highly volatile regions of the world. The global HR department is essentially responsible for both the safety and success of its global assignees.

GREATER EXTERNAL INFLUENCES

Global HR managers tend to be exposed to both problems typical in domestic HR as well as additional challenges associated with foreign governments, differing economic and political systems in host countries, and diverse legal systems throughout the world. Language and translation challenges add to the complexity of their role in a global enterprise. Global HR managers also need to spend more time interpreting and learning approaches, methods, and systems associated with the local subsidiaries abroad.

CROSS-CULTURAL DIVERSITY

As global HR management involves activities across national boundaries, cross-cultural diversity is a given. To add to earlier definitions, culture is a system of shared assumptions, beliefs, and values that guide behavior, the collective programming of the mind that is both learned and inherited.[6] Multinational and global corporations typically derive many of their values from the national culture in which they are headquartered. General Electric (GE), IBM, and General Motors have been greatly influenced by American cultural values. Similarly,

Matsushita, Toyota, Hitachi, and Mitsubishi have been affected by Japanese cultural influences. The challenge of managing cross-cultural diversity is a vital component of global HR and is pivotal to HR management's strategic significance in global operations.

◆ Worldwide Trends Reshaping Global HR Practices

Findings from Towers Perrin's 2006 Global Workforce Study,[7] suggest that in an increasingly competitive global economy, companies must ensure that money spent on reward programs is optimized to attract, retain, and engage the talent most critical to business success. The study surveyed 86,000 employees at all levels of the organization in midsize and large companies in 16 countries across four continents about attitudes, needs, work ethic, and personal commitment of people to their jobs and companies. The findings revealed that people tend to stay with organizations that have leading-edge work environments and HR practices. Recommendations from the study suggest employers consider five "macro factors" that are already reshaping business, workplace and workforce strategies, and practices around the world. These macro factors include the following:

GLOBALIZATION

The most predominant trend affecting business around the world is globalization. It has the twofold effect of reconciling the HR function with the strategic core of the organization, while changing the scope and content of HR management.[8] As Ulrich, the author of *Human Resource Champions*, suggests, HR will need to create models and processes for attaining global agility, effectiveness, and competitiveness to cope with the challenge of globalization.[9] He asserts that global competition requires more than creating products and generating services in a single market and transporting it to a new market abroad. It requires a complex network of global centers of HR excellence that share products, people, information, and ideas globally. Other leading strategists argue that as global corporations need to simultaneously achieve economies of centralized control and flexibility in local markets abroad, the old adage of "think globally, act locally" needs to change to "think globally and locally, and act appropriately."[10]

The following quotes further explain the concept of globalization:

> Globalization has rendered geographic boundaries porous, sometimes even insignificant. It has increased permeability of all kinds of borders—physical borders such as time and space, nation-states and economies, and industries and organizations, as well as less tangible borders such as cultural norms or assumptions about how "we" do things "here."[11]

> Globalization is not a trend; it is not a fad; it is not an isolated phenomenon. It is an inescapable force. If anticipated and understood, it is a powerful opportunity. If not, it can swiftly destroy businesses and drown careers.[12]

DEMOGRAPHIC SHIFTS

Younger populations in the developing nations form a crucial source of both labor and skills, as aging populations in developed countries begin to exhaust the workforce. These developments have rearranged the supply and demand for labor worldwide, generating shortages in both numbers of people and critical skills in some places, and surpluses in others.

This, in turn, influences where organizations do business and how they remain competitive. Finding, retaining, and transferring human resources and managing a far more diverse workforce are becoming very real challenges for multinational and global corporations.

NEW TECHNOLOGIES

The pace of technological innovation is redefining the business world. It requires organizations to continually reconfigure not only the work but how, where, and by whom it is to be done. This, in turn, is generating significant changes in the way people learn and communicate around the globe.

EVOLVING SOCIAL ATTITUDES AND INDIVIDUAL EXPECTATIONS

Employment relationships and perceptions of work and where and how it should be performed are changing dramatically worldwide. Not only is the workforce more diverse demographically, but their attitudes and expectations are as well. Identifying what motivates people from various nations to work and how best they learn and lead are a few of the competencies global organizations need to become more adept at doing.

PEOPLE-DEPENDENT BUSINESS STRATEGIES

All the predominant global trends have a significant variable in common—people. Human resources and the management thereof has become a more critical element of the global competitive equation than before. Sustained global competitiveness demands excellence in leadership, change, collaboration, communication, compliance, and customer service, all of which increasingly rely heavily on people for successful execution.

◆ Global HR Staffing

A natural consequence of globalization has been the increase in the complexity of staffing employees around the world. Today's workforce is not only more informed, connected, and demanding than at any other time in history, but it is also more critical than ever in sustaining competitive advantage in our service and knowledge-based world.[13]

The 2006 World Investment Report by the United Nations Conference on Trade and Development revealed that inflows of foreign direct investment worldwide rose by 29%, to reach $916 billion. The value of cross-border mergers and acquisitions rose by 88% over the previous year, to $716 billon. Of the 77,000 transnational corporations worldwide, the study showed that the largest 100 play a key role in the global economy.[14]

These reported trends, in turn, play a major role in increased global staffing activities in multinational and global corporations around the world. One of the primary distinctions between domestic and global HR management is the complexity of the mix of organizational members. Research in this field has categorized these global employees into three groups—namely, parent-country nationals (PCNs), host-country nationals (HCNs), and third-country nationals (TCNs).[15]

PARENT-COUNTRY NATIONALS (PCNS)

PCNs are employees who tend to be citizens of the country in which their organization's headquarters is located. PCNs are typically executives, specialists, or technicians who travel from the headquarters to assist overseas subsidiaries. One of the main advantages of using PCNs to staff subsidiaries abroad is that they tend to be experts in the way the parent organization operates. Additionally, when PCNs work abroad on temporary assignments, they gain access to host-nation practices and customer information and develop skills in cross-cultural diversity management. PCNs can play a vital interpretative role between the headquarters and the subsidiary. PCNs are expensive, however. In addition to direct compensation amounting to 4–20% of base pay, cost-of-living allowances, relocation and housing expenses, and family benefit packages all add to the total expense.

HOST-COUNTRY NATIONALS (HCNS)

HCNs are organizational members who are natives of the country in which the subsidiary they work for is located. For example, a Canadian manager working for a subsidiary of a U.S.-based company located in Canada. The advantage of staffing subsidiaries with HCNs is that they are familiar with the local customs and language, and they are not as expensive as PCNs. IBM, for example, hires HCNs believing that they have both a better appreciation for the local environment and that they are likely to develop better relations with local employees, customers, and suppliers.

THIRD-COUNTRY NATIONALS (TCNS)

TCNs are employees who work in a country other than their country of birth, in a subsidiary outside the country where the parent company is located—for example, a Portuguese manager working for a U.S.-based multinational's subsidiary in Belgium. The major advantage of staffing subsidiaries with TCNs is that they are less expensive than PCNs, often have extensive international experience, and are typically fluent in foreign languages. In Europe these TCNs have been called "Euro-Managers" as they view the whole of Europe as their domain of operation, not just their home country.

GLOBAL STAFFING APPROACHES

Ethnocentric Staffing Approach

The ethnocentric approach to staffing is one in which PCNs fill all the key positions in a multinational corporation. This approach is common for organizations at the early stages of internationalization. Some of the main reasons this approach is adopted include the following:

- A need to maintain control over subsidiaries abroad and ensure strong links with corporate headquarters

- A perceived shortage of qualified HCNs

Some disadvantages of this approach are these:

- Limited promotion opportunities for HCNs, which may increase turnover and reduce productivity.

- PCNs may not adapt effectively to host countries, thereby making poor decisions.

- PCNs are expensive and their pay may be significantly higher than HCNs, thereby generating tensions between PCNs and HCNs.

Polycentric Staffing Approach

The polycentric approach to staffing results in HCNs being recruited to manage subsidiaries in their own country and PCNs retain positions at headquarters in the home nation. The primary advantages of a polycentric approach include these:

- HCNs understand the local culture and help prevent cross-cultural insensitivities.

- HCNs are less expensive.

- HCNs are likely to remain at the subsidiary permanently unlike PCNs that are merely on temporary assignments.

Among the disadvantages of this staffing approach are these:

- Language and cultural barriers between the headquarters and host nation between PCNs and HCNs

- Limited career opportunities for HCNs outside their home nations

Geocentric Staffing Approach

The geocentric approach to staffing seeks to use the best people for key jobs throughout the global enterprise, irrespective of national origin. The main advantages of this approach include the following:

- International success is an essential ingredient for success in top positions.

- High-potential employees are constantly prepared to be transferred anywhere in the world.

- Flexibility and worldwide learning are enhanced as top performers continue to develop as they are repositioned.

- Highly competent individuals are available at both headquarters and subsidiaries.

The major disadvantages associated with this approach include these:

- Foreign governments may place constraints on the implementation of the geocentric policy.

- Increased training and relocation costs increase the overall costs associated with this approach.

- Successful implementation of this policy requires more centralized control and may diminish the autonomy of the subsidiaries abroad.

Regiocentric Staffing Approach

The regiocentric approach is similar to the geocentric approach but it divides its operations into regions (e.g., Europe, the Americas, and Asia–Pacific). The advantages of this approach are the following:

- It allows interaction between executives transferred to regional headquarters from subsidiaries in the region.

- It allows the multinational to gradually move from a polycentric approach to a geocentric one.

The disadvantages of this approach include these:

- It may produce federalism at a regional rather than national level and constrain the corporation's global efforts.

- Career prospects may become restricted to a regional level.

While organizations may adopt differing staffing approaches, all seek to tap the full range of available talent in the global marketplace. In addition to enlarging the pool of people available for key positions, organizations must develop criteria for selecting those most likely to succeed. At Matsushita, candidates for international assignments are selected based on characteristics expressed in the acronym SMILE: specialty (knowledge or skill), management ability, international

flexibility (adaptability and willingness to learn), language ability, and endeavor (perseverance and resilience in the face of difficulty).[16]

◆ Managing International Assignments

The success of global corporations is increasingly dependent on the effective management of expatriates. Expatriation is the process of moving from one country to another on a temporary assignment while staying on the payroll of the original employer.[17] It has been estimated that more than 250,000 employees of US firms work on overseas assignments.[18] According to the latest GMAC Global Relocation Trends (2006) study, more than two-thirds (69%) of multinational corporations reported an increase in the number of international assignments in 2006, as compared to 47% in 2005. Furthermore, the study revealed that 65% of companies as compared to 54% in 2005 anticipated an increase in the number of employees they have on assignment.[19] This represents the highest percentage in the history of the Global Relocation Trends survey, published annually by GMAC Global Relocation Services.

Although the booming global economy has increased the number of expatriates, the direct and indirect costs associated with failed assignments remain a serious concern.[20] Failed assignment rates have been reported to range between 25% and 40%.[21]

Results from the Global Relocation Trends (2006) study suggest that these trends continue. The study showed that 10% of assignments were not completed due to expatriates returning from their assignments prematurely. When asked to name the primary reasons for early returns from assignments, family concerns (32%) was the most common answer, followed by accepting a new position within the company

(23%), early completion of the assignment (14%), career concerns (6%), and cultural adjustment issues (4%). Twenty-four percent of expatriates left their company during an assignment and 28% left within a year of returning. This turnover may be the most costly effect of expatriate failure, but dissatisfaction, quit intentions, and decreased commitment represent harder to measure costs.[22] To overcome some of these challenges, scholars have sought to discover the key variables that enhance expatriate success abroad, thereby reducing the direct and indirect costs associated with premature returns. Palthe, for example, measured the relative importance of variables that predict expatriate adjustment abroad and found that socialization in the host nation and the expatriate family's adjustment were the two most critical determinants of expatriate success.[23] Where expatriates were well socialized in the host nation and where the expatriate's accompanying spouse and children were well-adjusted, the expatriate's likelihood of adjusting more effectively was enhanced. Other variables that were found to predict expatriate success abroad include the cultural similarity between the home and host nation, high role clarity and discretion, low role conflict, high learning orientation, and expatriate self-efficacy.

While global HR scholars spend much time examining the attributes necessary to produce expatriate success abroad, global companies also continue to search for ways to promote the success of their international assignees. Pepsi, for example, conducts extensive interviews with potential global assignees and their spouses to make sure they understand the host nation, culture, and markets. They also seek the following attributes: tolerance, patience, flexibility, and a sense of humor about unusual situations.[24] 3M encourages its employees to learn the language of the country of assignment and predicts that this ability will become more crucial to expatriate

success in the future. Global corporations are also increasingly recognizing that international work experience is a critical element in sustaining the competitiveness of their businesses.[25]

◆ Global Training and Development

Training and development is one of the primary responsibilities of the HR function. However, when organizations begin to develop global strategies, assign people abroad, and promote organizational learning across borders, this function takes on a new and more complex nature.

The American Society for Training and Development (2006) State of the Industry Report revealed that those business leaders who understand how to drive business results in an increasingly global environment recognize that a better-trained workforce improves performance, and investing in employee learning and development is critical to achieving success in the global marketplace. The report also stated:

> Globalization has emerged as a significant challenge for organizations that want to expand their learning functions outside their home countries. Organizations that already have a robust, well-functioning, centralized, domestic learning function have found it very difficult to "plug-and-play" in other regions of the world. Among the most common challenges are technology deficits, adaptation to the local culture, language barriers, territorialism, conflicts between standardization and localization, and inconsistent learning objectives across regions.[26]

Despite the rhetoric amongst executives that stress the importance of maintaining a well-trained global workforce, many organizations fail to give training the priority they suggest is necessary. Multinational and global corporations vary in the extent to which they emphasize training and development, the extent to which training is off-line (as contrasted with on-the-job training), and how much it focuses on divisional or corporate-wide perspective. IBM is an example of a global corporation highly committed to training its global workforce. Motorola and GE tend toward in-house training to support their global education initiatives, and Olivetti, on the other hand, tends to undertake more on-the-job training. Asian multinationals are renowned for the time their employees spend in training. To illustrate this, Mitsubishi and Nissan offer new employee orientation and development programs lasting 3 to 8 months.

Some of the major training challenges facing multinational and global corporations include the following:

- Who the training should be developed by (locals or those from headquarters?)

- Who should deliver the training (locals, independent trainers, or trainers from headquarters?)

- How the training should be delivered (appropriate methods, practices, and language relevant to the local culture)

- Contextual, language, and translation differences (keeping the meaning consistent while tailoring the content to the local culture)

- The transferability of the training material across diverse nations and learning perspectives (maintaining the relevance and applicability of the training content across diverse nations and trainees)

Worldwide, those corporations that have developed and sustained corporate-wide learning programs and institutions have achieved their objectives using various means. Accenture and Motorola, for example, have relied on corporate institutions to provide for the global training and development needs of their employees. BP, on the other hand, created group development forums in collaboration with Cambridge University to facilitate the enhancement of their employees' knowledge and skills worldwide. IBM has a more decentralized approach, having established education departments in each of its worldwide locations.

♦ Global Compensation and Benefits

The management of an organization's global compensation and benefits system is a major responsibility of global HR managers. The complexity of this function on a global scale is driven by considerations about pay for international assignees, subsidiary workforces, differing approaches to compensation, currency and exchange rate differentials, and diverse costs of living around the world.

The primary objectives of a typical global compensation program include the following:[27]

- Attraction and retention of employees qualified for international assignments

- Facilitation of transfers between international subsidiaries

- Development and maintenance of internal consistency and equity between employee compensation at home and abroad

- Establishment and maintenance of external competitiveness with compensation offered by competitors.

More specifically, the global compensation program should meet certain objectives for expatriates, including these:

- Providing incentives to expatriates to be assigned abroad

- Ensuring a reasonable standard of living for expatriates on assignment

- Considering career and family needs of the expatriate

- Facilitating repatriation upon return

Multinational and global corporations typically offer high premiums in addition to base salaries to encourage employees to accept international assignments. These premiums range from two to four and half times the cost of maintaining a manager in a comparable position in the home nation.

COMPENSATION APPROACHES

There are two main approaches to global compensation—the balance sheet approach (otherwise known as the build-up approach) and the going rate approach (also known as the market rate approach).[28]

Balance Sheet Approach

This approach is the most commonly used approach with the primary objective of keeping the home country standard of living while providing a financial inducement for expatriates. This approach integrates the base salary for PCNs and TCNs to the salary structure of the home country. There are three main advantages of the balance sheet approach. First, it provides equity between assignments and between expatriates of the same nationality. Second, it is easy to communicate. Third, because the compensation system is consistent with the compensation system in the parent country,

the repatriation process for expatriates is facilitated. The primary disadvantage of the balance sheet approach is that it can result in significant disparities between expatriates from different nationalities and between expatriates and locals doing the same work. It is also complex to administer.

Going Rate Approach

This approach is primarily based on local market rates. It relies heavily on survey comparisons among local nationals, expatriates of the same nationality, and expatriates of all nationalities. The main advantage of this approach is that pay equality with local nationals is facilitated. It also promotes equity amongst different nationalities doing the same work. The approach is simple and easy for expatriates to understand, and it provides greater identification with the host nation. The disadvantages of this approach, however, involve variations in pay between assignments for the same expatriate and pay discrepancies between expatriates from the same nationality doing similar work in different nations. This approach also causes potential reentry challenges, particularly when expatriates have been receiving significantly more pay while on assignment as compared to their home nation.

◆ Global Performance Management

Sound performance management is essential to balancing global HR strategies and local initiatives. Without systems for measuring individual and organizational accomplishments, commitment to continual improvement in global corporations will remain a mere token expression.[29] Performance management is a process that enables the multinational or global corporation to evaluate and continually improve individual and subsidiary performance. Performance-management techniques vary in purpose, design, and scope around the world. Not only do we observe differences in format and length but in the dimensions of performance deemed valuable by each organization and nation. For example, U.S. performance management systems tend to be more job-oriented and objective, possessing distinctive purposes from pay to promotion. In contrast, other nations administer more informal, subjective assessments of performance, incorporating traits such as honesty and trustworthiness. Irrespective of the type of system used, most global organizations spend substantial amounts of time and effort evaluating the performance of their global assignees. Some gather multiple evaluations for a single employee using input from the hierarchical boss, coworkers, and direct subordinates. It is essential that this process be well coordinated on a corporate rather than just a subsidiary or divisional level, to ensure that corporate-wide comparisons can be made. British Airways and Cathay Pacific are examples of organizations with sophisticated performance-management systems designed to facilitate cross-border comparisons and decisions regarding the development, pay, and promotion of their top performers worldwide.[30]

There are naturally some challenges associated with conducting performance assessments on a global scale. First, performance criteria may become more or less important depending on the context and nation of assignment. Certain criteria may be less applicable in one nation than another. For example, an expatriate may have more control over profitability figures in one nation than another. Distant evaluators at headquarters may not appreciate the contextual constraints placed on achieving profitability goals in the subsidiary nation. These constraints may include variables such as exchange-rate fluctuations, differences in accounting practices, depreciation, and overhead differentials. A second significant challenge associated with cross-border evaluations includes differences in rater styles and competence around the world. For example, parent-company raters may not fully understand the political, cultural, and economic context in which the expatriate is operating, and rater error and bias may increase. International assignees may also feel isolated and misunderstood. The adage "out of sight, out of mind" may be perceived as reality by some expatriates. Another major challenge associated with global performance management is the decision about who should do the evaluation. Home-country supervisors, host-country supervisors, coworkers, self-evaluations, and customers are all potential options, with the first two being the most common. The final key challenge involves the design of the assessment forms. Forms designed from a home-country perspective may not necessarily be relevant to the host-country context and may jeopardize performance ratings as a consequence.

Given the potential challenges associated with conducting global performance management listed above, Biscoe and Schuler offer some guidelines to improve the effectiveness of the process:[31]

Relevance: The performance criteria and assessment process should be relevant to the content and requirements of the job.

Acceptability: The performance criteria and assessment process should be acceptable to those using it, whether evaluators or raters.

Sensitivity: The appropriate cultural and contextual realities need to be taken into account in both the design and administration of the system.

Practicality: The system needs to be easy to use by all global parties involved.

◆ *Strategic Global HR Management*

Strategic international human resource management is increasingly being recognized as key to the success of the global corporation.[32] Global competition, rapidly changing workforce demographics, and changing technology are demanding that corporations rethink their global HR strategies. In a research effort undertaken to examine the linkages between HR management and the global strategic planning processes of multinational corporations, scholars found that if HR management is to begin to move away from merely responding to global strategic plans toward active participation in the strategic management process of multinational corporations, senior HR executives must begin to recognize and understand the nature of the services required to acquire, allocate, develop, reward, and evaluate managerial personnel on a global scale. They recommended several steps that global HR executives should follow to improve their degree of participation in the global strategic planning process:[33]

- Ensure that management considers HR issues as they plan and implement the global strategic planning process.

- Build a global HR strategy that is proactive in orientation and has the backing of senior managers.

- Build and maintain a strong, personal relationship with the CEO using effective listening and communication skills.

- Establish a supportive and consulting role with top managers.

Adler differentiates between five key potential global strategic options that effective global managers can use, depending on the challenges they are faced with, from strategic alliances to the development of a new HR system. The global strategic options involve balancing "my culture's way" with "their culture's way." The five strategic options include the following.[34]

CULTURAL DOMINANCE

The dominance option involves continuing to do things the way they are done in your home country. Relating this to HR management, it would mean applying the exact HR techniques and approaches used in the parent organization at the subsidiary abroad. At an individual level, this option tends to be adopted by managers that believe their way is the only or best way. At an organizational level, this option tends to be utilized by corporations that are in the early stages of global expansion.

CULTURAL ACCOMMODATION

The accommodation option is the complete opposite of the dominance option. It would involve, for example, choosing to imitate the HR practices employed by the host nation. Some refer to this approach as "going native" based on the premise that "when in Rome, do as the Romans do."

CULTURAL COMPROMISE

This approach is a blend of the dominance and accommodation options and implies that both parties make concessions to work more effectively together. An example of this approach would be for Japanese and American participants on global training to alternate training destinations each year so that attendees from both nations share in the amount of travel time abroad.

CULTURAL AVOIDANCE

This option involves acting as if there were no cultural differences in relationships between the parent and subsidiary organizations. It would imply that when new HR systems or programs are adopted, no consideration for cultural diversity would be given. An example of this approach would be for HR trainers to totally ignore the body language differences of their trainees, such as lack of eye contact, and continue conversing as though the listeners were paying attention. This approach is most commonly used when unresolved issues are less important than the overall relationship.

CULTURAL SYNERGY

This approach involves the joint development of new solutions to challenges while respecting all the parties involved. The synergistic option would foster the creation of new HR systems that combine the best HR practices of all participating operations. It also facilitates the development of creative solutions by embracing cross-cultural differences between the host and home nations.

◆ Global Organization Development and Change Management

In response to the accelerated pace of change around the world, organizations are becoming flatter and more agile, and they are manifesting more diverse forms of organizational designs and cultures.[35] The importance of effective change leadership and the critical role that the HR function plays in managing organizational change is gaining increasing attention amongst HR professionals worldwide. According to findings from a Society for Human Resource Management (SHRM) survey released in April 2007, HR needs to be involved from the beginning when major organizational changes take place. In a corporation operating in multiple nations, this is even more critical, given the complexity and scope of changes that occur on a global scale. Seventy-three percent of the employees surveyed said that their understanding of organizational changes improved when HR was involved in the change-management processes *before* it was introduced. The survey found that the key roles HR most often plays during major organization changes include the following:[36]

- Assisting employees in the transition through the process

- Coordinating meetings and communications about the changes

- Providing initial communication to employees of changes within the organization

- Developing related training programs, including designing training materials and/or contracting consultant services

- Preparing other informational documents, such as e-mails, meetings, and press releases

Sparrow, Brewster, and Harris argue that some of the main challenges facing global HR functions undergoing significant change include the following:[37]

- Dealing with the consequences of global process redesign

- The absorption of acquired businesses, the merging of existing operations, the staffing of strategic global teams, and the development of new HR processes

- The changing capability needs of international operations

- The capitalization on technological delivery of HR services while ensuring local cultural considerations

- The learning about how to operate through formal and informal global HR networks

- The offering of a compelling value proposition in the context of different beliefs and perceptions across the globe

- The identification of issues faced by HR professionals across constituent global businesses

◆ Global HR Leadership

"A global manager is someone with a strong interest and tolerance for other cultures and who understands how a particular decision might affect a company's many markets or competitors around the world."[38]

"The global business manager has to achieve an efficient distribution of assets and resources while protecting the competence at hand."[39]

Black, Morrison, and Gregersen have argued that globalization demands a new leadership model for the next generation of HR leaders.[40] They assert that old ethnocentric leadership models that once focused heavily on the domestic market and that emphasized hierarchical command and control structures no longer work in today's global marketplace. They argue that we instead need global leadership models that apply around the world, transcend national perspectives, and deliver a powerful tool for recruiting, developing and retaining a company's future leaders. From their research, they found that only 2–3% of firms have the

quantity and quality of global leaders that they need. This growing leadership gap represents not only a growing potential crisis but also a huge opportunity for those who have the interest and capabilities to be effective global leaders. They propose a model of global leadership that emphasizes four key characteristics that global leaders should possess.

INQUISITIVENESS

This is the central characteristic of effective global leaders. These leaders are passionate about learning and invigorated by diversity. Cultural, language, and business practice differences around the world excite them. They are driven to understand and master the complexities presented by an ever increasing diverse global marketplace.

PERSPECTIVE

Effective global leaders have a perspective on the world that allows them to view ambiguity and uncertainty as natural and invigorating features of global business. While some managers are paralyzed by this uncertainty, global leaders view it as an opportunity to discover innovative solutions.

CHARACTER

Character involves a global leader's ability to connect emotionally with people from diverse cultures and with an unwavering demonstration of personal integrity. This, in turn, engenders goodwill and trust in all cross-cultural relationships in the global marketplace.

SAVVY

Global leaders display tremendous organizational and business savvy. They can recognize global business opportunities and organize global resources to capitalize on them. They have a clear sense of what is to be done and how to access resources to make it happen.

In essence, Black and colleagues' model suggests that exemplary global leaders need to work at developing all four of these characteristics to be most effective. Consistent with their model, others, like Ferraro,[41] have highlighted some basic core competencies necessary for effective global leadership:

- Developing a broad global perspective

- Appreciating others' points of view

- Having the ability to balance contradictions and operate comfortably in ambiguous situations

- Working effectively in cross-cultural teams

- Being emotionally resilient, open-minded, autonomous, and perceptually alert

- Being willing to make decisions in the absence of all the facts

- IBM's 2005 Global Human Capital Study surveyed HR leaders from more than 300 organizations from around the globe. The study recognized that people make the competitive difference and that the potential of people can be transformed. The results also revealed that organizations can respond successfully to the challenges of a global marketplace, but it requires a corporate-wide commitment to the activities necessary to achieve these goals, with the senior HR professionals serving as the key thought leaders and champions.[42]

The Towers Perrin 2006 Global Workforce Study also suggested that HR leaders need to be more conscious of country, regional, and cultural differences when designing and implementing HR systems and practices.[43] For example, in Canada,

competitive base pay, work/life balance, and career advancement opportunities attract top talent; in India, the reputation of the organization as a good employer is the main driver; in the United States, competitive health benefits; in Germany, the level of autonomy; in Japan, the caliber of coworkers; and in the Netherlands, the collaborative environment. Thus, with this study in mind, global HR leaders need to carefully consider these cultural differences when formulating and executing HR activities worldwide.

While the field of multinational management and global human resource management is inundated with books on leadership competencies and traits needed to guide global organizations to greatness in the 21st century, scholars and practitioners alike are recognizing the criticality of attracting, developing, and retaining effective human talent. Today, the most successful organizations are the ones where senior executives recognize and appreciate the need to manage global competitive demands by focusing less on the quest for the ideal structure and more on developing the abilities, behavior, and performance of their people.[44]

◆ Conclusion

The globalization of world markets and the growing interdependency and connectivity among people from around the world are making the need for cross-cultural understanding and effective global HR management increasingly more imperative. The growing demand for HR talent to increase global corporate effectiveness has generated a renewed interest in this field. This chapter has served to highlight these trends and offer approaches to better managing this vital resource on a global scale. This chapter has also aimed to clarify how these predominant global trends are influencing each facet of HR, including HR staffing, training and development, international assignment management, performance management, compensation and benefits, strategic global HR, organizational development and change management, and global HR leadership.

The value of the HR function in a global organization lies in its ability to manage the balance between overall centralized HR systems and decentralized local needs. Consistent with this, the chapter has emphasized that contemporary global leadership points to the criticality of global HR management and the development of intercultural competencies for a sustained competitiveness in the global marketplace. Global HR management is no longer an afterthought in multinational management but is rather at the very heart of the mission and strategy of a truly global enterprise. If done right, it will set the great apart from the mediocre and will differentiate the international survivors from the global thrivers!

◆ Discussion Questions

1. What are some of the key distinctions between domestic and global HR management?

2. What are the main challenges facing global HR professionals?

3. What are some of the pros and cons associated with using PCNs, HCNs, and TCNs?

4. How does culture affect the management of global HR?

5. Why is it critical that HR be involved with global change management initiatives?

6. What are the main compensation approaches that companies can use to remunerate their expatriates?

7. What are some of the essential leadership characteristics associated with an effective global HR professional?

◆ Notes

1. Dowling, P. J., & Welch, D. E. (2004). *International human resource management: Managing people in a multinational context* (4th ed.). London: Thomson Learning.

2. Ulrich, D. (1997). *Human resource champions: The next agenda for adding value and delivering results.* Boston: Harvard Business School Press.

3. Tung, R. (2004). *Female expatriates: The model global manager.* Organizational Dynamics, 33(3).

4. Dowling & Welch (2005). *International human resource management.*

5. Adapted from Dowling, P. J. (1988). International and domestic personnel/human resource management: Similarities and differences. In S. Schuler, S. A. Youngblood, & V. L. Huber (Eds.), *Readings and cases in personnel and human resource management* (3rd ed.). West Publishing.

6. Hofstede, G. (1980). *Culture's consequences: International differences in work-related values.* Beverly Hills, CA: Sage.

7. Towers Perrin. (2006). *Global workforce study.* Retrieved June 4, 2007, from www.towersperrin.com

8. Pucik, V. (1992). Globalization and human resource management. In V. Pucik, N. Tichy, & C. Barnett (Eds.), *Globalizing management: Creating and leading the competitive organization.* New York: John Wiley & Sons.

9. Ulrich, D. (1997). *Human resource champions: The next agenda for adding value and delivering results.* Boston: Harvard Business School Press.

10. Moran, R. T., & Riesenberger, J. R. (1994). *The global challenge: Building the new worldwide enterprise* (p. 120). New York: McGraw-Hill.

11. Earley, P.E., Ang, S., & Tan, J. (2006). *CQ: Developing cultural intelligence at work* (p. 1). Stanford, CA: Stanford University Press.

12. Black, J. S., Morrison, A. J., & Gregersen, H. B. (1999). *Global explorers: The next generation of leaders* (p. 11). Routledge.

13. Towers Perrin. (2006, February). *Winning strategies for a global workforce.* Retrieved June 4, 2007, from www.towers perrin.com

14. United Nations Conference on Trade and Development. (2006). *World investment report, 2006.* New York: Author. Retrieved June 12, 2007, from www.unctad.org

15. Dowling & Welch (2005). *International human resource management.*

16. Bartlett, C. A., Ghoshal, S., & Beamish, P. (2006) *Transnational management: Text, cases, and readings in cross-border management* (5th ed.). New York: McGraw-Hill/Irwin.

17. Briscoe, D. R. (1995). *International human resource management.* Upper Saddle River, NJ: Prentice Hall.

18. Kraimer, M. L., Wayne, S. J., & Jaworski, R. A. (2001), Sources of support and expatriate performance: The mediating role of expatriate adjustment. *Personnel Psychology, 54*(1), 71–89.

19. Global Relocation Services. (2006). *Global relocation trends survey.* Retrieved June 11, 2007, from www.gmacglobalrelocation.com

20. Shaffer, M. A., Harrison, D. A., Gregersen, H., Black, J. S., & Ferzandi, L. A. (2006). You can take it with you: Individual differences and expatriate effectiveness. *Journal of Applied Psychology, 91*(1), 109–125.

21. McCaughey, D., & Bruning, N. S. (2005) Enhancing opportunities for expatriate job satisfaction: HR strategies for foreign assignment success. *Human Resource Planning, 28,* 21–37

22. Templer, K. J., Tay, C., & Chandrasekar, N. A. (2006) Motivational cultural intelligence, realistic living conditions preview, and cross-cultural adjustment. *Group and Organization Management, 31,* 154–173.

23. Palthe, J. (2004). The relative importance of antecedents to cross-cultural adjustment: Implications for managing a global workforce. *International Journal of Intercultural Relations. 28*(1), 37–59.

24. Geber, B. (1992). The care and breeding of global managers. *Training, 29*(7), 32–37.

25. Bhaskar-Shrinivas, P., Harrison, D. A., Shaffer, M. A., & Luk, D. M. (2005). Input-based and time-based models of international adjustment: Meta-analytic evidence and theoretical extensions. *Academy of Management Journal, 48,* 257–281.

26. ASTD. (2006). *State of the industry report.* Retrieved June 13, 2007, from: www.astd.org

27. Briscoe, D. R., & Schuler, R. S. (2004). *International human resource management.* London: Routledge Taylor and Francis Group.

28. Dowling & Welch (2005). *International human resource management.*

29. Pucik, V. (1992). Globalization and human resource management. In V. Pucik, N. Tichy, & C. Barnett (Eds.), *Globalizing management: Creating and leading the competitive organization.* New York: John Wiley & Sons.

30. Palthe, J. (2000). Globally managing human resources. In E. E. Kossek & R. N. Block (Eds.), *Managing human resources in the 21st century: From core concepts to strategic choice.* Cincinnati: OH: South-Western College Publishing.

31. Briscoe & Schuler (2004). *International human resource management.*

32. Dowling, P. J., Welch, D. E., & Schuler, R. S. (1999). *International human resource management: managing people in a multinational context.* Cincinnati: OH: South-Western College Publishing.

33. Miller, E., Beechler, S., Bhatt, B., & Nath, R. (1986). The relationship between the global strategic planning process and the human resource management function. *Human Resource Planning, 9*(2), 9–23.

34. Adler, N. (1997). *International dimensions of organizational behavior* (3rd ed.). Cincinnati: OH: South-Western College Publishing.

35. Palthe, J., & Kossek, E. E. (2003). Subcultures and employment modes: Translating HR strategy into practice. *Journal of Organizational Change Management, 16*(3), 287–308.

36. Gurchiek, K. (2007) *Survey: Change management needs HR from the start.* Society for Human Resource Management (SHRM). Retrieved from www.shrm.org/hrnews_pub lished/archives/CMS_021174.asp

37. Sparrow, P., Brewster, C., & Harris, H. (2004). *Globalizing human resource management.* London: Routledge Taylor and Francis Group.

38. Geber. (1992). The care and breeding of global managers.

39. Bartlett, C. A., & Ghoshal, S. (1992, September/October). What is a global manager? *Harvard Business Review, 70*(5), 124–132.

40. Black, J. S., Morrison, A. J., & Gregersen, H. B. (1999). *Global explorers: The next generation of leaders.* London: Routledge.

41. Ferraro, G. P. (2006). *The cultural dimension of international business* (5th ed.). Upper Saddle River, NJ: Pearson Prentice Hall.

42. IBM. (2005). *Global human capital study.* Retrieved June 15, 2007, from www.ibm.com

43. Towers Perrin. (2006). *Global workforce study.* Retrieved June 4, 2007, from www.towersperrin.com

44. Bartlett, Ghoshal, & Beamish (2008). *Transnational management.*

PART III

APPLYING CULTURAL VISION ORGANIZATIONS

8

TRANSFORMATIVE TRAINING

Designing Programs for Culture Learning

◆ Janet M. Bennett

"**E**lectrons don't have culture!"

This disarming comment brought the training program to a halt, while a room full of engineers nodded sagely. Indeed, why should they bother to learn about culture, when they were *scientists*? Everyone knows engineers all think the same the world over. And so begins another day of intercultural training—and learning why we need to learn about culture!

While few professionals would balk at learning to read their profit and loss statements or mastering a new computer program, they may tend to see intercultural relations as more peripheral to their work. However, intercultural competence is becoming more, not less, essential. It is not an accident that three recent business books are titled *Cultural Intelligence* (Earley & Ang, 2003; Peterson, 2004; Thomas & Inkson, 2004). While much of the past research has neatly divided global from local contexts, the trend is toward recognizing that intercultural competence is equally vital domestically and internationally. In the past, transferees, sometimes called "expatriates," have been given the greatest attention in the international business context, frequently receiving culture-specific predeparture, and sometimes reentry, seminars (Adler, 2007; Black & Gregersen, 1999; Mendenhall & Oddou, 1986; Mendenhall et al., 2004). Until the 1990s, few organizations prepared other employees or managers for the global interface. In contrast to the international arena, in the North American domestic context the range of so-called diversity programming has been enormous, often including organization-wide training for all levels and locations (Cox, 1994; Gardenswartz & Rowe, 1998; Hayles & Mendez Russell, 1997).

◆ Bridging Global and Domestic Contexts

Recently, however, there is a growing acknowledgment that many aspects of cultural competence bridge both areas, domestic and global (J. M. Bennett & M. J. Bennett, 2004; Cornwell & Stoddard, 1999; Gardenswartz, Rowe, Digh, & M. Bennett, 2003; Gundling & Zanchettin, 2006; Wentling & Palma-Rivas, 2000). Is the refugee from Somalia to be folded into the category of "African American"? Is the immigrant from Macedonia a member of the dominant culture because he is a White male? Is the non-English-speaking recent arrival from China an American now? Are their cultural identities based solely on their passport cultures or on a more complex framework? And what does this mean for the workplace, where these individuals attend meetings, perform on teams, and manage others? Can the similarity of electrons really erase the potential complications of these cultural intersections?

In fact, it is not a case of erasing cultural patterns but rather of recognizing those differences as contributions to the productivity of the organization. The *Workforce 2020* report sums it up succinctly, noting that "the rest of the world matters" (Judy & D'Amico, 1997, p. 3). Training now routinely emphasizes intercultural competence by integrating all of the complicated aspects of both global and domestic cultural differences: not only race, not only nationality, but also gender, class, sexual orientation, age, etc. (Carr-Ruffino, 2003; Fernandez, 1991; Hayles & Mendez Russell, 1997; Henderson, 1994). Many "diversity" programs have become "cultural competence initiatives," reflecting the new global thinking. To fulfill the potential of global interaction, we must attend to thriving in "a world lived in common with others" (Green, 1988).

Further, the programs do not address only upper management, nor do they focus merely on the transferees. Instead, comprehensive approaches for all segments of the organization are developed in recognition that every employee, from the reception desk to the president's office, interacts across cultural borders.

◆ Intercultural Competence

The field of intercultural communication is uniquely positioned to provide this bridge between the domestic and global perspectives, focusing as it does on the interactions between individuals and groups who have different learned and shared values, beliefs, and behaviors. Intercultural sensitivity can help leaders decode the workings of geographically dispersed virtual teams, discover culturally appropriate motivational strategies, and master negotiation across cultures. The interculturally skilled organization becomes the employer of choice for the best and the brightest applicants, avoids rapid employee turnover, and presents a welcoming face to clients and vendors.

Intercultural competence is being explored by researchers in many academic disciplines, including management and global leadership (Bird & Osland, 2004; Boyacigiller, Beechler, Taylor, & Levy, 2004; Gregersen, Morrison, & Mendenhall, 2000; Mendenhall, Kuhlmann, & Stahl, 2001), intercultural communication (Dinges & Baldwin, 1996; Hammer, 1989; Y. Y. Kim, 1991; Lustig & Koester, 2006; Martin & Hammer, 1989; Wiseman, 2002; Wiseman & Koester, 1993), and higher education (Deardorff, 2006; Hovland, 2006; McTighe Musil, 2006; Yershova, DeJaeghere, & Mestenhauser, 2000).

Yet, despite the variety of perspectives used in examining this topic, there is an emerging consensus around what constitutes intercultural competence, which is most often viewed as a set of cognitive, affective, and behavioral skills and characteristics that support effective and appropriate interaction in a variety of cultural contexts (J. M. Bennett & M. J. Bennett, 2004; Earley & Ang, 2003; Thomas & Inkson, 2004; Ting-Toomey, 1999). Listed below are the most salient intercultural competencies synthesized from the work of the authors noted above.

The cognitive dimension, or *mindset*, includes knowledge of culture-general maps or frameworks, of specific cultures, of identity development patterns, of cultural adaptation processes, and of cultural self-awareness.

The behavioral dimension, or *skillset*, includes the ability to empathize, gather appropriate information, listen, perceive accurately, adapt, build relationships, resolve problems, and manage social interactions and anxiety.

The affective dimension, or *heartset,* of attitudes and motivation includes first and foremost, curiosity, as well as initiative, nonjudgmentalness, risk taking, cognitive flexibility, open-mindedness, tolerance of ambiguity, flexibility, and resourcefulness.

An examination of the existing and desired intercultural competencies can provide a starting point for designing assessment and outcomes for interventions. But beyond the assessment, there is still a need for program design, creating a training format that addresses the needs of the learners with whom we are working. Perhaps too often, training programs aspire to develop consistent skills useful in the organization but fail to ground the skills in any theoretical rationale: People may learn *how* to do something, but they don't know *why* they are doing it.

This is a fairly shortsighted approach to a global workplace in which the leader that is carefully trained to go to Singapore may find herself quickly transferred to Boston or Dubai. Lacking a conceptual foundation for her skills, she may find them less transferable to the new environment. Truly educating such professionals requires a commitment to both the how *and* the why.

Understanding how to train and why we are training the way we are training are equally important for the educator. Clearly, having a conceptual rationale for the choices we make regarding instructional design, content, and methods affords a greater potential for achieving the desired learning outcomes. This chapter will explore frameworks for sequencing training design, addressing intercultural competencies, and selecting activities.

◆ Designing Developmentally

There are two models that can provide a substantial conceptual basis for intercultural training design. The first is the Developmental Model of Intercultural Sensitivity (DMIS) (M. J. Bennett, 1993; M. J. Bennett, 2001; J. M. Bennett & M. J. Bennett, 2004). The underlying assumption of the model suggests that as the learners' experience of difference becomes more sophisticated and cognitively complex, the degree of intercultural competence increases (J. M. Bennett & M. J. Bennett, 2004). There are six stages of increasing sensitivity to cultural difference, and each stage reflects a worldview configuration, as well as attitudes and competencies associated with it (see Figure 8.1). By identifying the underlying cognitive orientation that the audience has towards cultural differences, the trainer can tailor programming to intentionally and systematically address the learners' developmental needs, without engendering unnecessary resistance.

"The Frog Theory of Change" suggests that it is possible to boil a frog in a cauldron of water if you are careful to turn the heat up slowly. Turning the heat up too rapidly of course leads the frog to jump out,

foiling your dinner plans. As unsavory as this metaphor may be, it provides educators with a very apt strategy for teaching intercultural competence. We can teach the hottest intercultural issues effectively only when we've approached them gradually and developmentally (J. M. Bennett, 2003, p. 157).

Before delving into the application of the DMIS to training, we need to consider how to handle resistance—the frog jumping out of the kettle—while facilitating development. To address the issue of resistance, a second useful model considers how to balance the challenge of the training (topics and methods) with the nature of the support needed to take increasing risks (J. M. Bennett, 1993). Based on a concept from Nevitt Sanford (1966), the model of challenge and support suggests that for each learner, we need to examine what aspects of the learning context can provide support and what aspects present challenges (see Figure 8.1). Once again, we are mindful of the frog analogy; we are trying to turn the heat down on inappropriately risky training approaches.

Figure 8.1   The Challenge and Support Grid

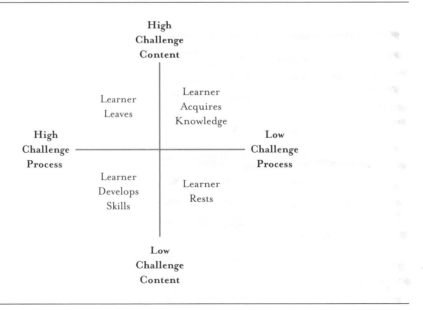

If the learner is overly supported, no learning takes place. This excessive support might occur if the learner was developmentally in ethnorelative stages, and the training focused on introductory material, acquainting the learner, for instance, with the fact that difference exists and that we should value it. In that case, the learner would be likely to yawn and detach from the program.

On the other hand, if the learner is overly challenged, the individual flees the learning context. This excess challenge might occur if the training began with powerful discussions of racism for a group of learners in ethnocentric stages. Tempting though it may be to confront ethnocentrism immediately, there is greater likelihood of transformation when the group has experienced a "learning edge" or teachable moment.

Further, the balance of challenge and support applies to both the content and the process of the educational program. By content, we refer to the subject being taught, whether lessons on culture shock or negotiation. By process, we refer to the methods we use, such as role-plays, exercises, lectures, simulations, and computer-based training.

Learners with different cultures and developmental worldviews may find certain content very challenging or affirming of their experience. For instance, the manager who has lived in multiple cultures may find discussions of complex value differences intriguing and validating of her experience. In contrast, an ethnocentric learner might find the same discussion alienating and threatening.

Depending on their culture, learning styles, cognitive styles, and communication styles, participants may find certain processes, such as role-plays, very rewarding or very risky. While *risk* can be variably interpreted, in general, activities that require self-disclosure, that risk loss of face, or that elicit strong conflict may involve high challenge for many (but not all) cultures. By first assessing the challenge in the content area, we can compensate for a difficult topic by selecting methods that do not intensify the challenge but that support the training goals.

When we know our learners find the idea of cultural difference quite challenging (as in the denial and defense stages), we create highly supportive training design. For instance, in creating a simulation on sexual orientation, one trainer developed a situation where participants would assume a gay identity and role-play telling his or her mother, boss, and best friend that he or she is gay. For someone in later stages of ethnorelativism, this is an engaging way to handle sexual orientation as a topic: low challenge and a fine learning opportunity. For someone in early stages of ethnocentrism, this would be a very high-risk activity and would likely engender strong resistance.

In general, a large proportion of our learners are likely to be in ethnocentric stages and therefore prone to finding intercultural competence challenging at best and quite threatening at worst. Since cultural topics become less challenging only in the ethnorelative stages, training methods for difference avoiders are typically more supportive and low risk, leaving the more complicated and demanding activities until the later stages.

By using both the DMIS and the challenge and support models, we are able to describe a theoretical rationale to our clients, our colleagues, and our learners for why we do our training the way we do.

◆ Training for Intercultural Competence

The DMIS model describes two fundamental approaches to difference: *difference avoidance*, an ethnocentric perspective that

Figure 8.2   The Developmental Model of Intercultural Sensitivity

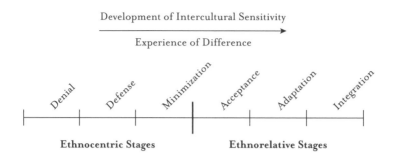

places one's own culture as the filter through which all other cultures are viewed, and *difference seeking*, an ethnorelative perspective that places one's own culture in the context of other cultures.

Within these two approaches are six stages that reflect different worldview orientation (see Figure 8.2). Within the ethnocentric, difference-avoiding perspective there are three stages: denial of difference, defense against difference, and minimization of difference. Within the ethnorelative, difference-seeking stages, the three stages are acceptance of difference, adaptation to difference, and integration of difference.

For the trainer, understanding each of these six stages allows for a diagnosis of potential learner resistance, for selection of both content and process elements of the program, and for sequencing the learning to address learner readiness. Trainers may choose to measure the stages through the Intercultural Development Inventory (Hammer, 1999; Hammer, Bennett, & Wiseman, 2003), discussed in Chapter 16 of this text. This tool assesses the worldview orientation of individuals or groups and, therefore, provides the basis for more precisely focused training design.

Further, the model allows for concentrating on stage-appropriate intercultural competencies—in essence, boiling the frog slowly. It is often the fond wish of educators

to conduct training programs that immediately develop tolerance of ambiguity and cognitive complexity, while eradicating racist attitudes and privilege. It is equally often that such ambitions are dashed in the sobering recognition that a day or two of training cannot eliminate beliefs and behaviors that have grown over a lifetime. By focusing on stage-appropriate competencies, the trainer may be able to influence greater change, because the training may foster less resistance.

The following discussion reviews the DMIS model, while describing the primary developmental task for cultivating intercultural competence, the implications for training design, the challenge and support patterns, and the stage-appropriate competencies and activities.

DENIAL ✓

Worldview of the Denial Stage

Frequently, the first sense of cultural difference that we experience is not to experience it at all. The worldview of the denial stage allows us to maintain isolation from other culture groups, either physically or psychologically. Those of us who view others through the denial filter may neglect to notice differences or may think in extremely limited categories. Perhaps we are just beginning to explore cultural differences. We may be unaware that we have a culture, or that certain privileges exist in our world that do not exist for other culture and racial groups. We may feel perplexed when asked about our own cultural filters and feel unconcerned about the impact of cultural differences on our lives. The typical manager may be surprised to find the subjects of culture or race on the training agenda, even a bit perplexed about their relevance to the workplace. Since the world is a global village, and the Internet brings us all together in a common language, why worry unnecessarily about culture differences?

Occasionally, we may even have a tendency to dehumanize others. By thinking in limited categories, we may come to see their world as simplistic, or somehow less vital than our own complicated world, where we have many categories for processing events. If we know little about another culture, we tend to reduce it to a few stereotypical images: the food they eat, their attitude toward time, the poverty we see on television.

Training at the Denial Stage

As trainers, our primary developmental task at the denial stage is to introduce learners to the existence of culture and its relevance to their careers: Culture matters. The intercultural competencies to prepare leaders at this stage include developing the initiative to recognize differences, to gather appropriate information, and to be comfortable with being culturally curious.

Participants with this worldview are quite challenged by the idea of cultural differences and offer a variety of resistances such as, "As long as we all speak the same language, it doesn't matter," "With my experience, I can be successful anywhere," "Live and let live," and "Cultural diversity will never happen here!" And, of course, "Electrons don't have culture!"

Realizing that cultural differences present such a high challenge, we can expose the learner to immediately relevant information such as human resource issues, local customs, and user-friendly activities that relate more directly to cultural differences. Many such methods expose the participants to mild and engaging disorientation, as does "Mixed Messages" (Myers & Lambert, 2000), an exercise that uses nonverbal signals in culturally contrastive ways, or "Working in Unfamiliar Surroundings" (Brandt, 2000), which uses simple math problems with a touch of cultural complexity. "Grocery Store Ethnography" (Kluver, 1998) involves the participants in an anthropological analysis of a familiar context. In each of these activities, the seemingly familiar is notably different, creating a stimulus for recognizing culture.

DEFENSE

Worldview of the Defense Stage

When we become aware of cultural differences in more powerful and penetrating ways, we may slip into a defense posture, where our worldview is polarized into us/them distinctions. For example, "Now that I've noticed the Indian culture is different, I recognize they're bad!" When we think in these bipolar categories, we tend to judge others or assert the superiority of our own culture. One intriguing variation on the defense perspective is what is called "reversal," which involves denigrating our own culture and exalting some other culture's ways of being and doing. While this may superficially seem to be more culturally sensitive, in fact it is nevertheless still dualistic and a defensive reaction to exposure to difference. The object of the defense has simply shifted.

Training at the Defense Stage

The developmental task at the defense stage is to promote recognition of cultural similarities, the only stage for which this is the primary goal. The intercultural competencies to prepare leaders at this stage are rather basic to intercultural interaction: developing the ability to manage anxiety, the discipline to maintain personal control, and the cultivation of patience and tolerance.

Learners with this worldview are maximally challenged by cultural difference and may appear to be resistant to culture learning—although perhaps *fearful* is a more accurate descriptor. Based on their powerful response to difference, they may view people from other cultures as rude or uncooperative, perhaps manipulative, or inefficient. When a supplier has agreed to deliver a product by a certain date and fails to do so, their first thought is not, "Something cultural is going on!" but rather, "They lied to me!" They may say, "When I visit other cultures, I realize how much better we have it here."

To address this powerful challenge, our task is to guide the learners to recognize that the manager from the other culture is "just like me!" It matters not what the commonality is, whether soccer, samba, or salsa. What matters is that the frame of reference shifts from "us/them" to "they're not so bad after all!" Supportive activities in the design may typically avoid the topic of culture and focus instead on Lego-block models of group interaction, team activities such as rope courses, and inventories such as the Myers–Briggs Type Indicator (Myers, McCaulley, Quenk, & Hammer, 1998) and the Kolb Learning Styles Inventory (Kolb, 2005). There is a reason karaoke is a popular business pastime in Asia; it bridges the barrier of the defense worldview. Each of these options allows the group to reflect on similarities and, incidentally, a few differences, while building comfort with the idea of working together across cultures.

MINIMIZATION ✓

Worldview of the Minimization Stage

When we adopt the minimization worldview, we typically feel that we have achieved intercultural sensitivity, since suggesting in most contexts that "we are all the same despite surface differences" is a vast improvement over the cultural biases that normally exist. However, this is perhaps the most complex strategy for avoiding cultural differences. Indeed, if we believe that deep down we are all alike, then we do not have to do the difficult work of recognizing our own cultural patterns, understanding others, and eventually making the necessary adaptations. This stage is thus characterized by the assumption that we are similar in some universal context, whether physical or philosophical. Superficial differences are absorbed through our own culture's filters and, fundamentally, we assume that people the world over are "just like us." This allows us to hire diverse staff only to expect them to walk, talk, and act like the dominant culture. If we explain culture through a minimizing worldview, we are often complacent and satisfied with our development and encourage others to share our perspective that we do not see color, the only race that matters is the human race, and class does not exist.

Training at the Minimization Stage

As trainers, our primary developmental task at the minimization stage is to develop cultural self-awareness. The intercultural competencies to prepare leaders at this stage include developing open-mindedness, listening skills, accurate cross-cultural perception, nonjudgmentalness, knowledge of our own culture, and culture maps for understanding other cultures.

Participants with this worldview are only moderately challenged by the idea of cultural difference. They are likely to think, "The best way to get along in any culture is just to be yourself." From the minimization perspective, technology is uniting the business cultures of the world into convergence, into a single set of values, values that are coincidentally more like my own culture than any other culture. Those in minimization often say, "People all over the world are alike. And of course they're just like me, or soon will be." Learners may feel uncomfortable with our discussions of difference, suspecting that we are being pejorative of other cultures. Their worldview dances between the previous stage (defense), where difference was bad, to the minimization perspective, where we are all alike. Suggestions that others are different and that this is *good* are not yet part of their cognitive constructs.

Since the idea of cultural difference is less threatening at this stage, the activities to develop cultural self-awareness can be more challenging. In fact, many exercise manuals are dominated by activities that are appropriate for minimization, activities that focus on recognizing your own culture and achieving a general sense of cultural patterns.

The classic intercultural exercise "Description, Interpretation, and Evaluation" (D.I.E., available at www.intercultural.org) helps learners suspend judgment long enough to examine multiple perspectives. The exercise differentiates what individuals actually see (description) from what they think it might mean (interpretation) and directs differential judgments. Further work on perception can be supported with a particularly useful module for the corporate context created by Osland, Kolb, and Rubin (2001, Chapter 8). Another intriguing tool is an introduction exercise ("Identity") developed by Steve Kulich (2000) for eliciting both commonalties and differences. Activities that ask participants to

reflect on culture maps of their own cultures, both personal and organizational, allow for initial recognition of interaction patterns across cultures (Brake & Walker, 1995; Kohls, 1996; Stringer & Cassiday, 2003). Asking participants to review annual corporate reports from the perspective of an outsider from another planet allows for amusing—and relevant—cultural analyses of power, values, and inclusivity (based on O'Mara's exercise "Magazines," 1994). In addition, structuring learning opportunities with selected and coached managers and leaders from other cultures can present a striking contrast to the idea that it's a small world after all.

ACCEPTANCE ✓

Worldview of the Acceptance Stage

As we become increasingly aware of our own culture, we begin to recognize how truly distinct other cultures are from our own, and we understand this distinction as *difference* without judging it to be "bad" or "less-developed." We move from the earlier three stages of difference avoidance into difference seeking. This movement into the stages of ethnorelativism reflects our capacity to acknowledge our own cultural filters and suspend our judgments temporarily in order to understand others. In a sense, for the first time, we may see the complexity and validity of another culture's worldview.

As we move to the acceptance stage, we are at first interested in behavioral differences ("They eat dinner at 10:00 p.m.!"), and then gradually we move into more complicated observations ("I've noticed that Masako observes our team discussion for a long time and thinks carefully before offering her comments"). Ultimately, we are able to decipher—and accept—profound value differences. However, it is essential to note that this does not mean *agreement with* or *preference for* those values, but rather acceptance of the reality of the other culture's worldview. In addition, at the acceptance stage, we tend to be more comfortable discussing culture, asking questions, and realizing that people in other culture groups may not share our worldview.

Training at the Acceptance Stage

As trainers, our primary developmental task at the acceptance stage is to increase the complexity of trainees' ideas about culture. Moving beyond the initial understanding of their own culture, they can explore culture more deeply, realizing with some degree of cultural humility that their own culture exists in a context of equally valid cultures.

The intercultural competencies to prepare leaders at this stage include culture-specific knowledge, cognitive flexibility, tolerance of ambiguity, and respect for other's values and beliefs.

Participants with this worldview are only mildly challenged by the idea of cultural differences. However, the challenge at this stage often emerges around a fear of compromising their own values and beliefs as they respect others. For the trainer, this issue requires walking a fine line of contexting behavior in a particular culture and honoring a participant's values, a capacity inherent in effective intercultural interactions. "Thus one can comprehend the context and meaning of certain business practices in other countries and at the same time adhere to U.S. standards. (See *Uncompromising Integrity: Motorola's Global Challenge* by R. S. Moorthy, et al. [1998] for a thoughtful model on how this can be approached)" (J. M. Bennett, 2003).

Since cultural difference is now intriguing rather than threatening, we can for the first time design training with more complicated and risky strategies, demanding complex analysis, such as simulations, role-plays, dialogues, and case studies. A useful resource for addressing the acceptance stage of development is a manual of 50 activities designed for the international business context. Titled *Global Competence* (Lambert, Myers, & Simons, 2000), the collection includes a simulation focusing on cultural patterns in a negotiation context (Simons & Hopkins, 2000); cross-cultural dialogues for analyzing communication (Storti, 2000); values analysis among Britain, Germany, and the United States (Lynn, 2000); and a team activity that explores both cooperation and interaction patterns (Halverson, 2000). In other volumes, "The Culture Compass" (Chu, 1996) contrasts personal values with the organizational culture, and Min-Sun Kim (1998) provides a set of critical incidents on communication styles. Within *The Managing Diversity Survival Guide* are multiple checklists, activities, and insights for training (Gardenswartz & Rowe, 1994). An extremely thorough lesson plan for using a *Star Trek* episode for managers at the acceptance stage has been designed by Greg Rossy and Margaret Phillips (2003).

ADAPTATION ✓

Worldview of the Adaptation Stage

The necessary motivation to move to adaptation often occurs when we need to be effective in our interactions with others in order to get something done. It is no longer enough to merely have the mindset (to know *about* a culture). Leaders now recognize that to succeed in the global economy, they need to moderate their approach; adaptation requires cultivation of the skillset, as well. And the premier skill of an interculturalist is empathy: that capacity to take the perspective of the other culture, to shift frames of reference, and to act in the context of the other's perspective.

Based on our appropriate frame shifts, we can adapt how we interact, a process called "code-shifting." For instance, we may adapt our greeting rituals, our problem-solving strategies, our negotiation style, or our apology patterns.

When we are at the stage of adaptation, we may wonder, "Do I have to abandon who I am to be interculturally sensitive?" For instance, "Do I have to give up being a feminist while I work in a male-dominated culture?" It may help us to understand that intercultural sensitivity is an *addition* to our personal repertoire of behavior, not a subtraction. We are who we are, but with adaptive intercultural expertise.

Training at the Adaptation Stage

When training participants at the adaptation stage, the primary developmental task is to improve the capacity to shift frames of reference and to function effectively and appropriately in that other perspective. The intercultural competencies to prepare leaders at this stage include developing skills in empathy, risk taking, problem solving, interaction management, social adaptability, and flexibility.

Participants with this worldview are at home discussing culture; therefore, the training design can present challenge in both content and process. The attention at this stage is focused beyond having the learners observe another culture, or merely analyze it. The challenge here is that they must be able to *do* it. Exercises such as "Communication Continuum" (Stringer, 2000), "Negotiating Across Cultural Boundaries" (Ady, 1998), "Decoding Indirectness" (Storti & Bennhold-Samaan, 1997), "The Cultural Detective" (Hofner Saphiere, 2007), and "The Role Play" (McCaffery, 1995) involve the participants in complex contexts that require code-shifting. Thiagarajan (2000, 2001, 2003, 2005, 2006) has developed

literally hundreds of games, simulations, and frame games that can be readily adapted for sophisticated audiences to structure complex learning at this stage. Finally, inventories that both reveal individual styles as well as require skill practice, such as the Intercultural Conflict Styles Inventory (Hammer, 2003) present useful challenges for managers.

INTEGRATION

Worldview of the Integration Stage

When we have experienced in-depth intercultural adaptation, one possible result is a bicultural identity in which we have internalized two or more cultures. This typically does not happen in brief sojourns in other cultures lasting fewer than 3 years but frequently results when we intentionally make a significant, sustained effort to become fully competent in new cultures. This adaptation may occur for nondominant group members to a dominant or colonial culture, for people who grew up in multiple countries, or for long-term sojourners who have lived for extended periods of time in other cultures. This is not a stage that most of us will achieve, and it cannot be developed through a training program, where most managers and leaders should be aspiring to acceptance and adaptation.

This bicultural or multicultural identity allows for lively participation in a variety of cultures but also for an occasional sense of never really being "at home." Home has become everywhere; our sense of who we are as cultural beings becomes quite complex. An African American living in the United States may experience this, as well as a Costa Rican sojourning in Brazil, or an individual with a passport culture of Japan, having lived in Denmark, Costa Rica, Peru, and Iran. The multicultural person brings many perspectives to every task, many ways to solve problems, and multiple possibilities for shifting codes.

Training at the Integration Stage

As trainers, our primary developmental task at the integration stage is to facilitate an individual's resolution of the multicultural identity. It is the rare training room that consists of a majority of participants at this stage. The intercultural competencies to prepare leaders at the integration stage include developing a culturally sensitive sense of humor, role and identity flexibility, and the ability to recognize new cultural patterns.

Once again, those with an integration worldview are not discomfited by culture differences; indeed, they likely thrive on them. Since they feel at home in the world and enjoy code-shifting, the last frontier of their intercultural exploration may be their own cultural marginality, living as they do on the edge of two or more cultures (J. M. Bennett, 1993). They may view the trainer's insights about their complex identity as a welcome support.

Therefore, one of the most appropriate approaches to training those at integration provides them with the opportunity to explore the nature of being a multicultural person, raising a multicultural/multiracial family, marrying across cultures, and transferring one more time to a new assignment abroad. They may appreciate validation of their expertise, enjoy serving as a resource person to other transferees, and meeting other professionals who share an integrated identity.

◆ Conclusion

For those new to the world of training, the variables to consider often seem overwhelming, particularly when the training concerns culture and the powerful attendant issues. Trainers often ask, "How can I keep all of these models in my head at once? How can I design with every participant and every issue in mind?"

The answer may very well be, "And how could we train leaders *without* doing that?"

By intentionally and systematically applying both the DMIS and the challenge and support model, trainers can design learning opportunities for leaders that transform their worldviews, develop their intercultural competence, and, yes, help them recognize that the engineers who talk about electrons *do* have culture!

◆ Discussion Questions

1. What is the business case for developing intercultural competence?

2. What is the human relations case for developing intercultural competence?

3. What benefits and limitations can you see in combining both domestic and global culture in training?

4. Imagine five statements of resistance to intercultural differences you might hear from managers. After listing them, try to diagnose what stage of the DMIS they might represent, and prepare a developmentally appropriate response.

5. Discuss why it is not appropriate to begin a training program with the topic of racism when you know the audience holds an ethnocentric worldview.

6. At which stages are participants open to learning about the more complicated aspects of culture and race? Why?

◆ References

Adler, N. J. (with Gundersen, A.). (2007). *International dimensions of organizational behavior* (5th ed.). Cincinnati, OH: South-Western College Pub.

Ady, J. C. (1998). Negotiating across cultural boundaries: Implications of individualism–collectivism and cases for application. In T. M. Singelis (Ed.), *Teaching about culture, ethnicity, & diversity* (pp. 111–120). Thousand Oaks, CA: Sage.

Bennett, J. M. (1993). Cultural marginality: Identity issues in intercultural training. In R. M. Paige (Ed.), *Education for the intercultural experience*. Yarmouth, ME: Intercultural Press.

Bennett, J. M. (2003). Turning frogs into interculturalists: A student-centered development approach to teaching intercultural competence. In N. A. Boyacigiller, R. A. Goodman, & M. E. Phillips (Eds.), *Crossing cultures: Insights from master teachers*. New York: Taylor & Francis.

Bennett, J. M., & Bennett, M. J. (2004). Developing intercultural sensitivity: An integrative approach to global and domestic diversity. In D. Landis, J. M. Bennett, & M. J. Bennett (Eds.), *Handbook of intercultural training* (3rd ed., pp. 147–165). Thousand Oaks, CA: Sage.

Bennett, M. J. (1993). Towards ethnorelativism: A developmental model of intercultural sensitivity. In R. M. Paige (Ed.), *Education for the intercultural experience* (2nd ed., pp. 21–71). Yarmouth, ME: Intercultural Press.

Bennett, M. J. (2001). Developing intercultural competence for global leadership. In R. Reineke & C. Fussinger (Eds.), *Interkulturelles management: Kozeptionberatung–training*. Germany: Gabler.

Bird, A., & Osland, J. S. (2004). Global competencies: An introduction. In H. W. Lane, M. L. Maznevski, M. E. Mendenhall, & J. McNett (Eds.), *The Blackwell handbook of global management: A guide to managing complexity*. Malden, MA: Blackwell.

Black, J. S., & Gregersen, H. B. (1999, March/April). The right way to manage expatriates. *Harvard Business Review*, 52–62.

Boyacigiller, N., Beechler, S., Taylor, S., & Levy, O. (2004). The crucial yet illusive global mindset. In H. W. Lane, M. L. Maznevski, M. E. Mendenhall, & J. McNett (Eds.), *The Blackwell handbook of global management: A guide to managing complexity*. Malden, MA: Blackwell.

Brake, T., & Walker, D. (1995). *Doing business internationally: The workbook for cross-cultural success*. Princeton, NJ: Princeton Training Press.

Brandt, M. (2000). Working in unfamiliar surroundings. In J. Lambert, S. Myers, & G. Simons (Eds.), *Global competence: 50 training activities for succeeding in international business*. Amherst, MA: HRD Press.

Carr-Ruffino, N. (2003). *Managing diversity: People skills for a multicultural workplace* (6th ed.). Needham Heights, MA: Pearson Custom.

Chu, P. (1996). The culture compass. In H. N. Seeyle (Ed.), *Experiential activities for intercultural learning* (pp. 155–170). Yarmouth, ME: Intercultural Press.

Cornwell, G. H., & Stoddard, E. W. (1999). *Globalizing knowledge: Connecting international and intercultural studies*. Washington, DC: Association of American Colleges & Universities.

Cox, T. (1994). *Cultural diversity in organizations: Theory, research and practice*. San Francisco: Berrett-Koehler.

Deardorff, D. (2006). Identification and assessment of intercultural competence as a student outcome of internationalization. *Journal of Studies in International Education, 10*(3), 241–266.

Description, interpretation, and evaluation. (n.d.). Retrieved August 24, 2007, from http://www.intercultural.org/documents/resources/die.doc/

Dinges, N. G., & Baldwin, K. D. (1996). Intercultural competence: A research perspective. In D. Landis & R. S. Bhagat (Eds.), *Handbook of intercultural training* (2nd ed., pp. 106–123). Thousand Oaks, CA: Sage.

Earley, P. C., & Ang, S. (2003). *Cultural intelligence: Individual interactions across cultures*. Stanford, CA: Stanford University Press.

Fernandez, J. P. (1991). *Managing a diverse workforce: Regaining the competitive edge*. Lexington, MA: Lexington Books.

Gardenswartz, L., & Rowe, A. (1994). *The managing diversity survival guide: A complete collection of checklists, activities, and tips*. New York: Irwin.

Gardenswartz, L., & Rowe, A. (1998). *Managing diversity: A complete desk reference and planning guide* (Rev. ed.). New York: McGraw-Hill.

Gardenswartz, L., Rowe, A., Digh, P., & Bennett, M. (2003). *The global diversity desk reference: Managing an international workforce.* San Francisco: Jossey-Bass.

Green, M. (1988). *The dialectic of freedom.* New York: Teachers College Press.

Gregersen, H. B., Morrison, A. J., & Mendenhall, M. E. (Eds.). (2000, Summer/Fall). Global leadership [Special issue]. *Human Resource Management, 39*(2&3).

Gundling, E., & Zanchettin, A. (2006). *Global diversity: Winning customers and engaging employees in world markets.* Boston: Nicholas Brealey.

Halverson, C. B. (2000). Building with differences. In J. Lambert, S. Myers, & G. Simons (Eds.). *Global competence: 50 training activities for succeeding in international business.* Amherst, MA: HRD Press.

Hammer, M. R. (1989). Intercultural competence. In M. K. Asante & W. B. Gudykunst (Eds.), *Handbook of international and intercultural communication* (pp. 247–260). Newbury Park, CA: Sage.

Hammer, M. R. (1999). A measure of intercultural sensitivity: The Intercultural Development inventory. In S. M. Fowler & M. G. Mumford (Eds.), *Intercultural sourcebook: Cross-cultural training methods: Vol. 2* (pp. 61–79). Yarmouth, ME: Intercultural Press.

Hammer, M. R. (2003). *The Intercultural Conflict Style (ICS) Inventory.* North Potomac, MD: Hammer Consulting.

Hammer, M. R., Bennett, M. J., & Wiseman, R. (2003). Measuring intercultural sensitivity: The Intercultural Development Inventory. In R. M. Paige (Ed.), *International Journal of Intercultural Relations, 27*(4), 421–443.

Hayles, R. V., & Mendez Russell, A. (1997). *The diversity directive: Why some initiatives fail and what to do about it.* Chicago: Irwin.

Henderson, G. (1994). *Cultural diversity in the workplace.* Westport, CT: Quorum Books.

Hofner Saphiere, D. (2007). *The cultural detective.* Available at www.culturaldetective.com

Hovland, K. (2006). *Shared futures: Global learning and liberal education.* Washington, DC: Association of American Colleges and Universities.

Judy, R. W., & D'Amico, C. (1997). *Workforce 2020: Work and workers in the 21st century.* Indianapolis, IN: Hudson Institute.

Kim, M. (1998). Conversational constraints as a tool for understanding communication styles. In T. M. Singelis (Ed.), *Teaching about culture, ethnicity, and diversity* (pp. 101–109). Thousand Oaks, CA: Sage.

Kim, Y. Y. (1991). Intercultural communication competence: A systems-theoretic view. In S. Ting-Toomey & F. Korzenny (Eds.), *International and intercultural communication annual: Vol. 15. Cross-cultural interpersonal communication* (pp. 230–275). Newbury Park, CA: Sage.

Kluver, R. (1998). Grocery store ethnography. In T. M. Singelis (Ed.), *Teaching about culture, ethnicity, and diversity* (pp. 23–28). Thousand Oaks, CA: Sage.

Kohls, L. R. (1996). U.S. proverbs and core values. In H. N. Seeyle (Ed.), *Experiential activities for intercultural learning* (pp. 79–81). Yarmouth, ME: Intercultural Press.

Kolb, D. A. (2005). *The Kolb Learning Style Inventory.* Boston: Hay Resources Direct.

Kulich, S. (2000). Identity. In J. Lambert, S. Myers, & G. Simons (Eds.), *Global competence: 50 training activities for succeeding in international business.* Amherst, MA: HRD Press.

Lambert, J., Myers, S., & Simons, G. (Eds.). (2000). *Global competence: 50 training activities for succeeding in international business.* Amherst, MA: HRD Press.

Lustig, M. W., & Koester, J. (2006). *Intercultural competence: Interpersonal communication across cultures* (5th ed.). Boston: Pearson.

Lynn, E. (2000). Germany, Britain, and the USA—Values and behavior patterns. In J. Lambert, S. Myers, & G. Simons (Eds.), *Global competence: 50 training activities for succeeding in international business.* Amherst, MA: HRD Press.

Martin, J. N., & Hammer, M. R. (1989). Behavioral categories of intercultural communication competence: Everyday communicators' perceptions. *International Journal of Intercultural Relations, 13*(3), 303–333.

McCaffery, J. A. (1995). The role play: A powerful but difficult training tool. In S. M. Fowler & M. G. Mumford (Eds.), *Intercultural sourcebook: Cross-cultural training methods: Vol. 1* (pp. 17–26). Yarmouth, ME: Intercultural Press.

McTighe Musil, C. (2006). *Assessing global learning: Matching good intentions with good practice.* Washington, DC: Association of American Colleges and Universities.

Mendenhall, M. E., Kuhlmann, T. M., & Stahl, G. K. (Eds.). (2001). *Developing global business leaders: Policies, processes, and innovations.* Westport, CT: Greenwood.

Mendenhall, M. E., & Oddou, G. R. (1986, Winter). Acculturation profiles of expatriate managers: Implications for cross-cultural training programs. *Columbia Journal of World Business,* 73–79.

Mendenhall, M. E., Stahl, G. K., Ehnert, I., Oddou, G., Osland, J. S., & Kühlmann, T. M. (2004). Evaluation studies of cross-cultural training programs: A review of literature from 1988 to 2000. In D. Landis, J. M. Bennett, & M. J. Bennett (Eds.), *Handbook of intercultural training* (3rd ed., pp. 129–144). Thousand Oaks, CA: Sage.

Moorthy, R. S., De George, R. T., Donaldson, T., Ellos, W. J., Solomon, R. C., & Textor, R. B. (1998). *Uncompromising integrity: Motorola's global challenge.* Schaumburg, IL: Motorola University Press.

Myers, I. B., McCaulley, M. H., Quenk, N. L, & Hammer, A. L. (1998). *MBTI manual (A guide to the development and use of the Myers Briggs Type Indicator)* (3rd ed.). Mountain View, CA: Consulting Psychologists Press.

Myers, S., & Lambert, J. (2000). Mixed messages. In J. Lambert, S. Myers, & G. Simons (Eds.), *Global competence: 50 training activities for succeeding in international business.* Amherst, MA: HRD Press.

O'Mara, J. (1994). *Diversity activities and training designs.* San Diego, CA: Pfeiffer.

Osland, J. S., Kolb, D. A., & Rubin, I. M. (2001). *Organizational behavior: An experiential approach* (7th ed.). Upper Saddle River, NJ: Prentice Hall.

Peterson, B. (2004). *Cultural intelligence: A guide to working with people from other cultures.* Yarmouth, ME: Intercultural Press.

Rossy, G. L., & Phillips, M. E. (2003). Building transpatriate skills: The *Star Trek* case. In N. A. Boyacigiller, R. A. Goodman, & M. E. Phillips (Eds.). *Crossing cultures: Insights from master teachers.* New York: Taylor & Francis.

Sanford, N. (1966). *Self and society: Social change and individual development.* New York: Atherton Press.

Simons, G., & Hopkins, W. (2000). The transcultural communicator. In J. Lambert, S. Myers, & G. Simons (Eds.), *Global competence: 50 training activities for succeeding in international business.* Amherst, MA: HRD Press.

Storti, C. (2000). Cross-cultural dialogues. In J. Lambert, S. Myers, & G. Simons (Eds.), *Global competence: 50 training activities for succeeding in international business.* Amherst, MA: HRD Press.

Storti, C., & Bennhold-Samaan, L. (1997). *Culture matters: The Peace Corps cross-cultural workbook.* Washington, DC: Peace Corps Information Collection and Exchange, 1998.

Stringer, D. M. Communication Continuum. (2000). In J. Lambert, S. Myers, & G. Simons (Eds.), *Global competence: 50 training activities for succeeding in international business.* Amherst, MA: HRD Press.

Stringer, D. M., & Cassiday, P. A. (2003). *52 activities for exploring values differences.* Yarmouth, ME: Intercultural Press, 2003.

Thiagarajan, S. (2000). *Facilitator's toolkit.* Bloomington, IN: Workshops by Thiagi.

Thiagarajan, S. (2001, May). *Fun in the workplace: Presentation skills and games.* #250105. Info-Line. Alexandria, VA: American Society for Training and Development.

Thiagarajan, S. (2003). *Design your own games and activities: Thiagi's templates for performance improvement.* San Francisco: Jossey-Bass.

Thiagarajan, S. (2005). *Thiagi's interactive lectures: Power up your training with interactive games and exercises.* Alexandria, VA: ASTD Press.

Thiagarajan, S. (2006). *Thiagi's 100 favorite games.* San Francisco: Pfeiffer.

Thomas, D. C., & Inkson, K. (2004). *Cultural intelligence: People skills for global business.* San Francisco: Berrett-Koehler.

Ting-Toomey, S. (1999). *Communicating across cultures.* New York: Guilford.

Wentling, R. M., & Palma-Rivas, N. (2000, Spring). Current status of diversity initiatives in selected multinational corporations. *Human Resource Development Quarterly, 11*(1), 35–60.

Wiseman, R. L. (2002). Intercultural communication competence. In W. B. Gudykunst & B. Mody (Eds.), *Handbook of international and intercultural communication* (2nd ed., pp. 207–224). Thousand Oaks, CA: Sage.

Wiseman, R. L., & J. Koester (Eds.). (1993). *International and Intercultural Communication Annual: Vol. 17. Intercultural communication competence.* Newbury Park, CA: Sage.

Yershova, Y., DeJaeghere, J., & Mestenhauser, J. (2000, Spring). Thinking not as usual: Adding the intercultural perspective. *Journal of Studies in International Education, 4*(1), 39–78.

LEADING ACROSS CULTURES

*Designing a Learning
Agenda for Global Praxis*

◆ L. Hyatt, Leslie A. Evans,
and Md Mahbubul Haque

Over 10,000 years ago, native peoples, indigenous to the
Western U.S. coastal regions, believed that the first people
were "People of the Sky" (birds) and occupied the world before
humans (Timbrook & Johnson, 1999, p. 1). Ethnographic records
show that birds appeared prominently in virtually all facets of life,
including ceremonies, medicine, rituals, clothing, music, art, astron-
omy, myths, language, and sociopolitical contexts. After studying with
and learning much from Native Americans, one of the authors created the following story intended to honor the genre of myth among
the Native American culture. It is used here to introduce cultural
awareness as an essential construct of a leadership learning agenda.

3 EAGLES 1 LESSON

Golden Eagle woke to the sounds of his 3 children quarrelling. They had been arguing about the value of other birds compared to eagles. After dismissing many types of birds as being of little or no significance, their conversation turned to birds that were most like themselves and therefore, of some merit.

"Surely, falcons are like us and therefore must be second to eagles," said one son.

"Hawks are second because they are most similar to eagles," asserted the daughter.

"Certainly the size of condors puts them in the running," claimed another son.

Their father listened from a distance, understanding that a certain amount of boastfulness was part of being a young eagle, but he also had some concerns about his children's limited views. He was scheduled to visit with Great Owl that day and thought he might seek his counsel on this matter.

Golden Eagle and Great Owl spoke of many things, including Golden Eagle's children. They were old friends whose relationship was borne out of respect. Golden Eagle said that he wanted his children to broaden their views and appreciate other birds. Great Owl suggested that before they can widen their perspective, they must first come to understand the narrow lens from which they view the world. The two friends then devised a plan to help the young eagles.

The next day Golden Eagle directed his children to meet with Great Owl. Once there, Great Owl asked the children if they had ever seen a lemon tree.

They shook their heads, "no."

"Very good," said Great Owl, "I have an errand for you."

The young eagles were eager to hear more.

"You will each travel thousands of miles in different directions to bring me a branch from a lemon tree," instructed Great Owl.

The young eagles asked, "How will we find the lemon tree?"

"You will use your excellent vision and hunting skills," Great Owl continued, "and there are many birds from these other places who can guide you."

One by one the young eagles took flight towards the west, the north, and the south.

Now, everyone knows that eagles can fly very far very fast. So, it wasn't long before the young eagles returned each with a branch from a lemon tree. Waiting for them were Golden Eagle and Great Owl.

The young eagle that had gone south told of birds that had blue feet and brought back a branch that had small budding flowers sprouting from it. The eagle that returned from the north delivered a branch with green leaves and spoke of very big birds that made honking sounds. The eagle that had gone west recounted tales of a bird that could not fly and returned with a branch that had yellow oval-shaped fruit attached.

Upon seeing the different looking branches, the young eagles started to argue over which was the branch from a lemon tree. Just then, Golden Eagle extended his wing to call for quiet. His wingspan was so massive that it blocked out the bright afternoon sun and effectively silenced the young eagles.

"Now then, all three of you are correct," said Great Owl.

The young eagles exclaimed, "But how can that be when all of our branches look so different?"

Great Owl cleared his throat, "Ahem . . . you were each sent to a different location with a distinct season. The lemon tree's appearance changes with each season. In fall and winter, green leaves grace the branches. In spring, the tree produces buds that blossom into flowers. As the weather becomes warmer the tree bears sour yellow fruit. So, you can see that broadening one's perspective opens up possibilities that even though something looks or acts differently, it can have similar value."

The young eagles listened attentively and began talking about their adventures and the many bird-friends they met along the way.

Golden Eagle and Great Owl nodded knowingly.

SOURCE: "3 Eagles 1 Lesson," by L. Hyatt, 2007, Organizational Leadership Doctoral Research Seminar, ULV, Los Angeles.

3 Eagles 1 Lesson is a story about learning to shift perspectives and expand awareness of the cultural landscape. "Culture as a set of basic assumptions defines for us what to pay attention to, what things mean, how to react emotionally to what is going on, and what actions to take in various kinds of situations" (Schein, 2004, p. 32). Increasing globalization obligates those engaged in leadership education to adequately prepare future leaders for the challenges that lie ahead. Central to this notion is the facilitation of capability and effectiveness within the context of global environments, and specifically the ability to function in a diverse cultural context (Kagan & Stewart, 2004; Laughton & Ottewill, 2000; Orpen, 2003; Starratt, 2005).

Cultural awareness consists of views and experience. The term *culture* connotes a surfeit of meanings, including education, experience, age, skill sets, ethnicity, religion, race, gender, marital status, geography, income, language, knowledge, occupation, generation, and communication and learning styles. Many of these elements have been individually addressed in writings by esteemed colleagues (Adler, 2002; Bhawuk, Landis, & Lo, 2006; Gardenswartz & Rowe, 1995; Hammer, Bennett & Wiseman, 2003; Hampden-Turner & Trompenaars, 1998; Paige, 2003; Palthe & Kossek, 2003; Schaetti, Watanabe, & Ramsey, 2000; Schmieder-Ramirez & McManus, 2007; Trompenaars & Woolliams, 2007; Van Dyne &

Ang, 2006). This chapter, then, considers these elements in combination and addresses cultural awareness from a global lens. The case for a global perspective is increasingly evident in our shrinking world (Kagan & Stewart, 2004). Curiously, the importance of a global perspective dates back to Aristotle's teachings that offer, "We cannot gain self-knowledge by turning our gaze unto ourselves . . . it is by looking outward on to the world that man's soul maps the structure of the world . . . self-understanding must be to some extent indirect" (Lear, 1988, p. 8).

◆ **Current Status of Integrating Global Teachings Into Education**

Reporting his findings on the state of global education today, Kenneth Tye (2003) noted that the global education movement started in the 1990s in the United States. The Association for Supervision and Curriculum Development (ASCD) Yearbook titled *Global Education: From Thought to Action* (Tye, 1991) defines global education as learning about those problems and issues which cut across national boundaries and about the interconnectedness of systems—cultural, ecological, economic, political, and technological. Global education also involves learning to understand and appreciate those who have different cultural backgrounds, to see the world through the eyes and minds of others, and to realize that other peoples of the world need and want much of the same things (Eble, 1988; Keller, 2003; Tye, 2003).

GLOBAL PROGRAM EXAMPLES

The major finding in Tye's (2003) study was that throughout the world, education is still seen as a major force in the building of national loyalties. This is true despite the growing interconnectedness of global systems. Global educators from 52 countries responded to the survey. The data revealed that only 14 countries had significant programs for global education. Moreover, the United States was not among the top seven, which comprised Australia, Canada, Japan, South Korea, Russia, the United Kingdom, and the People's Republic of China. Some of the highlights from each country's programs follow.

In Australia, many state education departments are considering significant rewrites of the curriculum to reflect the necessity to prepare people for life in a global society.

In Canada, there is a new Global Classroom Initiative that gives grants to teachers and educational entities. The main goal is to encourage the integration of a global perspective and to instill a sense of global citizenship and increased awareness of the difference that individual and collective actions can make on issues of global importance.

In the 1980s and 1990s, major corporations put pressure on the government of Japan to develop "education for global competitiveness." This movement led to an official policy that supports international educational exchanges of various kinds, promotes international understanding in the curriculum along with increased respect for Japan's traditional culture, and calls for improved foreign language instruction.

In South Korea, the Ministry of Education offers training to prepare teachers in dealing with global issues. A major development in global education in 2000 was the joint establishment of the Asia-Pacific Centre of Education for International Understanding (APCEIU) by the South Korean government and the United Nations Educational Scientific and Cultural Organization (UNESCO). The APCEIU will conduct research, strengthen curricula, create support in the civil society, train professionals, promote international exchanges, develop and disseminate educational materials and information, and encourage international cooperation and networking.

In Russia, there is a nationwide network of 10 Global Education Centers. Each center comprises a university, primary and secondary schools, and a center for in-service education. These Global Education Centers facilitate the exchange of teachers and students and engage the community in global learning content.

In 2000, global education was championed in the United Kingdom. In 2001 in Scotland, with its separate educational system, the minister of education went on record as supporting the inclusion of global studies in the curriculum.

"Global education" is not a term commonly used in China. However, there is a strong and growing concern for related issues such as international awareness and understanding, the global environment, population, globalization of the economy, and technology.

The list of countries instituting global programs continues to grow. In August 1997, the South African government published a paper that aims at fundamentally changing the higher education system. The paper advises that the world is increasingly becoming a global village, and, as a result, leadership educators need to incorporate a global perspective in all aspects of their curriculum (van der Colff, 2004).

Each of these programs has in common the realization that to compete in today's global arena, future leaders must be knowledgeable with regard to other countries: their customs, culture, geography, history, and values. In other words, knowledge is power.

◆ *Organizational Studies and Global Content*

Kagan and Stewart (2004) warn that "the nation's political and economic leaders have voiced concerns that we are not preparing our students to succeed in a globalized world. . . with global illiteracy the result" (p. 230). In the fifth global curriculum survey, Kwok, Folks, and Arpan (1994) found that among 500 respondent business schools from around the world, some progress had been made to integrate global literacy into education, but much more remained to be achieved. One of the most important findings of the study was that education relative to cultural and global efforts continued to fall short of fulfilling the needs of leaders who think and act in a global context. Surprisingly, only one-third of the business schools offered even a minimal amount of education with global content and one-third of the business schools offered none (Kwok et al., 1994).

In 2000, Kwok and Arpan (2002) repeated their global survey on curriculum. They found that significant progress had been made, but more work was definitely needed. Only about 25% of the doctoral programs had global content in organizational

studies. Bachelor's and master's programs, however, were more than double that figure. The study also revealed that faculty experience in the field of global business was significantly higher in non-U.S. schools (Kwok & Arpan, 2002). Despite the overall progress, only a minority of the programs were very satisfied with their efforts. The researchers suggested that the rapid pace of globalization had outpaced the universities' ability to respond.

◆ *The Need for Global Leadership Perspectives*

Future leaders must be informed in order to operate in a highly competitive environment. "The global economy is here to stay. . . . Businesses need employees who can think globally" (Kagan & Stewart, 2004, p. 232). Bryan, Rall, Fraser, and Oppenheim (1999) made an impelling prediction suggesting that by the year 2029, 80% of world output would be in global markets (p. 3). Alon and Higgins (2005) concluded that the rapid rise in globalization will compound the impact on leadership. First, the drastic shift in conducting business will necessitate leadership from individuals skilled in global aspects of business functions. Second, interpersonal skills necessary to conducting global business, comprising emotional and cultural intelligences, will become a precondition for effective leadership.

The Global Leadership and Organizational Behavior Effectiveness research program, commonly referred to as the GLOBE Study, resulted in the 800+ page book: *Culture, Leadership, and Organizations: The GLOBE Study of 62 Societies* (House et al., 2004). The study provided important findings regarding the impact of leadership and culture. The research involved more than 170 international investigators to study over 17,000 leaders in more than 950 organizations representing 62 countries. The purpose of the GLOBE Study was to examine how different cultures viewed leadership. A central question focused on the relationship between effective leadership behaviors and specific leadership attributes, and to what extent these attributes and behaviors are contingent upon culture.

The research found six global leadership behaviors: charismatic/value based, team oriented, participative, humane oriented, autonomous, and self-protective (House et al., 2004). Further, the study identified 22 leadership attributes, illustrated in Box 9.1.

BOX 9.1 The GLOBE Study's 22 Leadership Attributes

Trustworthy	Foresight	Positive	Confidence builder
Intelligent	Administrative skilled	Excellence oriented	Win–win problem solver
Just	Plans ahead	Dynamic	Motivational
Decisive	Communicative	Coordinator	Honest
Encouraging	Motive arouser	Dependable	Effective bargainer
Informed	Team builder		

The findings of the GLOBE Study should be considered in preparing future leaders to meet the challenges of the global environment. "At the present time there is a greater need for effective international and cross-cultural communication, collaboration and cooperation, not only for the effective practice of management but also for the betterment of the human condition" (House, et al., 2004, p. 1).

Culturally aware leadership essentially calls for a move from ethnocentrism to cultural relativity (Bennett, 1986). There is an urgent demand for people to understand that there are many valid centers of the world other than their own (P. Adler, 1977; Batchelder, 1977). Bennett (1986) notes that moving from ethnocentrism to ethnorelativism does not occur without education and experiences about and with other cultures.

Author Kamel Mellahi (2000) from the Coventry Business School in England writes in the *Journal of Management Development* that the proliferation of the ethnocentric approach to teaching leadership is due mainly to the lack of published empirical evidence outside the United States regarding alternative theories and global dimensions of effective leadership styles. The research proposes that there is a need for Western schools to adopt a more eclectic view of leadership and to cast perspectives beyond Western idiosyncrasies.

With decreasing acceptance of the generic leadership theory of one-size-fits-all common in the West, the universalistic approach is coming into question. There is increased recognition that the non-universality of Western leadership theories does not necessarily transfer across cultures (Mellahi, 2000).

◆ **Differences Between Western, Asian, African, and Arab Leadership Paradigms**

Western leadership theories place a high value on empowerment, coaching, performance management, rationality, delegation, vision, and strategic direction (Mellahi, 2000). In contrast, research reveals that Asian (Hofstede, 1984), Arab (Muna, 1980), and African (Dia, 1994) countries place more emphasis on directive and authoritarian leadership styles. Respect and obedience are expected from subordinates and harmony is a key value of leadership in Asian, Arab, and African countries. Harmony is achieved not by equality but by adherence to societal rules about behavior, which are moderated by Confucian values in Asian cultures (Kirkbridge, Tang, & Westwood, 1991), Islamic and tribal values in Arab cultures (Darwish, 1988), and religious and tribal values in African cultures (Blunt & Merrick, 1997). It is also important to note that the consensus leadership style is common to Asian, Arab, and African cultures. These non-Western cultures share conformity, loyalty, kindness, tolerance, forgiveness, consideration, and face-saving as valued leadership traits (Mellahi, 2000).

◆ **Ability to Function in a Cultural Context**

Trompenaars and Woolliams (2007) found that

> desirable characteristics or effective behaviors of leadership and other frameworks identified in the United States or Anglo-Saxon cultures do not transfer to modern global business. They also fail

at home for an increasingly diverse workforce. The question, then, is how can leaders deal effectively within multicultural surroundings? (p. 211)

Lorange (2003) asserts that it is imperative for future leaders to possess cultural awareness and a global perspective because global thinking can bring together people from different cultures, different backgrounds, different understandings, and different geopolitical viewpoints. "The quest to build a strong global position is no longer an option—it is a necessity. . . . Global thinking—truly acting across all borders—is becoming the fact of the day" (p. 216). This understanding can help each party benefit from the other.

A broader range of thinking can often create a truly innovative approach to collaboration. The antithesis of this would be the short-sighted nationalistic thinking inherent in the "we know best based on what works at home" attitude (Lorange, 2003, p. 220).

MYOPIC CONSEQUENCES

Mellahi (2000) has found that one of the key issues in integrating cultural awareness into leadership curriculum design is that leadership curricula is built on Western leadership models based on Western research and examples, and focuses primarily on Western leaders. This creates the impression that indigenous values are not suited to leadership positions. This conveys to international students that West is best, and, if they conform to the Western paradigms, they will be successful leaders.

House and Aditya (1997) found there is a heavy reliance on U.S. leadership literature due to the lack of materials published by non-U.S. sources. Kwok and Arpan (1994) discovered that faculty members are often more interested in the core subject of leadership rather than in its cultural and global dimensions. The consequence of this attitude is that international students do not typically challenge Western leadership theories, and they report that they feel coerced into adapting to the majority of the Western leadership paradigms. A recent examination of leadership materials has revealed that most, if not all, are based on leadership theories, models, and frameworks, authored by U.S. experts. "Almost all the prevailing theories of leadership, and about 98% of the empirical evidence at hand, are rather distinctly American in character" (House & Aditya, 1997, p. 420).

Nancy Adler (1997) found that most U.S. leadership theories masquerade as universal theories. Non-Western leadership values and norms are often left unelaborated or are depicted as a backward stage in the development toward enlightened leadership styles of the West. At the heart of cultural awareness is the belief that to be successful in the global arena, leaders must develop an appreciation of, and be responsive to, cultural differences. Patterns of behavior that simply reflect the values of the head office are no longer appropriate in today's global economy (Laughton & Ottewill, 2000).

KNOWLEDGE VELOCITY

While American sensibilities continue a hegemonic view of leadership, other international discipline-based literature continues to multiply. It is purported to have taken 1,750 years for discipline-based recorded international content to double the first time; after that it only took 150 years, then every 50 years, and currently it takes 5 years to double. By 2020 it is predicted that it will take less than 75 days for discipline-based global information to double. While knowledge continues to multiply, we are only able to attend to about 10% of current levels (Brunner, 2000).

Buendía (1998) posits that if man's entire existence on earth was represented by 1 hour, we could attribute 95% of our knowledge to the last 22 seconds. The chapter authors have termed this contemporary phenomenon of information proliferation and complexity as *knowledge velocity*. No longer will it be sufficient or even possible to manage and contain information. Instead, the complexity that parallels abundance will be mitigated by a generosity paradigm that encourages information sharing. Value-based initiatives will require knowledge leaders who possess the global acumen that exploits knowledge velocity and innovation through cultural heterogeneity of ideas, skills, education, and experiences.

COMPETENCE-BASED PREPARATION

Recent research in leadership development begins to delineate the competencies that constitute the constructs of global leadership (Brewster & Suutari, 2005; Bueno & Tubbs, 2004; Caligiuri & Santo, 2001; Lobel, 1990; Manning, 2003; Suutari, 2002; Suutari, Raharjo, & Riikkila, 2002; Suutari, 2003; Suutari & Taka, 2004; Tubbs & Schulz, 2006). The rationale behind competence-based inquiry is based on the notion that once the competencies can be identified, the leadership-development process can more effectively focus on improving the deficiencies identified in each individual.

Deardorff and Hunter (2006) reviewed studies that attempted to investigate programs designed to prepare students for the global workforce. The study concluded that both intercultural and global competencies are important for undertaking such initiatives. Fundamental intercultural competencies involve attitudes of openness, respect (valuing all cultures), curiosity, and discovery (tolerating ambiguity). The primary global competencies consist of developing a nonjudgmental and open attitude toward others. A comprehensive approach by Barham and Wills (as cited in Laughton & Ottewill, 2000) suggests that

> The deep-rooted competence, although holistic in nature, is composed of three interlinking parts, each of which is revealed by the existence of recognizable and distinct traits. First, cognitive complexity, observed through cultural empathy, the power of active listening and a sense of humility. Second, emotional energy, evidenced through emotional self awareness, emotional resilience and risk acceptance. Third, psychological maturity, manifested through a curiosity to learn, an orientation to time and a sophisticated approach to personal morality. (p. 381)

RECOMMENDATIONS

There is a call to better prepare leaders for the broad changes that accompany the current global environment (Smith, Hornsby, & Kite, 2000). Landis and Brislin (1983) have described fundamental cultural leadership education as having factual, analytical, and experiential components. This framework brings together the key dimensions of cultural awareness, skills development and competencies. Stewart Black, and Mendenhall (1991) recommend cultural leadership education be delivered on three levels: first, on a theory level using lectures, books, videos, and guest speakers; second, on an analytic level with training in communication skills, case studies, and interactive projects; and third, on an experiential level achieved through role-play, multicultural group work, simulations, and international travel, internships, work experience, and fellowships.

Sharma and Roy (1996) prescribe five emerging patterns of delivery of global leadership education. The most recognized among them is joint ventures between schools in different countries. The others include educational networks, multidisciplinary action projects, and international faculty exchanges.

In a recent study, Mendenhall (2006) proposed that the most effective type of global leadership development approach involves the use of expert coaches. Individualized coaching has three distinct advantages: first, it allows for assessment and evaluation of an individual leader's competencies; second, it is geared to develop the leader's competencies and personal strategies to deal with challenges that exist in the present; and third, it concedes confidentiality between the coach and the leader that provides the leader with the inner freedom to experiment with what he or she has been taught.

There is no substitute for person-to-person contact across international and cultural borders, whether it is the product of living abroad, travel in a study group, postgraduate research positions, hosting those from other countries, or even communication by e-mail. Christopher Orpen (2003) of MLS International College suggests interviewing local leaders who are from different cultures. The topic of discussion could revolve around differences and similarities that the leader perceives to exist between countries. Additional focus may be placed on preparation to cope successfully with the demands imposed by different cultures. A similar exercise would be to interview expatriates: those who have lived and worked abroad. It is important to remember that the goal is not to lead effectively in one country but instead to develop an understanding of the principles of diverse cultures so leaders can function reasonably well anywhere (Orpen, 2003).

Stice (1987) confirms the need to emphasize the degree of immediacy, relevance, and reality of education in order to bring it to life—a process that Wales and Stager (1977) call Guided Design. Relevance pertains to the degree of utility perceived for present or future application. Immediacy refers to the currency in terms of holding interest, and reality refers to the potency of content in meeting short- and long-term needs. Jon Franklin Ramsoomair (1997), professor at Wilfred Laurier University, Ontario, Canada, has developed graduate cultural courses based on Wales and Stager's Guided Design process. These courses serve as a model to others trying to integrate cultural awareness into leadership curriculum design. Goals of cultural awareness education for leaders are as follows:

1. Improving cultural communication skills to augment understanding of common problems and to develop skills that facilitate more effective cultural communication (immediacy)

2. Enhancing knowledge of specific cultures and related organizational practices relative to transition skills; promote an understanding of the issues involved in working and living in a different culture and to use this understanding to develop strategies for successful leadership cultural transitions (relevance)

3. Increasing cultural awareness to broaden and deepen an understanding of what culture is and how it affects organizational practices (reality)

Deardorff and Hunter (2006) made several recommendations for enhancing the understanding of intercultural issues. These include requiring culturally specific courses, incorporating culturally authentic materials into existing courses, directly experiencing others' cultures through education abroad or service learning (including within one's community), and having direct engagement with others from different cultural backgrounds.

◆ Conclusion

O'Hara-Devereaux and Johansen (1994) noted that cultural literacy is not simply desirable—it is a global organizational prerequisite.

The profile of the global leader today is one of a confident strategist, able to create global alliances and make decisions with non-nationalistic thinking. The competitive advantage of being culturally aware is that one benefits organizations both locally and in the global arena (Laughton & Ottewill, 2000). Moreover, culturally aware leaders employ a refined portfolio of skill sets that include adaptability, multiple-perspective thinking, effective communication, diplomacy, and culturally influenced decision making (Bigelow, 1994).

The studies reviewed here reveal a shortage of education (e) directed at developing competencies (dc) in preparing culturally aware leaders (CAL). The sense of urgency to integrate cultural awareness into leadership education is driven by the unprecedented expansion of globalization (g) and the phenomenon of knowledge velocity (kv) created by new technologies. Therefore, the authors propose that culturally aware leaders (CAL) are a function of education (e), developed competencies (dc), globalization (g), and knowledge velocity (kv), expressed as:

$$CAL = f (e + dc + g + kv)$$

Leadership competencies relative to cultural awareness can be gained through education, experiential activities, and coaching. Competence-based inquiry assists educators and/or coaches to better prepare leaders to face the cognitively complex tasks of a culturally diverse world (Mendenhall, 2006; Sharma & Roy, 1996).

The availability of global information on-demand has created the phenomenon of *knowledge velocity*. Abundance, speed, and complexity will create a paradigm shift from parsimonious information management to munificence through knowledge sharing. Cultural awareness in the context of heterogeneity of ideas, skills, education, experience, and communication, and learning styles will be ineluctable from leading innovation in a global environment.

Oscar Arias, former president of Costa Rica and recipient of the Nobel Prize for Peace in 1987, argued eloquently that we should not allow the process of globalization to be merely a material transformation; our times demand a corresponding change in consciousness. Enhancing cultural awareness education can make a significant contribution to such a change (Tye, 2003; Weathersby, 1992).

◆ Discussion Questions

1. In what ways has your education prepared you for leading in a global context?

2. Identify characteristics of a culture you are part of and contrast them with those of another culture.

3. If you were assigned to lead a project in another country, what preparations would you make to gain an understanding of the culture before arriving at the new location?

4. How would you prepare to mediate a disagreement involving a diverse group of employees?

5. Explain the impact of knowledge velocity on your industry in the last decade, and describe how your organization has adapted to the change.

6. In what ways could you seek out additional knowledge on cultural awareness through experiential activities including education and coaching to develop competencies?

7. Discuss the ideal characteristics of a culturally aware leader in this era of increasing globalization and knowledge velocity.

◆ References

Adler, N. J. (1997). Global leadership: Women leaders. *Management International Review, 37*, 171–197.

Adler, N. J. (2002). *International dimensions of organizational behavior* (4th ed.). Cincinnati, Ohio: South-Western.

Adler, P. (1977). Beyond cultural identity: Reflections upon cultural and multicultural man. In R. W. Brislin (Ed.), *Culture learning concepts: Application and research* (pp. 24–41). Honolulu: University of Hawaii Press.

Alon, I., & Higgins, J. M. (2005). Global leadership success through emotional and cultural intelligences. *Business Horizons, 48*(6), 501–512.

Batchelder, D. (1977). The green banana. In D. Batchelder & E. G. Warner (Eds.), *Beyond experience: The experiential approach to cross-cultural education.* Brattleboro, VT: The Experiment Press.

Bennett, M. J. (1986). A developmental approach to training for intercultural sensitivity. *International Journal of Intercultural Relations, 10*, 179–196.

Bhawuk, D. P. S., Landis, D., & Lo, K. D. (2006). Intercultural training. In D. L. Sam & J. W. Berry (Eds.), *The Cambridge handbook of acculturation psychology* (pp. 504–524). Cambridge, UK: Cambridge University Press.

Bigelow, J. D. (1994). International skills for managers. *Asia Pacific Journal of Human Resources, 32*(NP1), 1–12.

Blunt, P., & Merrick, J. L. (1997). Exploring the limits of Western leadership theory in East Asia and Africa. *Personnel Review, 26*(1/2), 6–23.

Brewster, C., & Suutari, V. (2005). Global HRM: Aspects of a research agenda. *Personnel Review, 34*(1), 5–21.

Brunner, J. J. (2000). Globalización cultural y posmodernidad. In F. López Segrera & A. Maldanado (Eds.), *Educación superior Latino Americana y organismos internacionales: Un análisis crítico.* Boston College and University of San Buenaventura, CA: UNESCO.

Bryan, L. L., Rall, W., Fraser, J., & Oppenheim, J. (1999). *Race for the world: Strategies to build a great global firm.* Boston: Harvard Business School Press.

Buendía, H. G. (1998). *Educación: La agenda del siglo XXI.* Bogotá: United Nations Development Program, TM Press.

Bueno, C. M., & Tubbs, S. L. (2004). Identifying global leadership competencies: An exploratory study. *Journal of American Academy of Business, 5*(1/2), 80–87.

Caligiuri, P., & Santo, V. D. (2001). Global competence: What is it, and can it be developed through global assignments? *Human Resource Planning, 24*(3), 27–35.

Darwish, Y. A. (1988). Correlates of perceived leadership styles in a culturally mixed environment. *Leadership and Organization Development Journal, 19*(5), 265–384.

Deardorff, D. K., & Hunter, W. (2006). Educating global-ready graduates. *International Educator, 15*(3), 72–83.

Dia, M. (1994). *Indigenous management practices: Lessons for Africa's management in the 90s.* Washington, D.C.: World Bank.

Eble, K. E. (1988). *The craft of teaching: A guide to mastering the professor's art.* San Francisco: Jossey-Bass.

Gardenswartz, L., & Rowe, A. (1995). *Diverse teams at work: Capitalizing on the power of diversity.* New York: Irwin McGraw-Hill.

Hammer, M. R., Bennett, M. J., & Wiseman, R. (2003). The Intercultural Development Inventory: A measure of intercultural sensitivity. *International Journal of Intercultural Relations, 27,* 421–443.

Hampden-Turner, C., & Trompenaars, F. (1998). *Riding the waves of culture: Understanding diversity in global business.* New York: McGraw-Hill.

Hofstede, G. (1984). Cultural dimensions in management and planning. *Asia Pacific Journal of Management, 1,* 81–99.

House, R. J., & Aditya, N. R. (1997). The social scientific study of leadership: Quo vadis? *Journal of Management, 23*(3), 409–474.

House, R. J., Hanges, P. J., Javidan, M., Dorfman, P. W., Gupta, V., & Associates (Eds.). (2004). *Culture, leadership, and organizations: The GLOBE study of 62 societies.* Thousand Oaks, CA: Sage.

Hyatt, L. (2007). *3 eagles 1 lesson.* Organizational Leadership Doctoral Research Seminar. ULV, Los Angeles, CA.

Kagan, S. L., & Stewart, V. (2004). International education in the schools: The state of the field. *Phi Delta Kappan, 86*(3), 229–235.

Keller, B. (2003). Teachers travel the globe for professional development. *Education Week, 23*(14), 8.

Kirkbridge, P. S., Tang, S. F. Y., & Westwood, I. (1991). Chinese conflict preferences and negotiating behavior: Cultural and psychological influences. *Organization Studies, 12*(3), 365–386.

Kwok, C. Y., & Arpan, J. S. (1994). A comparison of international business education at US and European business schools in the 1990s. *Management International Review, 34*(4), 357–380.

Kwok, C. Y., & Arpan, J. (2002). Internationalizing the business school: A global survey in 2000. *Journal of International Business Studies, 33*(3), 571–581.

Kwok, C. Y., Folks, W. R., & Arpan, J. (1994). A global survey of international business education in the 1990s. *Journal of International Business Studies, 25*(3), 605–624.

Landis, D., & Brislin, R. (1983). *Handbook on international training* (Vol. 1). New York: Pergamon Press.

Laughton, D., & Ottewill, R. (2000). Developing cross-cultural capability in undergraduate business education: Implications for the student experience. *Education & Training, 42*(6), 378–387.

Lear, J. (1988). *Aristotle: The desire to understand.* Cambridge, UK: Cambridge University Press.

Lobel, S. A. (1990). Global leadership competencies: Managing to a different drumbeat. *Human Resource Management, 29*(1), 39–47.

Lorange, P. (2003). Global responsibility—Business education and business schools: Roles in promoting a global perspective. *Corporate Governance, 3*(3), 216–226.

Manning, T. T. (2003). Leadership across cultures: Attachment style influences. *Journal of Leadership & Organizational Studies, 9*(3), 20–30.

Mellahi, K. (2000). The teaching of leadership on UK MBA programmes: A critical analysis from an international perspective. *Journal of Management Development, 19*(3/4), 297–308.

Mendenhall, M. E. (2006). The elusive, yet critical challenge of developing global leaders. *European Management Journal, 24*(6), 422.

Muna, F. A. (1980). *The Arab executive.* London: Macmillan.

O'Hara-Devereaux, M., & Johansen, R. (1994). *Global work: Bridging distance, culture & time.* San Francisco: Jossey-Bass.

Orpen, C. (2003). Teaching students to manage cross-culturally. *Cross Cultural Management, 10*(3), 80.

Paige, R. M. (2003). The intercultural development inventory: A critical review of the research literature. *Journal of Intercultural Communication, 6,* 53–61.

Palthe, J., & Kossek, E. E. (2003). Subcultures and employment modes: Translating HR strategy into practice. *Journal of Organizational Change, 16*(3), 287–308.

Ramsoomair, J. F. (1997). The Internet in the context of cross-cultural management. *Internet Research, 7,* 189–194.

Schaetti, B. F., Watanabe, G. C., & Ramsey, S. J. (2000). *The practice of Personal Leadership and the SIIC internship program.* Portland, OR: Intercultural Communication Institute.

Schein, E. H. (2004). *Organizational culture and leadership.* San Francisco: Jossey-Bass.

Schmieder-Ramirez, J., & McManus, J. (2007). *The accreditors are coming, the accreditors are coming! A monograph on the evaluation of experiential learning.* Dubuque, IA: Kendall-Hunt.

Sharma, B., & Roy, J. A. (1996). Aspects of the internationalization of management education. *Journal of Management Development, 15*(1), 5–13.

Smith, B. N., Hornsby, J. S., & Kite, M. (2000). Broadening the business curriculum via a cross-disciplinary approach: A mobile unit on cultural diversity. *Education, 120*(4), 713–721.

Starratt, R. J. (2005). Responsible leadership. *Educational Forum, 69*(2), 124–133.

Stewart Black, J., & Mendenhall, M. (1991). *A practical but theory-based framework for selecting cross cultural training methodologies.* Boston: PWS.

Stice, J. E. (Ed.) (1987). *Developing critical thinking and problem-solving abilities: New directions for teaching and learning, No. 30.* San Francisco: Jossey-Bass.

Suutari, V. (2002). Global leader development: An emerging research agenda. *Career Development International, 7*(4), 218–233.

Suutari, V. (2003). Global managers: Career orientation, career tracks, life-style implications and career commitment. *Journal of Managerial Psychology, 18*(3), 185–207.

Suutari, V., Raharjo, K., & Riikkila, T. (2002). The challenge of cross-cultural leadership interaction: Finnish expatriates in Indonesia. *Career Development International, 7*(6/7), 415–429.

Suutari, V., & Taka, M. (2004). Career anchors of managers with global careers. *Journal of Management Development, 23*(9), 833–847.

Timbrook, J., & Johnson, J. R. (1999, March). *People of the sky: Birds in Chumash culture.* Paper presented at the 22nd Ethnobiology Conference, Oaxaca, Mexico. Retrieved June 27, 2007, from www.sbnature.org/research/anthro/chbirds.htm

Trompenaars, F., & Woolliams, P. (2007). Developing global leaders: The critical role of dilemma reconciliation. In J. F. Bolt (Ed.), *The 2007 Pfeiffer annual leadership development.* San Francisco: John Wiley & Sons.

Tubbs, S. L., & Schulz, E. (2006). Exploring a taxonomy of global leadership competencies and meta-competencies. *Journal of American Academy of Business, 8*(2), 29–34.

Tye, K. A. (Ed.). (1991). *Global education: From thought to action* (ASCD Yearbook). Alexandria, VA: Association for Supervision and Curriculum.

Tye, K. A. (2003). Global education as a worldwide movement. *Phi Delta Kappan, 85*(2), 165–168.

van der Colff, L. (2004). A new paradigm for business education: The role of the business educator and business school. *Management Decision, 42*(3/4), 499–507.

Van Dyne, L., & Ang, S. (2006). Getting more than you expect: Global leader initiative to span structural holes and reputational effectiveness. In W. H. Mobley & E. W. Weldon (Eds.), *Advances in global leadership* (Vol. 4, pp. 101–122). New York: JAI Press.

Wales, C. E., & Stager, R.A. (1977). *Guided design*. Morgantown, VA: Center for Guided Design, West Virginia University.

Weathersby, R. (1992, December). Developing and global perspective: A crucial changing of our minds. *Journal of Management Education, 16*, 10–27.

10

FROM INTERCULTURAL KNOWLEDGE TO INTERCULTURAL COMPETENCE

Developing an Intercultural Practice

◆ Barbara F. Schaetti, Sheila J. Ramsey, and Gordon C. Watanabe

L et's begin with a story. Our lead character is Joan Raffert, an American posted to Europe for 3 months by the global corporation for which she works. Her primary objective is to lead the local training department on the design and implementation of a worldwide training initiative to be piloted in their region. As she says:

> I've worked internationally before, mainly in Asia, and have always done well. I find it exciting to work on new projects with people from different cultures and to learn about them and their countries. I did my MBA in a program that emphasized intercultural communication skills, so I understand both the challenges and the opportunities that multinational teams present.
>
> I was pleased when I arrived onsite to meet the four people with whom I'd be working most closely. They seemed to have a

good understanding of the objectives of the new training initiative and a strong commitment to implementing a successful pilot program. The creative energy of our work brought us close quite quickly. We worked long hours and laughed and debated and began to develop a design I knew was really good.

Finally we had the design completed, the materials prepared, things just about ready for the pilot launch in 2 week's time. That's when everything suddenly seemed to fall apart. We sat down to discuss who would facilitate which section of the program, and no one stepped forward. No one volunteered; no one took any initiative. Everything I suggested was met with resistance. No one actually refused, but it was clear no one wanted to co-facilitate with me. What should have been just a quick meeting to allocate responsibilities became two and then three meetings. They seemed to get more resistant with each meeting, and I know I got more frustrated. Clearly, the only way I was going to get anyone to co-facilitate was if I made mandatory assignments.

What should Joan Raffert do in this situation; if you were her boss, what would you coach her to do?

This chapter is not going to answer that question, at least not in the way that you might expect. Our focus here is not on the *content* of Raffert's decision and whether, for example, she mandates the co-facilitation assignments. Rather, we are interested in the *process* of how Raffert decides: We are interested in the dynamics of what we call Raffert's intercultural leadership *practice*.

We have organized the chapter as follows:

Reviewing three key concepts: leadership, intercultural competence, and practice

Merging these three concepts together and discussing various approaches for what we call an "intercultural practice for contemporary leadership"

Focusing on one of these approaches as the core of the chapter, the methodology of "personal leadership"

Concluding with a discussion of the power of an intentional self-reflective practice for the interculturally competent global leader

Toward the later half of the chapter, we will return to Raffert as an exemplar. By proxy, she will represent all those who lead in multicultural contexts and who, in so doing, are committed to transforming their intercultural knowledge into intercultural competence.

◆ Key Concepts

There are three concepts that take center stage in this chapter: leadership, intercultural competence, and practice.

LEADERSHIP

The concept of "leadership" has been of interest to humans since time immemorial. It has emerged as a renewed focus of fascination in the last 50 years, with easily hundreds of books being published every year for the past 5 years alone. Nevertheless, ask any 10 people to define *leadership*, to specify what leaders should or should not do and whether or not someone is an effective or ineffective leader, and you'll probably get 10 very different answers. Effective leadership is very much an assessment rooted "in the eye of the beholder."

In discussing what contemporary leadership means in relationship to intercultural communication, we're inspired by a segment of the leadership literature that focuses on the qualities, skills, and ways of being extraordinary leaders. These leaders operate in the transactional dimension, as all leaders must, ensuring that the tasks of the organization are accomplished (Burns, 1978). They also operate in the transformational dimension, bringing forth creativity in those with whom they work and developing leadership capacity in others (Sashkin & Rosenbach, 1998). What is most striking about extraordinary leaders, however, is that they also operate in the transpersonal dimension, living and leading in ways that are aligned with their own unique expressions of creativity and wisdom (Ramsey, Schaetti, & Watanabe, 2004).

Extraordinary leaders are involved in a continual and infinite dance of attention to self and attention to others, of leading self and leading others. They do three things: (1) they take a learning orientation, (2) they take an appreciative orientation, and (3) they take a receptive orientation.

Extraordinary leaders take a learning orientation when they engage every experience, every interaction and encounter, as an opportunity to learn more about themselves and the ways in which they move through and lead in the world. They demonstrate an enormous willingness and capacity for self-reflection and self-honesty. They take responsibility for their emotions (Goleman, Bayatzis, & McKee, 2002) and question the ways in which their assumptions and core values motivate them. They deconstruct their mental maps (Black & Gregersen, 2003), becoming curious about the ways in which their common sense and automatic reactions influence them. They expand into a state of presence we call "not knowing," from which creative direction is more readily accessed (Wheatley & Chodron, 1999).

In taking an appreciative orientation, extraordinary leaders actively look for "what is right" about a situation or interaction (Wright, 1998). They cultivate within themselves a positive (Fredrickson, 1998, 2003) and value-driven (Loehr & Schwartz, 2003) energy state and identify what it is that gives life, purpose, and energy to the organization (Cooperrider, Whitney, & Stravos, 2003; Schiller, Riley, & Holland, 2001). Refusing to engage in blame and resentment (Drucker, 2001; Nelson, 2005), extraordinary leaders find opportunities inherent in every situation. They look for, see, magnify, and connect the best in others and the world around them. They create safe and inclusive communities and support others to be successful in ways not originally thought possible. They accelerate learning and build organizational cultures that value difference, risk taking, and high performance (Schiller et al., 2001).

Finally, extraordinary leaders take a receptive orientation. They lead not just from their personalities but from a quality of connected awareness: They know themselves to be part of what physicist David Bohm called "the implicate order" (Bohm, 1980). This is a level of reality beyond our normal everyday thoughts and perceptions, a level of reality at which "the totality of existence is enfolded within each fragment of space and time—whether it be a single object, thought, or event" (Jaworsky, 1996, p. 78). Extraordinary leaders cultivate a deeply intimate relationship with the implicate order. Peter Senge and his colleagues (2004), world-renowned in the leadership and learning organization arenas, have named this relationship "presencing." They describe presencing as that state in which we become "totally present—to the larger space or field around us, to an expanded sense of self, and, ultimately, to what is emerging through us" (p. 19).

INTERCULTURAL COMPETENCE

A standard definition of "intercultural competence" is "the ability to communicate effectively and appropriately in a variety of cultural contexts" (J. M. Bennett, 2007, p. 1), with people who are different from one's self (i.e., who are from a different national, ethnic, religious, professional, organizational, generational, etc., culture).

An impressive body of scholarly work has been published over the past 50 years, and numerous academic and professional development programs now exist, designed to help people strengthen their intercultural competence. Together they reflect approaches to developing competence which can be categorized into what we call the three spheres: (1) culture specific, (2) culture general, and (3) intercultural practice. The spheres are "nested," with the first sphere nested within the second and the first and second spheres nested within the third.

The first sphere focuses on culture-specific competence. Here, the work of cultural anthropologists provides generalizable information about, for example, the communication styles or value orientations of a particular cultural group (e.g., Americans, Singaporeans, Brazilians) or subgroup (e.g., Muslim Americans, Singaporean Chinese, urban Brazilians). This approach to developing competence emphasizes learning about the specific cultural patterns exemplified by the chosen group and analyzing the impact of those cultural patterns when members of that group are involved in intergroup relations. While valuable, this approach alone is inadequate to build intercultural competence. The reasons are several. First, not all members of a particular group will manifest the same cultural characteristics as the mainstream of that group; learning about the mainstream teaches nothing about those on the margins let alone about individual variation. Second, given the rate of travel, of immigration and migration, and of international sojourning, more and more people in today's world are influenced by layers of diverse cultural influence. Third, most of us live in multicultural environments, making it nearly impossible for us to become competent in the culture specifics of every group we meet at the local neighborhood center or with whom we share office space.

The second sphere of intercultural competence takes a culture-general approach. The focus here is on the general cultural contrasts that apply in interaction, regardless of the particular cultural groups involved. The most famous of these cultural contrast patterns, also called cultural continua, include high-context/low-context communication, direct/indirect communication, individualist/collectivist orientation, high/low power distance, and high/low uncertainty avoidance (Hall, 1959; Hall & Hall, 1990; Hofstede, 1980). This approach offers great insight for those choosing to develop their intercultural competence. It allows them to assess, for example, to what extent the people with whom they are negotiating a contact may have a direct versus indirect communication style and how, given their own style, that is likely to affect the negotiations process. Even when taken in conjunction with a culture-specific approach, however, the culture-general approach is also inadequate to the task. For the most part this is for the simple reason that a culture-general approach to intercultural competence remains an intellectual exercise (and is too often focused exclusively on the "cultural other" rather than also on the "cultural self").

The third sphere is the sphere of practice; this approach to developing intercultural competence holds and encompasses the other two nested within it. It emphasizes moment-to-moment choice, moment-to-moment practice. It recognizes that "knowledge of content does not automatically translate into mastery of process" (M. J. Bennett, 1998, p. 10); that to be competent across cultures we "need to transform our knowledge of intercultural theories into appropriate and effective performance" (Ting-Toomey, 1999, p. 261). This requires a whole-person approach to building intercultural competence, for culture is as much an emotional and physical experience as it is an intellectual one (M. J. Bennett & Castiglioni, 2004; Cherbosque, Gardenswartz, & Rowe, 2004; Schaetti, Ramsey, & Watanabe, 2008; Schaetti & Ramsey, 1999; Schaetti, Watanabe, & Ramsey, 2000). This third sphere of intercultural competence is informed by the culture-specific and culture-general spheres, while emphasizing that leaders must always be learners and must practice for the specifics of intercultural context.

PRACTICE

To "practice" something is to do it with the deliberate aim of learning and improving one's competence. It requires a commitment to self-awareness, self-reflection, and self-monitoring (Goleman et al., 2002), as well as a commitment to engage the process of developing competence with intention. It implies a continual process of becoming, rather than the achievement of a completed end state.

Practicing for the sake of developing intercultural competence is different, it seems to us, from some other fields of practice. Plumbers and lawyers and gardeners and software engineers, for example, can focus their practice during set hours—perhaps within a 9–5 workday. They start their work and they put on their "plumber practice" coat; they finish work and they take off the coat and hang it up. A practice to develop intercultural competence doesn't work that way. It extends beyond the hours of any particular job we may have, into the whole of our lives. When we commit to developing an intercultural practice, to engaging the third sphere of intercultural competence, we are agreeing to transform our lives into a personal "living laboratory." Considered this way, every interaction, whether involving obvious cultural difference or not, offers an opportunity to apply

culture-specific and culture-general knowledge about self and other. This allows for the mindful and creative transformation of intercultural knowledge into intercultural competence.

◆ Intercultural Practice for Contemporary Leadership

The three concepts of leadership, intercultural competence, and practice come together as we now consider "intercultural practice for contemporary leadership." As a starting point, it is interesting to note that searching an online bookseller under the phrase "leadership practice" yields literally thousands of titles incorporating the two words into a single phrase. The same is not true for "intercultural practice," wherein the few hundred titles that do use the two words typically do so as separate ideas; they are linked together by such words as *therapy, literature, theater,* and *conflict.*

The idea that intercultural leaders might intentionally develop a personal intercultural practice, just as they are encouraged by the leadership literature to develop a personal leadership practice, is relatively new.

The Developmental Model of Intercultural Sensitivity (DMIS; see Chapters 8 and 16) and its related instrument, the Intercultural Development Inventory (IDI; see Chapter 16) reinforce the idea of an intercultural practice by asserting the developmental nature of intercultural competence. Advancement from the ethnocentric to the ethnorelative stages, as described by the DMIS and as measured by the IDI, is presented as a developmental journey that the intercultural leader can strategically and intentionally engage. The whole point of the IDI's feedback interview is to inspire the individual, team, and/or organization to actively participate in that journey. Although neither offers a specific practice methodology, the DMIS and the IDI each implicitly assert the importance of cultivating an intercultural practice.

Intercultural leaders are also called to cultivate an intercultural practice when they are charged with being a "mindful intergroup communicator" (Ting-Toomey, 1999). This is defined as a skill set rooted in the "practice of mindful intrapersonal communication . . . [which itself starts] with conscious monitoring of our reactive emotions in negatively judging or evaluating communication differences" (Ting-Toomey, p. 23). Parallel to this is the call for "authentic engagement" (Cherbosque et al., 2004), an approach that integrates the ideas of emotional intelligence, as mentioned earlier, with intercultural competence.

The Cultural Detective methodology (Saphiere, 2002) also emphasizes practice. It invites the intercultural leader to become a "cultural detective," using clues offered by another person's (potentially offensive) behavior to hypothesize the values that might be influencing that person's actions. By applying a similar lens to his or her own values, the intercultural leader can analyze how best to bridge between the differences so that effective communication becomes possible. The Cultural Detective methodology is now being used as the structure for an immensely popular series of culture-specific products, primarily but not exclusively focusing on national cultures. The series offers an excellent example of one way in which the first sphere of intercultural competence (culture-specific knowledge) can potentially be linked with the third (intercultural practice).

At the core of all these mandates to develop "cultural intelligence" is an emphasis on practice as process: as an "experiential, iterative way in which each repetition of the [intelligence] cycle builds on the previous one" (Thomas and Inkson, 2004, p. 183).

We come now to the methodology of Personal Leadership (Schaetti et al., 2008; Schaetti et al., 2000). Providing one of the most explicit calls to intercultural practice to date, Personal Leadership is unique in the kind of articulated pathway it details for the intercultural leader who wants to translate intercultural knowledge (both culture specific and culture general) into competence.

The methodology emerged out of the authors' recognition that even people who have a lot of intercultural experience, when in the stress of the moment, tend to judge one another from their personal cultural frames and to leap to culturally based conclusions. They may even end up entrenching themselves within those conclusions, making it difficult to engage the personal and cultural shifts usually necessary for success. In 1995 the authors began holding a question as the lens through which we did our work: When people are able to interact effectively as intercultural leaders across difference and in times of change, what specifically are they doing? By 1998, we had articulated the first iteration of the methodology that has, in the 10 years since, become the core curriculum in graduate-level education (in the master's teaching program at Whitworth University and in the master's of arts in intercultural relations program jointly sponsored by the Intercultural Communication Institute and the University of the Pacific), in professional development programs (at the Summer Institute for Intercultural Communication), and in international study programs (for example, through Randolph College, Whitworth University, and the Scholar Ship). Recognized facilitators of the methodology consult and facilitate with intercultural leaders worldwide, in sectors as diverse as global corporations and international cooperation/ humanitarian relief. For more information on where the Personal Leadership methodology is being used, please visit www.pl seminars.com.

◆ *Intercultural Practice Through Personal Leadership*

Personal Leadership is a methodology of two principles and six practices. The methodology is called "Personal Leadership" because it is about taking leadership of our own personal experience. Its purpose is to help the contemporary leader—for example, Joan Raffert, with whose story we began this chapter—transform intercultural knowledge into intercultural competence.

Personal Leadership's two principles are "mindfulness" and "creativity." Mindfulness is about being aware, being "awake," and paying attention. Creativity is about bringing forth what's right for the particular moment and cultivating a connection to our deepest source of joy and inspiration.

Where the two principles of Personal Leadership come together, we find presence: the state of being "here" now. Visualize the ouroboros, the mythological dragon that, in eating its tail, is said to represent the interconnection of all things. Like the ouroboros, mindfulness and creativity together nurture our capacity for presence, and presence emerges out of our expression of mindfulness and creativity.

For Raffert, mindfulness means understanding that experience is subjective: She feels and thinks and behaves in the way that she does, she sees what she sees and hears what she hears, because of the way she's been taught by her family, her school, the cultural mores of the country in which she grew up. She understands that she has developed automatic reactions that influence her to feel, think, and behave in habitual ways however new or unfamiliar the circumstances may be. And so she has committed to waking up, noticing, attending, and being curious.

The principle of creativity, for Raffert, means seeking the response or action uniquely appropriate for the situation she is in with her European team. It asserts that she will know when she has identified her best possible course of action as long as she pays attention to the quality of inspiration she experiences in contemplating that action; when she experiences joy, interest, hope, contentment, appreciation, and gratitude, she is likely to be applying the deepest levels of her creativity and intellectual resources.

Personal Leadership offers Raffert a three-phase process model to help her take these two principles from theory into competence.

1. Recognize "something's up"—Her team is in resistance to the idea of co-facilitating, she's frustrated, and doesn't know what to do other than to make mandatory co-facilitation assignments.

2. Invite reflection—She takes a learning, appreciative, and receptive orientation to the situation. She considers what culture-specific and culture-general knowledge she has that might be applicable and engages this situation with her team as an opportunity to deepen her intercultural leadership practice.

3. Discern right action—She determines what, if anything, is to be done, to be said, to whom, when, how.

Recognizing "something's up" is a relatively easy first step, as long as Raffert is willing to be mindful of her experience. But how is she to actually invite reflection? How is she to actually take a learning, appreciative, and receptive orientation? What does that really mean, in practice, when confronted by a seemingly recalcitrant team? How is Raffert to transform these concepts into action?

This is the unique contribution that Personal Leadership makes to the translation of intercultural knowledge into intercultural competence. It offers six very tangible practices with which Raffert can work.

- Attending to judgment
- Attending to emotion
- Attending to physical sensation
- Cultivating stillness
- Engaging ambiguity
- Aligning with vision

The first three practices in the list above, the ones that begin with "attending," are the three "sensory input" practices. That is, we interface with the world through our cognition (which manifests as judgment), through our emotions, and through our physical bodies. Our judgments, our emotions, and our physical sensations are how we know what kind of meaning we're making about the world around us; becoming attentive to them allows us to take leadership of the kind of our personal experience. Becoming attentive to them simply means noticing them (mindfulness) and becoming curious and inquisitive about them (creativity).

The last three practices in the list above are the three "container" practices. They help keep us motivated to engage in the first three practices, help us be attentive even when we'd rather just move forward on autopilot.

Using Raffert's story, we will now walk you through the six practices, beginning with a short single-paragraph description of each practice. We will also give you a practice-by-practice summary of Raffert's reflective process and the "right action" which she then discerned.

arned that the best way to get to ·eal meaning and value of the to live your way into them. We :o have no more than a first-level

understanding from reading this chapter. Your understanding will only take off as you engage the practices for yourself. You have to live these practices, not just think about them, if you want to get their full value.

Here now are the six practices, with Raffert's accompanying reflection.

1. *Attending to judgment.* Automatic judgments prevent us from mindfully observing and creatively engaging what is going on in the present moment. Watch your thoughts. Examine your judgments, both positive and negative. Inquire about the sources and consequences of your judgments before you act on them.

> I'm judging the team members as resistant, recalcitrant, as lacking in initiative. I'm judging them as being dishonest in some way; there's something behind their resistance that they're not telling me about.

> From the very beginning of being given this assignment I've assumed it would go easily. I've assumed that all of my experience in Asia would be easily transferable. And certainly since I'm an American of European ancestry, cultural differences would be less of an issue than they were in Asia.

> I certainly wasn't expecting this resistance around assigning co-facilitation roles. I was pretty sure who would want which sections and was pleased that it looked like we'd have even roles—no one standing out as the star but all equally sharing in the implementation of our design.

2. *Attending to emotion.* Emotion paradoxically both blocks and offers an opportunity to learn about the specific situation or encounter. Rather than engage or suppress your emotion, move into the neutral perspective of "witness" and observe yourself. Follow the emotion to its source and to the insight it has to offer. Notice how your emotion changes.

I'm frustrated! I don't have time for this right now! We're less than 2 weeks away from the rollout and there's this big mess that shouldn't be a mess at all.

I'm angry with myself for waiting to do the assignment of facilitation roles so late in the process. It never occurred to me it would be a problem, so I left it until the last minute, and now look at it. And I'm angry with them. This whole thing is just silly.

And I feel stressed, too, and at risk of failure. This project is important to my career. I want to do a good job on this pilot rollout. I also care about this team. I've spent almost 3 months working with them and getting to know them. I don't want things to end with me having to order them to do something that apparently they don't want to do. I value positive, collaborative working relationships. I value co-facilitation relationships—being out on that training floor with trusted co-facilitators is one of the most exciting and professionally rewarding experiences I know. I'm being cheated of that.

3. *Attending to physical sensation.* The routines and patterns that we have developed to get along in the world live in our nervous systems and in our muscular patterns. Values and assumptions are embodied experiences and talk to us through physical sensation. Distinguish the knot in your shoulder, twist in your gut, expansion in your heart. Receive your body's guidance.

I feel like I have a ball of something hard and stringy caught in the base of my throat. I feel tense, too, and haven't been sleeping well; I wake up in the night, and this is the first thing on my mind.

This thing about the ball caught in the base of my throat—it's like I want to just

yell at the team. Behaving "properly" around this is choking me.

I need to do something to clear out my throat. I'll go put on some music and sing along. And I'll dance around while I'm doing that so I release some of the tension in my gut, between my shoulders . . .

4. *Cultivating stillness.* Internal stillness makes possible a receptive space through which to receive information from our deep, creative connection. Quiet your mind. Disentangle internal experience from external circumstance. Breathe. Meditate through movement or sitting. Attend to what resonates as truth from deep within.

That was good. I feel much more clear and centered. I still don't know what to do, but the stuck feeling in my throat is gone. And I feel much more energized, not so trapped by this whole situation, not so entangled.

So, taking a few breaths now, just letting myself get quiet . . .

It was interesting—one of the songs I played was Aretha Franklin's "Respect." As I was swirling madly around and singing along, I realized what I was saying. I wonder how this whole situation might shift if I actually continued to hold a feeling of respect toward the members of this team even though they're not responding the way I expected them to, or want them to, or the way I would have if I were them . . . ?

I'm realizing as I reread some of what I've written that my career probably isn't at risk if I end up facilitating by myself. No one but me cares about that. What they care about is the pilot rollout and the results they get throughout the region. Maybe, instead of putting so much attention on who's going to co-facilitate which sections with me, I should keep it focused on the big picture of the rollout . . .

Hmmmm. There's something important about that recognition. I can feel a sense of "rightness" about that. A lightness in my body.

5. *Engaging ambiguity.* Change and difference create a time of uncertainty, a liminal state, between what was and what will be. Embrace that time. Become comfortable with the sense of not knowing what to do. Allow possibilities to arise. Open yourself to inspiration and tap your infinite creativity for constructing appropriate responses.

Well, I don't know why they're so resistant to co-facilitating. No one's been willing to tell me, which in and of itself has been frustrating to my direct/low-context communication style. I guess I may also be much more low power distance than them—seeing us all as equal facilitators and as equally responsible for deciding who will facilitate what parts.

Hmmm. I just realized that I've been thinking no one's been communicating with me when in fact they've all been communicating with me but in a more indirect/high-context kind of way. When I pay attention, it's pretty clear that it's not just that they don't want to commit to what they'll facilitate; they may, in fact, not want to facilitate at all!

So what might that be about? They might not like to facilitate, they might not like to co-facilitate, they might not like to co-facilitate a program they've designed, they might not like to co-facilitate a program in English . . . wow, I hadn't thought of that before. They all speak English as a foreign language, and even though they strike me as perfectly fluent, maybe they don't feel it themselves. Could it be this—a matter of language?

What more can I not know? Maybe they don't know how to facilitate. Could

that be part of it? It would be unlikely in the United States; there you don't end up on a design team unless you're also able to facilitate the implementation. But this is Europe. I've been assuming they're skilled facilitators just because they design as if they are.

6. *Aligning with vision.* Visions provide direct support as we live and work in situations of difference. Craft your guiding vision. Commit to being an expression of your highest and best. Make choices that support you living in alignment with that vision.

My vision includes being inspired by differences and using them as a creative resource, so there's a bit of a gap here in the way that I've been dealing with this situation! At least now by applying Personal Leadership I'm separating a bit from my "stuff." I already feel clearer and aligned with my vision. I'm feeling much more open to the whole situation, to my team members.

Also, this whole "something's up" situation confirms my vision. I really am committed to being an effective intercultural leader; I really do have a committed intercultural leadership practice.

So what about my "right action"—what, if anything, do I need to do or say?

This seems so obvious to me now. I need to give up this idea that we're all supposed to co-facilitate and just take it on myself. There's plenty of other work to be done during the rollout to make sure it's a success. I'll keep my "antennae" out as we talk about this, but I suspect they've just been waiting for me to "get" that they want me to facilitate on my own.

And I think I'll just check some of this out with my original contact. Even though he's not been willing to speak out directly in the team meetings, I think if I go to him in private he'll be willing to talk to me about it. I can even frame it as asking him to be my "cultural informant."

I feel so totally different than when I began this process of self-reflection. I feel reconnected to inspiration and possibility, much more open-hearted and creative. And I'm clear about my next steps.

Epilogue. That is the end of the story, at least the part that concerns us as intercultural leadership practitioners. You may remember that at the beginning of the chapter we said we weren't so concerned with the "what" of Raffert's decision but with the "how"—less with the outcome and more with the process of practice. We've therefore done what we needed to do with Raffert's story and can leave her here. At the same time, however, we're aware that some readers may like to have an epilogue, to know what happened to Raffert and to the pilot rollout.

She met with her contact and he indeed confirmed that the team members had very little training as facilitators and that they were nervous about facilitating the rollout in English. At the next team meeting, she offered to facilitate the whole training herself, and immediately two of the team members volunteered to co-facilitate some of the region-specific aspects of the program that she would have been hard-pressed to do herself without a lot of extra preparation. The rollout was a success, with the rest of the team taking full responsibility for all the behind-the-scenes work and Raffert coaching her co-facilitators in the process. Years later, Raffert still returns to the region periodically and still gets together socially with several of the team members.

Leaving behind the "what" of Raffert's decision, let us now focus on the "how" of her intercultural leadership practice. If you review her story, you'll see that her practice of

Personal Leadership helped her demonstrate the orientations of an extraordinary leader. She took a learning orientation toward her own cultural programming and to the situation overall. She consistently committed to an appreciative orientation, even when she felt most frustrated by the behaviors of her team members. She engaged a receptive orientation as she maintained her own sense of "presencing." Overall, she operated from not only the transactional dimension of leadership (getting the job done) but also the transformational (developing the skills of her team members) and the transpersonal (aligning with her unique vision and creative wisdom).

Raffert certainly used her culture-specific knowledge: She drew upon her understanding of American culture and recognized that European cultures likely operated differently. She also used her culture-general knowledge: She assessed the differences between her direct/low-context communication style and what she realized were her team members' more indirect/high-context styles. She used all this content knowledge in talking with her contact, her "cultural informant," to confirm what she was discerning as the right action to take.

Raffert was able to translate this knowledge into competence because she was able to step back from the "stuff" of the problem and reflect with clarity. This is specifically where her Personal Leadership practice came in to serve her. She paused, she took a breath, she intentionally created the space that then allowed her to access all her knowledge and wisdom. In using the six practices to guide her, she was able to go beyond what she consciously knew to discern her right action.

Raffert understood that every instance of leading across cultures is new and different. As a contemporary leader operating effectively in an intercultural context, she proceeded on that assumption. If she had not, rather than engaging with mindfulness and creativity, she would have operated, at best, on the automatic pilot of her own culturally driven beliefs of what was "right" to do. She might have made those mandatory co-facilitation assignments she was considering, the results of which would likely have been a terrible implementation, a team demoralized by its lack of facilitation competence, and a failed rollout. In other words, Raffert would have been subject to the consequences that all contemporary leaders risk when they act out of habit in the face of difference.

Ultimately, no amount of culture-specific and culture-general knowledge will save us, no amount of preplanning will serve us, unless we have an intercultural practice that helps us translate it into moment-to-moment competence. The methodology of Personal Leadership offers contemporary leaders like Raffert a very specific form for that practice.

You'll have seen that, with just two principles and six practices, Personal Leadership is a very simple methodology. That simplicity is part of its power. Put into actual application, and the practices into interaction, Personal Leadership can facilitate a profoundly powerful pathway through the potential turbulence of intercultural leadership.

◆ *Conclusion*

A key dimension to "discerning the right action" is that there is no "should." There is no "one size fits all" when it comes to discerning the appropriate response to any given intercultural leadership challenge. Discernment arises out of the creative spaciousness we cultivate by mindfully reflecting upon, and disentangling from, our automatic, habitual reaction. "Right" action thus conveys no sense of ultimate truth but rather a sense of wholeness and completion, of matters clearly perceived and well considered. In the practice of Personal Leadership, mindfulness and creativity supersede any claim that a right action for one moment is necessarily a right action in any other.

It's important to know that we may end up doing or saying, or not doing or saying,

exactly as we would have done had we ignored our "something's up" and gone right ahead with our habitual reaction. However, having invited reflection and released ourselves from habit, we can be sure that we're responding to the situation with as much intercultural competence as possible.

And of course, whatever we do or don't do, do or don't say, we then again mindfully notice any "something's up" that may arise in consequence, again invite reflection, and again discern our most right and creative action.

So how do we know when we've discerned our right action? It comes through practice, through an increasing sophistication in discerning the quality of feeling or energetic experience in our bodies. Certainly it helps to have an intellectual appreciation for why a particular action seems to be the right one. Ultimately, we are best guided by a deeper level of knowing. Are we feeling energized and inspired as we contemplate the potential action (or non-action)? Is there a sense of expansion rather than constriction, a sense of relaxation rather than tension? The more we learn to distinguish for ourselves the nuanced messages from our physical body, the more we will be able to go forward in confidence with our right action.

Ultimately what we're looking for through this integrative process is what we call the "Personal Leadership shift." This is the shift from entanglement into disentanglement, from attachment into witness, from righteousness into curiosity, from uncertainty into discernment.

And how long does all this take, from the first recognition of a "something's up" through to the discernment of right action? It depends—on our skill in practicing Personal Leadership, on the extent of our entanglement and identification, and on how momentous the situation or interaction actually is. When the situation is relatively straightforward or easy, we can easily move through the process of reflection as a kind of "gestalt" in a matter of minutes or even seconds. When the entanglement is great, disentangling can evolve over days, weeks, or even months.

Intercultural leaders sometimes ask if they're practicing Personal Leadership "right." The only answer to that is to ask a question in return: Are you practicing? There isn't any wrong way to practice except not to practice. In every moment, literally in every one, we have a choice about whether to practice. We call it the Personal Leadership "choice point."

This moment-to-moment choice is a choice between automatic pilot on the one hand and, on the other, the tremendously enlivening process of opening up to new learning, to inspiration, and to the possibility of strengthened relationships with ourselves and with others. The more we engage our lives with mindfulness and creativity, the more we experience the world as a vibrant and deeply fulfilling place. There's always a new vista around the corner, a new understanding or insight to achieve, a new level of applied competence to actualize. We discover that even the most mundane of leadership activities has the potential to be full of wonder.

And there's no shortage of opportunity in which to practice Personal Leadership, in which to exercise this choice. We're surrounded by difference and the unfamiliar, all the time. We don't have to wait until we're with someone from the other side of the planet whose language we don't speak; we don't have to wait until we're negotiating an important contract. We can practice Personal Leadership in any context of difference—even in the context of a simple difference of opinion between siblings over what movie to rent from the video store. Practicing Personal Leadership when the stakes are relatively low helps us build our skill level for when the stakes are higher. This is the "living laboratory" to which we all have access. Wherever we are, whatever we're doing, we can build our intercultural leadership competence. It's a bit like learning

to swim in the shallow end of the pool: We can drown just as easily in an inch of water as in 6 feet, but the illusion of safety allows us to focus on improving our stroke.

◆ Discussion Questions

1. What are the pros and cons of using the culture-specific and culture-general spheres of intercultural competence, and what contribution does the methodology of Personal Leadership offer?

2. Think of a time when you demonstrated one or more of the three orientations of an extraordinary leader (learning, appreciative, and receptive); what were the circumstances?

3. Which of the six practices of Personal Leadership do you already intentionally use?

4. In what ways do you currently cultivate stillness in your personal and professional life?

5. What is your vision of yourself as an extraordinary leader in an intercultural context?

6. How do you define your own personal/professional intercultural practice?

◆ References

Bennett, J. M. (2007, March 29). *Curiosity: The key to intercultural competence.* Paper presented at the Families in Global Transition (FIGT), Houston, Texas.

Bennett, M. J. (1998). *Basic concepts of intercultural communication: Selected readings.* Yarmouth, ME: Intercultural Press.

Bennett, M. J., & Castiglioni, I. (2004). Embodied ethnocentrism and the feeling of culture: A key to training for intercultural competence. In D. Landis, J. M. Bennett,

& M. J. Bennett (Eds.), *Handbook of intercultural training* (3rd ed., pp. 249–265). Thousand Oaks, CA: Sage.

Black, J. S., & Gregersen, H. B. (2003). *Leading strategic change: Breaking through the brain barrier.* Upper Saddle River, NJ: FT Prentice Hall.

Bohm, D. (1980). *Wholeness and the implicate order.* London: Routledge and Kegan Paul.

Burns, J. M. (1978). *Leadership.* New York: Harper and Row.

Cherbosque, J., Gardenswartz, L., & Rowe, A. (2004). In search of authentic engagement: The emotional intelligence and diversity (EID) way. In J. Cherbosque & L. Gardenswartz (Eds.), *Emotional intelligence and diversity.* Portland, OR: Summer Institute for Intercultural Communication.

Cooperrider, D. L., Whitney, D. L., & Stravos, J. M. (2003). *Appreciative inquiry handbook: The first in a series of AI workbooks for leaders of change.* Bedford Heights, OH: Lakeshore Communications.

Drucker, P. (2001). Forward. In *Appreciative leaders: In the eye of the beholder.* Chagrin Falls, OH: The Taos Institute.

Fredrickson, B. (1998). What good are positive emotions? *Review of General Psychology, 2*(3).

Fredrickson, B. (2003). The value of positive emotions. The emerging science of positive psychology is coming to understand why it's good to feel good. *American Scientist, 91.*

Goleman, D., Bayatzis, R., & McKee, A. (2002). *Primal leadership: Learning to lead with Emotional Intelligence.* Boston: Harvard Business School Press.

Hall, E. T. (1959). *The silent language.* New York: Anchor/Doubleday.

Hall, E. T., & Hall, M. R. (1990). *Understanding cultural differences.* Yarmouth, ME: Intercultural Press.

Hofstede, G. (1980). *Culture's consequences: International differences in work related values.* Beverly Hills, CA: Sage.

Jaworsky, J. (1996). *Synchronicity: The inner path of leadership.* San Francisco: Berrett-Koehler.

Loehr, T., & Schwartz, J. (2003). *The power of full engagement: Managing energy, not time, is the key to high performance and personal renewal.* New York: Free Press.

Nelson, N. C. (2005). *The power of appreciation in business: How an obsession with values increases performance, productivity, and profits.* Malibu, CA: Mindlab.

Ramsey, S., Schaetti, B. F., & Watanabe, G. C. (2004). *Personal leadership: Making a world of difference.* Portland, OR: Intercultural Communication Institute.

Saphiere, D. H. (2002). *Cultural detective.* Retrieved from www.culturaldetective.com

Sashkin, M., & Rosenbach, W. (1998). A new vision of leadership. In W. Rosenbach & Taylor (Eds.), *Contemporary issues in leadership* (4th ed.). Boulder, CO: Westview Press.

Schaetti, B. F., Ramsey, S. J., & Watanabe, G. C. (2008). *Making a world of difference. Personal Leadership: A methodology of two principles and six practices.* Seattle, WA: FlyingKite.

Schaetti, B. F., & Ramsey, S. J. (1999). The expatriate family: Practicing Personal Leadership. *Mobility: Magazine of the Employee Relocation Council, 20,* 89–94.

Schaetti, B. F., Watanabe, G. C., & Ramsey, S. J. (2000). *The practice of Personal Leadership and the SIIC internship program.* Portland, OR: Intercultural Communication Institute.

Schiller, M., Riley, D., & Holland, B. M. (2001). *Appreciative leaders: In the eye of the beholder.* Chagrin Falls, OH: The Taos Institute.

Senge, P., Scharmer, C. O., Jaworsky, J., & Flowers, B. S. (2004). *Presence: Human purpose and the field of the future.* Cambridge, MA: Society for Organizational Learning.

Thomas, D. C., & Inkson, K. (2004). *People skills for global business: Cultural Intelligence.* San Francisco: Berrett-Koehler.

Ting-Toomey, S. (1999). *Communicating across cultures.* New York: The Guilford Press.

Wheatley, M., & Chodron, P. (1999). *It starts with uncertainty.* Retrieved from www.berkana.org/articles/uncertainty.html

Wright, K. (1998). *Breaking the rules: Removing the obstacles to effortless high performance.* Boise, ID: CPM.

THE STRESS DYNAMIC AND ITS INTERSECTION WITH INTERCULTURAL COMMUNICATION COMPETENCE

◆ LaRay M. Barna

Perhaps the greatest attribute of intercultural communication competence is that it makes it possible for employees who are culturally different to work together effectively. One aspect that can enhance such effectiveness is for there to be a harmonious atmosphere in the organization, a place where there is friendly cooperation and an absence of unwanted stress. The latter is not easy to achieve in any workplace, let alone one where cultural diversity is present.

This chapter will explain why stress, that feeling of anxiety and tension, often coincides with face-to-face contact with one who is culturally different. The chapter will also explore the physical and emotional manifestations of stress, its positive effects, and ways for members of organizations to cope if stress is perceived negatively.

◆ Difference as a Cause of Stress

Perhaps adventurous people feel that sameness is boring, but most others prefer to associate with people who look and act like they do. When individuals have the same background or are well known to each other, conversations can be easy—they know that the way they speak will be understood and they know what is safe to say. They share ways to enter a conversation appropriately instead of impolitely interrupting. Banter flows freely. They can predict what response there will be to certain behaviors so they can knowingly choose how to act.

Contrast this with a time when people from diverse cultures make their initial encounter. There is now the possibility of confusion due to differing communication styles or of a possible challenge to one's worldview or a way of life. Such unknowns place them on the alert. Their innate bodily system is at work being forever watchful for anything that might place it off balance. If the individual encounter goes smoothly such individuals can relax, resulting in their heart rate and blood pressure returning to normal. If not, the tension they may hold makes them ready to react to a possible challenge.

Physiologists understand this tendency to avoid difference. Humans are hard-wired to react with alertness when a strange occurrence comes into focus. Sometimes it is an unusual sound in the middle of the night, a loud quarrel in the aisle of a supermarket, or a car weaving in and out of its lane of traffic. Nothing will raise a mother's blood pressure faster than the cry of her child in distress. The alarmed feeling that comes along with any event such as these will partially subside as one prepares to deal with the situation, but a stress reaction remains as long as the body senses a demand that is serious enough to need an extra energy supply.

In an organization where diversity is ever present, that alarm system may work overtime, causing extra and unneeded stress on the members of the organization who are already subjected to the everyday pressures of getting the job done. It does not matter that no actual threat can be seen or heard. The presence of difference is a subliminal signal that the body cannot ignore until it receives assurance that all is well.

◆ Stress Research

The term *stress* was first used in 1936 by Hans Selye, a young doctor who emigrated from Hungary to Canada. He defined it as the "nonspecific response of the body to any demand made upon it" (Selye, 1974, p. 27). He explained that this generalized aroused state of the body will partially subside as one "gathers one's wits" and prepares to deal with the problem.

Selye (1956) observed stress as a process of three parts, which he labeled the "Alarm Reaction," the "Resistance Stage," and the "Exhaustion Stage." Together they comprise the "General Adaptation Syndrome." The Alarm Reaction, when the body's defensive forces are sparked into a reaction, is what he would observe as happening if members of an organization would interpret diversity as potentially threatening. Toffler (1970) referred to this as a "novelty-detection apparatus."

SELYE'S RESISTANCE STAGE

Selye's (1956) second stage was called the Resistance Stage. This occurs when the body defends itself by such means as the secretion of adrenocorticotropic hormone (ACTH). Carried through the vascular system, this substance acts directly on the adrenal cortex, stimulating it to release various hormones, including cortisone. In essence, this is the alarm stage settled in for a long period of time. The heart beats faster, breathing rate increases, blood-clotting mechanisms are released to reduce loss of blood, muscles are tightened, the digestive system is shut down, and sugar is extracted out of the liver into the bloodstream to provide extra energy to take care of the emergency, whatever it may be (Oken, 1974).

The stage of resistance remains until the danger is perceived to have passed or can be controlled by one's normal resources. Obviously, the longer a person remains in this stage the more wear and tear there will be on the body. There are other hazards as well. One is that the anxiety and tension, which was noticeable at first, may be adjusted to and no longer remain in awareness. The highly activated state would then change to a trait and be accepted as normal. As the person becomes habituated to the "revved-up" feeling, she or he does not perceive the need to rest and "let down" to protect the body (Barna, 1983, p. 23). Physically, the body's natural inhibitors have been affected. This could account for the overreaction to normal stressors, such as the presence of people who are culturally different.

Another result of remaining in a highly aroused state is that this predisposes one to perceive a wide range of objectively non-dangerous circumstances as threatening (Janis, 1974). Such is the position of those people in an organization that are carrying stress from everyday hassles, which could potentially be composed of a large majority. The aforementioned research states that if their stress level is fairly high to begin with, they might be more disturbed than others by the diversity that surrounds them.

SELYE'S EXHAUSTION STAGE

Selye (1974) explains that the length of the resistance period depends on the body's innate adaptability and the intensity of the stressor. If the pressure continues too long the organism may lose its ability to resist, and the third stage,

the Exhaustion Stage, would ensue. Selye believed that in this final stage of the syndrome, where there is a depletion of energy reserves, fatigue would occur and, eventually, death. He said, "Superficial adaptation energy is immediately available upon demand [replenished by sleep] but 'deep' adaptation energy is like a reserve tank that can be drawn upon but not refilled" (pp. 39–40).

The above statements by Selye (1974), which proclaimed that adaptation energy is a finite substance, have been discounted. It's still believed, however, that a person who has not learned how to cope with constant and severe pressure will have a shorter lifespan. This will be because of the physical problems that have resulted from stress, such as heart disease.

◆ *Early Research*

An important predecessor of Hans Selye and the General Adaptation Syndrome was Walter B. Cannon (1915), who is credited with providing the foundation for systematic experimental research on the effects of stress. Barna (1983) states:

Others were working concurrently and the term "psychosomatic" was introduced by Felix Deutsch in 1929 (Silverman, 1968, p. 9). Only six years later, a massive compilation of studies on the mind-body relationship appeared in the first edition of Dunbar's *Emotions and Bodily Changes.* By 1954 the fourth edition appeared (Dunbar, 1954) containing a bibliography of over 5,000 sources. Harold G. Wolff was another pioneer whose studies in psychosomatic medicine demonstrated that the organism responds with the same physiological reactions to numerous stimuli, including emotional conflicts (Wolff, 1950, 1953). That somewhere between 50 and 80 percent of all diseases are believed to have their origins in stress

(Pelletier, 1977; Schindler, 1954) and that treatment of the "whole person" is becoming fashionable is testimony to the impact of the research begun by these scientists. (p. 25)

Writers in the 50s and 60s referred to that period of time as the "Age of Anxiety" (e.g., May, 1950; Fromm-Reichman, 1960). Many suggested that it was a cultural trait to be in a constant state of alarm. If that was true at that time, it must be even worse now considering the complexity of the state of affairs in today's world.

Holmes and Rahe (1967) started a new surge of interest in stress and psychosomatic disease with their publication of the Life Change Index, a 43-item checklist representing fairly common life situations that are differing enough from an individual's daily routine to require a certain amount of adjustment. These items ranged downward from the death of a spouse to Christmas. The higher a person's life-change score, the more likely that person would be to experience illness.

Early writers concentrated on proving that stress was indeed rampant in the culture, but now that seems to be taken as a given. A search today for books on stress at Amazon.com will reveal thousands of entries. Many self-help books are included, describing ways to manage the stress that seems to follow leaders everywhere.

◆ Stress Management Procedures

In organizations, the following procedures could be deemed helpful:

BECOMING AWARE OF SIGNS OF STRESS

When a deadline threatens or one's workload is over the top, it's not hard to notice signs of stress. Muscles are tense, breathing is shallower, and relief is looked for by means of coffee, complaints, and some way to avoid the inevitable. In the case of diversity in the workplace, these same symptoms are present, but because they are dulled by constancy and the cause is more or less hidden, they are often ignored. Like any ailment, if it is not within one's attention span it never gets treated. For these reasons it's important to scan the body often to detect the signs of stress while they are still manageable.

LEARNING THE TECHNIQUES OF PHYSICAL RELAXATION

There is good reason for any program of stress-management to include training in muscle relaxation. Barna (1983) found that "it is impossible to respond to any situation with an emotion of anxiety or apprehension if one's musculature is relaxed" (p. 38). Jacobson (1938, 1957) was among the first to demonstrate the relationship between the physical aspect of muscle tension and the emotion of anxiety.

Newspaper, magazine, and journal articles abound with instructions on how to physically relax. Most individuals within the United States, with an orientation of "doing," need these step-by-step instructions, but they are tedious to follow because they consist of admonitions to let go and exercise by doing nothing, a total oxymoron. It is only when tight muscles become achy that relief is sought by using relaxation techniques. Eventually the vulnerable learn that even 1-minute breaks several times a day to allow the stress to ease out of muscles improves their physical, mental, and emotional state.

PERUSING STRESS-MANAGEMENT LITERATURE

Information on stress management is abundant. One of the most recent books is by Dr. Claire Michaels Wheeler titled *10 Simple Solutions to Stress* (2007, New Harbinger), which she based on the field of psychoneuroimmunology. Her commonsense advice includes such things as venting one's emotions, getting regular aerobic exercise, cultivating close friendships, and advancing toward optimism.

REALIZING THAT IT IS THE EMOTIONAL REACTION TO SOMETHING THAT BRINGS FEELINGS OF STRESS, NOT THE THING ITSELF

It is a mind twist to know that one's reactions are separate from their cause, but that is a vital step. For a simple example, it is not the fan blowing on someone all day that made him get a spasm in his neck; it was his muscle resistance to that blowing air that caused the spasm. Reactions can be changed, whereas whatever caused the reaction may not be malleable. Know that diversity in the workplace is here to stay and, in itself, does not cause stress. Individuals can, however, change their reactions to diversity or improve their stress tolerance.

APPRECIATING THE POSITIVE ASPECTS OF STRESS

As explained earlier, a stress reaction is not inherently bad. It is a state of activation, nature's way of preparing the body to handle what has been perceived as an unusual circumstance that needs special attention. It could be the challenge of a ski jump, perceived as exciting, or a dash to avoid a speeding car, perceived as frightening. In either case it is a useful biological resource. It is imperative for members of an organization to make use of it but not let it use them by wearing them down.

AVOIDING DEFENSIVE MECHANISMS THAT LEAD TO TROUBLE

When individuals feel stressed or threatened by anything, big or small, their tendency is to defend themselves. As important as that is, some of these efforts to make them feel better cause problems of their own. Here are a few reactions, sometimes caused by the perceived threat of diversity, that members of organizations should avoid:

- Becoming aggressive or hostile
- Shunning interactions
- Ignoring or tuning out of situations
- Becoming dependent on others
- Being excessively concerned with unimportant details
- Using palliative measures, such as drinking or drug use

COPING WITH STRESS

Coping methods are different from defensive ones where the only purpose is a temporary fix, a way to feel better at all costs. To cope means to face and emotionally deal with those situations that cannot or should not be changed, such as organizational diversity. A few suggestions to accomplish this are as follows:

- Moving stress out of the body physically with long walks, massage, participation in athletic events, etc.
- Using support systems; sharing feelings with others
- Relabeling felt emotion; interpreting body signals as interest or curiosity rather than irritation
- Being confident; knowing one can handle stress
- Developing a sense of humor
- Toughening up

◆ Conclusion

Diversity, in itself, is neutral, but it affects everybody differently. Some individuals will be energized with positive feelings when they encounter diversity, but others will have negative feelings of overstimulation, unpredictability, helplessness, uncertainty, a lack of situational control, or a threat to self-esteem. These are sure signs of someone being under stress (Barna, 1983, pp. 31–32). Organizations would do well to consider all aspects of diversity, including methods to reduce stress.

◆ Discussion Questions

1. Recall being in a situation in a university setting where there was a stressful atmosphere. What could you, as an individual, do to keep your own stress level under control?

2. Do you believe that current circumstances might cause students to suffer from more stress than they did 15 or 20 years ago? Justify your answer.

3. Why could one person have a stress reaction to an event whereas someone else would not?

4. Pelletier wrote a book titled *Mind as Healer, Mind as Slayer.* Explain the dichotomy in that title.

◆ References

Barna, L.M. (1983). The stress factor in intercultural relations. In D. Landis & R. W. Brislin (Eds.). *The handbook of intercultural training* (Vol. 2). New York: Pergamon Press.

Cannon, W. B. (1915). *Bodily changes in pain, hunger, fear and rage.* New York: Appleton-Century-Crofts.

Dunbar, F. (1954). *Emotions and bodily changes* (4th ed.). New York: Columbia University Press.

Fromm-Reichmann, F. (1960). Psychiatric aspects of anxiety. In M. R. Stein, A. J. Vidich, & D. M. White (Eds.), *Identity and anxiety.* Glencoe, IL: The Free Press.

Holmes, T. H., & Rahe, R. H. (1967). The social readjustment rating scale. *Journal of Psychosomatic Research, 11*, 213–218.

Jacobson, E. (1938). *Progressive relaxation* (2nd ed.). Chicago: University of Chicago Press.

Jacobson, E. (1957). *You must relax.* New York: McGraw-Hill.

Janis, I. L. (1974). Vigilance and decision making in personal crises. In G. V. Coelho, D. A. Hamburg, & J. E. Adams (Eds.), *Coping and adaptation.* New York: Basic Books.

May, R. (1950). *The meaning of anxiety.* New York: Ronald Press.

Oken, D. (1974). Stress—Our friend, our foe. In *Blue print for health.* Chicago: Blue Cross Association.

Pelletier, K. R. (1977). *Mind as healer, mind as slayer.* New York: Delta.

Schindler, J. A. (1954). *How to live 365 days a year.* New York: Prentice-Hall.

Selye, H. (1956). *The stress of life.* New York: McGraw Hill.

Selye, H. (1974). *Stress without distress.* Philadelphia: J. B. Lippincott.

Silverman, S. (1968). *Psychological aspects of physiological symptoms.* New York: Appleton-Century-Crofts.

Toffler, A. (1970). *Future shock.* New York: Bantam Books.

Wolff, H. G. (1950). *Life stress and bodily disease—A formulation.* Baltimore: Williams & Wilkins.

Wolff, H. G. (1953). *Stress and disease.* Springfield, IL: Charles C Thomas.

12

BEYOND BORDERS

Leading in Today's Multicultural World

◆ Sangeeta R. Gupta

"One cannot manage change. One can only be ahead of it."

—Peter Drucker[1]

"I think that it was a pretty good job . . . for a girl," stated Mikel. The other members of the team sat in stunned silence. Raj, the team leader, sighed and continued the meeting, knowing that he was going to have to take Mikel aside, yet again, and talk to him about his communication and his attitude toward women. The team took their cue from Raj and ignored Mikel's comment, although the tension was palpable in the room. The team members, especially the women, were really getting tired of Mikel's comments.

Raj is leading a 16-person team that is scattered throughout the United States. The majority of the time they work remotely from Los Angeles, Seattle, Chicago, and Boston; however, they meet every other week in Chicago or Boston. Therefore, the bulk of the traveling is done by the people from the West Coast and some of it by the team members from Chicago. Raj's team is very multicultural and consists of individuals who are native-born Americans and first-generation Americans[2] from China, Pakistan, India, Vietnam, England, Turkey, Brazil, and Russia. Raj is an experienced manager, but this is the first time he is managing a team and a budget of this size. This is an important project for his career, and there is a promotion at stake. He is mild mannered but firm and is well liked and respected by his team. He is aware that there are underlying tensions within his team but is not sure what to do about them. His schedule is very tight and he wants to keep the focus on meeting the deadlines and their upcoming launch. This scenario is being repeated throughout the United States and, in fact, the world. Teams are no longer homogeneous entities but very much a part of our new multicultural environment. This change has come fast, and most individuals and companies are not prepared.

Within a generation, the world has changed. My parents emigrated from India in the late 1960s when the United States opened its doors to professionals willing to travel thousands of miles for a different life. There were very few Indians in the United States at this time, and my grandmother had to send care packages full of Indian spices and lentils. My mother wore Western-style pants and dresses, and Indian clothes were purchased by mail order or from India. In the blink of an eye, my sister and I were working professionals ourselves and could buy Indian spices, lentils, and even frozen entrees at Trader Joe's and regular grocery stores.

In one generation, the world has changed. Now there are ethnic enclaves, ethnic restaurants, and grocery stores dotting our increasingly multicultural landscape. The world my parents experienced in the United States a generation ago has changed dramatically.

Today's working professional is also experiencing this dramatic shift—both professionally and personally. One has only to look around to see a kaleidoscope of national origins, religions, ethnicities, races, and cultures. Leading in today's multicultural business environment presents challenges not experienced a generation ago. The skills that leaders utilized have to

be updated so that they can lead in the new reality of today's workplace.

This chapter will examine some of the new skills that today's leaders must possess to lead effectively. This new skill set consists of the development of a global mindset, cultural competency, and cultural adaptability. Today's leaders will flounder without a deep understanding of global dynamics, cross-cultural dynamics and how they play out in today's business arena, and the ability to adapt to a multicultural environment. They must understand the various dimensions of culture and how to recognize and adapt to cultural differences. Encompassed within cultural competency is the recognition and awareness that business etiquette is also culturally determined. It is very easy to offend someone if you are not aware of the subtle differences in modes of introduction, how business meetings are conducted, or when to refuse or accept offered refreshments, to name just a few potential minefields. Also contained under the cultural competency umbrella is the ability to lead both onsite and virtual or geographically dispersed cross-cultural teams. It is vital that today's leaders are able to inspire and motivate across cultures and across national and other boundaries. And last, today's leaders must develop cultural adaptability—the ability to adapt oneself to the current cultural environment without losing a sense of self and without judgment.

Is this chapter relevant to you? If you are leading or working on a team of Americans, do you need multicultural skills? Yes! Multiculturalism within the United States is increasing by leaps and bounds. The American workplace mirrors the general population, and the vast majority of people regularly encounter individuals from different ethnic, religious, racial, and cultural backgrounds from an ever-increasing number of countries. It is imperative to understand how culture, ethnicity, national origin, race, and gender intersect within our multicultural business environments. In addition, the multicultural landscape also extends into our personal lives. Look at your neighbors, or the children in your children's school or on their sports teams. Look at the different cultures and national origins of the individuals you encounter as you buy your groceries or gas or go to a movie theater. The United States is a multicultural environment, and everyone must develop effective skills to interact with and lead this new diverse workforce. These challenges are brought home to me day in and day out in my work as an intercultural specialist. My clients are in every industry . . . they are midsize to large companies completely located in the United States or are global players. These issues are ones they face on a daily basis.

◆ *Leading Across Borders: Developing a Global Mindset, Cultural Competency, and Cultural Adaptability*

Today's leaders must develop a global mindset—a way of looking at business on a global level rather than just at a domestic or regional one. Today's leaders are working in a borderless world, and they need to develop both a mindset and a skill set that facilitates and supports their transition to the new reality of our business environment. A global mindset gives an individual the ability to see the world as a holistic entity and not as something that functions in isolated sections. They are able to see how the different parts interconnect.

The first step in developing this mindset is to build a foundation of knowledge. This foundation will start with understanding culture—what it is and how it affects and directs our lives, both personally and professionally. Next, leaders must develop these general cultural competency skills: communication

styles, concepts of time, leadership and decision making, negotiation, motivation, and an understanding of how to lead onsite and geographically dispersed cross-cultural teams. These skills will create the foundation that leaders will use to interact effectively and as a springboard to the next step: developing cultural adaptability. The third step, once leaders possess information about the different styles and preferences that are present in today's multicultural business environment, is to develop the ability to adapt to different ways of looking at the world without judgment. This part of the foundational skills is a journey—some will progress faster than others, and some may linger in one area longer than others, and it will take time to travel this path. The ability to adapt is a crucial skill, and its importance cannot be emphasized enough.

Cultural competency and cultural adaptability are foundational skills vital to the success of anyone working in a cross-cultural environment, domestically or internationally. I would argue that *all* leaders today must possess these skills due to the tremendous diversity found in many working environments. Even if their company is located completely within one country, they may have clients, customers, suppliers, distributors, manufacturers, etc., who are of a different nationality, culture, religion, ethnicity, or race. One can think of cultural competency and cultural adaptability as the foundation of a house—everything else is built on top of this foundation. You can utilize beautiful and expensive trappings, but without a strong and skillfully constructed foundation, the walls of the house will eventually collapse. Cultural competency and cultural adaptability are the bedrock of today's new leader who will build their foundation with extensive background information about a particular culture or set of cultures, be able to experience the culture(s) without judgment, and will be able to skillfully adapt to situations with subtle cultural nuances. When developing this foundation, do leaders need to focus on a particular culture, or should they develop overall cross-cultural skills? From my experience, all leaders need to develop general cross-cultural competency, and *if* they are primarily dealing with a culture or a few cultures, they need to develop deeper expertise in that particular culture or set of cultures.

After developing cultural competency and cultural adaptability, some leaders may find the need to develop specialized knowledge to enable them to dive deeper into a specific culture or set of cultures. For this, a leader needs to understand the historical, political, linguistic, religious, cultural, and social background of the culture or cultures with which he or she will be interacting. The depth of knowledge needed will depend of the level of interaction anticipated. For example, business travel to another culture requires a different level of knowledge than interacting in the United States with a client from that culture. My clients share some interesting, sometimes amusing, stories of their interactions with other cultures and with individuals who have not taken the time to develop the skills that I believe *all* leaders must possess in today's cross-cultural environment. The stories shared by my amused Indian clients range from one of their clients who purchased snake bite insurance when traveling to New Delhi to a vice president in the IT industry who traveled with 2 weeks' of food and water in her luggage when she went to Bangalore, India. It is clear that neither had done even the most basic research prior to their trip. Even 30 minutes spent on the Internet would have given them enough knowledge to avoid these very basic mistakes. Anyone who is interacting with other countries or with individuals from other countries who are conducting business in the United States must take the time to learn enough specialized knowledge about that country and culture to operate professionally and effectively.

Development of cultural competency skills enables leaders to adapt their communication and negotiation styles in subtle ways based on the individuals with whom he or she is interacting. Savvy leaders understand that being able to adapt to multiple communication styles is a necessary skill in today's business environment. They will adapt their concepts of time and management styles also. In short, today's leaders must be able to adapt their preferred styles and do so without judgment.

I have clients who are unable to grasp that certain cultures view time differently. They insist on a fixed interpretation of time where time is closely and rigidly measured. They state over and over again that "it's rude to be late!" They cannot get beyond their own thought processes and see that other cultures have a different but equally valid sense of time. This has led to some extremely frustrating interactions and team meetings. Why is this relevant in today's business environment? If you are not able to view and interact with another culture without judgment, then your interpersonal relationships will suffer and your ability to lead, team morale, and productivity will eventually be negatively affected. By developing the ability to see beyond your ethnocentric lens, you are literally opening up another dimension of understanding and collaboration.[3] You are now able to enhance your team's performance by incorporating multiple perspectives and you are able to tap into the full potential of your team.[4] Your team will be collaborating in the true sense of the word.

◆ What Is Culture?

I've been discussing how a global mindset, cultural competency, and cultural adaptability are skills necessary for anyone leading in today's business environment. Before we continue on to discuss the various components of cultural competency, I would like to offer my brief overview of culture, to add to the definitions presented in Chapter 2. What do we mean when we talk about culture? What *is* culture? How does it develop, and is it something that everyone experiences? Or is it limited to certain parts of the world? Certain parts of the United States? What is tradition? Some cultures claim to have hundreds or thousands of years of culture and tradition. Does that mean that it has not changed in centuries? These are all valid questions regarding culture.

Quite simply, culture is something that is a part of each and every one of us. It is something that we learn as we are growing up. We learn it from our parents, extended family, faith-based organizations, educational environments, and society in general. We learn about culture without even realizing that we are learning. We are taught that "this is the way that things are done—in our family, in our society." Therefore, culture is knowledge that we acquire as we are growing up. Culture is also fluid, which means that it changes as the world around us changes, as we change through our experiences. The culture that your grandparents grew up with is different than the culture your parents grew up with and it is different from the culture you experienced and are still experiencing. Culture is also selective. By this I mean that you select which aspects of your cultural heritage you will incorporate into your life. You may choose to incorporate everything you have learned and experienced or you may reject it all or you may select something in between. The choice is yours. Culture is also ethnocentric, and by this I mean that everyone thinks that their way of doing things is the "right" way, the "best" way. We view other cultures through our ethnocentric lens and decide whether they are "right" or "wrong." We make judgments about other cultures based on our culture. So, for example, if our culture says that a direct style of communication works best, we may have

negative associations toward individuals who have an indirect communication style. When we look through our ethnocentric lens, we believe that our direct style is "right" and that the indirect style is "wrong."

Culture is often described as an iceberg. The vast majority of the iceberg is what you do not see under the water. The part that is visible, above the water, is a small fraction of the complete iceberg. People and culture are also like this. We can only see a fraction of a person from the outside, from the part that is visible. The majority of the person and who they are is under the water; it is hidden from our sight. And yet, we make the majority of our assumptions about a person based on the small part that is visible, the small part that we can see. You can easily see why misunderstandings can arise when we base our opinions and often decisions on a small portion of the total picture. How does this play out in the business world? Our interactions with our business colleagues are often of short duration and mainly focused on the task at hand, particularly in those cultures that are task oriented, like that of Americans. Given the pace of business, we make quick decisions based on the small amount of information we have—what we have observed and interacted with at the surface level. Task-oriented cultures often do not take the time to go deeper, to develop the relationship that promotes a deeper understanding of the individual. Relationship-oriented cultures, like many Asian and Middle Eastern cultures, prefer to get to know a person before they think about conducting business. They try to find out information that tells them something about the individual, about their values and beliefs.

I am often asked whether we can make general assumptions about a group of people, religion, a culture, or a country. Making generalizations provides a framework for understanding a group of people or a culture. However, it is important to distinguish between generalizations and stereotypes.

Generalizations are fluid concepts; they adapt as new information comes in. Generalizations allow us to see certain trends and patterns, but it is understood that this information does not apply to everyone within that group, religion, culture, or country. On the other hand, stereotypes are fixed concepts—"everyone" in this group or from this culture acts this way or believes this. When you stereotype and you receive new information that does not fit into your preconceived ideas about a group of people, a culture, religion or country, it is rejected and your worldview stays the same. Take, for example, the statement that "all Indians like spicy food." If you have lunch with me and I order my food medium spicy and you are generalizing, you will use this new information to adjust your worldview to "some Indians like spicy food and some do not." If you are stereotyping, you will reject this new information and say, "She's an exception to the rule and my viewpoint stands." This is why stereotyping is problematic when interacting in a multicultural environment. It limits your ability to understand other people.

Now that we have defined culture, let us discuss the various cultural dimensions. They include but are not limited to communication, time, power, individualism, structure, and thinking. In this chapter, I will focus on communication styles and concepts of time, as these are the areas that my clients have the greatest difficulty with and which, based on my work with them, have the greatest impact on team dynamics and productivity. Before I discuss these dimensions in detail, I want to make the point that there are individual variances within each culture. There will be both direct and indirect communicators in any one culture. These dimensions are generalizations and provide a starting place for us to understand individual differences. They provide a framework within which to understand multiculturalism. They are not definitive characteristics or preferences of any given culture.

◆ Communication: Are You Hearing What I Am Saying?

There are two aspects of communication that my clients have problems with: what they understand has been said and how it is said. In simpler terms, do the words they are hearing convey the entire message (direct communication), or are they required to "read between the lines" in order to receive the entire message (indirect communication)? Some cultures, like those of Americans, Germans, and Israelis, prefer and utilize direct communication, in varying degrees of directness. They say exactly what they mean and they believe that this type of communication sends a clear message to the listener. In fact, they find indirect communication to be evasive and often misleading. They consider indirect communicators to be dishonest and believe that they increase tension by not addressing any disagreements or issues in a direct manner. "You can take my words to the bank" is a saying that Americans in particular are fond of. They believe that verbally saying exactly what you mean is the best way to handle business and personal matters because it lets the other party know exactly where you stand. Their ethnocentric lens tells them that this is the way to conduct business.

On the flip side, indirect communicators, such as most Asians and Middle Easterners, believe that they convey the entire message by utilizing both verbal and nonverbal communication. They believe that not everything needs to be verbalized—things can be alluded to or implied. Indirect communicators believe that this is a more polite way of communicating; in this manner, they enable someone to "save face,"[5] an important concept in many cultures. They use words, facial expressions, body language, tone, and manner of speaking to send and receive the entire message. They, in turn, find direct communicators to be harsh, rude, insensitive, and insulting and believe that tension is increased as a result of their direct communication style. So, which is the better way to communicate? Neither; both are equally valid styles of communication, and it depends on who you are interacting with. It is vital to know your audience and have the ability to switch comfortably between communication styles.

◆ What Do I Call You?

Another aspect of communication that my clients frequently encounter is the degree of formality one should use when they interact cross-culturally. Some cultures prefer a more informal interaction, whereas other cultures like to follow a more formal protocol. Informal cultures often tend also to have a more egalitarian outlook. They prefer to use first names and their organizational structure tends to be more of a flat structure. Subordinates are encouraged to say what they think even if they do not agree with their supervisor/manager. Differences of opinion are explored and the interactions are more casual. Individuals will often make decisions on their own and take ownership of a section of the work plan. They will use this ownership to highlight their individual skills and contributions.

Formal cultures are more hierarchical: Individuals have "status" based on factors such as age, education, and seniority. Individuals prefer and expect to use titles until they are encouraged or requested to use first names. There is a protocol to how things are done, and there is a chain of command. Most subordinates would not openly disagree with their supervisor/manager, as this would be considered disrespectful. They wait for the decision and then support it, at least in public. This plays out in multicultural teams in the following manner: Individuals are reluctant to take personal ownership or responsibility of a stream of

work or deliverables. They are reluctant to openly contradict their supervisors or managers in meetings. They will often not speak their minds. In addition, they will wait their turn to speak and when they are mixed in with individuals with an informal outlook, they are often perceived to be very quiet or "having nothing to contribute," particularly because informal communicators will interrupt or speak over them. In addition, individuals from a formal culture will often not make eye contact as this is considered disrespectful. When leading multicultural teams, leaders need to be aware of these tendencies and take the time to create a space for these individuals to express themselves and to perhaps coach them on how they are being perceived. Individuals from formal cultures are often passed over for promotion or not given management responsibilities in these situations because it is mistakenly believed that they do not have the ability to lead.[6]

So, how should you conduct yourself? My recommendation is to be conservative in the beginning and take your cue from what others around you are doing. If everyone is using first names, then follow their example. The same applies if everyone is using titles. Observe meeting styles and how other people are interacting. This will give you an indication of the interaction styles that are being used. Your goal is to make everyone feel comfortable and for you to blend in.[7]

◆ Am I On Time or Am I Late? Task Versus Relationship Orientation

An area of intense frustration for many individuals operating in a multicultural environment is different concepts of time. Most individuals believe that there is one way to look at time, and they are dumbfounded by the fact that other cultures view time in any other way than their own. Every culture only has 24 hours in a day, after all. This is pretty much the only thing that they agree on! There are basically two orientations toward time: fixed and fluid. Someone with a fixed time orientation takes time and structures it in a precise manner. Schedules are developed and maintained. Meetings start and end on time. People are expected to be on time. If someone is late, there is a domino effect on the rest of their daily schedule. Individuals with a fixed time orientation believe that people who are perpetually late are disrespectful and not very professional.

I have a global client who hangs up if people are late to his conference calls. If the call is scheduled for 9:00 a.m., he hangs up at 9:02. He feels that there is no excuse for them to be late. For him it shows disrespect for his time. When I asked if he does that with his colleagues down the hall or in his onsite office, he said no. When we explored this issue, we discovered that he was so frustrated with working with fluid-time-orientation individuals and cultures that it became a hot-button issue whenever he interacted with them. On the flip side, however, if one of his colleagues whom he interacted with frequently and with whom he had a relationship was late, he hardly noticed. However, for his cross-cultural colleagues, because he did not have a relationship with them, he was not willing to accommodate what was a common business practice for them.[8]

I always have at least one person in my workshops with a fixed orientation toward time who simply cannot understand why anyone would be late. They are not able to get past the idea that being late is rude and constitutes unprofessional behavior. They are unable to understand individuals with a fluid orientation to time. Let us discuss what a fluid orientation is and why it causes so much difficulty for people with a fixed orientation.

An individual with a fluid orientation toward time also obviously works with 24 hours. However, they perceive those hours to be loosely organized. They also have scheduled appointments—after all, they are business professionals. However, they are willing to let a meeting run longer if the business at hand has not been completed. They are more concerned about the relationship with the individuals they are interacting with and in completing the task at hand to everyone's satisfaction than they are in keeping to a rigid schedule. They will more likely open a first meeting by getting to know the persons before they start conducting business. Subsequent meetings will also have a few minutes of chitchat before moving into the meeting. They believe that people with a fixed orientation to time should be a bit more relaxed and that they cause stress by being so rigid. So, who is right? Neither one of them. This is a preference and a different orientation toward time. There is no right or wrong to this issue. I generally advise my clients to be flexible.

When I go to India, my time orientation becomes more fluid, but in the United States and other fixed-time-orientation countries, I operate as people there do. For example, I went to Bangalore and New Delhi, India, to do some research and meet with clients. I had set up appointments before leaving the United States and I purposely arranged my appointments so that I had quite a bit of time in between. My meetings always started out with a cup of tea or coffee and several minutes of questions about my personal and professional background. Not one of my meetings started on time. In fact, one meeting was almost 2 hours late—it was suggested that since the person I was meeting was "on his way in," it would be a great idea for me to take a look at the new technology park that was being built. So, that's what I did. When I returned, my meeting was ready to start and the CEO was very cordial, and after our meeting was finished, he took the time and initiative, while I sat in his office, to set up another appointment for me with a friend of his, also a CEO. Now, this second gentleman was extremely busy; however, he made time to speak to me as a favor to his friend (relationship aspect of the fluid-time orientation) and of course, that was time out of his already packed schedule, so obviously someone was waiting while he spoke to me. However, he considered our meeting important enough to push his other meetings back. And his administrative assistant was not calling everyone to reschedule their meeting. People simply waited. This is the fluid preference of time in practice. This works for him in his business environment; however, it may or may not work in another business environment. When he is somewhere where they prefer a fixed-time orientation, if he has developed his cultural competence and cultural adaptability skills, he will be able to adapt to that environment. This is why there is no "right" or "wrong" when it comes to a preferred orientation. This is why being flexible and understanding that people are not being rude or rigid is critical to your success—keep in mind that they simply utilize time in a different manner.

◆ *Do I Bow or Shake Hands?*

Included under the umbrella of cultural competency is a thorough knowledge and understanding of business etiquette. It is vital to understand the details of the business etiquette practiced by those with whom you interact. Business etiquette includes everything from introductions, when to start discussing business, acceptance or refusal of refreshments, attire, personal grooming, dining etiquette, and hostess gifts, to name a few categories that multicultural leaders need to be aware of. It takes only a few minutes to peruse some basic information; this knowledge can make the difference between a smooth interaction and a potential disaster.

I have a global client who lost a huge contract over a handshake. My client was represented by an Israeli orthodox Jewish man who was introduced to the female head of a company. She put her hand out to shake his hand as the introduction was taking place. He backed away in horror, and she was humiliated. Hardly the way to start delicate negotiations! Someone should have explained to him that it was everyday business etiquette to shake hands with the opposite gender in the United States. He would have been prepared for the situation and could have simply acknowledged her greeting and said, "I am unable to shake your hand for religious reasons." In addition, no one had thought to explain to the female head that orthodox Jewish men do not shake hands with women. It would have taken a few minutes to explain to her that she should acknowledge the introduction verbally and not extend her hand. This basic information should have been conveyed to both parties so that they were not caught unaware and in an awkward situation. This company has now mandated cultural awareness training for all their global offices. In addition, they have a series of advanced training workshops for individuals who interact with specific cultures that provide more in-depth information and advanced skill-development. An expensive lesson to be sure.

Not only must one be mindful of religious sensitivities but also of gender and what interactions are appropriate across gender lines. One of my American IT clients went on a business trip to his company's branch in Bangalore, India, and as he was leaving the Indian office, he hugged and kissed each of the women he had interacted with. He recounted this story to me several months later as I was training them on how to work across cultures. Although the Indian women did not say anything directly to him, he was able to pick up from their expressions and body language that they were uncomfortable with his actions. Knowing that India is a formal-orientation country would have provided this client with the necessary framework and he would have interacted in a more accepted manner. We discussed that when working or socializing across cultures and genders, it is much safer to take the lead from the woman. If she extends her hand, then it is appropriate to shake it. If she initiates a hug or a kiss on the cheek, then it would be considered appropriate to follow her example. In general, it is a safer practice to start with the more conservative approach when dealing across cultures.

Knowledge of business etiquette also includes adhering to accepted standards of dress and grooming. Another American IT client, who has a very casual, almost beach-like, dress code in Southern California, wore T-shirts and shorts in their Bangalore office during a visit and noticed that he received some interesting stares. If he had taken a few minutes to research the Indian business environment, he would have realized that adult males do not wear shorts to the office. It is not considered acceptable business attire in the Indian business environment, and it will affect how people view and interact with you.

Grooming can also present some interesting challenges for today's business leaders. How do you handle a situation where an individual has different notions of grooming? A fairly common grooming issue recently developed for a client where a coworker would work out during lunch but would not shower afterward; instead she would spray a generous amount of cologne. A situation I have encountered myself on a cross-cultural team was one where an individual (we'll call her Mona) would shower every day but would not use deodorant, and the shower proved not to be enough. As the team leader, this situation was brought to me to handle. Both of these examples are ones that must be handled with tact and sensitivity in order to not humiliate the individual. In the first example, the coworker who had to interact with the cologne user in the afternoon had a tactful conversation with her and gently suggested that the cologne was not effective in masking the body odor generated

from the workout. The offending coworker was embarrassed but quickly corrected her behavior. In the second example, I had to tread carefully as the use of deodorant was not something that was an accepted practice in Mona's culture. I had to approach it in such a way that I was not insinuating that she was unclean but rather that for Americans, it is important to mask everyday body odor and that it would be beneficial for her interaction with the American team if she would adopt this practice. She agreed and the situation was resolved without her losing face in front of the team. It is important to remember when dealing with these extremely personal situations that different cultures have different belief systems regarding grooming and that any requests to act outside of these belief systems should be addressed in a respectful and nonjudgmental manner so that the individual does not feel embarrassed. The end goal is for people to work together in a more productive and harmonious way, not to impose on or even request a standard of behavior from someone in a judgmental way. This goes back to my earlier statement about seeing behavior outside of our ethnocentric lens. If we can see behavior within the context of the other culture, we can begin to address issues and concerns without judgment.

◆ Onsite and Geographically Dispersed Cross-Cultural Teams

An expanded set of leadership skills are required when leading cross-cultural teams. With onsite cross-cultural teams, team leaders will be utilizing the cultural competency and cultural adaptability skills discussed earlier. When leading virtual or geographically dispersed teams (GDT), today's leaders need to add additional competencies.

Let's start with a few definitions. Onsite teams, also known as co-located teams, are structured like the traditional teams with which many of us are familiar. The members are physically in the same location and are able to have frequent, sometimes daily, interactions. They may be working in a joint team room or may meet frequently for meetings, over a cup of coffee or for lunch. Team members are able to develop relationships as a result of these interactions, and therefore their exchanges are often smoother than those of GDT or virtual teams. Geographically dispersed teams deal with all the normal issues (for example, communication, personality differences) that onsite teams face and in addition handle the complications that arise when team members are separated by distance, time, and culture (local, regional, and national). Add in the fact that team members have limited to sometimes no face-to-face interaction and you can easily see how team morale and productivity can decrease unless the team is handled with skill. Geographically dispersed teams, whether domestic or global, also face cross-cultural issues. In addition to the issues of communication and time that we discussed earlier, GDTs have to work through additional issues to be highly functional teams.

Geographically dispersed teams have to work through issues of communication and trust in addition to more complicated logistics. They lack a sense of team or "team feeling" because of their structure. As most members have limited to no face-to-face contact, they do not form the interpersonal relationships that smooth over many rough spots in team interactions. When someone does not have a relationship with their team members, small things become an irritant and the ability to overlook small issues and give individuals the benefit of the doubt are lost. In addition, GDTs frequently have individuals who are working in different time zones, and without that sense of camaraderie, something as simple as scheduling conference calls can become a power and prestige struggle. When the time difference

is substantial, this can be even more contentious, particularly when different members have different perceptions regarding time. If you do not have a relationship with the individuals on the other end of the phone line, it becomes easier to hang up at 9:02 as your party is 2 minutes late for the call. Now add in multicultural issues and you are facing additional layers of subtlety that will damage your team cohesiveness and productivity.

So, how can these issues be resolved, short of meeting in person every week? Focusing on team building, preferably when the team is first formed, will put you ahead of the curve. Simple things like taking the first few minutes of the conference call to share news and reconnect or having a quarterly team-building conference call where the purpose is not to conduct any business but to build the team are quick and effective. A few simple icebreaker exercises will get you past the awkwardness of "where do we start?" The team leader can even create a few exercises from the content we have discussed in this chapter. One idea would be to talk about the different communication styles or time-orientation preferences and how they affect team dynamics. Another effective team-building exercise is to create a team Web page where members post some professional and personal information and where members can share news about an engagement, marriage, new baby, new pet, etc. These things, while sounding simple, are important because it is much easier to form a relationship when you personalize someone. You are more likely to give them the benefit of the doubt if they are a few minutes late to the call because you happen to know that they are sleep deprived because of a new baby in the family or because they face a long commute. They may be a little late on a deadline because they have had a death in the family and are observing a culturally set number of days of mourning. The basic point is that because you have formed a relationship with them and see them as individuals, you are less likely to be irritated by the same things that you would overlook with a colleague you have spent time with.

So, let's get back to Raj's team, whom we met at the beginning of this chapter. This is a real-live team I am currently advising. Raj's team has members in Los Angeles, Seattle, Chicago, and Boston. The team has approximately 16 members of both genders who represent almost as many different cultural and subcultural backgrounds. This team is pretty standard in today's multicultural and global business environment. Raj's multicultural team is working through issues of gender role expectations due to cultural differences, different concepts of time, power issues, communication, logistics, time zones, and providing effective feedback, to name a few. In other words, the typical multicultural team I frequently encounter! This team is handling a high-profile project with millions at stake, and due to the pressure they are focusing on the work stream and have not taken the time to deal with the "softer" issues. While individual members have attended some leadership training, no one has had team effectiveness training, nor have they spent any time trying to understand the dynamics of their particular team structure. The issues they are encountering are not "soft" issues but *core* issues that will contribute to their success or failure. By addressing these issues in a constructive manner, they will be able to maximize their potential and really harness the strength of their diverse team or they will be handicapped from the beginning.

Raj, the team leader, is a savvy individual with strong leadership skills; however, this is his first time leading a GDT. The team is in place for 1 year, and various members travel several times a month for a week at a time, so there is plenty of in-person contact. Although they have a team kickoff for each of the various phases of the project, it focuses on the work plan and they have yet to do any official team building. Their corporate culture has not recognized the unique characteristics of a GDT, and while they are diligent about providing a variety of training programs, they do not provide training in communication, cultural competency, cultural adaptability, and team effectiveness. Therefore, Raj is leading his team without the tools he needs to manage them effectively. This is a highly visible major project for his company and millions of dollars are at stake. Not to mention, Raj's promotion and bonus.

What are some of the issues that Raj is managing on this multicultural GDT? Let's start with the fact that the members are working across three time zones. A sticky situation recently occurred when someone high up in Boston wanted to do update conference calls several times a week at 7:30 a.m . . . EST! That was 4:30 in the morning for the L.A.- and Seattle-based individuals. Another issue arose when this same individual scheduled daily update calls at 3 p.m. EST; that's noon for the West Coast team members. These calls lasted several hours and cut into their lunch hour every single day. This was hardly the way to develop team camaraderie. Although this individual was in a higher position of authority, Raj felt that he had to make some changes to the schedule for the sake of team morale. Although it seems like a simple and reasonable enough request, it became an issue that had to be carefully negotiated because it was tied to issues of power, prestige, and corporate culture. Another issue that arose had to do with gender roles. Mikel, a first-generation Russian member of the team in his late 30s, had very traditional gender role expectations. He would often make disparaging remarks about the technical expertise of the women on the team, specifically linked to their gender. For this team member, making disparaging comments about the women on the team was acceptable behavior as seen through his personal cultural lens. These comments were felt to be even more abrasive when communicated as a disembodied voice coming out of a speaker phone. Raj had to coach this individual on how to interact with women on a U.S.-based team, not only for team morale and the respect of the talented women on the team but also for legal purposes.

Although this team was already in place, Raj took one morning when they were all together and had them do some of the simple team-building exercises we discussed earlier in the chapter. He gave a short overview of some of the issues that GDTs experience and then talked about communication styles, as this was a major factor within his team. Raj felt that some progress had been made, and he decided to add these discussions to their work plan. He found definite value in helping his team understand the dynamics of GDTs and how different people communicate. He has already decided that gender interactions, particularly around communication, will be the topic of their next team-building session. In addition, he is planning on writing a white paper to circulate within his company on the learnings from his GDT experience.

◆ Conclusion

Today's leaders are operating in a business environment that is different from what business leaders experienced even a decade ago. Population demographics and technology have created a dramatic shift and one that will continue to change the landscape of business at a speed never experienced before. To keep up with the face of business in our new multicultural world, today's leaders need to develop strong cross-cultural skills. These skills are not limited to global players. The development of a global mindset, cultural competency, and cultural adaptability are critical foundational skills that every leader needs to possess to maximize

his or her own impact and productivity as well as that of the team.

NOTE: I would like to thank Ravikumar Bodla, John Mitchell, and Michael Moodian for their helpful comments on earlier drafts of this chapter.

◆ Discussion Questions

1. What are some of the issues that individuals face when they have a direct style of communication and they are dealing with someone who has an indirect style of communication? What are some things that they could do to communicate more effectively?

2. What are some of the issues that could affect the work plan and timeline when your team has both fluid- and fixed-time-orientation individuals? What are some things you could do to help the team work more effectively and meet its deadlines?

3. What are some aspects of culture that would fall below the waterline—i.e., that are not visible? What are some that are visible? What happens when we make assumptions about people based on the very small part that we can readily see?

4. Discuss some generalizations and stereotypes you have about different groups of people or cultures. What are some different ways that you can work toward understanding these groups or cultures without stereotyping?

5. Have you ever worked on a multicultural team? What are some of the issues that you faced? After reading this chapter, are there things that you would have done differently? How would you now handle those situations?

6. Have you worked on a geographically dispersed team? What are some of the issues that you faced? If you had 5 minutes to give someone advice on how to lead a GDT, what would you say?

◆ Notes

1. Drucker, P. (1999). *Management challenges for the 21st century*. New York: HarperCollins.

2. The term "first generation" refers to individuals who immigrated to the United States as adults. "Second generation" refers to those individuals who are born in the United States. Asian American studies also uses the term "1.5 generation" to refer to individuals who came as small children. The 1.5, or "knee-high," generation are culturally between the first and second generations and demonstrate some characteristics of each group. Unfortunately, due to space limitations, I am not able to discuss the subtleties of the cultural behavior exhibited by the second and subsequent generations in the United States in this chapter.

3. When someone is exhibiting ethnocentric behavior, they are viewing and judging other cultures based on their own culture. Individuals believe that their way of doing things is the right and usually, the only way, of doing things. Other cultures are viewed through this filter and are, quite often, found lacking.

4. I am using the term *team* to refer to all colleagues and not just a specific team.

5. Saving face refers to a way of interacting that enables both parties to maintain their position of respect and a graceful way of conceding that does not cause any shame or lowering of prestige in their own and in others' view of them.

6. I have explained this to many individuals, and once they understand this tendency and create this space, they are often amazed at the management potential of these individuals, which was previously overlooked due to a simple difference in cultural outlook. I particularly remember one CEO who was not impressed by one of his directors until he became aware of this tendency. He provided cultural executive coaching to the director, who is now performing above expectation.

7. I coach individuals not to do anything that goes against their values and beliefs; however, stepping out of your comfort zone can help you adapt to different cultural situations.

8. Cross-cultural executive coaching has significantly decreased the frustration level of this executive and his interactions are much smoother as he continues to build his cross-cultural competence and his ability to interact with other cultures without judgment.

PART IV

MEASURING INTERCULTURAL COMPETENCE

GETTING THE MEASURE OF INTERCULTURAL LEADERSHIP

◆ Fons Trompenaars
and Peter Woolliams

◆ The New Challenge

The challenge today in leadership models and an associated competence framework is to include a perspective that transfers to modern global business and international leaders. During the last 20 years, the fact that national and organizational cultures both need to be considered in modern business management has been increasingly recognized. Some authors and practitioners have responded by seeking to add "culture" as yet another factor like "quality" to be taken into account when planning, marketing, and doing business and managing. We have argued consistently that culture is not simply another variable to be "bolted on," but that it provides the whole contextual environment defining much of the essence of the relationship between an organization and the environment in which it operates. If we agree that culture is a system of shared meaning, then we begin to understand why every organization is a cultural construct.

Many of the conceptual frameworks for explicating culture are based on describing how different cultures give different meanings to relationships with other people, the meaning they give to their interaction with the environment and to time, and by other similar cultural dimensions. Trainers and consultants have been keen to ply their own respective models across the practitioner and academic press, conferences, and workshops—and are still doing so. We often hear that the world of business and management does not need to further the proof that people are different. Many authors, trainers, and consultants are still stuck in this anthropological time warp.

Much attention has been given to the recognition and respect for cultural differences. However, if we stop at only these first two stages, we run the risk of supporting only stereotypical views on cultures. In our extensive cross-cultural database, we have found enough variation in any one country to know it is very risky to speak of a national, corporate, or even functional culture in terms of simple stereotypes. Our response was to progress from basic cross-cultural awareness training and consulting to developing global minds and beyond.

We claim that our work is unique in that our focus has been to extend research on culture to giving much more attention to the reconciliation of differences after the identification of these differences. We have accumulated a significant body of evidence that wealth through effective business is created by reconciling values. This is true for alliances (including mergers and acquisitions) and in recruitment and for marketing across cultures—indeed throughout the complete management spectrum. It is also true in leadership as well as for nations speaking peace unto nations.

The starting point is to ask how leaders deal effectively within multicultural surroundings. Take these alternate descriptions. Which would you choose?

(a) Good leaders are people who continually help their subordinates to solve the variety of problems that they face. They are like parents, not teachers.

(b) Good leaders occupy a position between that of a private coach and a teacher. Their effectiveness depends on how they balance both roles.

(c) Good leaders get things done. They set goals, give information, measure results, and let people do their own work in that context

(d) Good leaders give a lot of attention to work streams, so that goals, tasks, and achievements are aimed at improving those processes.

(e) Good leaders complete the task at hand. They lead the process so that everyone is embedded in continuous work streams.

We posed this question to many top leaders during our research into globalization and organization sustainability. Answers are consistent with our proposition that leaders such as Richard Branson of Virgin, Michael Dell of Dell, Inc., Kees Storm of AEGON, and Laurent Beaudoin of Bombardier made significantly different choices from people in our database of more "ordinary" managers. Do you know what the difference was?

The leaders described in answer (a) look like those of the beginning of the last century: Listen to father and everything will be OK. This style is still very popular in Latin America and Asia, where we have also collected research data, compared to Europe and the United States. There is nothing wrong with this approach, simply that it is limited in its applicability outside these regions.

Answer (b) is a typical compromise and will not work very well anywhere—certainly not the optimum approach.

Answer (c) is very popular amongst Anglo-Saxons and northwest European managers. The ever-popular "Management by Objectives" is again applied recklessly. Add some vision and mission, and you're the modern leader; but the French would quickly argue: "Whose vision and mission is it?"

Answers (d) and (e) are two alternative ways to integrate seemingly opposing values on a higher level and would therefore have our approval. Answer (d) suggests that good leaders guide people who make mistakes and learn from them, while (e) integrates the dichotomy of task orientation with work streams beginning from the opposite direction. More successful leaders selected the last two choices much more frequently.

Once you are aware of and respect cultural differences, the way is open for this next step, which is based on this concept of reconciliation. The new question is therefore to ask what we can do with the differences to make business more effective once we cross cultural or diversity boundaries.

◆ The Importance of Reconciliation

The above helped to identify and define behaviors and actions that vary across the world and across companies but which all integrate differences to a higher level—much more significantly than compromise solutions. The approach informs managers how to guide the people side of reconciling any kind of values. It has a logic that integrates differences. It is a series of behaviors that enables effective interaction with those of contrasting value systems. It reveals a propensity to share an understanding of others' position in the expectation of reciprocity. We found from our research that successful leaders have this propensity to reconcile dilemmas to a higher level and that it is this underlying construct that defines transcultural competence.

◆ Why Do Leaders Face Such Dilemmas and Why Are They Important?

All organizations need stability and growth, long-term and short-term decisions, tradition and innovation, planning and laissez-faire, order and freedom. The challenge for leaders is to fuse these opposites, not to select one extreme at the expenses of the other. As a leader you have to inspire as well as listen. You have to make decisions yourself but also delegate, and you need to centralize your organization around local responsibilities. You have to be hands-on and yet hands-off. As a professional, you need to master your materials and at the same time you need to be passionately at one with the mission of the whole organization. You need to apply your brilliant analytic skills to place these contributions in a larger context. You are supposed to have priorities and put them in a meticulous sequence, while parallel processing is in vogue. You have to develop a brilliant strategy and at the same time have all the answers to questions in case your strategy misses its goals.

Thus we know for example that American, British, or Australian managers tend to be more individualistic and Japanese more teamwork oriented. So as long as American managers remain in the United States managing all Americans and the Japanese stay in Japan, then presumably there is no problem. However, in today's multicultural world, an American manager could be running a team overseas with Korean, Japanese, and French members. So does the manager focus on leading the individual or the team? In our findings, all cultures and corporations share similar dilemmas but their approach to them is culturally determined. The success of a company will depend, among other things, on both the autonomy of its people and on how well the information arising from this autonomy has been centralized and co-coordinated. If you fail to exploit fully centralized information, you're scattered but highly self-motivated personnel might as well remain totally independent. If various teams are not free to act on local information, then centralized directives are subtracting, not adding, value. In this example, reconciliation is where the team is led, so that it serves the individual and how well individuals contribute to the team.

We have found that this component of intercultural competence in reconciling dilemmas is the most discriminating feature that differentiates successful from less successful leaders and thereby the performance of their organizations. These dilemmas that derive from value (i.e., cultural) differences also mean, increasingly, that the culture leads the organization. The leader defines what an organization views as excellent and develops an appropriate environment in which the (ideographic) culture of the workforce is reconciled with the (nomothetic) needs of the organization. As a result, the organization and its workforce cannot do anything other than excel.

As our own work progressed to be focused on the development of intercultural competence, we refocused our interventions for our client organizations to address the need to consider what behaviors were effective in being not only able to recognize cultural differences but to respect these differences and moreover to be able to reconcile these differences.

Readers of our more recent books and other publications will know that we make extensive use of the Internet for collecting primary data from participants from our client organizations. In addition to the main Trompenaars cross-cultural database, we have also collected and indexed some 6,500 dilemmas faced by our client respondents in their respective organizations across the world gathered over the last 5 years. Coding and subsequent analysis of these dilemmas using clustering and data-mining algorithms reveals a frequently recurring series of "Golden Dilemmas" that provide a basis for a structured approach to diagnosing organizational challenges that owe their origin to cultural differences.

From this beginning, we extended our own earlier cross-cultural instruments to account for and assess how successful leaders reconcile cultural differences and thus realize the business benefits that they offer.

◆ The Need for a New Holistic Competence Framework

We all know that the world of business is changing ever more rapidly due to the internationalization of business and migration of people from their fatherlands. Yet we still observe that the major instruments and methods used for evaluating and assessing leaders and the performance of their business units owe their origins to Anglo-Saxon or American philosophies and are still dominated by an Anglo-Saxon or American signature. One might conjecture that there is a bountiful supply of diagnostic instruments to determine individual or company-based cross-cultural profiles and competence. Not surprisingly, we can all observe how each is promulgated by their originators, all claiming their own is the best. These varying authors usually claim degrees of "reliability," but this is not the same as them being "valid." And are they seeking to measure what we should be measuring to inform the HR function and corporate strategy in order to improve business performance in 2009 and beyond?

On critical evaluation one finds that most are not free of cultural bias and are stuck in the time warp of focusing on cultural differences—and not how to assess (and thereby develop) the competence to deal with multicultural situations. We have similarly developed our own series of such instruments over the last 20 years that have sought to assess different aspects of cultural competence. These have ranged from assessing fundamental awareness, determining cultural orientation, the propensity to reconcile differences, through to the competence to realize the business benefits of cultural differences—and in the context of both country and corporate cultural frameworks. As individual instruments they have served their purpose well. However, we have recognized limitations in earlier versions of our own cross-cultural frameworks and have been searching for solutions that overcome common problems faced by all consultants and HR professionals in coming to grips with intercultural competence.

Even without the complexity of the cultural context, confusion begins over the use of the term *competence*. *Competences* and *competencies* are more than just a difference between American English and European English spelling. The descriptions are applied variously to denote the capacity in an individual but also as an element of a job role. The term *competence* has its origins in the research of the McBer Consultancy in the late 1970s in the United States as part of the initiative by the American Management Association to identify the characteristics that distinguish superior from average managerial performance (Iles, 1999). The work was encapsulated in the seminal book *The Competent Manager* (Boyatzis, 1982). This has spawned a mass of literature and initiatives in organizational attempts to identify and construct the "competent" manager.

However, the term and its related concepts have become problematic as they have been taken and adapted to different environments. Boyatzis (1982) defined the term as "an underlying characteristic of a person." It could be a motive, trait, skill, aspect of one's self-image or social role, or a body of knowledge that he or she uses. However, as Woodruffe (1993) has pointed out, there is a mass of literature attempting to define the terms *motive, trait, skill*, etc. This again opens up the term to a multitude of interpretations. Woodruffe for example, defines *competency* as "a set of behaviour patterns that the incumbent needs to bring to a position in order to perform its tasks and functions with competence." Others have used the terms *skill* and *competence* interchangeably: "Perhaps the most fundamental implication of moving to a skill- or competency-based

approach to management concerns the area of work design" (Lawler, 1994). For Rhinesmith (1996), "If mindsets and personal characteristics are the 'being' side of global management, then competences are the 'doing' side." As a basis for management training needs analysis or organizational review and development, most authors fail to clarify which of these meanings they are ascribing to "competence."

Additionally we then have the challenge of how to design an instrument that covers the spectrum of cultural effects. When we begin to incorporate non-Western types of logic, such as yin–yang or Taoism, we soon realize that we have all been restrictive in basing any profiling on bimodal dimensions. For example, we were trying to place respondents along a scale with "individualism" at one end and "communitarianism" (collectivism) at the other. But in a multicultural environment, a highly individualized leader will agonize over the fact that many subordinates prefer to work with their team. Conversely, the group-oriented leader will fail because of an apparent lack of not recognizing the efforts of individuals. Thus we have a dilemma between the seemingly opposing orientations of individualism or communitarianism. Similarly, do we find undue criticisms of staff in a business unit or an excess of support? Someone criticized by authorities feels attacked, where support is absent, or indulged where criticism is withheld. Any instrument that seeks to be free of cultural bias needs to avoid being based on this type of Western Cartesian logic, which forces us to say if it is "either/or."

◆ The Intercultural Competence Profiler

With the above in mind, we have recently assembled our ICP (Intercultural Competence Profiler). It is an attempt to describe and measure certain modes of thought, sensitivities, intellectual skills, and explanatory capacities that might in some measure contribute to the formation of an intercultural competence.

We used a range of methods to determine what components of competence should compose this integrative model. They include the following:

- A critical review of extant knowledge of established competence frameworks

- Observations of best practice of high-performing leaders (see Trompenaars & Hampden-Turner, 2002)

- Inductive analysis of our own cultural databases

- Job analysis of global leaders and senior managers that shows how they have to deal with dilemmas

- Our own THT Academy that included supervision of PhD students researching in these areas

The ICP is multifunctional instrument that enables a participant to assess his or her current Intercultural Competence or that of their organization or business unit. Unlike other competence tools, our ICP does not focus on a single basic area of cultural knowledge or behavior but addresses the complete spectrum from cross-cultural awareness through to the business benefits deriving from effective action in multicultural situations. It has been developed by combining our earlier frameworks based on our extensive research and intellectual property that originally addressed each area separately. Each component has been subject to rigorous research and testing through extensive application in many client situations across the world. Recently we have confirmed the reliability of the combined integrated instrument with a sample base that has included MBA students as well as senior managers and business leaders from our client base.

The ICP is normally completed online. Participants can download and save their own personal profile report as a PDF file for archiving and printing.

Additional basic biographical data of the respondent provide more extensive benchmark comparisons across our rapidly evolving ICP database. Extensive feedback, extended interpretations, and theoretical background to the ICP are available in a series of interactive pages from the Web-based ICP support center. Participants can explore their own personal profiles through these online tutorials, which offer further insights, "coaching" advice, and suggestions for competence development. Figure 13.1 displays the four components of the Intercultural Competence Profiler.

We distinguish four aspects of Intercultural Competence:

1. **Recognition:** How competent is a person to recognize cultural differences around him or her?

2. **Respect:** How respectful is a person about those differences?

3. **Reconciliation:** How competent is a person to reconcile cultural differences?

4. **Realization:** How competent is a person to realize the actions needed to implement the reconciliation of cultural differences?

Note that we define "intercultural competence" based on all four quadrants. What we also describe as "transcultural competence" refers to the quadrant on reconciliation, as described in more detail below.

Figure 13.1 Intercultural Competence Profiler Model

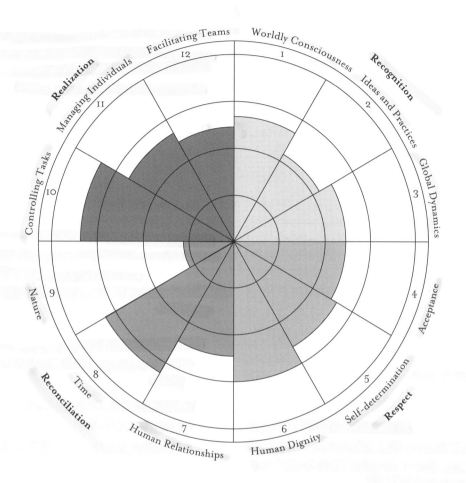

RECOGNITION

The first cluster is concerned with the individual's capacity to understand his or her condition in the community and the world and thereby make effective judgments. It includes the respondents' awareness of nations, cultures, and civilizations, including their own societies and the societies of other peoples. The focus is on how these are all interconnected, how they change, and the individual's responsibility in this process. It defines some key elements of what we call a global consciousness—to flesh out some of the relevant constructs if we are to cope with the challenges of an increasingly interdependent world.

Operationally, it consists partly of the modes of thought, skills, etc., but as conceived here, a recognition competence is not a quantum—something you either have or do not have. It is a blend of many things, and any given individual may be rich in certain elements and relatively lacking in others. A very crucial part of intercultural awareness, as Eileen Sheridan (2005) found in her Delphi-based research, is self-awareness.

In this cluster of recognition, we distinguish three main competence areas that take account of the conceptualization developed by Robert G. Hanvey (2004):

1. Worldly consciousness, which comprises perspective consciousness and "state of the planet" awareness

2. Fundamental cross-cultural awareness

3. Global dynamics, which comprises knowledge of global dynamics and awareness of human choices

The diagnostic questions we have assembled and developed to measure this first cluster have been based on many sources, such as the ideas developed by Van der Zee and Brinkmann (2004) and in particular Robert G. Hanvey (2004) in the essay "An Attainable Global Perspective."

RESPECT

How respectful is a person about those differences? Respect serves as the basis for our attitudinal, cognitive, and behavioral orientation toward people who hold a diversity of values.

In our professional practice we have focused a significant part of our work on helping people to recognize cultural differences and structure their international experiences. The risk of stopping at the level of awareness and recognition without progressing further is that one might be supported in one's (negative) stereotypes. But respect of these differences is crucial for one's competence to deal with cultural differences.

According to Webster's, the noun *respect* is defined as the giving of particular attention, high or special regard, and expressions of deference. As a verb, *to respect* is to consider another worthy of esteem, to refrain from obtruding or interfering, to be concerned, and to show deference. A composite definition of *respect* that reflects these characteristics can be presented as follows:

Respect is a basic moral principle and human right that is accountable to the values of human dignity, worthiness, uniqueness of persons, and self-determination. As a guiding principle for actions toward others, respect is conveyed through the unconditional acceptance, recognition, and acknowledgment of the above values in all persons. Respect is the basis for our attitudinal, cognitive, and behavioral orientation toward all persons with different values.

In our model, we have based the three components of respect on the research by Kelly (1987), as they are appropriate for organizing the measurement of respect as an attitude:

1. Respect for human dignity and uniqueness of a person from another culture

2. Respect for the person's rights to self-determination

3. Acceptance of other culture's values

RECONCILIATION: THE TRANSCULTURAL COMPONENT

This third cluster deals with the propensity of a person to deal with the differences of which one is both aware and that one respects. We have identified three levels of reconciliation that are linked to the main constructs that we have used to organize the seven dimensions of culture:

Reconciling Aspects of Human Relationships

1. *Standard and adaptation.* Do we have to globalize our approach or do we just have to localize? Is it more beneficial for our organization to choose mass production

than just focus on specialized products? High performers find the solution in the "transnational organization" where the best local practices are being globalized on a continuous basis. "Mass customization" is the keyword for reconciling standardized production and specialized adaptations.

2. *Individual creativity and team spirit.* This demands the integration of team spirit with individual creativity and a competitive mindset. High performers are able to make an excellent team out of creative individuals. The team is stimulated to support brilliant individuals, while these individuals deploy themselves for the greater whole. This has been called coopetition.

3. *Passion and control.* Is a competent person an emotional and passionate person or does he or she control the display of emotions? Here there are two clear types. Passionate people without reasons are neurotics, and neutral individuals without emotions are robots. An effective performer regularly checks passion with reason, and if we look at the more neutral people, we see individuals who give controlled reason meaning by showing passion once in a while.

4. *Analysis and synthesis.* Is the competent person a detached, analytical person who is able to divide the big picture into ready-to-eat pieces, always selecting for shareholder value? Or is it somebody whose behavior puts issues in the big picture and gives priority to the rather vague idea of "stakeholder value"? At Shell, Van Lennep's "helicopter view" was introduced as a significant characteristic of a modern leader—the capability to ascend and keep the overview, while being able to zoom in on certain aspects of the matter. This is another significant attribute of the competent reconciler—namely, to know when and where to go in deep. Pure analysis leads to paralysis, and the overuse of synthesis leads to an infinite holism and a lack of action.

5. *Doing and being.* "Getting things done" is an important characteristic of a manager. However, shouldn't we keep the rather vulgar "doing" in balance with "being," as in our private lives? As a reconciler you have to be yourself as well. From our research we found that successful reconcilers act the way they really are. They seem to be one with the business they are undertaking. One of the important causes of stress is that "doing" and "being" are not integrated. Excessive compulsion to perform, when not matching someone's true personality, leads to ineffective behavior.

Reconciling Aspects of Time

1. *Sequential and parallel.* Notably, effective reconcilers are able to plan in a rigorous sequential way but at the same time have the ability to stimulate parallel processes. This reconciliation, which we know as "synchronize processes to increase the sequential speed"—or "Just in Time" management—is also very effective in integrating the long and short term.

Reconciling the Inner and the Outer Worlds

1. *Push and pull.* This final component is the competence to connect the voice of the market with the technology the company has developed and vice versa. This is not simply about technology push or market pull. The competent reconciler knows that the push of technology finally leads to the ultimate niche market, that part without any clients. If you only choose for the market, the client will be unsatisfied.

REALIZATION

After one has recognized, respected, and reconciled cultural differences, the emphasis shifts to processes in which the resolutions are implemented and rooted in the organization.

Components of this competence are captured in John Adair's Action-Centered Leadership model (2005). Competent managers and leaders should have full command of three main areas and should be able to use each of the elements contingent upon the situation. Being competent in each component delivers results, builds morale, improves quality, develops teams and productivity, and is the mark of a successful manager and leader.

The key to nurturing leaders is to ensure that your company recognizes excellence at three levels: strategic, operational, and team. It is a mistake to believe that all an organization needs is a strategic leader in charge, asserts Adair (2006).

The fourth cluster, after recognizing, respecting, and reconciling cultural differences, comprises these tasks:

- Achieving the task
- Managing the team or group
- Managing individuals

Based on the above clusters, the full ICP comprises some 100 questions that are used in different combinations to contribute to the total profile. Ratings are not simply added and averaged for the different scales. In many cases the sectors are computed from the root mean square of competing questions to assess their mutual interaction. This is especially important for assessing the competence to reconcile in Cluster 3.

To accommodate different client/participant needs we have developed several versions. Thus in the 360° version, a participant's own self-assessment scores can be triangulated with peer feedback. This can even be based on additional input from clients, customers, or suppliers. The "organization version" is oriented to an analysis of the "competence" of the business unit and/or wider organization rather than the individual. In the "diversity" version, the focus is on diversity and ethnicity rather than country-derived cultures.

◆ From Intercultural Competence to Business Performance

The really exciting part of this new wave based on our new dilemma database is that we have been able more recently to converge on a number of key diagnostic measures that reveal how these competences manifest as effective behaviors for the leader and how these link to bottom-line business performance. We first help leaders make such "Golden Dilemmas" explicit and therefore tangible through our structured "Dilemma Reconciliation Process." We then assess the current status of the dilemma against an ideal state that would result when the business benefits had been realized. A typical result, as shown in Figure 13.2, is that there appears to be a wide variation in the assessment of the current state from an international leadership team, but much more consensus about what is needed in the ideal state. However, closer examination reveals that such assessments are culturally determined. In the example shown, American leaders tend to adhere to the top left, Europeans toward the center, and leaders from Asia in the bottom right in terms of current practices. And thus, although our Golden Dilemmas may be universal, how they are interpreted and the starting point for their reconciliation need to account for culture.

Leaders are now in a position to evaluate various business. The example summarizes the top-level descriptions of the

Figure 13.2 Measuring Current Versus Ideal Status of Golden Dilemmas

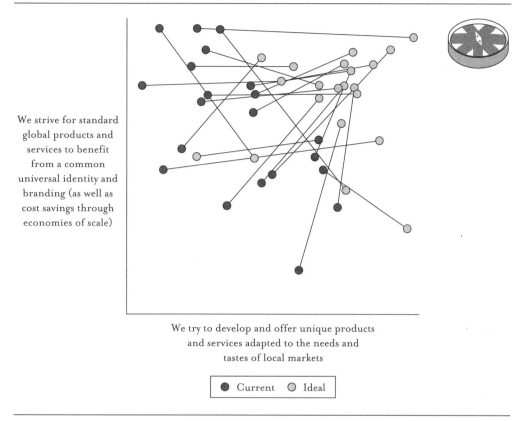

We strive for standard global products and services to benefit from a common universal identity and branding (as well as cost savings through economies of scale)

We try to develop and offer unique products
and services adapted to the needs and
tastes of local markets

● Current ○ Ideal

Golden Dilemmas faced by the top leadership of a major American organization and how they were subsequently placed on the dilemma relationship matrix using our new measurement techniques. In Figure 13.3, we present the Dilemma Portfolio Analysis.

This type of analysis provides the leader with an objective evaluation of where the highest return on investment can be achieved and thus secures the best benefits to the business. In this particular case, the most important dilemma that warranted addressing was the need for a technology push (what the company can make from its own intellectual capital) versus what the different markets want (what the organization could sell). When leaders are faced

with major decisions involving high levels of funding and human capital, such analytical approaches help them to validate their tacit insights by making them explicit and open to debate.

As the world marketplace becomes ever more oligopolistic and more competitive, leaders need such frameworks and their associated tools to provide a decision-making framework that prioritizes actions. How does this new approach deal with this aspect? Leaders are increasingly confronted with questions from clients regarding how their knowledge can be embedded into the company's long-term learning processes or how they can help the organization build and sustain "cultures of learning," "cultures of continuous

Figure 13.3   Dilemma Portfolio Analysis (Where Is the Biggest Bang per Buck?)

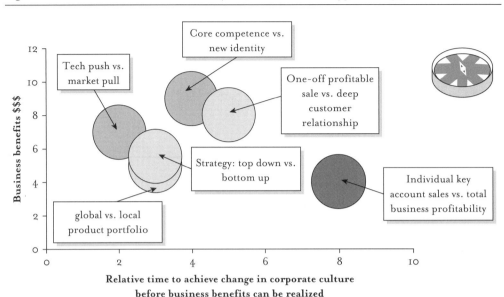

development," and "cultures that embrace change and diversity."

We believe that the existing dominant theories of leadership, categorized in three main paradigms known as trait, behavioral and situational theories, do not resolve the main dilemmas leaders are facing today. Furthermore, they do not give sufficient attention to the variations in which different cultures approach frequent leadership challenges. Trait theory claims a single best set of traits for the leader and ignores the culture in which these traits are needed to come to fruition. Behavioral theory claims that there are different styles of leaders vis-à-vis tasks and followers. The weakness of this approach is that one hardly enters the complexity of the world of the relationship between both styles. Again, the cultural context is not taken into consideration. Finally the situational theory of leadership introduces the (cultural) context as an important aspect in the effectiveness of leadership. One aspect, however, has not been resolved. How

can a leader be effective in a multicultural environment? We believe our proposed metatheory resolves most black spots in existing leadership models.

◆ *Conclusion*

Nobody claims that combining values is easy; nevertheless, it is possible. The ever-expanding system of satisfaction of values will form the ultimate test for the leaders of this century. However complex this world is, in all these dilemmas, one discovers the underlying organizational principle that is based on the idea of integration.

To meet the challenges of today's ever-globalizing world, leaders need to develop a new mindset of inquiry and support centered on the reconciliation of dilemmas and thereby finally reveal these leaders' true worth. One approach to help leaders develop this capability we are currently exploring is to develop a competency framework that specifies effective behavioral criteria based on our conceptual framework. Thus a conventional competency model that prescribes criteria for demonstrating integrity might include statements such as "to be direct, open, frank, and honest." Such statements are often (unintentionally) culturally biased and do not embrace reconciliation. Thus, "to be direct, open, frank, and honest" may work in the United States but might be less effective in China (or dealing with Chinese members of your team located in the United States) for whom matters of "face" are different when facing criticism (even if the criticism is constructive). The equivalent behavior description that engenders a reconciliation approach would be "to develop your relationship with your team so that you can be open, direct, frank, and honest." Extending this idea to the complete portfolio of competence descriptors can thereby induce a change of mindset through prescribing behaviors that are reconciling. Living and practicing these develops the aspiring leader to this new level.

We are now researching a further phase in which we can quantify the dilemmas between the organization and its societal responsibilities. These will become increasingly important to organizations in the future, as G8 world leaders reconcile their own needs with those of an unhealthy and hungry Third World, declining (finite) raw materials, global warming, and poverty—not forgetting the threat of terrorism.

The need for a competence framework with both high reliability and validity poses a difficult challenge, first made by Lord Kelvin in his lecture to the Institution of Civil Engineers, London, 3 May 1883: "When you can measure what you are speaking about, you know something about it. But when you cannot measure it, your knowledge is of a meagre and unsatisfactory kind."

◆ Discussion Questions

1. What are the critical challenges for global managers today? What can be done about them?

2. What are some ways that cultural differences can be reconciled?

3. What is an example of a behavior that may be acceptable in the United States but not in another country?

4. How significant is the ability to achieve cultural integration to a business's bottom line?

◆ References

Adair, J. (2005). *Effective leadership development*. London: Chartered Institute of Personnel and Development.

Adair, J. (2006). *How to grow leaders: The seven key principles of effective leadership development*. London: Kogan Page.

Boyatzis, R. E. (1982). *The competent manager: A model for effective performance*. New York: Wiley.

Hanvey, R. G. (2004). *An attainable global perspective*. New York: the American Forum for Global Education. Retrieved from www.globaled.org/An_Att_Glob_Persp_04_11_29.pdf

Iles, P. (1999). *Managing staff selection and assessment (Managing work and organizations series)*. Buckingham: Open University Press.

Kelly, B. O. (1987). *Perception of professional ethics among senior baccalaureate nursing students*. Unpublished doctoral dissertation, the Ohio State University.

Lawler, E. E., III. (1994). From job-based to competency-based organizations. *Journal of Organizational Behavior, 15*, 3–15.

Rhinesmith, S. (1996). *A manager's guide to globalization: Six skills for success in a changing world*. New York: McGraw-Hill.

Sheridan, E. (2005). *Intercultural leadership competencies for U.S. business leaders in the new millennium*. Unpublished doctoral dissertation, University of Phoenix.

Trompenaars, F., & Hampden-Turner, C. (2002). *21 leaders for the 21st century: How innovative leaders manage in the digital age*. New York: McGraw-Hill.

Van der Zee, K. I., & Brinkmann, U. (2004). Construct validity evidence for the Intercultural Readiness Check against the Multicultural Personality Questionnaire. *International Journal of Selection and Assessment, 12*, 285–290.

Woodruffe, C. (1993) *Assessment centres: Identifying and developing competence* (2nd ed.). London: Institute of Personnel and Development.

14

ASSESSMENT INSTRUMENTS FOR THE GLOBAL WORKFORCE

◆ Douglas Stuart

Spurred by the demands of economic globalization, the international relocation industry, and the increasingly multicultural workplace, assessment instruments have proliferated in the last decade. The increasing supply of instruments reflects, of course, the increasing importance of selecting appropriate people for international assignments or positions in multicultural work environments and preparing them for these unfamiliar circumstances. Because such positions often require competencies beyond the standard set of professional knowledge and skills needed for familiar first-culture work environments, international human resource professionals responsible for selection and development look for new tools to assess and enhance aptitude, awareness, and skills.

Now, there are dozens of commercially available and increasingly sophisticated instruments purporting to measure various aspects of intercultural adaptability or suitability; intercultural sensitivity, development, or competence; or work style and/or cultural values orientation. It has become increasingly difficult to keep up with what tools are available in the market, what they measure, and whether they are appropriate for particular needs.

This chapter discusses the various aspects of competence required for successful performance in the global environment, organizes commercially available instruments that attempt to measure some aspects of that competence according to their appropriate application—selection or development—and describes several appropriate instruments in each category with respect to purpose and design, supporting research, presentation languages, source, and other pertinent or unique attributes. Part 1 focuses on instruments applicable particularly to the selection process, while Part 2 focuses on instruments primarily designed for the development process.

PART 1: INSTRUMENTS FOR THE SELECTION PROCESS

◆ *Global Competencies for Global Work*

Although a lot of research has examined the traits and skills associated with success in international assignments and, more recently, success in the multicultural workplace (one need not always leave home to experience a multicultural workplace), the selection and development process is still more of an art than a science. With respect to international assignments, there are so many variables affecting the outcome that predictability of success or failure is difficult. One must look at the personal situation of the candidate—single or married, with or without children, of what ages, separation issues from extended family or support group, point in career path, etc. Variables in the assignment itself include location (developed or undeveloped economy, urban versus rural setting, remoteness, degree of cultural difference and language challenge, climate, number of other expatriates at workplace and in the community, experience of the local workforce with foreigners, etc.) and the nature of the work (a technical versus a management focus, the relative importance of external relationship building with client, customer, local government, and community versus internal management, etc.).

So, there are many variables affecting the nature and the degree of challenge of an assignment. The fundamental question is, what factors (beyond technical competence) predict success in the global business environment? *In general, the global workplace requires the ability to operate comfortably and effectively within a broad spectrum of difference—human, cultural, and environmental.* (These three categories, of course, overlap.) While research has identified attitudes, traits, and skills that make up this broad ability or competence, here is a short but reasonably comprehensive list:

- Action orientation (conscientiousness)
- Flexibility
- Openness (open-mindedness)
- Emotional stability
- Sociability (extraversion, agreeableness)
- Cultural empathy (cultural sensitivity, cultural intelligence)

Taken as universal across cultures, the first "big five" attributes (terminology sometimes varies) are transparent and make sense with respect to fostering comfort and competence in unfamiliar and diverse situations. One can argue that these items are traits that are not learned but rather part of one's personality, their presence or absence appearing early in life. While the more personal traits like sociability and openness may be strengthened through life experience and perhaps coaching, in general such traits are not amenable to training.

Cultural empathy, however, differs from the rest. Research in social neuroscience confirms ever more strongly that empathy, the major component of cultural sensitivity, is learned (Goleman, 2006) and that cultural sensitivity plays a primary role in intercultural competence.

What is the role and importance of cultural sensitivity or empathy? If we consider cultural difference as expressed in the workplace, five factors have been revealed to be of considerable importance through the research of Geert Hofstede (2001). Hofstede identified the dimensions of individualism (individual vs. collectivism), power distance (hierarchical vs. participative orientation), masculinity (task vs. relationship orientation), uncertainty avoidance (structure vs. risk orientation), and long-term orientation (pragmatic future vs. conventional historical or short-term orientation). These differences in attitudes and behaviors are profound, change slowly over time, and are more related to national or ethnic culture than to organization, profession, age, or gender. Such differences need to be recognized, understood, acknowledged, and managed in the global work environment. When the need arises to work in a cultural environment where values very different to one's own are the norm, it may be necessary (depending on a variety of factors) to adapt to these differences. This is where cultural sensitivity and empathy become an important part of intercultural competence.

◆ *Global Intercultural Competence: A Cluster of Attitudes, Knowledge, and Skills*

The successful global manager, whether expatriating, simply working in a multicultural environment, or supporting a multicultural workforce, exhibits a complex global competence that includes cultural empathy. This empathy consists of four related components:

- Knowledge of one's own and other pertinent cultures

- Recognition of specific differences between cultures

- Understanding of how culture influences behavior in the workplace

- Ability to adapt to and/or manage differences, as expressed in business structures, systems, and priorities, within multicultural work environments

Underlying these components is *attitude*—namely, openness to difference and a willingness to suspend judgment. As referenced in other chapters of this text, this requires a movement in stages from a natural ethnocentrism toward an acceptance of otherness typically called ethnorelativism (Bennett, 1993). Acceptance increases sensitivity to cultural difference and leads to conscious *knowledge* of the particularities of one's own and other pertinent cultures. From this knowledge base one begins to observe the impact of cultural differences on the workplace. One then develops the *skill* of adapting to or managing specific differences in order to operate successfully in another cultural milieu or in a multicultural situation. Cultural empathy thus leads to the development of *global intercultural competence*—the emotional, cognitive, and behavioral skill set required for successful participation in global business.

Whether the task is selecting employees to fill sensitive positions or development planning for managers, there are increasingly sophisticated tools for measuring and developing various aspects of intercultural competence. It is crucial to understand the new skills needed for management of the global workplace and to be able to measure and develop these. The instruments that follow can be extremely valuable in these processes.

◆ *Tools for the Selection Process: Adaptability*

When selecting candidates for international or multicultural assignments from a pool of personnel of roughly equal technical qualifications, it is useful to assess both adaptability/suitability and intercultural competence. Ideally candidates are offered the confidential opportunity to complete instruments relating to both categories in order to self-select into or out of consideration for a specific assignment. Often, however, human resources personnel elect to review the results from these instruments. (Be aware that use of such instruments in employment decisions has important legal implications, since they are generally not job specific.) In either case, there are several instruments designed to assess adaptability or intercultural competence, or some combination of both. We will first look at adaptability instruments.

Adaptability instruments were the first assessment tools developed in response to the globalization of business and the increase of international assignments. Some have been available for more than 30 years, and new ones continue to be developed. Most of these instruments are based primarily on a self-assessment of a set of personality traits (listed previously under Global Competencies for Global Work) associated with adaptability to new situations. Here are six quite different instruments that assess variations of these traits, or these plus other competencies. Four of these tools below were developed in the United States, one in Canada, and one in the Netherlands:

- Cross-Cultural Adaptability Inventory (CCAI)

- International Assignment Profile (IAP)

- International Personnel Assessment tool (iPASS) *Canada*

- Overseas Assignment Inventory (OAI)

- Multicultural Personality Questionnaire (MPQ) *Netherlands*

- Self-Assessment for Global Endeavors (SAGE)

CROSS-CULTURAL ADAPTABILITY INVENTORY (CCAI)

The CCAI, developed by Colleen Kelley, PhD and Judith Meyers, PsyD, was copyrighted in 1987. It is designed to provide information to an individual about his or her potential for cross-cultural effectiveness. Both versions consist of 50 questions that assess four components of cross-cultural adaptability. Initial statistical studies indicated that the CCAI had sufficient reliability and validity for a training instrument. While some recent research has questioned the validity of the four-factor structure, other research has correlated it with emotional intelligence. The CCAI remains a convenient tool for the self-selection process because of its simplicity and low cost. The instrument can be purchased in any quantity and does not require certified administrators. It can be used as a stand-alone instrument for self-selection for international assignments, as part of a larger selection battery, for pre- and post-testing, or as part of cross-cultural training. There is a follow-up training tool called the CCAI Action-Planning Guide that suggests actions to address factors assessed as weak, and there is also a Facilitator's Guide and Cultural Passport to Anywhere for use in group debriefs. The Multi-Rater Kit provides 360° feedback with three observers. The CCAI is available in two versions: a self-scoring paper and pencil instrument that provides immediate turnaround and an online version that provides the scoring and a printed feedback report.

INTERNATIONAL ASSIGNMENT PROFILE (IAP)

It is common knowledge that family adjustment is the most significant threat to the success of an international assignment. The IAP, from International Assignment Profile Systems, is a unique and technologically sophisticated tool designed primarily as a preparation instrument to assist those selected for international assignment to prepare well for their destination. Its goal is to make a good match between the employee, the family, and the particular destination. However, the tool has selection implications; if the IAP report indicates that the required support is too onerous or extensive, the manager and employee may want to reconsider the timing or destination. The IAP is a multifaceted process that gathers and organizes extensive information about a family anticipating international assignment and integrates it with information about the destination to which they are being sent. It also provides the means of archiving this information for learning and future research. (The IAP recognizes the client company and can be customized to convey specific information; it can be modified, customized, or "branded" to fit a client's or vendor's specific requirements.)

The IAP report summarizes family information in a comprehensive, easily understood format identifying core issues that need to be addressed prior to departure, such as the following:

- Critical planning issues and adjustments that must occur to ensure assignment success

- A list of "sleeper" issues that could emerge post-arrival to compromise the assignment

- Information on "back home" issues that may affect the assignment

- "Pleasant surprises"—essential or important things to the family that will meet or exceed expectations in the destination

- Destination information on spousal employment and spousal impact

- Traits and behaviors that may hinder or enhance cultural adjustment

The two-part questionnaire can be completed in approximately 35 minutes per section for employee and spouse. The survey is secure and does not have to be completed in one sitting. The report is typically generated within 24 hours but can be received more quickly if necessary. Although information on how to use and interpret the IAP is available from IAP Systems, the IAP requires no special training.

INTERNATIONAL PERSONNEL ASSESSMENT TOOL (IPASS)

With Part 2 still under development, iPASS is already a comprehensive behaviorally based tool to assess intercultural effectiveness and readiness for undertaking an international assignment. Designed for HR and recruiting specialists in the international field, iPASS is being developed by the Centre for Intercultural Learning, Foreign Affairs Department, Canada. In contrast to most intercultural assessment instruments, iPASS is intended to provide a strong, reliable basis for HR and management in employment decisions. Part 1, available now in French and English, is the Behavioral-Based Interview Kit, providing a reliable intercultural competency interview. Based on 35+ years of research, the interview kit employs seven Competencies for Intercultural Effectiveness: cultural adaptation, knowledge of the host country, sensitivity and respect, network and relationship building, intercultural communication, intercultural leadership, and personal and professional commitment. Each competency has four levels of mastery. A client chooses three competencies necessary for success in the intended assignment as well as the level of each competency required for adequate functioning. Based on this, a customized interview kit is then prepared for the iPASS-certified HR/recruiter specialist with a set of comprehensive questions for a 2-hour interview appropriate to the selected competencies and levels; this set also includes questions on motivation, interest, and attitude toward cultural difference.

Part 2, a 40-question Situational Judgment test based on actual intercultural conflict situations, will provide an additional screening tool when completed. Qualification for use of the Behavioral-Based Interview Kit is obtained through a 3-day training session delivered for 8 to 12 people wherever required.

OVERSEAS ASSIGNMENT INVENTORY (OAI)

Developed by Michael Tucker, currently of Tucker International, the OAI was the first major instrument assessing suitability for an international assignment. Available since the early 1970s (first version designed for the U.S. Navy) the self-awareness questionnaire examines 14 attributes and motivations found crucial for successful adaptation to another culture as well as motivations for accepting or wanting an international assignment. Studies of validity and reliability have been conducted at intervals on various populations since its implementation, and the OAI has undergone significant redevelopment. It continues to be well known and respected in the relocation industry.

The questionnaire is conveniently available online, although the reports (two versions; one to the candidate and another to HR or management) are furnished in hard copy only. They are individually prepared, further validated by a telephone interview, and may take up to a week for delivery. Reports are self-explanatory and do not require debriefing by certified administrators. The OAI is appropriate for self-selection as well as support for HR in its decision-making process. The OAI provides a limited basis for professional development in preparation for an international assignment, and its debrief can become a major component of cultural training.

MULTICULTURAL PERSONALITY QUESTIONNAIRE (MPQ)

Karen I. Van der Zee, PhD, and Jan Pieter Van Oudenhoven, PhD (University of Groningen, the Netherlands) developed the Multicultural Personality Questionnaire of 91 items as a multi-dimensional instrument to measure intercultural effectiveness. Developed in 1998 and revised in 2000, the MPQ measures five traits: cultural empathy, open-mindedness, social initiative, emotional stability, and flexibility. Designed primarily for self-assessment, it can be used as well for risk assessment as part of the selection process. While personalities are generally considered stable rather than learnable competencies, the more social dimensions—open-mindedness, social initiative, and cultural empathy—have been shown to increase as a result of training or living abroad.

SELF-ASSESSMENT FOR GLOBAL ENDEAVORS (SAGE)

The SAGE was developed by Paula Caligiuri, PhD, who is currently director of the Center for Human Resource Strategy at

Rutgers University. Available since 1997, the instrument was designed to assist individuals and families as a confidential tool in their decision process of whether to accept an international assignment. The tool's three sections address issues of personality (six factors), motivation, and family. Validity and reliability are supported by considerable research. The SAGE is available in two versions—one for the employee and a second for the accompanying partner—online in English with the report immediately available for reading online or via printing. (Paper-based versions are also available in French, Japanese, Mandarin, and Taiwanese. These versions are not merely translation/back translations but recreations of the instrument using cultural resources to assure the appropriateness of the questions.) The first two sections are scored with ranges marked in greed, yellow, or red as indications of one's suitability and readiness for assignment. The third section is not scored but is designed to facilitate the family conversation necessary for an informed decision about seeking and accepting an assignment. The SAGE is designed to facilitate the self-selection process, but the report can also be used to structure a pre-departure or post-arrival cultural training program.

◆ **Tools for the Selection Process: Competence**

While the dividing line is blurry because many instruments have more than one focus, there are a number of instruments designed more for the assessment of competencies than for adaptability. The OAI and iPASS above contain elements of this, while the CCAI, SAGE, and MPQ are primarily focused on adaptability traits (and life situation, in the case of the SAGE). The next four disparate instruments focus more on the complex skills essential for effective functioning in international assignments.

- Global Candidate Assessment (GCA 360°)
- Intercultural Development Inventory (IDI)
- Intercultural Readiness Check (IRC) *Netherlands*
- Survey on Intercultural (Relocation) Adaptability (SIA, SIRA)

GLOBAL CANDIDATE ASSESSMENT (GCA 360°)

Very different from the tools discussed above, the Global Candidate Assessment is an elaborate three-step online assessment process developed by Aperian Global that involves self-assessment and assessment by up to 10 colleagues, supervisors, and subordinates on the same items (not identified in the available description), including written commentary on selected questions about the candidate's attitudes and abilities. While the assessment examines workplace behaviors and adaptability, the instrument does not focus specifically on intercultural competencies as defined above. Once the surveys are completed, the tool generates an instant compilation, the Candidate Summary Report, which is viewable by the client assessment administrator. This includes overall scores, a combined visual display, a gap analysis indicating difference between the candidate's and others' scores, and a compilation of written comments. Administrative functions can be performed by Aperian or by a client HR person. Step 2 is a 3-hour interview with the candidate conducted by an Aperian consultant. This may include the spouse or partner as well and covers motivation, challenges, relocation issues, career impact, personal strengths/weaknesses, and self-rating of adaptability, all resulting in a verbal summary report to client HR. Step 3 is a candidate meeting with client HR to debrief the process and indicate current level of commitment to an international assignment. As an optional Step 4 after the candidate has been accepted, the candidate and key colleagues in the new position can take the GlobeSmart Assessment Profile (GAP), which compares a profile of the candidate with that of the selected colleagues and generates a report to each suggesting various behavior modifications to enhance collaboration. (No information on research support was offered.)

INTERCULTURAL DEVELOPMENT INVENTORY (IDI)

The IDI, covered thoroughly in Chapter 16, is a theory-based instrument developed by Mitchell Hammer, PhD, and Milton Bennett, PhD, that measures intercultural sensitivity as conceptualized in Bennett's Development Model of Intercultural Sensitivity (DMIS 1986, 1993). First developed in the mid-1990s, the recently revised 50-item instrument measures people's reaction to cultural difference along a developmental six-stage scale of cognitive structures or "worldviews" reflecting increasing intercultural sensitivity or competence. These worldviews range from denial and defense through minimization to acceptance, adaptation, and integration, with the first three labeled as ethnocentric and the last three as ethnorelative. Intercultural competence minimally requires development into the acceptance/adaptation stage of intercultural sensitivity. The IDI is supported by impressive reliability and validity studies and can be used with confidence in both the selection process and developmental planning, where it predicts the kind of intervention most effective for development according to the revealed stage of intercultural sensitivity. It is

equally applicable for measuring the intercultural competence of work or leadership teams (as an average) and for planning further competence development.

The IDI is available as a paper and pencil instrument or online in nine languages: Chinese, English, German, Italian, Japanese, Portuguese, Spanish, Korean, and Russian. While quite inexpensive to purchase, it must be debriefed by a certified interpreter.

INTERCULTURAL READINESS CHECK (IRC)

The Intercultural Readiness Check was developed in 2002 by Ursula Brinkman, PhD, of Intercultural Business Improvement in the Netherlands. Focused entirely on learnable skills crucial to effective intercultural interaction, the IRC examines the following four competencies: intercultural sensitivity, intercultural communication, building commitment, and preference for certainty (defined as the "ability to manage the greater uncertainty of intercultural situations"). Reliability and validity research was conducted on an international business population of Europeans, Americans, and others. Studies show high reliability (reconfirmed based on a population of more than 2,600 individuals) and sufficient validity to make the IRC a useful instrument for specific developmental training on any of the four competencies. Research continues on the instrument, and scores can be compared to a large database of more than 7,000 respondents. The questionnaire can be accessed online, but results must be presented by a licensed intercultural consultant. The tool can be used before entering a multicultural environment or during an international assignment, and the results provide an excellent basis for building a development plan and ongoing coaching.

SURVEY ON INTERCULTURAL (RELOCATION) ADAPTABILITY (SIA & SIRA)

From Grovewell LLC, SIA and SIRA are online 360° assessment instruments for global leadership or relocation candidates. For global leadership candidates, the SIA assesses seven skills/qualities that facilitate successful adaptation to global realities: flexibility, nonjudgmentalness, interest in different views and values, awareness of others' feelings, attention to relationships, responding well in unclear situations, and self-confidence. The 360° process (up to 12 raters) also assesses 20 behaviors that undermine relationships with diverse counterparts. For global relocation candidates, the SIRA adds a self-assessment (not 360°) for the candidate and separately for the spouse or partner of motivations, concerns, and expectations around long-term living and working in an unfamiliar environment. The Feedback Report of these instruments is provided directly and solely to the user, who is advised to share results with HR or management. While no certification is required for the administration of these instruments, a separate manual plus phone consultation is provided to HR and EAP professionals in contracting firms.

◆ Conclusion: Part I

Part 1 describes 10 varied instruments in support of the selection process for international assignments or any entry into the multicultural workplace, with respect to both adaptability and intercultural competence. These were selected from a larger pool for various reasons including design, research support, proven utility, and application to varied needs. As a final comment, users of selection instruments are often concerned about their reliability and validity. It is important to understand that, although many of these instruments are well supported by significant research, the linking of their results to the probability of assignment success is problematic since such instruments (with the exception of iPASS and GCA 360°) are not job specific in their design. That is, the need for adaptability and intercultural competence varies greatly with the job and the business and living environments. Therefore, results of these instruments (again with the exception of iPASS, GCA 360°, and, to some extent, the IDI) should not be used as the sole or even the primary basis of employment decisions.

Part 2 below describes another set of instruments primarily suited for the development of intercultural competence.

PART 2: INSTRUMENTS FOR THE DEVELOPMENT PROCESS

◆ Tools for the Development Process: Intercultural Awareness

The contrast of cultures through the lens of value dimensions has been inspired by intercultural research from Florence Kluckhohn & Fred Strodbeck in the 1950s through Edward Hall in the 60s and 70s and Geert Hofstede and his protégé Fons Trompenaars (with Charles Hampden-Turner) in the 80s and 90s, plus the large value surveys such as the World Values Survey, Shalom Schwartz's work in Europe, and most recently the seminal publication of *Culture, Leadership, and Organizations: The GLOBE Study of 62 Societies* (House, Hanges, Javidan, Dorfman, & Gupta, 2004). This contrast has provided a research-supported, practical means of comparison in which values can be predictably linked to patterns of behavior in a variety of situations. Such information forms the basis of the knowledge component of intercultural competence and can be invaluable in the preparation for an international assignment, working in a multicultural environment, or leading a global team. It is no surprise, then, that a number of assessment instruments have been developed to enable people to understand their own cultural value preferences and compare these with core values of other cultures to understand the challenges these differences might present in the work environment. Below are descriptions of five instruments (one from the United Kingdom and one from the United Arab Emirates) with a focus on cultural values and their impact on how we work.

- Argonaut Assessment (AA) *UK*

- Cultural Mapping and Navigation Assessment Tool (CMNAT) *U.A.E.*

- Cultural Orientation Indicator (COI)

- Culture in the Workplace (CWQ)

- Peterson Cultural Style Indicator (PCSI)

ARGONAUT

Developed by Coghill & Beery International in the United Kingdom, ArgonautOnline is actually a suite of cross-cultural e-learning tools that includes an assessment instrument. The Argonaut Assessment (AA) instrument, available in English only, employs a 20-minute questionnaire involving 12 dimensions (communication, conflict, problem solving, space, use of time, time spans, fate, rules, power, responsibility, group membership, and tasks) to produce a graphical map allowing comparison of the learner's self-perception, home culture, and target cultures from a list of more than 50 countries. This

contrastive mapping provides a basis for the formation of "personal strategies for international success." Results from the AA instrument can be combined with other online learning tools including personalized feedback and interactive tutorials. Access to the AA is gained through accreditation as a trainer or coach to use the ArgonautOnline tool suite.

CULTURAL MAPPING AND NAVIGATION ASSESSMENT TOOL (CMNAT)

Created by Knowledgeworkx in the United Arab Emirates, this tool employs a 72-question online inventory to produce a personal profile that details preferences on 12 bipolar cultural dimensions affecting workplace behaviors: growth, relationship, outlook, destiny, context, connecting, expression, decision making, planning, communication, accountability, and status. The CMNAT profile is incorporated in the second level of a four-level program (3 days of training for Levels 1–3 and ongoing coaching toward intercultural excellence in Level 4). The goal is the growth and application of intercultural intelligence to achieve intercultural excellence within multicultural teams. The assessment tool is also integrated with other (noncultural) assessment instruments (the Diamond Profiling Process) as part of intercultural leadership consultation. There is a 5-day intensive program for certification in the delivery of Levels 1–3 of the Cultural Mapping & Navigation Program suite of products; certification is granted only after delivery of the first program within 2 months of completing the accreditation training.

CULTURAL ORIENTATIONS INDICATOR (COI)

The COI is a Web-based self-reporting instrument developed by TMC (Training Management Corporation) that assesses individual preference within 10 cultural dimensions (environment, time, action, communication, space, power, individualism, competitiveness, structure, and thinking) drawn from the social science research mentioned above, plus other contributors, such as Edward Stuart, Milton Bennett, and Stephen Rhinesmith. The 108-question inventory yields a profile of preferences along a series of continua—17 in all, as several of the 10 dimensions have subcontinua. The profile of preferences (restricted to work-related behaviors and situations) enables comparison to other team members and national norms, allowing "gap analysis" and the coaching of strategies for bridging differences. Group or team aggregate reports are also available. The COI is also integrated into the Cultural Navigator, an online learning portal, and other programs offered by TMC. Test construction has been psychometrically validated, but one should note that not all the 10 dimensions have been equally researched globally. (On the other hand, having additional dimensions is useful to distinguish national cultures, which may appear quite similar with respect to a few dimensions.) The COI is available in Chinese, English, French, German, Italian, Japanese, and Spanish. The COI is supported by the *Cultural Orientations Guide* (4th edition), which supplies a context for understanding the instrument and its applications.

CULTURE IN THE WORKPLACE QUESTIONNAIRE (CWQ)

Based on the research and developed with the support of Geert Hofstede (2001), the CWQ, recently revised and now fully Web enabled, provides individual cultural profiles incorporating five cultural dimensions: individualism, power distance, certainty (uncertainty avoidance), achievement (masculinity), and time orientation (longterm orientation). The revised and more powerful version of the instrument was released in December 2006 by ITAP International, which licenses the Culture in the Workplace Questionnaire from Professor Hofstede and has the worldwide exclusive rights to its use. Profiles can be compared to average national values (established through the research of Hofstede and others) of 60 countries.

The 60-question inventory is completed online, resulting in nine-page personal reports, which can be immediately downloaded and printed by the user or saved for later distribution by a facilitator. The individual profile illustrates the user's score on each dimension in comparison with national averages of up to 15 selected countries. The report explains each dimension, lists the impact on work style of values at either end of the dimension (such as individual versus group orientation), and illustrates in a scenario the misunderstanding and conflict typical of interaction between individuals holding different orientations. It also provides specific analyses on the user's score on each dimension and the implications of the differences between the user scores and the comparison country scores.

The CWQ can be used with individuals or groups and also provides team reports for printing or download. Group averages can be compared in PowerPoint slides to numerous countries' average values, and the scores of individual members of the group can be confidentially compared with respect to each dimension, which is very useful for global teams. For both user and team reports, users or facilitators have a choice of how the data is graphically displayed, either in horizontal or vertical bar charts. Clients can also add special demographic fields so that, for example, data can be analyzed by location of multiple users.

The CWQ assists in the following:

1. Understanding how to work more effectively with people from different cultures

2. Harnessing the diversity of teams for greater effectiveness and productivity

3. Developing a common conceptual base and vocabulary for understanding and managing team diversity

4. Coaching executives with global responsibilities or with employees from different countries

5. Conducting cultural audits—e.g., determining the cultural preferences of classroom participants in different locations for tailoring instructional designs

CWQ profiles must be requested and debriefed by trainers or consultants certified in CW profile interpretation.

PETERSON CULTURAL STYLE INDICATOR (PCSI)

The PCSI, designed by Brooks Peterson of Across Cultures, Inc., consists of a 20-question online inventory that generates a five-dimensional profile (fifth dimension added in 2004). The dimensions are hierarchy/equality, direct/indirect, individuality/group, task/relationship, and risk/caution. One's profile is comparable to 70 country "norms" (chosen scores based on comparing various studies), with strategic recommendations for increasing business success. Research supporting the instrument is discussed on the Web site, which includes a list of corporate clients. The PCSI, designed as a stand-alone instrument, can be accessed immediately online for a fee, including the comparison of one's profile with other countries and suggestions for bridging gaps based on one's score. Peterson has also authored a book (*Cultural Intelligence: A Guide to Working With People From Other Cultures,* Intercultural Press, 2004).

◆ Tools for the Development Process: Intercultural Coaching

It is important to note that two of the tools introduced in Tools for the Selection Process: Competence (above) are equally suitable for the development process, particularly in a coaching environment. These are the Intercultural Readiness Check and the Intercultural Development Inventory.

The IRC yields a self-assessment of development with respect to four complex skills. In the debrief of the personal profile, a participant is advised of potential pitfalls and provided practical suggestions for development. The participant then creates, in collaboration with an intercultural trainer or coach, a plan for applying strengths and addressing weak points, which can be carried out with or without continued coaching.

The explanatory material provided with an IDI profile also contains descriptions for each of its scales, which list behaviors or attitudes associated with particular scores, the strengths associated with these, and the developmental tasks. Again with the help of an intercultural coach, a user can create and implement a developmental plan.

Here are three more instruments, developed in the United Kingdom and intended to be used developmentally. The first two instruments focus on adaptability and workplace behaviors, while the third incorporates values and workplace behaviors.

- The International Profiler (TIP)

- Global View 360°

- The Spony Profiling Model (SPM)

THE INTERNATIONAL PROFILER (TIP)

TIP, developed by WorldWork Ltd., in the United Kingdom, is a Web-based questionnaire and feedback process, available in English, German, French, and Italian, to assess the development needs of managers and other professions for international work. It is based on a set of 10 competencies (with 22 associated skills, attitudes, and areas of knowledge) derived from intercultural research and the practical experience of international professionals. The competencies are openness, flexibility, personal autonomy, emotional strength, perceptiveness, listening orientation, transparency, cultural knowledge, influencing, and synergy. TIP is an online psychometric inventory of 80 questions requiring about 45 minutes and generating a scored report (a hefty Feedback Book) for the certified consultant and client that provides structured feedback in terms of the energy, emphasis, and attention the user typically brings to a competency set. The feedback session, face-to-face or by telephone, consists of a structured discussion of the report with respect to the user's present or future international challenges. The intent is to identify three or four qualities requiring greater energy in the future. This results in a completion of a Personal Development Plan by the user entailing developmental areas, expected benefits from the development, and a S.M.A.R.T. action plan. The licensing process, required in order to employ TIP, provides a coaching manual.

GLOBAL VIEW 360°

Global View 360° is a panoramic version of the TIP providing feedback from 6 to 10 international colleagues, clients, friends, etc. who have observed the user in international contexts. It employs a reduced questionnaire (55 questions) focusing solely on the 10 key competencies and provides a gap analysis in the feedback report of the difference between the level of importance given to selected behaviors as compared with the perceived level of performance. Two free fields allow for open-ended commentary. The Global View 360° can be administered totally by its subject.

THE SPONY PROFILING MODEL (SPM)

The SPM is a unique integrated online instrument offered by FutureToBe in the United Kingdom that combines aspects of cultural values and work style instruments with 360° reporting on communication style (three work colleagues). It can be used to produce individual, team, and organizational culture profiles using the same concepts and frameworks, thereby providing consistency, rigor, and integration between the development of individuals, the building of teams, and the strategic alignment of organizations. Developed over 8 years of research and testing in Britain and France by Dr. Gilles Spony at the Cranfield School of Management, the SPM incorporates the work of cross-cultural psychologist Shalom Schwartz as well as the research of Geert Hofstede to produce profiles of work style preferences. These are graphically displayed on a values framework of two perpendicular universal axes: the vertical RELATIONSHIP axis of Self-Enhancement versus Consideration for Others and the horizontal TASK ORIENTATION axis of Group Dynamics versus Individual Dynamics. This results in a profile of 12 attitudinal orientations that yield 12 operational styles with a total of 36 subdivisions. The individual profile is then overlaid on a cultural values map to understand how work style may fit into or clash with various national cultures. The 230 questions of the work style questionnaire require about 45 minutes, while the communication style questionnaire for colleagues takes about 15 minutes. Because of the SPM's sophistication and complexity, accreditation in its use requires a 3-day training plus 1 day of assessment to use the instrument to a professional standard with respect to individuals, teams, and organizations. Candidates for accreditation are preferred to be holders of a Certificate of Competence in Occupational Testing (Level A) from the British Psychological Society and/or to have experience of other management models.

◆ Conclusion: Part II

The five value orientation tools described in Tools for the Development Process: Intercultural Awareness all incorporate the concept of behaviors (generally in a business context) differing rather predictably according to deeply held cultural preferences on values spectra that have been extensively researched globally over the last 50+ years. The instruments differ with respect to the value dimensions they employ, but they all produce personal profiles for comparison with other individuals and group or national averages. Such instruments can be powerful teaching tools for the knowledge component of intercultural competence, both before and during an assignment or while in a multicultural team; they provide a structured comparative basis for intercultural training and can also be used for coaching.

The two instruments described in Tools for the Development Process: Intercultural Coaching both look at workplace behaviors, one from an adaptability perspective and the other from a cultural values perspective. These tools lend themselves less to training and more to a coaching process.

◆ Assessment Instruments for the Global Workforce: Conclusion

The increasing demands of globalization raise the stakes of the cultural due-diligence process, both in the selection of appropriate personnel for sensitive positions in the multicultural workforce both at home and abroad and in employee preparation for intercultural demands of these assignments.

In making employment decisions with intercultural implications, no assessment instrument, by itself, can replace a thorough and systematic selection process including job-specific performance evaluation, interviews with candidates, colleagues, superiors, direct reports, and family (in the case of international assignments). On the other hand, with the availability of the instruments described above, it is equally inexcusable to make such decisions without the support of an appropriate intercultural assessment tool.

Whether one intends to do any task in the following list, or affect any other situation involving a need to select for or further develop intercultural competence, there are competitive choices among the sophisticated and powerful assessment tools described in this chapter to assist in that task:

- Help an employee or family decide whether to accept an international assignment

- Gather significant information for HR and management to assist in an culturally sensitive employment decision

- Choose the most culturally competent manager from a pool of candidates to lead a virtual multicultural team

- Determine the intercultural competence of a work group or leadership team

- Prepare a manager for an international assignment or a multicultural leadership position

- Prepare a team for work with a specific cultural group

- Coach an international transferee or the leader of a multicultural team

- Provide developmental input to a multicultural team

I encourage you to investigate further those that seem most relevant to your needs.

◆ *Discussion Questions*

1. Why is it powerful to be able to quantitatively assess one's level of intercultural competence?

2. Describe cultural empathy.

3. How can assessments like the ones described in this chapter assist in preparing an individual for an expatriate assignment?

4. How can some of the assessments described in this chapter be used to measure the effectiveness of an international assignment or study abroad?

◆ *References*

Bennett, M. J. (1993). Towards ethnorelativism: A developmental model of intercultural sensitivity. In R. M. Paige (Ed.), *Education for the intercultural experience* (2nd ed., pp. 21–71). Yarmouth, ME: Intercultural Press.

Goleman, D. (2006). *Social intelligence: The new science of human relationships.* New York: Bantam.

Hofstede, G. (2001). *Culture's consequences: Comparing values, behaviors, institutions, and organizations across nations* (2nd ed.). Thousand Oaks, CA: Sage.

House, R. J., Hanges, P. J., Javidan, M., Dorfman, P. W., & Gupta, V. (2004). *Culture, leadership, and organizations: The GLOBE study of 62 societies.* Thousand Oaks, CA: Sage.

ASSESSING LEADERSHIP BEHAVIOR AS IT RELATES TO INTERCULTURAL COMPETENCE

◆ Charles M. Fischer

The effective contemporary leader displays a unique blend of behaviors, motivations, and skills that enables him or her to guide an organization to successful outcomes. During this process the leader is challenged to sustain vision, energy, and optimal personal interrelationships simultaneously, so that the organization may confront new objectives and challenges in the future.

As stated in Chapter 1, Northouse (2004) explained that "Leadership is a process whereby an individual influences a group of individuals to achieve a common goal" (p. 3). A homogeneous and familiar cultural environment permits a leader to focus on general communication styles and predictable group dynamics, but in today's global environment, the blend of ethnicities, religions, race, and lifestyles demands that to be a transformational leader, one must also focus on being interculturally competent. Earley, Ang, and Tan (2006) concurred by stating, "A deep understanding of cultures around the world becomes imperative for effective leadership" (p. 185).

Are all leaders capable of functioning in multicultural settings? Probably not. What types of leadership behavior, then, suggest a predisposition toward being sensitive and open to other cultures? Does appreciating other cultures also mean that a leader can successfully lead culturally diverse organizations? Perhaps.

In this chapter I will investigate select leadership behavior that is foundational for intercultural competence; behavior that facilitates learning about, understanding, and working with people of varied and complex backgrounds. I will also review several popular leadership, communication, and style assessments to determine which aspects of their behavioral profiles may provide management with indicators of potentials for intercultural competence and when additional training may be necessary.

◆ *Leadership Qualities That Relate to Intercultural Competence*

Harris, Moran, and Moran (2004), defined global leadership as

> being capable of operating effectively in a global environment while being respectful of cultural diversity. This is an individual who can manage accelerating change and differences. The global leader is open and flexible in approaching others, can cope with situations and people disparate from his or her background, and is willing to reexamine and alter personal attitudes and perceptions. (p. 25)

When culture diversity exists within an organization, certain behaviors are favored and others repressed (Adler, 2002). Diversity, if positively managed, can increase creativity and innovation in organizations as well as improve decision making by providing different perspectives on problems. While a modern leader may lead from the top down and be transactional, he or she also empowers, motivates, and focuses followers

by allowing them to make key decisions and helping them identify with the organizational vision. Furthermore, for a leader to be followed and respected, he or she must engender trust as well as be an excellent cross-cultural communicator.

VISION AND ALIGNMENT

A successful organization, like a ship navigating its way to a faraway destination, must have a clear vision of where it is going and why. The captain must communicate this information clearly to his crew, who may often consist of different nationalities, in a manner that allows everyone to work together toward that objective. The positive impact of an alignment to a vision is consistently cited as essential to excellence. Leaders must not only believe in and support the purposes and visions of their organizations, but they must communicate them frequently to all stakeholders in a manner *that can be embraced by all players* to ensure alignment (Collins & Porras, 1994; Maull, Brown, & Cliffe, 2001). Childress and Senn (1995) identified clear alignment and common focus of leadership at the top as a major characteristic found in high-performance organizations.

TRUST AND OPENNESS

When employees are working in an environment that is friendly and supportive, higher productivity and loyalty result. High trust and openness among people is a major characteristic found in high-performance organizations (Childress & Senn, 1995). Empowering leaders believe that employees enjoy work, want responsibility, and are able to exercise self-direction and control. Different cultures require different approaches to authority, task structure, and accountability, so team management and independence need to be adjusted accordingly. But in all cases, when leaders are trusted, their followers are confident that they will be treated fairly and are more open to sharing information and feedback with those leaders (Robbins, 2005).

COMMUNICATION

Organizational communication is optimal when it is open, is culturally contextual, and exists at all levels. Successful organizations communicate clearly, ethically, and regularly. Robbins (2005) stated that communication creates motivation because it clarifies for staff what needs to be done, how well they are doing, and what they can do to improve. Happiness on the job is improved by communication because it provides a means for employees to express emotion in accordance with their cultural mores and folkways and offers fulfillment of their social needs. Job satisfaction is an important factor in organizations, although it may vary in its nature from culture to culture.

DECISION MAKING

Good leaders recognize the importance of allowing decisions to be made at the appropriate levels. Leaders should empower their followers to decide (Maull et al., 2001).

When leaders are thought to be in command, a different organizational culture is formed than when the leader's role empowers others to act (Reigle, 2001). Different cultures respond in unique ways to empowerment, and the interculturally competent leader understands these nuances and directs appropriately.

RESPECT AND VALUE

Ulrich (1996) pointed out that successful organizations treat individuals as long-term critical investments to be nurtured and maintained. Childress and Senn (1995) noted that in high-performance organizations people feel valued and appreciated. Leaders treat their followers as valuable and respected members of the team (Barrett, 2003). Maull and colleagues (2001) noted in their research that low work satisfaction resulted from companies that did not show loyalty and respect to employees. Being treated with respect and value is a leadership quality that is embraced by all cultures.

EMOTIONAL INTELLIGENCE

Goleman (1998) pointed out that "When I compared star performers with average ones in senior leadership positions, nearly 90% of the difference in their profiles was attributable to emotional intelligence factors rather than cognitive abilities" (p. 8). What exactly is "emotional intelligence," and how does it impact cultural competence?

EQ, or emotional intelligence, consists of two main categories of behavior: self-management and relationship skills. Self-management skills include (a) *self-awareness*, which, besides knowing one's strengths and weaknesses and having confidence in one's self-worth, also includes the ability to intuitively understand how ones actions may be affecting others. The latter quality is absolutely critical to cultural competence, (b) *self-regulation*, which deals with controlling one's emotions and having integrity, and (c) *motivation*, which relates to desire for achievement. Relationship skills include *empathy*, the ability to sense how others are feeling and an absolute requisite to becoming interculturally adept, and *social skills*, the ability to build rapport, to effectively communicate, being able to inspire people to work together in a cooperative manner, and to defuse conflicts. Social skills are arguably the most important quality for a leader to have in managing diversity.

Although one might think that a leader with a high EQ would possess the ideal qualities to manage a multicultural workforce, Earley, Ang, and Tan (2006) posed an interesting example of how this might not be necessarily true. They discuss an example of how a popular, high-EQ American "boss" had been assigned to run a factory in Mexico.

In an effort to create an initial bond with his Mexican management, he invited two managers to his home to visit. The managers quit the company shortly thereafter. After investigation, the American boss was surprised to discover that he had inadvertently lowered the power differential between himself and his managers, a value important in their culture, and they felt that they had no recourse but to leave the company.

Being sensitive and open to cultural differences and having social skills and empathy are simply not enough to make one a competent leader in a company with an abundance of diversity or, as in the Mexican factory example, if one is transferred to an American firm's foreign operation. Knowledge about a culture's traditions, practices, and patterns is also essential. However, the ability to appreciate, learn, embrace, and apply this knowledge is optimized by one's level of EQ.

TASK ORIENTATION VERSUS RELATIONSHIP ORIENTATION

The Contingency Theory of leadership is partially based on one's motivation by tasks or relationships. Meanwhile, Carl Jung proposed four personality types that are measured by several popular behavior assessments, including the DISC and MBTI, which will be discussed later in the chapter. Task orientation and relationship orientation are two of these characteristics, which are significant from a cultural point of view. Thomas and Inkson (2004) stated that "people from different cultures react to task-oriented leadership in different and often unpredictable ways" (p. 127). This inability of a culturally naive manager to predict reactions can lead to ineffective leadership.

FLEXIBILITY AND ADAPTABILITY

The ability for a leader to adapt his or her style to the circumstances at hand, or in the case of cultural diversity, to adjust one's approach to the particular nature of the individual that is being managed, is referred to as situational leadership. Although situational leadership is most often thought of in reference to how leaders favor or blend supportive or directive styles of leading, it can also refer to the manner in which the leader adjusts approaches as required by the subordinates.

Various scholars have developed theories on this concept. For example, Trompenaars and Hampden-Turner (1998) developed a model of cultural/transnational difference based on multiple dimensions. Additionally, another significant concept is that of national cultural differences manifested within organizations, as described by Geert Hofstede (1980). Through his study of the cultural dimensions of business, Hofstede determined that the dimensions of culture and national influences are power distance, individualism versus collectivism, masculinity versus femininity, uncertainty avoidance, and long- versus short-term orientation.

As Hofstede (1993) points out, management theories vary with cultures. In different countries there can be striking differences in management philosophies and practice; hence one can also surmise that to be an effective intercultural leader one must be able to grasp those disparities and use them accordingly when leading diverse groups, transactionally or transformationally. As we examine how behavioral assessments of leaders can relate to intercultural competence, this must be considered.

In reference to Hofstede's (1980) dimensions of cultural values (power distance, individualism, masculinity-femininity, uncertainty avoidance, long-term vs. short-term orientation), leaders may possess varying amounts of these organic tendencies based on their individual cultures and their degree of American acculturation. The behavioral assessments reviewed in this chapter will always be slightly skewed by that influence of one's culture. Unfortunately, "U.S. psychology is clearly a more respectable discipline in management circles than sociology" (Hofstede, 1993, p. 11), and this prejudice needs to be recognized as we look for behavioral characteristics that may relate to intercultural competence.

◆ *Leadership Assessments That Measure Parameters of Cultural Competence*

TAYLOR-JOHNSON TEMPERAMENT ANALYSIS (T-JTA)

The T-JTA is designed to measure nine common personality traits for the assessment of individual adjustment. These traits are considered important components of personal adjustment and significantly influence interpersonal relationships. The results enable one to compare self- and other perceptions:

Self-disciplined versus impulsive

Nervous versus composed

Depressive versus lighthearted

Subjective versus objective

Expressive–responsive versus inhibited

Sympathetic versus indifferent

Dominant versus submissive

Hostile versus tolerant

Active–social versus quiet

Over half of the traits measured on the T-JTA have a direct relationship to how an individual may interface with others from different cultures. The sympathetic, tolerant, and active–social leader behavior can be helpful with subordinates from many cultures, while expressive–responsive and dominant characteristics can be helpful with a limited number of cultures.

CALIFORNIA PSYCHOLOGICAL INVENTORY (CPI)

The California Psychological Inventory (CPI) is an assessment for adult development and is effective for assessing normal adult behavior. The results provide data on personality style, dealing with others, self-management, motivation and thinking style, and work-related measures. In each of these categories are a number of scales that provide useful data for exploring everyday behaviors such as dominance, conceptual fluency, tolerance, responsibility, leadership potential, and many more facets of development.

The Coaching Report for Leaders is a special report that combines CPI scale results for comparison with leaders from the database from the Center for Creative Leadership. This report covers the following core performance areas of leadership: self-management, organizational capabilities, team building and teamwork, problem solving, and sustaining the vision.

The parameters of dominance, conceptual fluency, and tolerance are particularly important in assessing the individual's ability to successfully interact with other cultures.

THE THEMATIC APPERCEPTION TEST (TAT)

The Thematic Apperception Test is a widely used psychological test. It uses a standard series of provocative yet ambiguous pictures about which the subject must tell a story. A subject is asked questions such as, "What dialogue might be carried on between these characters?" and "How might the 'story' continue after the picture shown?" Each story created by a subject is carefully analyzed to uncover underlying needs, attitudes, and patterns of reaction.

The TAT is a projective test in that, like the Rorschach test, its assessment of the subject is based on what he or she projects onto the ambiguous images. It assesses motives, including needs, for achievement, power, intimacy, and problem-solving abilities. Since the results are interpreted by the examiner, factors including race, gender, and social class, and ethnicity of both examiners and subjects influence the stories told and how they are evaluated. Cross-cultural interpretation can be problematic if the examiner is not interculturally competent; however, with optimal testing conditions, the results can reveal many insights into how the person being assessed feels about other cultures.

FUNDAMENTAL INTERPERSONAL RELATIONS ORIENTATION–BEHAVIOR (FIRO–B)

This instrument is used to uncover how personal needs affect behavior toward others and what one wants from them in return. It shows compatibility with other people as well as individual characteristics. This report is useful for identifying leadership operating styles. The FIRO–B instrument is based on the assumption that all human interaction may be divided into three categories: issues surrounding inclusion, issues surrounding control, and issues surrounding affection. Each item is measured in two dimensions: the expressed behavior of the employee and the behavior they want from others. This tool can provide insight into the employee's compatibility with other people.

All of the dimensions have components that reflect upon an individual's intercultural competency. The need for inclusion deals with forming new relations and associating with people and determines the extent of contact that a person needs.

The need for control is connected with decision making, influence, and persuasion between people and determines the extent of dominance that a person seeks. The need for affection is linked with emotional ties and warm connections between people and determines the extent of closeness that a person seeks.

MYERS-BRIGGS TYPE INDICATOR (MBTI)

According to the developers of the MBTI, all people can be classified using four basic criteria: extraversion–introversion, sensing–intuition, thinking–feeling, and judging–perceiving. Determining one's natural Myers-Briggs type or cognitive style is affected by our life-long learning experiences. After the onset of puberty, adult learning begins to overlay core personality, and there is blending of nature and nurture that can lend multiple facets to a personality. The different combinations of the criteria determine a type, and there may be sixteen types.

Sensing–intuition defines the method of information perception by a person. Sensing means that a person relies mainly on information received directly from the external world. Intuition means that a person relies mainly on information received from the internal or imaginative world. This correlates with Trompenaars and Hampden-Turner's (1998) model of cultural/transnational difference dimension of internal-external (environmental control) orientation.

Thinking–feeling defines how the person processes information. Thinking means that a person makes a decision mainly through logic. Feeling means that, as a rule, decisions are based on emotion. Assumptions about other cultures should come from both spectrums, appropriately.

Judging–perceiving defines how a person implements the information he or she has processed. Judging means that a person organizes all his or her life events and acts strictly according to plans. Perceiving means that the person is inclined to improvise and seek alternatives. As Harris and colleagues (2004) pointed out, "The global leader is open and flexible in approaching others, can cope with situations and people disparate from his or her background, and is willing to reexamine and alter personal attitudes and perceptions" (p. 25).

LEADERSHIP PRACTICES INVENTORY (LPI)

The consistency of results and the demonstration that leadership can be learned makes the Leadership Practices Inventory one of the most widely used assessments of its kind. From an analysis of the personal-best cases, a model of leadership was developed that consists of the Five Practices: challenging the process, inspiring a shared vision, enabling others to act, modeling the way, and encouraging the heart.

The approach to "inspiring a shared vision" involves "Enlisting others in a common vision by appealing to shared aspirations" (Kouzes & Posner, 2002, p. 22). In the global environment, the ability to articulate a common vision, cross-culturally, is a prime quality for a contemporary leader as is the ability to "enable others to act" by encouraging collaboration and cooperative goals. The alignment of shared values that the practice of "modeling the way" implies

can determine the success of a leader. So can celebrating the spirit of community in the culturally blended organizational subculture as is suggested in the practice of "encouraging the heart." Both can be assessed to some degree by the LPI.

Measurement of the Five Practices does not vary from industry to industry, profession to profession, community to community, and country to country, which makes the LPI an excellent cross-cultural instrument. It underscores the fact that good leadership is a universal and learnable process.

EMOTIONAL QUOTIENT (EQ)

As discussed earlier in this chapter, emotional intelligence is a set of acquired skills and competencies that predict positive outcomes for leaders. Having a high EQ also suggests that a leader is more open-minded and apt to achieve intercultural competence, given the proper experience and training.

The Rapid Emotional Quotient (REQ) inventory measures seven broad dimensions of emotional intelligence that are closely linked to Daniel Goleman's (1998) research. Besides providing a single score of emotional intelligence to give one a succinct indication of current overall EQ, it breaks down the total score across seven dimensions: innovation, social skills, self-awareness, motivation, emotions, intuition, and empathy. The cultural significance of each dimension was explained in the leadership qualities section of this chapter.

THE DISC ASSESSMENT

The DISC instrument is perhaps the most used behavioral assessment in industry throughout the world today. Its applicability is, therefore, cross-cultural. It measures four key personality factors: dominance, influence, steadiness, and compliance (from which the DISC assessment takes its name).

At the core of personality is the manner in which one responds to stimulus. Sets of circumstances or individual events (stimuli) cause people to act or react (respond) to them. A personality is defined, in this instance, as the sum of all a person's varying response styles to varying stimuli. Different kinds of DISC responses are grouped together into traits.

Dominant individuals are not naturally trusting of others and will seek to attain success on their own merits, without asking for or expecting help or support from those around them. Dominant, competitive behavior is characterized as a masculine trait by Hofstede (1980) in his discussions of culture and national influences. This trait may fly in the face of many cultures, as Trompenaars and Hampden-Turner (1998) pointed out when they discussed the individualism–communitarianism continuum and how different cultures respond to those ranges of behavior. Most leaders have higher "D" scores, but interculturally competent leaders usually also have strong "I" scores to offset the negative characteristics of dominance.

Influence is another factor described by a DISC assessment. The communicative and socially confident style of those with high influence can be important in multicultural settings. They are interested in other people and their backgrounds and seek to understand behavior. They are open and are natural communicators. A high "I" score usually indicates a potential for cultural competency; however, their desire to be open with other people sometimes can also be construed as lacking in tact.

The third of the four factors is *steadiness*. Personalities showing a high level of steadiness take a measured, steady approach to life. They are patient and undemanding, often showing sympathy for and loyalty to those around them. Culturally, in Western countries, steadiness is relatively rare in comparison with the other three factors. This is perhaps because the unassuming,

amiable type of personality associated with this factor tends to be less valued by society than those connected with the other three DISC factors. People of this profile are patient and sympathetic listeners, with a real interest in the problems and feelings of others, and are particularly capable of fulfilling support roles.

High-S personalities are resistant to change and will prefer to settle into a predictable and constant environment. They have an intrinsically passive approach and work best when given clear instructions and a high level of support. Because of this, they avoid conflict or confrontation. Hofstede (1980), in his forth dynamic, discusses the avoidance of uncertainty in Mediterranean and Japanese cultures, both preferring a heavy adherence to rules and structure.

The final DISC factor is *compliance.* Individuals who have a high "C" tend to be rule oriented and appreciate structure and order. They like detail, fact, precision, accuracy, and rules, which Trompenaars and Hampden-Turner (1998) described as particularism and specific in their cultural/transnational difference model. Personalities of this kind usually have personal codes of behavior and tend to regard etiquette and tradition as important, which is complimentary to some cultures.

◆ Measuring Leadership in Other Cultures

While the assessments that are included in this chapter may be used to identify intercultural competence proclivities in primarily American leaders, they may, in addition, be used to recognize and measure certain universal leadership qualities that are embraced by a host of other cultures. A number of the aforementioned assessments are also available in different languages and have had their format and content culturally adjusted. For example, the DISC instrument is marketed throughout North and South America, Europe, the Middle East, Africa, and Asia.

In the extensive GLOBE study of 17,000 leaders in 62 countries, 22 universal leadership qualities were determined as well as 8 universal impediments, or characteristics that detracted from an individual's ability to lead effectively. Some of the positive, pancultural characteristics the study found included the following: trustworthy, foresight, positive, administrative skilled, excellence oriented, win–win problem solver, just, plans ahead, dynamic, motivational, decisive, communicative, coordinator, honest, encouraging, motive arouser, dependable, effective bargainer, and team builder (House et al., 2004). The assessments that have been discussed are capable of measuring all of these attributes to varying degrees.

◆ Integrating Behavioral, Leadership, and Intercultural Competence Assessments

Behavioral assessments are widely used in industry today, primarily for recruitment screening. Although employment law does not permit a company to use test results as the sole basis for hiring an individual, the data derived from these types of tools can be immeasurably valuable in the overall selection process. Unfair discrimination occurs when employment decisions are based on race, sex, religion, ethnicity, age, or disability. Therefore, assessment instruments should be unbiased and fair to all groups.

The assessment products I have chosen to discuss in this chapter are tests that are commonly used by businesses, human resource professionals, industrial psychologists, and major human resource consulting companies.

Some are used routinely for screening and team building while others are specifically used to identify leaders. These instruments have been used for many years and are recognized for their insight and validity. To investigate other assessments, it is suggested that the *Mental Measurements Yearbook* be referenced. It consists of a continuing series of volumes that contain reviews of nearly all commercially available psychological, educational, and vocational tests published. New volumes do not replace old ones; rather, they supplement them.

Although cultural sensitivity assessments can be exceptionally valuable in choosing and training leaders, not all organizations can incorporate such assessments quickly and easily into their existing human resource and leadership development programs. If it is possible to infer predispositions to intercultural competence using existing employee records and currently used assessment batteries, organizations can immediately begin to, in some measure, evaluate this inclination. More important, however, assessments, such as the ones mentioned in this chapter, indicate cultural *trainability*, a behavioral factor that may be normally overlooked in preparing leaders for diversity.

To best use assessments to determine leadership and cultural competence, specific *position profiles* should be determined to reveal if an individual is suitable or where his or her training and development needs reside. Available assessment research data and the creation of benchmarks by assessing clearly identified culturally competent leaders can establish a valuable baseline. Candidates can then be compared to this standard. This is commonly referred to as a *gap analysis*. The objective should be to devise a simple system that will allow a human resources department to read and use the information gathered without having to mull over stacks of reports, have extensive training to understand the results, or require hours of study to interpret someone's scores.

Leaders are expected to provide direction to the organization, define and drive critical business opportunities, exercise power responsibly, obtain resources, sponsor the development of others, and represent the organization on crucial strategic issues. Organizations with diversity must identify interculturally competent leaders and address the gaps in their skill sets, behavior, values, and competencies.

◆ Conclusion

Although commercially available leadership assessments do not specifically address intercultural competence, they do reveal a great deal about an individual's potential to function and lead in today's multicultural workplace. By understanding which psychometric parameters to look for, one may predict competency and trainability.

In today's multicultural organizations, developing an ability to work effectively across cultures is considered a vital trait from which members of organizations will benefit immensely (Earley & Mosakowski, 2004). To explain the importance of CQ (cultural intelligence) for leadership success, Earley, Ang, and Tan (2006) state that "leadership behaviors that are effective in one culture are not necessarily effective in others. While some leadership qualities or practices may be universal, other leadership qualities, styles, and principles are situational or culture specific" (p. 175).

The need for leaders to establish high levels of CQ is detailed by Thomas and Inkson (2004), who proclaim that "the idea of great individuals [such as Gandhi, Abraham Lincoln, and Joan of Arc] is one that has had a great deal of influence on how we think about leadership" (p. 125). They pose incisive questions to consider when evaluating great leaders: "Would these people have been great leaders at another time, in another place, or indeed in another

culture?" and "Would these people have been great leaders with different followers, particularly followers who were culturally different from them?"

◆ Resources

1. California Psychological Inventory (CPI)
   - Center for Psychological Studies, Nova Southeastern University: www.nova.edu
   - Consulting Psychologists Press: www.cpp.com

2. DISC Assessment
   - Profiles Global, Inc.: http://profiles global.com/main.asp
   - Inscape Publishing: www.inscape publishing.com

3. Fundamental Interpersonal Relations Orientation–Behavior (FIRO–B)
   - Consulting Psychologists Press: www.cpp.com/products/firo-b/index.asp
   - Office of Organizational & Employee Development: http://training.usgs.gov/Leadership/FIRO-BAssess.html

4. Leadership Practices Inventory (LPI)
   - Kouzes, J. M., & Posner, B. Z. (2002). *The leadership challenge.* San Francisco: Jossey-Bass.

5. Myers-Briggs Type Indicator (MBTI)
   - The Myers & Briggs Foundation: www.myersbriggs.org

6. Rapid Emotional Quotient (REQ)
   - My Skills Profiles: www.myskills profile.com/tests.php

- Goleman, D. (1998). *Working with emotional intelligence.* London: Bloomsbury.

7. Taylor-Johnson Temperament Analysis

   - Psychological Publications: www.tjta.com/abouttjta.htm

8. Thematic Apperception Test (TAT)

   - University of Tennessee: http://utk.edu

   - Encyclopedia of Mental Disorders: www.minddisorders.com/PyZ/Thematic-Apperception-Test.html

◆ Discussion Questions

1. Is it possible to be a transformational leader without a moderate to high degree of intercultural competence?

2. Does a higher EQ automatically mean that one is able to interact effectively with individuals from other cultures?

3. How does the MBTI stage of Sensing correlate with Trompenaars and Hampden-Turner's Internal–External orientation?

4. How does an effective leader align a multicultural team toward the vision and goals of the organization?

◆ References

Adler, N. J. (2002). *International dimensions of organizational behavior* (4th ed.). Cincinnati, OH: South-Western.

Barrett, R. (2003). Improve your cultural capital. *Industrial Management, 45*(5), 20.

Childress, J., & Senn, L. (1995). *In the eye of the storm: Reengineering corporate culture.* Long Beach, CA: Leadership Press.

Collins, J., & Porras, J. (1994). *Build to last: Successful habits of visionary companies.* New York: HarperCollins.

Earley, P. C., Ang, S., & Tan, J. S. (2006). *CQ: Developing cultural intelligence at work.* Stanford, CA: Stanford University Press.

Earley, P., & Mosakowski, E. (2004, October). Cultural intelligence. *Harvard Business Review, 82*(10), 139–146.

Goleman, D. (1998). *Working with emotional intelligence.* London: Bloomsbury.

Harris, P. R., Moran, R. T., & Moran, S. V. (2004). *Managing cultural differences: Global leadership for the twenty-first century* (6th ed.). Oxford, UK: Elsevier-Butterworth-Heinemann.

Hofstede, G. (1980). *Culture's consequences: International differences in work-related values.* Beverly Hills, CA: Sage.

Hofstede, G. (1993). Cultural constraints in management theories. *Executive, 14,* 81.

House, R. J., Hanges, P. J., Javidan, M., Dorfman, P. W., Gupta, V., & Associates (Eds.). (2004). *Culture, leadership, and organizations: The GLOBE study of 62 societies.* Thousand Oaks, CA: Sage.

Kouzes, J. M., & Posner, B. Z. (2002). *The leadership challenge.* San Francisco: Jossey-Bass.

Maull, R., Brown, P., & Cliffe, R. (2001). Organizational culture and quality improvement. *International Journal of Operations and Production Management, 21*(3), 302.

Northouse, P. (2004). *Leadership: Theory and practice* (3rd ed). Thousand Oaks, CA: Sage.

Reigle, R. (2001). Measuring organic and mechanistic cultures. *Engineering Management, 13*(4), 3.

Robbins, S. (2005). *Essentials of organizational behavior.* Upper Saddle River, NJ: Pearson/Prentice Hall.

Thomas, D. C., & Inkson, K. (2004). *Cultural intelligence: People skills for global business.* San Francisco: Berrett-Koehler.

Trompenaars, F., & Hampden-Turner, C. (1998). *Riding the waves of culture: Understanding cultural diversity in global business* (2nd ed.). New York: McGraw-Hill.

Ulrich, D. (1996). *Human resource champions.* Boston: Harvard Business School Press.

THE INTERCULTURAL DEVELOPMENT INVENTORY

An Approach for Assessing and Building Intercultural Competence

◆ Mitchell R. Hammer

◆ *Mary's Dilemma*

Consider the following situation.[1] It was 9 months ago that Acme Pharmaceutical Company formally agreed to a limited partnership arrangement with Jaca Marketing of Japan. The purpose of this partnership is to permit Acme to introduce a line of pharmaceutical products in Japan. Jaca is a well-respected and established marketing firm in Japan that knows the "ins and outs" of obtaining government approvals so that the medicines developed by Acme can be formally approved for sale to Japanese consumers. At the time of the signing of the agreements, both the president of Acme and the president of Jaca expressed their enthusiastic support for and confidence in the newly formed partnership. For Acme, Jaca represents an essential method of introducing pharmacological products into the Japanese arena. For Jaca, the opportunity to represent a large, U.S.-owned multinational corporation that wants to do business in Japan solidifies Jaca's position as a premier partner for foreign corporations desiring to bring their services and products to the Japanese consumer.

You are an intercultural management consultant, recently hired by Acme to help ensure the success of the partnership with Jaca Marketing. Your main contact at Acme is Mary Jones, a European American female, age 35. Mary has been employed in the pharmaceutical industry for the past 15 years and is currently the director of international marketing for Acme and team leader for this critical project.

Soon after the contracts were signed, problems began to emerge that were largely unanticipated among key Acme and Jaca team members (who are responsible for coordinating this large project). Mary, as team leader from Acme, has particularly felt the brunt of confusion and misunderstanding with her marketing counterparts from Jaca. The following portrait seems to be emerging.

Acme team members are quite frustrated as their carefully negotiated business goals for each quarter during the past 9 months appear, from their perspective, to have been either ignored or incompetently addressed by the Jaca team. On numerous occasions, Mary has been briefed by her confused team about how they feel their Jaca counterparts are dropping the ball and not trying hard enough to obtain the proper government approvals. Until these approvals are given, the overall marketing effort remains in a holding pattern. In addition, many of the frontline Acme team members have commented that they feel they are not taken seriously and rarely receive a "straight answer" from Jaca.

Mary has heard from some of the Jaca team members that the American team members don't understand how "things are done" in Japan. Recently, the Jaca team leader communicated in an email to Mary that the Americans involved in this project are making the situation most difficult for the project to move forward in a timely manner. When Mary shared this information with her Acme team, they erupted with, "A timely manner! We are already 6 months behind on our agreed-upon objectives!"

Mary is perplexed. It is clear to her (and the Acme and Jaca team members) that (a) both organizations genuinely desire success for this partnership, (b) both organizations are in agreement concerning the goals and timeline, and (c) both organizations have committed sufficient financial and human resources to make this effort successful. After reviewing this situation, Mary has called you to come and help. What recommendations would you give Mary that would help restore confidence among both the Acme and Jaca team members? What actions would you suggest Mary take to specifically assess how cultural differences may be negatively affecting each group's effort at working collaboratively toward an agreed-upon set of goals?

In formulating your response, the information presented in this chapter will likely be most helpful in developing a strategic intervention for the Acme team members (and later, possibly, for the Jaca team as well). One of the key tools you may wish to add to your toolkit is the Intercultural Development Inventory (IDI). For example, you can administer the IDI to the Acme team members, and this will produce a profile of their collective capability to recognize and adapt to cultural differences between the American members and their Japanese colleagues. The IDI profiles can also be developed for individual team members. With this information, you would be able to engage in targeted, intercultural coaching of key team leaders that focuses on those cultural differences that are making a difference in the communication between the Acme and Jaca teams. In short, the IDI can provide the Acme team a clear picture of the way in which they approach the cultural aspects of their working relationship with Jaca. Armed with this information, targeted interventions can be undertaken to help the team members more effectively deal with the cultural differences that are negatively affecting the success of the project.

◆ Introduction

Corporate leadership gurus and educators alike recognize that the sin qua non of effective management in our global community is the development of intercultural competence at both the individual and organizational level (Adler, 1997; Barnlund, 1998 Harris, Moran, & Moran, 2004). Indeed, the ability to engage in effective interaction across cultures is a core capability in the 21st century not only for our business leaders but for our political leaders as well. Without systematic efforts at developing intercultural competence, our world community may well devolve into increased conflict and violence, fulfilling Samuel Huntington's (1996) observation that human conflict and violence in the new millennium will not be primarily generated from economic or ideological grounds but rather from the divide of cultural differences.

Historically, we have not had a sufficient "intercultural competence toolkit" from which to assess how "competent" an individual or an organization is in terms of working across cultures nor a framework from which systematic efforts at developing increased intercultural competence can be undertaken. With the development of the Intercultural Development Inventory (IDI) (Hammer, 2007; Hammer, Bennett, & Wiseman, 2003), our "toolkit" has been greatly expanded.[2] The IDI is the premier cross-culturally valid and reliable measure of intercultural competence. The IDI has direct application to global leadership, defined by Harris and colleagues (2004) as "being capable of operating effectively in a global environment while being respectful of cultural diversity" (p. 25). While a relatively new assessment tool, the IDI is already demonstrating significant impact with over 1,200 qualified IDI administrators from over 30 countries. Further, the IDI has been rigorously "back translated" (Brislin, 1970, 1976, 1980) into 12 languages, thus ensuring both linguistic and conceptual equivalence.

◆ What Is the IDI?

The IDI is a 50-item paper and pencil (and online) questionnaire with selected demographics that can be completed in about 15 to 20 minutes. Accompanying the IDI questionnaire are four open-ended "contexting" questions individual respondents may complete. These open-ended questions help further capture the experiences around cultural differences of the respondent. Once the IDI is completed, the IDI analytic structure generates an individual (or group) graphic profile of the respondent's overall position on the intercultural development continuum. This continuum, presented in Figure 16.1, identifies specific orientations toward cultural differences that range from more monocultural perspectives to more intercultural mindsets.[3]

The intercultural development continuum represents a progression from a less complex perception of and consequently a less complex experience of culturally based patterns of difference to a more complex experience around cultural diversity. What does it mean to say that an individual has a less complex or a more complex perception and experience of cultural difference? In general, it suggests that individuals who have a more detailed set of frameworks for perceiving and understanding patterns of cultural differences between themselves and others have the capability of then experiencing observed cultural differences in ways that approximate how a person from that other culture might experience the world (M. J. Bennett, 2004). The capability of shifting cultural perspective and adapting behavior to cultural context represents an intercultural mindset. In contrast, perceiving cultural differences from one's own cultural perspective is indicative of a more monocultural mindset.

Figure 16.1   Intercultural Development Continuum

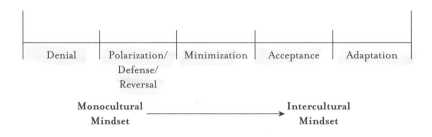

◆ Dimensions of Culture Differences

While there are many and varied patterns of cultural difference that can be identified, Harris and colleagues (2004) offered a useful framework of 10 "culture general" dimensions of cultural difference that often can make a difference in our effectiveness in interacting with people from different cultural communities: (1) sense of self and space, (2) communication and language, (3) dress and appearance, (4) food and feeding habits, (5) time and time consciousness, (6) relationships, (7) values and norms, (8) beliefs and attitudes, (9) learning, and (10) work habits and practices. The underlying intercultural development continuum that is assessed by the IDI posits that individuals and groups have a greater or lesser capability to perceive differences between themselves and others that are "culturally grounded."

DEVELOPMENTAL AND TRAILING ISSUES

The IDI assesses a respondent's or group's primary orientation toward cultural differences (such as intercultural conflict styles; Hammer, see Chapter 17, this volume; Hammer, 2005) along this developmental continuum outlined in Figure 16.1. In addition, the IDI profile indicates key developmental,

or "leading," issues that directly face the respondent that, when systematically addressed, can result in further progression along the continuum. Also, the IDI profile identifies "trailing" issues that are currently holding back the respondent or group from moving further along the developmental continuum. These trailing issues represent unresolved aspects associated with an earlier orientation. In this sense, the IDI profile identifies an individual's or group's primary orientation but also reflects the individual's experience of cultural differences in terms of the degree to which the respondent has resolved issues associated with earlier (and less complex) perspectives toward cultural differences. It also indicates the immediate challenges the individual faces in further developing a deeper set of perceptions and consequently a more complex experience of cultural diversity.

WHAT ARE THE CORE ORIENTATIONS TOWARD CULTURAL DIFFERENCES?

The intercultural development continuum identifies five core orientations that reflect a distinct set of perceptions and experiences around cultural differences. Movement along the continuum begins with the more monocultural orientations of denial and polarization (defense/reversal), through a more transitional mindset of minimization, to the more intercultural or global mindsets of acceptance and adaptation. The capability to more deeply shift cultural perspective and adapt behavior to cultural context is most fully realized through the orientation of adaptation.

The monocultural orientations of denial and polarization (defense/reversal) reflect a view that "one's own culture is central to reality" (M. J. Bennett, 1993, p. 30) and is, therefore, more ethnocentric in the way individuals perceive and experience cultural diversity. At the other end of the development continuum lie the intercultural orientations of acceptance and adaptation. These orientations reflect a sense that one's own cultural patterns are "not any more central to reality than any other culture," that cultural differences need to be understood relative to one another, and culturally based actions and behavior must be seen within a specific cultural context (M. J. Bennett, 1993, p. 46). Between the more monocultural mindset and the intercultural orientations is minimization. Minimization is a transitional state between the more ethnocentric orientations of denial and polarization (defense/reversal) and the more intercultural states of acceptance and adaptation (M. J. Bennett, 2004; Hammer et al., 2003).

To add to the explanations in Chapter 8, the earliest developmental state is that of *denial*. Denial is most reflective of dominant culture individuals who have sparse experience with people from different cultural backgrounds. As a result, they often have a limited, stereotypic set of perceptions of the cultural "other." Other cultures and the differences they bring into social interaction are typically not recognized. Further, a denial orientation maintains a sense of disinterest and even avoidance of cultural diversity. In contrast, nondominant culture members are less likely to maintain a denial orientation toward cultural diversity, as these members often need to deal with cultural differences (in terms of the dominant group's practices)

within the larger society. Denial represents a low level of capability for understanding cultural differences and adapting to these differences (which are likely to go unnoticed).

Denial in an organization can be expressed in terms of emphasizing the need for newly hired "diverse" members to fit in the culture of the company, the offer to help diverse members "learn the organization," and an overemphasis on maintaining historically derived core values and practices. The primary issue to be resolved is to begin to notice and confront cultural differences (M. J. Bennett, 2004; Hammer, 2007). This process begins to establish a set of categories for understanding cultural diversity.

Unfortunately, these emerging categories often take the form of stereotypes. It is this developmental process that typically leads an individual to adapt a more polarization (defense/reversal) orientation. A second factor that moves individuals from denial to polarization is that as more people from different culture groups move into one's community or organization, the need to increase interaction with people from these different groups arises.

This creates conditions for the emergence of *polarization*, a judgmental orientation grounded in a sense of "us" and "them." A polarization orientation can take the form of a defense or reversal perspective. *Defense* is an orientation in which perceptions are polarized in terms of "us versus them," where "our" ways of doing things are seen as superior to the way things are done in other cultural communities. There can also be a sense of denigration toward other cultural patterns. Overall, cultural differences are experienced as divisive and threatening. Cultural difference is seen as an obstacle to be overcome, and this sense of superiority can lead to overconfidence and a view that "our" way of doings things is the best way.

In an organization, defense can manifest itself in terms of an insistence that "minorities need to figure out how to get things done in this organization" and an assumption that the goal of diversity efforts should be to help diverse members adopt our ways (with little awareness of the need or value of adapting to the ways of other, diverse groups).

A distinct orientation—yet a variation within polarization is that of *reversal*. Reversal, as the name implies, polarizes cultural differences into "us and them" but reverses that polarization, where the cultural practices and values of the "other cultural group" are viewed as superior to one's own culture. This can take the form of "going native" or "passing." Unlike defense, however, reversal consists of generally positive evaluations toward other cultures. However, these evaluations are also stereotypic and reflect little deeper cultural understanding of the other cultural community. In reversal, individuals are often uncritical toward other cultural practices and overly critical toward their own group. As such, they may idealize or romanticize the other culture (M. J. Bennett, 2004).

Whether polarization is more defense or reversal, the key resolution issue is to recognize the stereotypic nature of one's perceptions and experience of the other culture and to actively identify commonalities between one's own views, needs, and goals and that of the other.

This effort at focusing on shared commonalities (rather than what is experienced from a defense/reversal orientation as divisive differences) creates the conditions for the emergence of *minimization*—an orientation in which cultural difference is subsumed into more culturally familiar categories (M. J. Bennett, 2004). Minimization is a state whereby an individual may well be familiar with different cultures and aware of differences in cultural patterns (e.g., values, beliefs, communication styles). However, the approach taken in minimization toward these recognized cultural differences is to focus on more unifying frameworks within which the cultural differences may be better understood—albeit understood largely from one's own cultural

perspective. A minimization perspective is able to recognize some patterns of cultural difference; but the orientation emphasizes dealing with these identified differences through a commonality lens that can mask underlying differences. Typical commonality frameworks can include an over-application of human (i.e., physical, psychological) similarity as well as universal values and principles.

For dominant group members, this emphasis on commonalities (generated largely from one's own cultural framework) may mask a deeper awareness of "privilege" and may lead to an overestimation of one's own cultural sensitivity or competence. For nondominant members, the experience of minimization can be different. That is, often nondominant members are aware of how privilege functions in the community and organization. Minimization therefore functions more as strategy for getting things done within a dominant cultural context. This can take the form, for instance, of "go along to get along." In this sense, minimization (the use of commonality strategies) is a way to focus attention away from deeper cultural differences to accomplish some set of goals (e.g., maintain cordial relations in the workplace).

At the organizational level, minimization tends to pursue efforts at structural integration and equity concerns and elimination of bias, prejudice, and discrimination. This is accomplished by establishing common policies, practices, and universal principles and values in the organization that clearly spell out the firm's commitment and activities to eliminate cultural, ethnic, gender, age, sexual orientation, and other group stereotypes and discriminatory behavior. Clearly these goals support improved intercultural relations. Nevertheless, they do not adequately address issues focused on valuing diversity and, even less, on adapting to cultural differences.

The issue for resolution in minimization is to deepen understanding of one's own culture (cultural self-awareness) and to increase understanding of culture-general and specific frameworks for making sense (and more fully attending to) culture differences.

Resolution of this core minimization issue creates conditions for progression into an *acceptance* orientation—that is, as individuals begin to more deeply explore cultural differences, they recognize that these cultural patterns need to be understood from the perspective of the other culture. As this develops, an appreciation of the complexity of cultural differences arises. From this vantage point, individuals are now able to experience their own cultural patterns of perception and behavior as one of a number of different but equally complex sets of perceptions and behavioral patterns. Acceptance, therefore, involves increased self-reflexiveness in which one is able to experience others as both different from oneself yet equally human.

Individuals at the acceptance level are typically curious and interested in cultural differences and committed to the cultural diversity agenda. However, while they recognize and acknowledge the relevance of culture and cultural context, they are unclear on how to appropriately adapt to cultural difference. Within an organization, acceptance reflects a genuine desire to learn about and adapt to cultural differences.

The main issue of resolution for an acceptance orientation concerns value or ethical relativity. As Milton J. Bennett (2004) comments, "to accept the relativity of values to cultural context (and thus to attain the potential to experience the world as organized by different values), you need to figure out how to maintain ethical commitment in the face of such relativity" (p. 69). In other words, the primary task for further development is to reconcile the "relativistic" stance that aids understanding of cultural differences without giving up one's own cultural values and principles. Movement through acceptance therefore involves deepening one's perceptions of other cultures, demonstrating a willingness to understand different (and even abhorrent) cultural practices from

that other cultural perspective, and an increased capability to weigh one's own cultural values alongside the values from the other cultural perspective in such as way as to make ethical judgments in which cultural differences are fully taken into consideration. These judgments are made, however, not by employing completely culturally relativistic criteria (i.e., what is judged good in another culture should remain so), but rather employing reflective consideration of one's cultural values and those of the other group that ultimately address the existential question, "What kind of world do we want to live in?" As Milton J. Bennett (2004) comments, "resolution of the issue of value relativity and commitment allows you to take the perspective of another culture without losing your own perspective" (p. 70).

As this occurs, conditions for the emergence of *adaptation* arise. Adaptation involves the capability of shifting perspective to another culture and adapting behavior according to cultural context. Adaptation involves the capability to at least partially take the perspective of one or more cultures, bridge between different cultural systems, and change behavior in culturally appropriate and authentic ways (Hammer, 2007). Adaptation is characterized by an increased repertoire of cultural frameworks and behaviors available to reconcile unity and diversity goals and a sense that one's living in a multicultural world demands intercultural competence (performance in adaptation). Within organizations, adaptation orientations encourage the development of intercultural competence/adaptation among *all* members. Further, domestic and international cultural differences are often used as a resource for multicultural teams and the organization as a whole.

The major issue to resolve in adaptation is how to maintain an authentically competent intercultural experience—one in which substantial cognitive frame shifting and behavioral code shifting is occurring such that an individual is able to experience the world in ways that approximate the experience of the cultural "other."

The obvious question arises, "How can you have the *same* experience of someone who is from another culture?" Of course, the answer to this phrasing of the question must be, "I cannot have the same cultural experience as you do because I am not you nor am I a member of your cultural community." Yet this prompts the more important question: "Can you develop a perceptual set of categories of cultural difference as a new lens within which to sufficiently shift your perspective and adapt behavior to a culturally different context in ways that allow you to *approximate* the cultural experience of the other?" The answer to this question is yes. After all, many, many individuals achieve just this level of adaptation—we often call this being bicultural or multicultural. That is, the individual possesses a deep capacity to experience the world from two or more different cultural platforms. In short, they are authentically able to shift perspective and adapt behavior to cultural context. In this sense, to demonstrate complex intercultural competence is grounded in this adaptation capability.

Being bicultural/multicultural in adaptation does not suggest, however, that the individual also has developed a bi/multicultural identity. Indeed, the development of such an expanded identity "does not represent a significant improvement in intercultural competence" (M. J. Bennett, 2004, p. 72).

THE DISTINCTIVENESS OF CULTURAL IDENTITY

The IDI also assesses, as a separate and distinct dimension from those orientations placed along the developmental continuum, the degree of *cultural disengagement* an individual or group possesses. Cultural disengagement reflects a sense of being disconnected and not feeling fully a part of one's cultural group (Hammer, 2007). This sense of cultural alienation from one's own cultural group can arise from any number of experiences, including significant adaptation to one or more cultures. In this latter case, Bennett and Bennett (2004) suggested that "at some point, their sense of cultural identity may have been loosed from any particular mooring, and they need to reestablish identity in a way that encompasses their broadened experience. In so doing, their identities become 'marginal' to any one culture" (p. 157; see also J. M. Bennett, 1993).[4]

It is important to recognize, however, that cultural disengagement may arise from any number of other experiences—experiences that are not grounded in the developmental state of adaptation. For example, cultural disengagement may derive from an individual's collective experience of being rejected or made to feel deviant from his/her own cultural group. When this occurs, the individual may have the experience of alienation from his or her own group. This sense of cultural disengagement does not necessarily mean, therefore, that the individual is functioning at the developmentally complex level of adaptation. In fact, the individual may have limited experience with other cultural groups and therefore likely will not feel stuck between two cultural identities.

From the perspective of the intercultural development continuum, cultural disengagement is not developmentally a core orientation. Cultural disengagement as assessed by the IDI is therefore an independent dimension of one's experiences around cultural identification but is not an orientation that falls along the intercultural development (competence) continuum described in Figure 16.1.

To conclude, the IDI measures a number of core orientations toward cultural difference along an intercultural development continuum. These orientations range from more monocultural mindsets (denial, polarization, defense, reversal) through minimization to more intercultural mindsets (acceptance, adaptation). In addition, the IDI also assesses cultural disengagement (alienation from one's own cultural group identity). This measure of cultural disengagement is independent, however, from the progression of core orientations that comprise the intercultural development continuum.

IS THE IDI VALID ACROSS CULTURES?

The psychometric testing of the IDI indicates that the IDI is a cross-culturally generalizable, valid, and reliable assessment of an individual's and group's core orientations toward cultural differences (Hammer, 1999; Hammer et al., 2003; Hammer, 2007). There have been three distinct versions of the IDI (v.1, v.2, and v.3).[5] Overall, these various tests clearly demonstrate that the IDI is a robust measure of the core orientations of the intercultural development continuum (and cultural disengagement) and that the assessment is generalizable across cultures.

IDI v.1

IDI v.1 was a 60-item measure derived from a sample of 312 culturally diverse respondents. The following scales and reliabilities were identified: Denial (10 items, α = .87), Defense (10 items, α = .91), Minimization (10 items, α = .87), Acceptance (10 items, α = .80), Cognitive Adaptation (10 items, α = .85), and Behavioral Adaptation (10 items, α = .80). In this first version, individual scale scores were obtained, but placement along the intercultural development continuum was not determined (Hammer, 1999).

IDI v.2

IDI v.2 was a 50-item measure, the development of which was undertaken based on a desire to develop additional measures for reversal and integration (as specified in the

original DMIS theory) as well as the results from factor analytic research conducted on IDI v.1 by Paige, Jacobs-Casuto, Yershova, and DeJaeghere (1999). Therefore, a new sample of 591 individuals responded to 122 items. Analysis of these responses using confirmatory factor analysis (CFA) resulted in the best fit to the data of a five-factor model that consists of 50 items divided into the following scales: DD scale (13 items, denial/defense, α = .85), R scale (9 items, reversal, α = .80), M scale (9 items, minimization, α = .83), AA scale (14 items, acceptance/adaptation, α = .84), and an EM scale (5 items, encapsulated marginality, α = .80)[6] (Hammer et al., 2003).

IDI v.3 (Current Version)

Recently, I decided to undertake a more comprehensive testing of the IDI across culturally different groups (see Hammer, 2007, for a more detailed description of this additional research effort). I administered the 50-item IDI to a significantly larger, cross-cultural sample of 4,763 individuals from 11 distinct cross-cultural sample groups. These individuals came from the profit sector, international organizations, nonprofit organizations, and high schools and colleges. All participants completed the IDI in their native language using rigorously back-translated versions of the IDI unless English was the language of the organization (e.g., managers from the international organization took the IDI in English due to exceptionally high English language fluency).

Results from this more comprehensive confirmatory factor analysis (CFA) of the data enable empirical distinctions to emerge between the denial and defense orientations and between acceptance and adaptation perspectives, resulting in the following seven scales: Denial (7 items, α = .66), Defense (6 items, α = .72), Reversal (9 items, α = .78), Minimization (9 items, α = .74), Acceptance

(5 items, α = .69), Adaptation (9 items, α = .71), and Cultural Disengagement (5 items, α = .79). In addition, two composite measures were created. The Perceived Orientation score, computed using an unweighted formula, reflects where the individual or group places itself along the intercultural development continuum (PO, α = .82). The Developmental Orientation score (DO, α = .83) is computed using a weighted formula and identifies the main or primary orientation of the individual or group along the intercultural development continuum. The developmental orientation is the perspective the individual or group is most likely to use in those situations that involve cultural difference. Further, comparative CFA testing also shows these seven core orientations are the best fit to the data compared to either a two-factor model of monoculturalism and interculturalism or the five-factor model used in IDI v.2.[7]

Overall, these results testing IDI v.3 persuasively demonstrate the generalizability of the IDI across cultural groups. Additional analysis of the data by distinct sample groups also clearly demonstrates the culture-specific applicability of IDI v.3 (i.e., across specific cultural communities). In addition, the intercorrelations among the seven dimensions of the 50-item IDI v.3 support the developmental continuum and the relationships among the core orientations: (a) there is a strong correlation between defense and denial (r = .83), (b) there is a strong correlation between acceptance and adaptation (r = .64), (c) reversal is positively correlated with denial (.34) and with defense (.37) and not significantly correlated with acceptance (.01) or adaptation (.12), and (d) there are negative correlations between the Defense and Denial scales and the Acceptance and Adaptation scales. Cultural disengagement is most correlated with reversal (.43) and, secondarily, denial (.22) and not significantly correlated with defense, minimization, acceptance, or adaptation, supporting the sense that cultural disengagement is focused on the disconnection experienced toward one's own cultural group.

WHAT ARE THE MOST EFFECTIVE APPLICATIONS OF THE IDI (V.3)?

The IDI assesses how individuals and groups construe their social interactions with people from different cultural communities. To date, over 1,200 individuals have attended the IDI Qualifying Seminar (QS) to learn how to administer this assessment tool. Additional, more advanced seminars are currently offered to help these qualified IDI administrators effectively implement IDI guided-development efforts in areas such as individual coaching, team building, training needs assessment, program evaluation, organizational development, and basic research efforts.

A key area of IDI impact is helping individuals (e.g., managers) better assess their capability for recognizing and effectively responding to cultural diversity. Prior to the development of the IDI, managers and employees from different cultures in organizations often engaged in fruitless and at times divisive conversations around such questions as the following:

- Is there conscious or unconscious bias in the way we hire, train, and promote people from different cultures in our organization?

- To what extent is prejudice and racism present in our company?

- To what degree do our own organizational practices reinforce "privilege" in the way we do things in our firm?

- What does it mean when our annual employee survey indicates that people of color and/or women feel our organization is less open and less welcoming to culturally diverse managers and employees?

- How prepared are our human resources to fully engage the contributions of customers, clients, employees, and managers who are from different cultures?

- In our multicultural, global organization, how do we establish common frameworks, policies, and practices that create a sense of shared vision and at the same time value diversity?

These and other critical challenges around cultural diversity face our organizations in the 21st century. The IDI provides a powerful assessment platform from which to effectively engage these important questions in a deeper conversation. The IDI provides key insights on the capabilities of managers and employees for dealing with cultural differences. It provides a picture of both an individual's and a group's primary orientation toward cultural differences—and this orientation frames how each of the questions above will be addressed.

WHO SHOULD
ADAPT TO WHOM?

One common question I am often asked when I consult with organizations around issues of cultural diversity is, "Who should adapt to whom?" Answers to this question range from neither party should adapt to the other to mutual adaptation among the parties. If one's goal, however, is to more deeply understand and relate to cultural practices, values, and behaviors different from one's own, then intercultural mindsets (e.g., adaptation orientation: the capability to shift cultural perspective and appropriately adapt behavior to cultural context; Harris et al., 2004; Wurzel, 2004) are more helpful than monocultural (ethnocentric) mindsets (e.g., denial, defense, reversal orientations; M. J. Bennett, 1993; 2004). An IDI profile of key leaders and the larger group profile of

the organization can reveal what perspectives will be taken in answering the question "Who should adapt to whom?" and what specific company policies, training programs, and other interventions will likely be recommended. Further, the IDI profile results also indicate which of these perspectives and actions taken will likely be more or less effective in achieving a more interculturally capable and responsive organization.

For individuals and groups with a primary orientation of denial or defense, this question often reflects an underlying concern that an increase in cultural diversity in the organization is threatening the core values and practices upon which this organization's success and viability is based. From this orientation, it is often recommended that the organization create opportunities for newly hired, culturally diverse managers and employees to "learn the ropes" and gain a sense of how things need to done "around here." Unfortunately, this approach demands assimilation (one-way adaptation) from cultural diversity. The result is that culturally diverse resources are not able to fully contribute to the organization's core mission: They often feel less a part of the company, they are often at a disadvantage for promotions, and they perceive little opportunity to bring culturally different perspectives, values, or practices to the attention of the organization at large.

In contrast, a primary orientation of minimization would answer the question, "Who should adapt to whom?" by recognizing some of the differences culturally diverse groups bring to the organization and be open to changing current policies and practices based on this understanding of differences but would attempt to find or establish a set of common standards and policies believed to apply equally (i.e., better) to all members of the organization. This effort will serve many productive purposes when focused on issues of racism and prejudice in the organization.

However, this effort will fall short when applied to management practices, performance appraisal processes, and other "interactive" arenas within which cultural differences emerge. In these more interactive situations, a limited focus only on common solutions will likely mask culturally grounded, different ways people may deal with disagreements, how emotion is expressed, how problems are addressed, how feedback is given, how goals are established, and how work is organized. In these areas, minimization can create a situation in the organization where culturally diverse resources are not valued and the insights and practices available to the organization from this cultural diversity in the areas of human management and performance are not activated. For people who possess these culturally different resources, they will likely employ minimization as a strategy to get along in a minimization-dominated organization. The result is that culturally diverse resources are not fully integrated into the life of the firm.

Finally, a developmental orientation of acceptance or adaptation would likely respond to the question of "Who should adapt to whom?" with a clear statement that mutual adaptation is expected among all managers and employees. From these perspectives, a deeper search for and consequently a deeper recognition of those cultural differences that are present among diverse resources in the organization is completed. With this more complex understanding of how people construe their experiences in the organization (e.g., planning, organizing, leading, communicating), more effective decisions around cultural differences and their contributions can be realized. From the acceptance and, even more, the adaptation orientation, all members of the company are learning to adapt to cultural context and are gaining valuable intercultural skills in the process.

Overall, the IDI is appropriate to use with a wide variety of people and organizations. It

can be effectively employed for individual assessment and coaching. When used in this way, the IDI profile becomes an important tool for the individual—one in which developmental issues and trailing issues are identified and learning activities agreed upon in order to progress along the intercultural development continuum.

The IDI can be used to assess a group's capability to deal with cultural differences. When used in this way, the IDI becomes a blueprint of the group's overall capabilities and can help identify the struggles the group will likely encounter as they attempt to work together to accomplish tasks that involve bridging across cultural difference.

The IDI provides a benchmark assessment of an organization as a whole. This can help pinpoint areas of development in various divisions and management levels throughout the company. The IDI can also be used as a training needs assessment. Knowing, for instance, the percentage of denial, defense/reversal, minimization, acceptance and adaptation developmental orientations within a training population can better target and leverage the specific training interventions created. For example, training programs that emphasize a more sophisticated understanding of patterns of cultural difference will likely be more effective with minimization, acceptance, and adaptation orientations. These same programs might reinforce simpler stereotypes among denial and polarization (defense/reversal) orientations, as these orientations do not have a sufficiently complex understanding of what a cultural difference is (compared to a personality difference, for instance) to adequately apply these more complex frameworks to understand patterns of cultural difference.

Finally, the IDI can be used to evaluate various programs. It has been successfully used, for example, to evaluate a range of programs, from corporate training to study-abroad programs in high schools and colleges. Additional areas where the IDI shows promise is in law enforcement, the court system, military operations, and the diplomatic community.

To conclude, the IDI provides a conversational platform within which to engage the "other" in a deep and genuine conversation around cultural diversity concerns. In addition, the intercultural development continuum provides a blueprint for how to encourage and assist individual and group development toward greater capability to shift cultural perspective and adapt behavior to cultural context. Why is this important? To quote the Vulcan greeting from *Star Trek*: "Greetings. I am pleased to see that we are different. May we together become greater than the sum of both of us."

◆ Discussion Questions

1. As you reflect on your own experiences with cultural differences, where do you think your primary orientation is located along the intercultural development continuum?

2. Identify specific situations you have observed or been involved in which a denial, defense or reversal orientation was used.

3. Identify specific situations you have observed or with which you have been involved in which a minimization orientation was used.

4. Identify specific situations you have observed or with which you have been involved in which an acceptance or adaptation orientation was used.

5. How might minimization strategies be useful in reducing prejudice and even violence between cultural or ethnic groups in our world?

◆ Notes

1. This is a composite case based on a set of real events that reflects issues around cultural differences that can be involved in startup operations and joint-venture operations that are initiated outside one's own culture. The names of the individuals and the companies are hypothetical and do not represent real persons or corporations.

2. All versions of the IDI (v.1, v.2, and v.3) are solely owned by Mitchell R. Hammer, PhD. The current version (v.3) of the IDI and its analytical structure was developed by Mitchell R. Hammer, PhD. The IDI v.3 is revised from earlier work on the IDI (v.1 and v.2) developed by Dr. Hammer and Milton Bennett, PhD (see Hammer, Bennett, & Wiseman, 2003, for a detailed review of the methodology used in developing earlier versions of the IDI).

3. This intercultural development continuum and the associated orientations toward cultural differences are adapted from Bennett's (1986, 1993, 2004) Developmental Model of Intercultural Sensitivity (see, for example, recent application of this developmental approach to international education in Wilkinson, 2007). An additional orientation initially identified by Bennett (1986), termed "integration," is concerned with the construction of an intercultural identity. This orientation is not, however, conceptually related to the development of increased intercultural competence (Bennett, 2004). In addition, the IDI also assesses cultural disengagement—the degree to which an individual or group is experiencing a sense of alienation from their own cultural community. This is a separate dimension assessed by the IDI and is conceptually located (and empirically verified) outside of the developmental continuum.

4. Bennett and Bennett (2004) and J. M. Bennett (1993) have termed this sense of marginality "encapsulated marginality" and theorize that encapsulated marginality is one form of the DMIS orientation of integration (the other form being constructive marginality). As proposed by the DMIS model, the condition of encapsulated marginality is where "one's sense of self is stuck between cultures in a dysfunctional way" (Bennett & Bennett, 2004, p. 157). The notion of *cultural disengagement* assessed by the IDI is not the same as encapsulated marginality.

Cultural disengagement involves a sense of alienation from one's own cultural group. This does not imply that the individual's identity is somehow between two different cultures in a dysfunctional way. What it measures is simply this sense of feeling disconnected from one's own group identity. The empirical results suggest that cultural disengagement as assessed by the IDI in fact is not significantly more related to an adaptation orientation than any of the other orientations. That is, an individual can experience high or low levels of cultural disengagement across all of the developmental orientations (Hammer, 2007). In this sense, as stated earlier, cultural disengagement functions within the IDI as a distinct and separate construct and measure and is not conceptually situated as a "developmental orientation" along the continuum.

5. Developing the IDI (v.1, v.2, and v.3) involved a number of protocols, including (a) in-depth interviews of 40 individuals from a variety of cultures and preparation of verbatim transcripts of these interviews, (b) inter-rater reliability testing to determine whether the discourse of the respondents reflects core orientations delineated in Milton J. Bennett's (1993) DMIS model, (c) listing of all statements made by each respondent that are indicative of the agreed-upon developmental orientation followed by a review (for redundancy, word clarity, etc) of these statements by two cross-cultural pilot groups, (d) rating of the remaining statements (randomly arranged) by a group of seven cross-cultural experts (expert panel review method) in terms of whether the items clearly reflect an identifiable core orientation, (e) submission of the remaining items to factor analysis (IDI v.1) and confirmatory factor analysis (IDI v.2 and v.3), and (f) content and construct validity testing of the IDI with modified versions of the Worldmindedness Questionnaire and an Intercultural Anxiety questionnaire. Additional testing found no significant correlations of the IDI with social desirability (Crown Marlow Social Desirability Index) and no significant systematic effects on the IDI in terms of gender, educational level, and age.

6. In version 2 of the IDI, the Cultural Disengagement scale referred to earlier in this chapter was labeled the Encapsulated Marginality

scale. However, as more data have been gathered since the development of IDI v.2 concerning the correlations of this scale to other scales in the IDI, this scale has been renamed Cultural Disengagement in IDI v.3 to better reflect its independent status within the developmental continuum.

7. Byrne (1998) noted that "evaluation of model fit should derive from a variety of sources and be based on several criteria that can assess model fit from a diversity of perspectives" (p. 103). This suggests that a number of criteria should be brought to bear on assessing the adequacies of different models. These criteria typically include parsimony, cross-sample consistency, inter-pretability, and theoretical relevance. In some cases, the application of these various criteria may result in equivocal recommendations. When this occurs, it is the researcher who ultimately determines what is best, given the empirical evidence and theoretical constructs being tested. This speaks directly to the validation study for IDI v.2 (Hammer et al., 2003) in which there was evidence that could have led to the choice of the seven-dimension model and evidence that led to choice of the five-dimension model. At that time, the criterion of parsimony suggested that the five-dimension solution rather than the seven-factor model (the original DMIS conceptualization) be accepted. However, research should be evolving and developmental; it should assist in refining and amending our theoretical notions of the phenomenon under study. The current results testing IDI v.3 on a more extensive sample that is more culturally diverse clearly indicate the following core orientations, denial, defense, reversal, minimization, acceptance, and adaptation, which comprise the developmental continuum along with the separate measure of cultural disengagement.

◆ References

Adler, N. J. (1997). *International dimensions of organizational behavior* (3rd ed.). Cincinnati, OH: South-Western College Publishing.

Barnlund, D. (1998). Communication in a global village. In M. J. Bennett (Ed.), *Basic concepts of intercultural communication* (pp. 35–51). Yarmouth, ME: Intercultural Press.

Bennett, J. M. (1993). Cultural marginality: Identity issues in intercultural training. In R. M. Paige (Ed.), *Education for the intercultural experience* (2nd ed., pp. 109–135). Yarmouth, ME: Intercultural Press.

Bennett, J. M. & Bennett, M. J. (2004). Developing intercultural sensitivity: An integrative approach to global and domestic diversity. In D. Landis, J. M. Bennett, & M. J. Bennett (Eds.), *Handbook of intercultural training* (3rd ed., pp. 147–165). Thousand Oaks, CA: Sage.

Bennett, M. J. (1986). A developmental approach to training for intercultural sensitivity. *International Journal of Intercultural Relations, 10*(2), 179–196.

Bennett, M. J. (1993). Towards ethnorelativism: A developmental model of intercultural sensitivity. In R. M. Paige (Ed.), *Education for the intercultural experience* (2nd ed., pp. 21–71). Yarmouth, ME: Intercultural Press.

Bennett, M. J. (2004). Becoming interculturally competent. In J. Wurzel (Ed.), *Towards multiculturalism: A reader in multicultural education* (2nd ed., pp. 62–77). Newton, MA: Intercultural Resource Corporation.

Brislin, R. W. (1970). Back-translation for cross-cultural research. *Journal of Cross-Cultural Psychology, 1*(3), 185–216.

Brislin, R. W. (1976). Comparative research methodology: Cross-cultural studies. *International Journal of Psychology, 11*(3), 215–229.

Brislin, R. W. (1980). Translation and content analysis of oral and written materials. In H. C. Triandis & J. W. Berry (Eds.), *Handbook of cross-cultural psychology* (Vol. 2, pp. 389–444). Boston: Allyn and Bacon.

Byrne, B. M. (1998). *Structural equation modeling with LISREL, PRELIS, and SIMPLIS: Basic concepts, applications, and programming.* Mahwah, NJ: Lawrence Erlbaum Associates.

Hammer, M. R. (1999). A measure of intercultural sensitivity: The Intercultural Development Inventory. In S. M. Fowler & M. G. Mumford (Eds.), *Intercultural sourcebook: Cross-cultural training* (Vol. 2, pp. 61–72). Yarmouth, ME: Intercultural Press.

Hammer, M. R. (2005), The Intercultural Conflict Style Inventory: A conceptual framework and measure of intercultural conflict approaches, *International Journal of Intercultural Research, 29,* 675–695.

Hammer, M. R. (2007). *The Intercultural Development Inventory manual* (Vol. 3). Ocean Pines, MD: IDI, LLC.

Hammer, M. R., Bennett, M. J., & Wiseman, R. (2003). The Intercultural Development Inventory: A measure of intercultural sensitivity, *International Journal of Intercultural Relations, 27,* 421–443.

Harris, P. R., Moran, R. T., & Moran, S. V. (2004). *Managing cultural differences: Global leadership strategies for the 21st century* (6th ed.). New York: Elsevier.

Huntington, S. P. (1996). *The clash of civilizations and the remaking of world order.* New York: Simon & Schuster.

Paige, R. M., Jacobs-Cassuto, M., Yershova, Y. A., & DeJaeghere, J. (2003). Assessing intercultural sensitivity: An empirical analysis of the Hammer and Bennett Intercultural Development Inventory [Special issue: Intercultural development; R. M. Paige, Ed.], *International Journal of Intercultural Relations, 27,* 467–486.

Wilkinson, L. C. (2007). A developmental approach to uses of moving pictures in intercultural education. *International Journal of Intercultural Relations, 31,* 1–27.

Wurzel, J. (Ed.). (2004). *Towards multiculturalism: A reader in multicultural education* (2nd ed.). Newton, MA: Intercultural Resource Corporation.

17

SOLVING PROBLEMS AND RESOLVING CONFLICT USING THE INTERCULTURAL CONFLICT STYLE MODEL AND INVENTORY

◆ Mitchell R. Hammer

◆ A Conflict Brewing

It's 7:00 p.m. on a Friday night—and you're still at the office.[1] It's been a tough day, you think, as you plant your tired feet on the edge of your well-worn, mahogany desk. As manager for project development for an international aid organization, it is your responsibility to oversee a half-dozen international projects that range from basic infrastructure development (e.g., roads, purification of water supplies) to community development efforts (e.g., family planning programs, literacy development).

Two weeks ago, you selected four key employees in your organization to begin to plan and develop a more effective emergency-response effort when natural disasters (e.g., typhoons) occur in remote areas in India and Indonesia. The team is culturally diverse, with two European American members from the United States (Jim and Mary), one member from India (Geetha), and one member from Indonesia (Slamet). Once assembled, you reminded everyone that "time is of the essence," and you need an identified set of goals, responsibilities, and a task time-line in 1 week. It is now the end of the second week of the project, and the team has not submitted any plan at all! Further, there is increasing tension—even conflict—emerging among the team. You are very concerned. This is an important project, and the staff to complete the effort is not getting along. You are surprised at their inability to effectively establish the core goals and identify key tasks needed to be undertaken. Further, you have heard confusing reports in one-on-one discussions with each of the project members.

The two Americans comment that neither Geetha nor Slamet are truly interested in moving forward on this project. They complain that Geetha and Slamet seem unprepared and rarely contribute during a number of brainstorming meetings. Further, they feel Geetha and Slamet are deceptive and feel that it is much too early to formulate goals and tasks.

However, you have heard a very different story from Geetha and Slamet. From their perspective, the Americans are becoming too "pushy" in meetings and are unwilling to really listen. After all, they commented, we are from these countries—the Americans need to respect our experience! Interestingly, the two Americans and Slamet also commented that Geetha is trying to dominate the meeting and has shown her frustration and anger with the group in inappropriate ways. One situation recently occurred where Geetha "yelled" at the other team members about their lack of commitment—yet she did not propose any solutions!

You know you need to do something—but you are not sure what actions you can take to deescalate the growing tensions and problems among the team members. You know you selected very competent people for this particular project. They all have a strong background in delivering humanitarian aid and services in conflict zones as well as during times of emergencies. Further, Geetha is from India, Slamet from Indonesia, Mary

has lived 3 years in India, and Jim has lived 2 years in Indonesia. It seems the problems among the team members have already compromised the development of their plan. What should you do? What insights might you bring to the group to help them work more effectively in solving problems and dealing with an increasing conflict situation?

◆ Introduction

The purpose of this chapter is to outline a powerful model and assessment tool that can be used in these types of situations to help individuals and groups solve problems and resolve conflicts. In this chapter, I describe the Intercultural Conflict Style (ICS) model and ICS Inventory. I conclude the chapter by showing how the ICS model and Inventory can be used to help this multicultural project team meet its important mission in India and Indonesia.

◆ NASA and Cultural Conflicts

I had the opportunity to consult with two important organizations in the United States: the National Aeronautics and Space Administration (NASA) and the National Institutes of Health (NIH). With NASA, I worked with the Behavior and Performance Laboratory to address the question, "Do cultural differences affect mission success and astronaut and ground crew relations?" We designed a critical incident protocol and interviewed selected astronauts and ground crew members from different cultures who flew on multicultural space flights (including early space station MIR deployments). What we discovered is that the extensive technical training astronauts and ground crews received over many years was effective in preparing these space explorers to achieve mission objectives in a variety of space flight scenarios. This was especially true concerning routine, less complex flight tasks and responsibilities. In these situations, the space and ground crews were able to work effectively with one another across cultural boundaries. In these more mundane, less demanding activities, cultural differences did not emerge as particularly troublesome or problematic.

However, we found that in situations where uncertainty increased, conflicts erupted, emergencies arose, and interpersonal relations were stressed—cultural differences did arise and powerfully affected the ability of the space and ground crews to accomplish mission goals. In short, under conditions of stress and conflict, people reverted to their cultural programming rather than relying on the training protocols developed over years of effort (NASA Behavior and Performance Laboratory, 1989).

This was a surprising finding for NASA in view of the fact that the organization maintained some pride in its ability to properly prepare these crews to effectively relate and work with one another. I continued to work with the Behavior and Performance Laboratory in developing protocols for offering intercultural training, with an important element focusing on conflict and culture, for all astronauts and ground crews involved in multinational space endeavors. This training is continuing with the multicultural crews assigned to the construction and manning of the International Space Station.

SCIENTIFIC CONFLICT

The National Cancer Institute (NCI) of the National Institutes of Health (NIH) undertook over a 4-year period in the mid-1990s Phase II clinical trials of A10 and AS2–1 (antineoplastons) infusion therapy developed by Dr. Stanislow Burzynski in patients with primary malignant brain tumors. At the end of the 4 years, the research was terminated before it was determined whether the antineoplaston therapy was effective. Both the NCI and Dr. Burzynski asserted that the "other party" deliberately undermined the study.

Dr. Wayne Jonas, then director of the Office of Alternative Medicine of the NIH, commissioned me to conduct a study addressing the conflicts that arose that led to the ending of this promising line of cancer research. My team and I reviewed hundreds of documents and memoranda and conducted interviews with key researchers involved in this 4-year research program (see Hammer & Jonas, 2004, for a full analysis of this case). We identified 10 areas of contention between NCI and Dr. Burzynski (e.g., production, quality and delivery of antineoplastons, role of Dr. Burzynski in the clinical trial, need for communication, and criteria for patient selection). These 10 areas of substantive disagreements were all located within the canons of science—of which the NCI researchers and Dr. Burzynski were well trained. Each of these disagreements could—and probably should—have been easily resolved by focusing on identification of socially agreed-upon research protocols for conducting Phase II clinical trials. Yet this did not happen. These disagreements were "scientific" only so far as the substantive issues were largely concerned with research methodology. The actual conflict communication and interaction between the NCI researchers and Dr. Burzynski reflected conflict in attunement—issues of trust, power, and affiliation between Dr. Burzynski and the NCI that accounted for the lack of progress in completing this important research (Hammer & Jonas, 2004). This lack of attunement created conditions of frustration and at times anger, which permeated the research effort.

In both the NASA and NIH assessments, the failure to effectively manage and resolve disagreements and conflict had life-and-death consequences. It was clear that the way individuals communicated with one another in their attempts to solve problems or resolve conflicts, differences in the approach or style the parties used to address the substantive disagreements, and the level of emotional upset present in these kinds of stressful interactions contributed to an escalating situation.

Each of these events took place before I created the Intercultural Conflict Style (ICS) model and ICS Inventory. As I reflect on the way in which the various individuals attempted to deal with substantive disagreements in both of these events, I am convinced that one critical difference involved very different styles or approaches for solving problems and resolving conflicts.

◆ Conflict and Style

Conflict is a form of social interaction in which substantive disagreements arise between two or more individuals (Geist, 1995) which gives rise to an affective or emotional reaction, often based on a perception of threat or interference by one or more other parties to the disagreement (Hammer, 2001, 2005). Therefore, conflict involves two core elements. The first is substantive disagreements. In this sense, conflict is more than a simple misperception or misunderstanding. Rather, it involves real disagreements between individuals over goals, values, or other issues. Second, conflict interaction is stressful and involves some degree of emotional upset or even distress.

Our "conflict style" refers broadly to how we attempt to resolve our disagreements and deal with emotional upset when interacting with one another. Ting-Toomey and colleagues (2000) defined conflict style as "patterned responses to conflict in a variety of situations." Further, they posited that differences in conflict styles are a central factor that can escalate difficulties between contending parties.

Conflict style has been conceptualized in a number of ways (see Hammer, 2005, for a brief summary of various taxonomic models). Common to these typologies is a focus on two personal goal dimensions: a high/low concern for attaining one's own goals and a high/low concern for the other party obtaining their goals.

Pruitt and Carnevale (1993) identified four conflict styles from this vantage point (see Table 17.1). *Problem solving* involves a high concern for self and other goal attainment, *contending* or dominating a high concern for one's own goals and low concern for the other party's goals, *yielding* or accommodating a low concern for one's own goals and high concern for the other party's goals, and *avoiding* or inaction a low concern for self and other goal attainment.

Table 17.1 Dual Concern Model

		High Concern for others' goals	Low Concern for others' goals
Concern for own goals	High	Problem Solving	Contending
	Low	Yielding	Avoiding

SOURCE: Pruitt & Carnevale (1993).

Not overtly discussed in many of these conflict style models is the observation that conflict style is also culturally learned (Ting-Toomey et al., 2000; Hammer, 2005). Ting-Toomey (1994) persuasively argues that because these models were not developed along intercultural dimensions, they may not possess sufficient cross-cultural generalizability. She points out that an avoiding/yielding strategy from a Western cultural definition reflects a low concern for achieving one's own interests and a low concern for the other party's goals. However, within more collectivistic, Asian cultural contexts, avoiding/yielding approaches are used to maintain or restore harmony between the contending parties and actually indicate a high concern for achieving one's own goals and a high concern for the attainment of the other party's interests.

Because there was not a model and assessment tool of conflict style based on an overt consideration of "etic" (culturally generalizable) dimensions of cultural difference related to the way disagreements are addressed and the way emotion is dealt with in a conflictual interaction, I embarked on a process to develop such a framework and measure of an individual's intercultural conflict style. This resulted in the Intercultural Conflict Style (ICS) model and ICS Inventory.[2]

◆ **Theoretical Basis of the Intercultural Conflict Style Model**

Above, I offer Ting-Toomey and colleagues' (2000) definition of conflict style as patterned responses to conflict across situations. Yet what is a "patterned response"? Is it, for instance, predispositions or personality traits characteristic of an individual? The problem with viewing patterned responses in terms of personal characteristics is that, as Folger, Poole, and Stutman (2005) cogently pointed

out, "although people certainly develop habitual ways of responding to conflict, they also have the capacity to change or adapt their behavior from situation to situation" (p. 216). Viewing conflict style in terms of personal traits does not adequately address how our responses change depending on different demands of the situation. A second approach to "patterned responses" defines conflict styles as particular types of behavior individuals employ (Cosier & Ruble, 1981). The problem with viewing conflict styles strictly in terms of behaviors is that the same action can be used in different identified styles due to functionally different meanings of that specific behavior, depending on the situational context (Folger, et al., 2005).

The Intercultural Conflict Style (ICS) model is most consistent with the view of patterned responses in terms of *behavioral orientations* (Folger et al., 2005) individuals adapt toward negotiating disagreements and dealing with emotional upset during a conflictual interaction. By behavioral orientation, I mean an interpretive *frame* within which an individual "makes meaningful" messages and behavior that arise from interaction with the other party. As Folger and colleagues (2005) remarked, "behavioral strategies and general orientations are bound up with each other because behaviors are not meaningful outside the context of the style they represent" (p. 218).

On the broadest level, frames are viewed as interpretations of interaction that serve to define the activity in which individuals are engaged (Hammer, 2007). Bateson (1954/ 1972) defined a frame as "a class or set of messages (or meaningful actions)" (p. 186) that functions as a map providing cues about how the interaction is to be defined and how to interpret the communicative acts within the specific context. At a general level, framing is the process by which people attach idiosyncratic definitions, interpretations, and meaning to a class of objects, persons, and events (Watzlawick, Bavelas, & Jackson, 1967).

At a more precise level of meaning, frames reflect a person's expectations about the issues at hand. According to Lewicki, Saunders, and Minton (1999), frames "are abstractions, collections of perceptions and thoughts that people use to define a situation, organize information, determine what is important, what is not, and so on" (p. 31). Yet frames do not exist as abstract forms disconnected to how people behave. As Gray (2006) cogently pointed out, "how we frame a situation also affects how we respond to it" (p. 194). Frames, as applied to conflict interaction, are interpretive lenses through which individuals perceive and behave in relation to a particular issue, problem, or concern.

THE INTERCULTURAL CONFLICT STYLE (ICS) MODEL

Based on the above discussion, conflict style and intercultural conflict style are defined as "the manner in which contending parties communicate with one another around substantive disagreements and their emotional or affective reaction to one another" (p. 679).

◆ Direct Versus Indirect Cultural Patterns

Two intercultural dimensions of cultural difference provide the foundation for how individuals solve problems and resolve conflicts: (1) direct versus indirect approaches for communicating about substantive issues (disagreements) and (2) emotionally expressive versus emotionally restrained strategies for dealing with emotional upset.[3]

Direct culture strategies focus attention on the specific words participants use when discussing particular issues. That is, direct cultures emphasize precise, explicit language use to increase understanding of the issues or disagreements. For direct cultures, it is each party's responsibility to verbalize their own concerns and perspective and to verbally confront misperceptions and misunderstandings that can arise in a dispute. Direct cultures prefer direct face-to-face methods for resolving conflict. From this perspective, there is a greater opportunity for productive dialogue and resolution of the disagreement when the parties can finally sit down and talk to one another. In fact, for many direct culture systems, the process of conflict resolution is considered to be finally initiated and maintained when the contending parties are able to directly address their disagreements with one another. Direct cultures value individuals who speak their mind and can verbally assert (albeit tactfully) differences in viewpoints. Direct cultures value persuasion that is conducted largely through logically ordered arguments supported by verifiable, objective facts, concluding with logically related recommendations or solutions. In this sense, direct cultures emphasize a "solution oriented" approach to problem solving.

In contrast, indirect cultures look to identify meaning in one another's statements and actions by looking outside the verbal messages being exchanged between the parties. This includes greater attentiveness to history, context, and nonverbal behaviors. Words are more often used in indirect cultural systems to meet social or situational expectations and less to communicate what each party actually believes or wants. Indirect cultures prefer to use third-party intermediaries (TPIs) to mediate a conflict-resolution process. From an indirect culture view, engaging in direct, face-to-face meetings when tensions are escalating only increases discomfort among the parties. Indirect cultures value discretion in voicing one's own views and goals as direct statements may threaten the harmony that needs to be maintained during the conflict episode. Consequently, indirect culture systems prefer to "talk around" disagreements through such strategies as hinting, analogies, historical examples, and metaphors. For indirect cultures, persuasion is accomplished by sensitivity to face—publicly supporting the social position or reputation of the other party. This influence is wielded incrementally and framed relationally, with less overt emphasis on the factual basis of the dispute. Evidence is suggested more than asserted, relational connections and obligations are reinforced, and solutions are "adjusted" depending on the response of the other party. In this sense, indirect cultures employ a "relationship repair" framework for dealing with substantive issues.

EMOTIONALLY EXPRESSIVE VERSUS EMOTIONALLY RESTRAINED (CONTROLLED) CULTURAL PATTERNS

Emotionally expressive cultures value more overt displays of emotional experience during a conflict event. There is a sense that when someone is upset, it is important to braid how one feels with one's position on the substantive disagreement. For emotionally expressive systems, emotional upset is controlled by externalizing, or letting out emotion. Trying to control or hide emotional upset can escalate rather than deescalate the situation. More visible displays of affect through nonverbal behaviors along with more expansive vocalization characterize emotionally expressive approaches. Sensitivity is found toward perceived or actual constraints being placed on an ability to fully express one's emotional reality. The sometimes well-intentioned comment to "take a break so we can all calm down" is often negatively perceived by emotionally expressive individuals. Advice to calm down or soften one's emotional expressiveness is experienced as a statement that directly challenges one's sense of authenticity. From this cultural perspective, to divorce how one feels from how one addresses substantive issues

during a conflict is to be insincere to the difficult process of "working through our issues." Emotional authenticity is central for resolution as it is through emotionally expressive commitment that relational trust is gained and credibility established. In emotionally expressive cultures, conflict is deescalated after the personal credibility and sincerity of each party is demonstrated through more emotionally expressive and authentic displays.

In emotionally restrained systems, the focus is on maintaining emotional control even when one is upset. Strong feelings should be hidden to some degree to avoid upsetting the other party. Emotions are controlled by internalizing. Unlike emotionally expressive cultures, where humor is a comfortable strategy to reduce tensions, humor for emotional restrained cultural systems is risky when tensions are high because it may be negatively interpreted as diminishing the situation or the experiences and feelings of the other party. Minimal displays of emotion through nonverbal behavior and a more constrained vocal pattern characterize resolution strategies often employed in emotionally restrained cultures. Sensitivity is directed toward not hurting the feelings of the other party; thus, emotionally controlled cultures are uncomfortable with more overt expressions of emotion. Relational trust and credibility is established and maintained through emotional control or suppression. Maintaining calm in the face of emotional upset also communicates sincerity. More overt displays of emotion send a message of insincerity, questionable intentions, and suspicious motives. Each of these approaches, when combined, produces four distinct conflict resolution styles.

THE FOUR INTERCULTURAL CONFLICT STYLES

Table 17.2 presents the four-quadrant model of intercultural conflict style differences.

Table 17.2   Intercultural Conflict Style Model

	Emotionally Restrained	Emotionally Expressive
Direct	Discussion	Engagement
Indirect	Accommodation	Dynamic

The *discussion* style uses direct strategies for communicating about substantive disagreements and emotionally restrained or controlled approaches for dealing with emotional upset. This style resolves issues through a focused, problem-solving process in which objective facts and information are presented in a logical argument format. Clarity in expressing one's goals or position is important as is maintaining emotional calm when tensions rise. This style follows the American maxim, "Say what you mean, and mean what you say."

Strengths from the *discussion* style perspective include an ability to directly confront problems and elaborate arguments so people do not misunderstand your views and a willingness to maintain a calm atmosphere. From the perspective of other styles, however, the discussion style can appear logical but unfeeling and appear to overemphasize verbal clarity to the exclusion of recognizing other, more emotional and relational concerns that arise during a conflict. A few exemplar cultures that normatively function largely within a discussion style are those of the United States (European American), Australia, and northern Europe.[4]

The *engagement* style also emphasizes verbal direction in communicating about substantive issues. Unlike the discussion style, however, the engagement style couples this form of directness with an emotionally expressive demeanor. This style is comfortable with more emotionally intense dialogue and in fact participants feel that when each party "puts their emotion on the table" the resolution of the dispute is satisfactorily progressing. This style, because of its more emotional expressive focus, follows the Irish proverb, "What is nearest the mouth is nearest the heart."

Strengths from the engagement style viewpoint include an ability to provide detailed information and explanations and a sincerity and commitment to the other party through more emotional expressions and a positive sense that sharing one's feelings is how conflicts are successfully resolved. From the orientation of other styles, the engagement style can appear unconcerned with the views and feelings of others and dominating and rude. A few examples of engagement-style cultural systems are those of African Americans in the United States and people of southern Europe, Cuba, Nigeria, and Russia.

The *accommodation* style uses indirect strategies for solving problems coupled with an emotionally restrained approach. This style emphasizes ambiguity, stories, metaphors, and use of third parties to soften verbal confrontation between contending individuals. Relational harmony is maintained in a tense conflict situation by masking or controlling one's own emotional discomfort. The accommodation style follows the Japanese maxim, "Hear one and understand 10."

Self-perceived strengths of the accommodation style are an ability to consider alternative interpretations of ambiguous messages and sensitivity to the feelings of the other party. From the view of other styles, however, the accommodation style can reveal difficulty in clearly voicing one's own opinion, problems in providing detailed explanations, and an appearance of being uncommitted and perhaps dishonest. Some cultural exemplars of the accommodation style are those of Native Americans (United States), Somalians, Mexicans, Japanese, and Thai.

The *dynamic* style uses indirect messages to negotiate substantive disagreements along with more emotionally intense and expressive verbal and nonverbal communication. This style may use language elements that include strategic hyperbole, repetition of one's position, ambiguity, stories, metaphors, and humor along with greater reliance on third-party intermediaries for resolving an escalating dispute. Prioritization of concerns may be communicated more through the level of emotional expression than a direct statement of what is important and what is unimportant.

Individuals with a dynamic style may describe themselves in terms of being comfortable with other people interjecting themselves into a disagreement and offering solutions to the contending parties, skilled at observing behavior, and comfortable with strong emotional displays. From the perspective of the other styles, a dynamic style may be seen as unreasonable, too emotional, volatile, and rarely able to "get to the point." Some dynamic cultures include those of a number of Arab Middle Eastern countries and Pakistan.

◆ Development of the ICS Inventory

The ICS Inventory is an 18-item, self-scoring questionnaire that assesses an individual's core approach for solving problems and resolving conflicts.[5] Based on an extensive review of the literature, a total of 122 items were generated that reflect direct and indirect strategies and emotionally expressive and emotionally restrained approaches for resolving conflict. Once these items were identified, a panel of 16 intercultural conflict experts rated these items in terms of the degree to which they are clear indicators of the cultural dimensions examined. Following this review, 52 items were retained for further statistical analysis.

A total of 510 respondents from a variety of cultures then responded to the (randomly assigned) items using a Likert agree/disagree scale format. Confirmatory Factor Analysis (CFA) was then completed. The results clearly indicated that the dimensions of direct/indirect and emotionally expressive/restrained provided a good fit to the data. A review of these items (e.g., factor/item correlations, redundancy of meaning) resulted in an 18-item direct/indirect scale and an 18-item emotionally expressive/restrained scale. The reliability (coefficient alpha) for the direct/indirect scale was .71 and .86 for the emotionally expressive/restrained scale. Additional analysis was then conducted examining the effects of gender, educational level, and previous experience living in another culture. No significant differences were found on either scale by gender, education, or previous intercultural experience.

The ICS items were then formatted as follows: The nine direct style items and the nine indirect style items were paired with one another as two separate options (A, B) to the question, "In general, when resolving conflict with another party, my preferred approach is to. . . ." This produced nine questions. The same was then done for the nine emotionally expressive items and the nine emotionally restrained items. These questions were than randomly arranged in the questionnaire. This newly formatted questionnaire was then administered to a new sample of 487 culturally diverse respondents. Coefficient alpha was then calculated, resulting in a reliability of .73 for the direct/indirect scale and .85 for the emotionally expressive/restrained scale. Overall, these tests demonstrate the ICS Inventory is a cross-culturally valid and reliable assessment of an individual's core approach for resolving conflict.

◆ Uses of the ICS Model and Inventory

There are currently over 600 intercultural and conflict resolution professionals using the Intercultural Conflict Style Inventory in various coaching and training efforts. It is employed in the U.S. military, education, the court system, mediation, health care, industry, and the diplomatic community both within the United States and internationally.

The ICS model and Inventory shed a needed light on an area of the human landscape that is only dimly understood. Differences in the way we attempt to authentically interact with one another when we disagree and are frustrated or angry are often misinterpreted as negative personal characteristics. Thus, discussion styles are falsely judged to be unfeeling, engagement approaches are evaluated as dominating and rude, accommodation styles are dismissed as uninvolved and unclear, and dynamic styles are avoided because the individual is thought to be volatile and unstable.

When the discussion style is the normative approach expected of managers and employees in our organizations, then individuals whose approach is different are likely to be marginalized. In the training programs I conduct on the ICS, I have heard countless stories from individuals who, after receiving feedback on their ICS Inventory, for the first time are able to look at these differences between their own approach for solving problems and the "way things are expected to be done" in their organization. As they reflect on these differences, they realize how differences as identified in the ICS model and Inventory have affected their personal and work lives. Here are some examples of how—and why—intercultural conflict style differences often "make a difference":

- An accommodation-style middle manager was told by his boss that he "needs to speak up, to not be shy, to believe in something, to assert himself—or he will never get anywhere in this company." From his accommodation perspective, however, he was working very hard in maintaining effective relations in the company and he thought his contributions were being recognized.

- An engagement-style employee stated that she was overlooked for promotion because she was too dominating in meetings and she needed to "better control" her emotional outbursts. She was flabbergasted at this suggestion! From her perspective, she did not feel she offended anyone! In fact, she was passionate!

- A dynamic-style executive (Mari) was confused. A customer previously received a price quote from the company and now was personally asking for a better price for some steel strapping. Mari immediately called the customer and invited him out to what ended up being a 2-hour lunch. When Mari returned to work, she was shocked when her boss said to her, "Your customer just called. He says he wasted two hours with you at lunch. He thought you were meeting him to discuss his product needs, but all you did was ramble on about how long they have worked together!" Mari thought the customer knew that the invitation to a long lunch was a way to inform the customer that he was very important to Mari and the company but that it was not possible to lower the prices further.

♦ *A Return to "A Conflict Brewing"*

It is now time to return to the case presented at the beginning of this chapter. As manager for project development for an international aid organization, you are facing a difficult situation. Your newly formed work team is having significant difficulties in articulating a plan to develop a more effective emergency-response effort in the more remote areas of India and Indonesia. As you reflect on this escalating problem, you come to the following conclusion. The very different (and largely negative) perceptions the various team members have of one another have a lot to do with differences in the way they attempt to solve problems and deal with frustration and stress—in short, how they handle conflict. Much of what is interfering with their ability to have more cooperative interactions with one another has to do with differences in intercultural conflict styles.

The two American members operate within a discussion style frame for dealing with disagreements. They value maintaining emotional control and they place particular importance on group brainstorming sessions as a verbally direct method for making progress on the assigned tasks. During these meetings, they fully participate by sharing not only ideas that they have given some serious thought to but also ideas that just occur to them while the meeting is going on. From their perspective, isn't that what brainstorming is all about?

Geetha's intercultural conflict style is dynamic. She participates in these brainstorming meetings only reluctantly—and frankly, she finds them more of a waste of time and effort than they are worth. From her perspective, effective participation means being well prepared and being very careful when voicing your opinion. She is frustrated because these sessions rarely have a specific agenda of topics, so she feels she comes to the meetings unprepared. She attempts to let the others know her frustrations, often through a past example of how a project was conducted. When she is frustrated, she is comfortable showing her emotional reality to others—after all, she thinks, "How will everyone know my views if they don't know how I feel?"

Slamet's style is accommodation. She also has difficulty fully participating in these brainstorming meetings, for reasons similar to those expressed by Geetha. Slamet has attempted to share her concerns with another colleague, Bill, but he does not seem willing to act as a third party in communicating her thoughts, particularly to the American team members. Consequently, she has remained quiet during many of the meetings. She is also somewhat offended that her team members do not seem to recognize that she has personal experiences around disasters. After all, don't they know that in Indonesia, when difficulties or disasters occur, it is not uncommon to rename your child "Slamet" (which means good fortune) as a way to help ensure more positive experiences later in life?

As you reflect on this state of affairs, you realize that you will need to help the team members better understand how these patterns of differences in intercultural conflict styles are affecting their relations. Further, you believe that after reviewing this with the team, the team will need to spend some time deciding how they can better adapt to one another's styles so that the full contribution of each member is obtained. To get them started, you may suggest that they develop an agenda for the brainstorming meetings. This will allow Geetha and Slamet to better prepare for each session. Further, you might suggest that each member be permitted to present his or her ideas first rather than beginning with a more freeform discussion format. Again, this can be helpful to Geetha and Slamet, and, frankly, it would also demand that Jim and Mary do a bit more preparation for the brainstorming sessions as well. Finally, it would be helpful if the team members met with one another individually prior to the brainstorming session. By doing this, Geetha and Slamet can "check out" everyone's views prior to the meeting. These more informal sessions would also allow all team members to get to know one another better, which will solidify the relational context within which the work is being done. By doing this, all team members will likely be more comfortable joining the discussion.

◆ Conclusion

Intercultural conflict style differences represent an important, although largely unexamined, aspect of how conflict escalates—even when individuals genuinely desire to cooperate and work out their disagreements. Developing awareness of these style differences begins with oneself. How an individual profiles on the ICS Inventory provides a clear window on how that person will likely frame and respond to a problem that arises or a conflict that erupts. Recognizing how one's own approach differs from others then becomes the basis for increased sensitivity to difference and an improved ability to better bridge across these intercultural style patterns of difference.

The preliminary results from individuals using the ICS Inventory have been most encouraging. An international financial organization trained their full team of over 20 mediators with the ICS Inventory. Reports from the field indicate that the use of the ICS Inventory is being effectively integrated in the mediation process when disputes arise across cultures. Further, insights from this effort have enabled the disputants to more cooperatively

resolve their disagreements. In another international development organization, training with the ICS Inventory has resulted in documented benefits in conflict resolution, more effective decision making, and improved relations across cultures. Within the United States, the ICS has been productively used to help judges and attorneys better recognize intercultural style differences in working with clients and within the courtroom protocols. Managers within the corporate sector are modifying the way they provide performance feedback and coaching based on differences in intercultural conflict/problem-solving styles identified by the ICS Inventory and model.

Finally, in one situation, I mediated a conflict-resolution process between two high-level company presidents. One president exhibited leadership through an accommodation style and the other president operated within an engagement style. After individually completing the ICS Inventory, we engaged in a productive conversation on these differences in how each president attempted to resolve substantive issues and how each president brought into the dialogue varying degrees of emotional expressiveness. They discovered that while there were clear, substantive disagreements, these disagreements were exacerbated by different misinterpretations each made of the other about directness/indirectness and emotional expressiveness/restraint. As a result, progress was made and more cooperative behavior was elicited as these individuals worked with one another in the future.

◆ Discussion Questions

1. How would you describe your general communication approach toward others? Is it the same as your conflict-resolution style?

2. After reading about intercultural conflict styles in this chapter, do you think your approach for resolving disagreements (when you are upset) is more similar to a discussion, engagement, accommodation, or dynamic style?

3. Think of some situations you have observed or in which you have been involved in which different intercultural conflict styles were used by people to solve a problem or deal with a disagreement. What did you think, feel, or do in these situations?

4. "Code words" refer to more negative (often personal characteristic) statements made about a different intercultural conflict-resolution style. Generate a list of at least 10 code words that have been said about the discussion, engagement, accommodation, and dynamic styles.

◆ Notes

1. The cases presented in this chapter are composite descriptions based on a set of real events. The names of the individuals and the companies are hypothetical and do not represent real persons or corporations.

2. Accompanying the ICS Inventory is the ICS Participant's Guide (Hammer, 2003a) and the ICS Facilitator's Manual (Hammer, 2003b). The ICS Inventory and accompanying materials can be obtained at www.hammerconsulting.org.

3. These two dimensions were identified based on an exhaustive review of relevant research that focused on cultural differences in resolving disagreements and cultural differences related to how individuals express how they feel toward one another during a conflict event. See Hammer, (2005, 2003b) for a summary of this literature.

4. For a more comprehensive discussion of the normative intercultural conflict styles characteristic in some countries, see Hammer (2003b).

5. See Hammer (2005) for a summary of the psychometric testing completed on the Intercultural Conflict Style Inventory.

◆ References

Bateson, G. (1954/1972. *Steps to an ecology of mind.* New York: Ballantine Books.

Cosier, R. A., & Ruble, T. L. (1981). Research on conflict handling behavior: An experimental approach. *Academy of Management Journal, 24,* 816–831.

Folger, J. P., Poole, M. S., & Stutman, R. K. (2005). *Working through conflict.* Boston, MA: Pearson.

Geist, P. (1995). Negotiating whose order? Communicating to negotiate identities and revise organizational structures. In A. Nicotera (Ed.), *Conflict and organizations* (pp. 45–64). Albany: State University of New York Press.

Gray, B. (2006). Mediation as framing and framing within mediation. In M. S. Herrman (Ed.), *Handbook of mediation* (pp. 193–216). Malden, MA: Blackwell.

Hammer, M. R. (2001). Conflict negotiation under crisis conditions. In W. F. Eadie & P. E. Nelson (Eds.), *The language of conflict and resolution.* Thousand Oaks, CA: Sage.

Hammer, M. R. (2003a). *The Intercultural Conflict Style Inventory: Interpretive guide.* Berlin, MD: Hammer Consulting.

Hammer, M. R. (2003b). *The Intercultural Conflict Style Inventory: Facilitator's manual.* Berlin, MD: Hammer Consulting.

Hammer, M. R. (2005). The Intercultural Conflict Style Inventory: A conceptual framework and measure of intercultural conflict resolution approaches. *International Journal of Intercultural Relations, 29,* 675–695.

Hammer, M. R. (2007). *Saving lives: The S.A.F.E. model for negotiating hostage and crisis incidents.* Westport, CT: Praeger.

Hammer, M. R., & Jonas, W. B. (2004). Managing social conflict in complementary and alternative medicine research: The case of antineoplastons. *Integrative Cancer Therapies, 3,* 59–65.

Lewicki, R. J., Saunders, D. M., & Minton, J. W. (1999). *Negotiation* (3rd ed.). New York: McGraw-Hill/Irwin.

NASA Behavior and Performance Laboratory. (1989). *Space shuttle intercultural crew debrief study.* Houston, TX: NASA Center.

Pruitt, D. G., & Carnevale, P. J. (1993). *Negotiation in social conflict.* Pacific Grove, CA: Brooks/Cole Publishing.

Ting-Toomey, S. (1994). Managing intercultural conflict effectively. In L. Samovar & R. Porter (Eds.), *Intercultural communication: A reader* (pp. 360–372). Belmont, CA: Wadsworth.

Ting-Toomey, S., Yee-Jung, K. K., Shapiro, R. B., Garcia, W., Wright, R. J., & Oetzel, J. G. (2000). Ethnic/cultural identity salience and conflict styles in four U.S. ethnic groups. *International Journal of Intercultural Relations, 24,* 47–82.

Watzlawick, P., Bavelas, J. B., & Jackson, D. D. (1967). *Pragmatics of human communication: A study of interactional patterns, pathologies, and paradoxes.* New York: W. W. Norton.

18

CULTURAL INTELLIGENCE

Measurement and Scale Development

◆ Linn Van Dyne, Soon Ang,
and Christine Koh

Although globalization has increased the importance of intercultural competencies, and although a large number of constructs have been used by practitioners to assess intercultural competencies, much of this research is not based on a firm theoretical foundation, and much of this research does not provide rigorous evidence of the construct validity of the measures. Responding to the importance of intercultural competencies and this gap in the measurement literature, this chapter discusses the development and validation of the CQS: the Cultural Intelligence Scale.

Cultural intelligence (referred to here as CQ) is the capability to function effectively in culturally diverse settings (Earley & Ang, 2003). Cultural intelligence is based on contemporary conceptualizations of intelligence as multidimensional (more than general mental ability), which includes the capability to adapt to others and to situations (Sternberg & Detterman, 1986). Specifically, CQ focuses on adaptive capabilities focused on culturally diverse situations. Building on this framework, we explain the process we used to develop and validate a 20-item, four-factor measure of cultural intelligence that includes meta-cognitive CQ, cognitive CQ, motivational CQ, and behavioral CQ.

In this chapter we report results of a cumulative series of studies (using over 1,350 respondents with diverse demographic and cultural backgrounds) that provide construct validity evidence for the four-factor measure of CQ. Confirmatory factor analysis demonstrates a clear four-factor model of cultural intelligence, with high internal consistency and test–retest reliability for each factor. Additional analyses demonstrate other essential psychometric properties (e.g., discriminant, incremental, and predictive validities) of the scale and demonstrate that cultural intelligence can be differentiated from other capabilities such as cognitive ability and emotional intelligence. Results also demonstrate that CQ increased explained variance in cultural judgment and decision making as well as mental well-being, over and above the effects of demographic characteristics, cognitive ability, and emotional intelligence. In sum, results suggest that the four-factor model of cultural intelligence has important selection and training implications for those who function in situations characterized by cultural diversity.

Selecting and developing individuals who can function effectively in culturally diverse domestic and international settings is a significant challenge facing most organizations (Adler, 2002; Black, Gregersen, Mendenhall, & Stroh, 1999; Caligiuri, 2000; Gelfand, Erez, & Aycan, 2007; Kraimer, Wayne, & Jaworski, 2001; Lievens, Harris, Van Keer, & Bisqueret, 2003; Takeuchi, Tesluk, Yun, & Lepak, 2005; Tsui & Gutek, 1999; Williams & O'Reilly, 1998). Based on the rigorous development of the CQS measure of cultural intelligence, we argue that cultural intelligence provides an important and practically relevant measure of intercultural competencies that has direct relevance to managers and employees. We also suggest that cultural intelligence has important relevance to those in culturally diverse domestic settings as well as those who have cross-border international responsibilities.

◆ The Four-Factor Model of Cultural Intelligence

Cultural intelligence (CQ) is a theoretical extension of contemporary approaches to understanding intelligences (Earley & Ang, 2003). Traditionally, the study of intelligence focused mainly on "g," the academic or cognitive factor intelligence. More recently, multiple intelligence theory (Sternberg, 1988) proposed nonacademic intelligences (Hedlund & Sternberg, 2000) that emphasize the capability to adapt to others. These newer forms of intelligence include interpersonal intelligence (Gardner, 1993), emotional intelligence (Goleman, 1995; Salovey & Mayer, 1990), and social intelligence (Cantor & Kihlstrom, 1985; Ford & Tisak, 1983). Each of these formulations of intelligence, however, assumes that familiarity with culture and context guides individual thoughts and social behaviors. As elaborated in Earley and Ang, these relatively general capabilities may not apply when individuals have different cultural backgrounds.

Although those doing research on emotional and social intelligence do not limit their models to a single culture, they also do not acknowledge the importance of cultural diversity and they do not consider forms of intelligence that specifically include the capability of functioning effectively in situations characterized by cultural diversity. Cultural intelligence (the capability to cope and interact effectively in situations that are culturally diverse) is an etic construct (Aguinis & Henle, 2003) that can meaningfully be applied across cultures. Although cultural intelligence is associated closely with culture, it is not an emic, indigenous, culture-bound or culture-specific construct. In other words, CQ does not represent capability within a single culture—such as those of France, Brazil, or China.

Cultural intelligence is an important individual capability that is consistent with contemporary conceptualizations of intelligence: the ability to adapt and adjust to the environment (Cantor & Kihlstrom, 1985; Gardner, 1993; Mayer & Salovey, 1993; Sternberg, 2000). Specifically, we argue that just as nonacademic intelligences such as EQ (emotional intelligence) complement IQ (cognitive intelligence) because both are important for high-quality personal relationships and effectiveness in this increasingly interdependent world (Earley & Gibson, 2002), cultural intelligence is another complementary form of intelligence that explains adapting to diversity and cross-cultural interactions. In sum, cultural intelligence differs from other types of intelligence such as IQ and EQ because it focuses specifically on settings and interactions characterized by cultural diversity (for additional information on CQ, see Ang and colleagues [2007]). Also, consistent with contemporary views of intelligence, we theorize that cultural intelligence is a complex set of individual capabilities that reflect different loci of intelligences (see Sternberg, 1986). Following a symposium of intelligence experts, Sternberg and Detterman (1986) developed a framework that locates intelligence at multiple levels—as attributes of individuals (e.g., biological, mental, motivational, behavioral) and as an attribute of the environment (e.g., context, societal demands). Biological approaches focus on the genetics of intelligence (e.g., understanding the biological process related to intelligences and locating the genetic code for intelligences). Mental approaches focus on metacognitive and cognitive capabilities (e.g., the knowledge and cognitive processes that an individual possesses). Motivational approaches argue that there is more to intelligence than mental capability (e.g., most cognition is motivated, and motivation to think determines quality and quantity of cognition). Thus, the magnitude and direction of an individual's

energy represent motivational intelligence. Finally, behavioral approaches focus on what individuals do (i.e., their actions), rather than on what they think or feel. In our research, we focus on the three loci of individual intelligence with direct relevance to human interaction: the mental (metacognition and cognition), motivational, and behavioral aspects of intelligence. Further, we argue that differentiating multiple forms of cultural intelligence will enable more fine-grained understanding of key individual capabilities that enhance functioning in culturally diverse settings.

So far we have differentiated cultural intelligence from existing nonacademic intelligences and have used Sternberg's (1986) work on loci of intelligence as a conceptual basis for proposing four factors of CQ (metacognition, cognition, motivation, and behavior). Before describing these four aspects of CQ in more detail, we acknowledge the large and increasing amount of research with relevance to CQ: culture (Adler, 2002; Erez & Earley, 1993; Hofstede, 1991; Nisbett, 2003; Triandis, 1994), expatriate adjustment (Bhaskar-Shrinivas, Harrison, Shaffer, & Luk, 2005; Black, Mendenhall, & Oddou, 1991; Black & Stephens, 1989; Caligiuri, Hyland, Joshi, & Bross, 1998; Mendenhall & Oddou, 1985; Shaffer, Harrison, Gregersen, Black, & Ferzandi, 2006; Takeuchi, Yun, & Tesluk, 2002), expatriate selection and training (Spreitzer, McCall, & Mahoney, 1997), expatriate performance (Caligiuri, 2000; Hechanova, Beehr, & Christiansen, 2003; Kraimer et al., 2001; Ones & Viswesvaran, 1997; Tung, 1988), global leadership (House, Hanges, Javidan, Dorfman, & Gupta, 2004), global teams (Kirkman, Gibson, & Shapiro, 2001), cross-cultural training (Black & Mendenhall, 1990; Bhawuk & Brislin, 2000; Landis, Bennett, & Bennett, 2004; Lievens et al., 2003), and intercultural communication (Ting-Toomey, 1999; Gudykunst & Ting-Toomey, 1988).

It is also important to differentiate cultural intelligence from prior research on the general topic of cultural competence. This is because it is important to avoid proliferation of constructs and scales. It is also critical to show that new constructs (a) are strongly grounded in theory, (b) have strong psychometric characteristics, and (c) improve our ability to predict and understand meaningful outcomes. To date, scholars and consultants have introduced numerous constructs focused on the general topic of cultural competence. Most of these constructs and measures, however, do not fit the three criteria outlined above. More specifically, review of the numerous intercultural competency scales included in Paige's (2004) summary of the literature highlights several gaps that CQ addresses. First, most intercultural competencies scales mix ability and personality (a partial list includes the CCAI: Cross-Cultural Adaptability Inventory; CCWM: Cross-Cultural World Mindedness; CSI: Cultural Shock Inventory; ICAPS: Intercultural Adjustment Potential Scale; MAKSS: Multicultural Awareness-Knowledge-Skills Survey; OAI: Overseas Assignment Inventory, and Prospector). Although personality characteristics can be relevant to cross-cultural adjustment, including stable dispositional traits in competency models muddies the validity and precision of these models. Second, although many scales include items that are similar to CQ, none of the existing scales are based explicitly on contemporary theories of intelligence, and none of the scales systematically assess the four aspects of intelligence.

In sum, contemporary globalization and the breadth of existing research on intercultural competencies show the potential benefits of a measure of cultural intelligence that is theoretically based and psychometrically rigorous. Second, since none of the existing research focuses specifically on

intelligence as the conceptual basis for differentiating individual capabilities to function effectively in situations characterized by cultural diversity, CQ is unique in its focus. Third, cultural intelligence has the potential to enrich these other streams of research, just as this existing research can inform future research on cultural intelligence. In sum, this chapter introduces a new measure that has a strong conceptual foundation based explicitly on theories of multiple loci of intelligence, including metacognition, cognition, motivation, and behavior. In the next section, we describe each of the four factors of CQ in more detail.

METACOGNITIVE CQ

Metacognitive CQ is an individual's cultural consciousness and awareness during interactions with those who have different cultural backgrounds. The metacognitive factor of CQ is a critical component of cultural intelligence for at least three reasons (O'Neil & Abedi, 1996; Pintrich & DeGroot, 1990). First, it promotes active thinking about people and situations when cultural backgrounds differ. Second, it triggers critical thinking about habits, assumptions, and culturally bound thinking. Third, it allows individuals to evaluate and revise their mental maps, consequently increasing the accuracy of their understanding.

COGNITIVE CQ

Cognitive CQ is an individual's cultural knowledge of norms, practices, and conventions in different cultural settings. Given the wide variety of cultures in the contemporary world, cognitive CQ indicates knowledge of cultural universals as well as knowledge of cultural differences (Triandis, 1994). The cognitive factor of CQ is a critical component of cultural intelligence because knowledge about cultural similarities and differences is the foundation of decision making and performance in cross-cultural situations.

MOTIVATIONAL CQ

Motivational CQ is an individual's capability to direct attention and energy toward cultural differences. Using the expectancy–value framework of motivation (Eccles & Wigfield, 2002; Kanfer, 1990), we conceptualize motivational CQ as a special form of self-efficacy (Bandura, 1986) and intrinsic motivation (Deci & Ryan, 1985) in cross-cultural situations. Self-efficacy and intrinsic motivation play an important role in CQ because successful intercultural interaction requires a basic sense of confidence and interest in novel settings.

BEHAVIORAL CQ

Finally, behavioral CQ is an individual's capability to exhibit appropriate verbal and nonverbal actions when interacting with people who differ in cultural background. Behavioral CQ is based on having and using a broad repertoire or range of behaviors and is a critical component of CQ because behavior is often the most visible characteristic of social interactions (Gumperz 1982; Gudykunst & Kim, 1984; Scollon & Scollon, 1995; Wiseman, 1995). Cultures vary in their behavioral repertoires in three ways: (a) the specific range of behaviors that are enacted; (b) the display rules for when specific nonverbal expressions are required, preferred, permitted, or prohibited; and (c) the interpretations of specific nonverbal behaviors (Lustig & Koester, 1999). In cross-cultural interactions, nonverbal behaviors are especially critical because they function as a "silent language" that conveys meaning in subtle and covert ways (Hall, 1959).

Given the proliferation of constructs and measures in management, organizational behavior, and psychology, it is essential to show that cultural intelligence can be differentiated from other capabilities. It is also important to show that CQ increases our understanding (above and beyond existing related constructs in cross-cultural research) and that CQ predicts meaningful outcomes. For discriminant validity, we focus on differentiating CQ capabilities from cognitive ability and emotional intelligence capabilities (Mayer & Salovey, 1993) as well as adjustment and mental well-being (Ward & Kennedy, 1999). For incremental validity, we propose that cultural intelligence will make an incremental contribution to the literature only if it increases predicted variance in outcomes above and beyond that of demographic characteristics, cognitive ability (IQ), and emotional intelligence (EQ). For predictive validity, we examine the extent to which CQ predicts the outcomes of cultural judgment and decision making (CJDM), adjustment, and mental well-being.

◆ Scale Development of the 20-Item Cultural Intelligence Scale (CQS)

Based on review of the intelligence and intercultural competencies literatures, supplemented by interviews with eight executives who had extensive global work experience, we developed operational definitions of the four theoretically based aspects of CQ. Metacognitive CQ is the capability for consciousness during intercultural interactions. We drew on educational and cognitive psychology operationalizations of metacognition (e.g., O'Neil &

Abedi, 1996; Pintrich & DeGroot, 1990) for awareness, planning, regulating, monitoring, and controlling cognitive processes of thinking and learning. Cognitive CQ is knowledge of norms, practices, and conventions in different cultural settings. We used cultural knowledge domains identified by Triandis (1994) and supplemented these with Murdock's (1987) Human Relations Areas Files. Cultural knowledge includes knowledge of the economic, legal, and social systems in other cultures (Triandis, 1994). Motivational CQ is the capability to direct attention and energy toward learning and functioning in intercultural situations. We drew on Deci and Ryan (1985) for intrinsic satisfaction and Bandura (2002) for self-efficacy in intercultural settings. Finally, behavioral CQ is the capability to exhibit appropriate verbal and nonverbal actions when interacting with people who differ in cultural background. We drew on intercultural communication research for verbal and nonverbal flexibility in cross-cultural interactions (Gudykunst et al., 1988; Hall, 1959).

ITEM POOL GENERATION

Hinkin (1998) suggested starting with twice as many items as targeted for the final scale to allow for psychometric refinement. We aimed for a parsimonious scale with four to six items for each CQ dimension to minimize response bias caused by boredom and fatigue (Schmitt & Stults, 1985) while providing adequate internal consistency reliability (Hinkin & Schriesheim, 1989). Using the above operational definitions for the four CQ dimensions, we started with 53 items for the initial item pool (13–14 per CQ dimension). Each item contained one idea, was relatively short in length, and used simple, direct language. Since negatively worded items can create artifacts (Marsh,

1996), we used positively worded items. Next, a non-overlapping panel of three faculty members and three international executives (each with significant cross-cultural expertise) independently assessed the randomly ordered 53 items for clarity, readability, and definitional fidelity (1 = very low quality; 5 = very high quality). We kept the 10 best items for each dimension, resulting in an initial set of 40 items.

STUDY 1: SCALE DEVELOPMENT

Business school undergraduates (n = 576; 74% female; mean age 20; 2 years of work experience) in Singapore voluntarily completed the 40-item initial CQ questionnaire (1 = strongly disagree; 7 = strongly agree) for partial fulfilment of course requirements. In our analysis, we expected to confirm a four-factor structure since we designed the measure to reflect the four theoretical dimensions of CQ. Accordingly, we assessed dimensionality with confirmatory factor analysis (CFA: LISREL 8: maximum likelihood estimation and correlated factors). We used CFA for this analysis because our items were based on an a priori four-factor structure of intelligence.

Starting with the initial 40 items, we conducted a comprehensive series of specification searches in which we deleted items with high residuals, low factor loadings, small standard deviations or extreme means, and low item-to-total correlations. We retained 20 items with the strongest psychometric properties as the Cultural Intelligence Scale (CQS): four metacognitive CQ, six cognitive CQ, five motivational CQ, and five behavioral CQ (see the Appendix for the Cultural Intelligence Scale, page 240). CFA demonstrated a good fit of the hypothesized four-factor model to the data: χ^2 (164df) = 822.26, (p < .05) since the Comparative Fit Index (CFI = .92) was over .90 and the Root Mean Squared Error of Approximation (RMSEA = .08) was less than .09. Standardized factor loadings for items in the four scales (.52–.80) were significantly different from zero (*t*-values: 9.30–17.51, *p* < .05).

We compared this four-factor correlated model with alternate theoretically possible models to assess relative fit compared to (a) an orthogonal four-factor model (Model B), (b) three factors—metacognitive CQ and cognitive CQ versus motivational CQ versus behavioral CQ (Model C)—(c) two factors—metacognitive CQ and cognitive CQ versus motivational CQ and behavioral CQ (Model D)—(d) two factors—metacognitive CQ versus cognitive CQ , motivational CQ , and behavioral CQ (Model E)—and (e) one factor (Model F).

Nested model comparisons (see Table 18.1, page 241) demonstrate the superiority of the hypothesized four-factor model because each of the $\Delta\chi^2$ statistics exceeds the critical value based on degrees of freedom. Model A (correlated four factors) demonstrated a better fit than Model B (orthogonal four factors) ($\Delta\chi^2$ [6*df*] = 377.50, *p* < .001). Model A (four factors) also had a better fit than Model C (three factors), which combined metacognitive CQ and cognitive CQ ($\Delta\chi^2$ [3*df*] = 411.91, *p* < .001). Likewise, Model A (four factors) was a better fit than the two alternate two-factor models: Model D (metacognitive CQ and cognitive CQ versus the other two factors: $\Delta\chi^2$ [5*df*] = 1314.99, *p* < .001) or Model E (metacognitive CQ versus the other three factors: $\Delta\chi^2$ [5*df*] = 1631.17, *p* < .001). Finally, Model A (four factors) was a better fit than Model G with one factor ($\Delta\chi^2$ [6*df*] = 1931.52, *p* < .001).

In sum, Model A, the hypothesized model, had the best fit. We averaged items for each factor to create scales representing each of the four CQ factors. Table 18.2 (page 242) reports means, standard deviations, correlations, and alphas. The four

factors were moderately related (.21–.45), with acceptable variances (.75–1.03). The corrected item-to-total correlations for each subscale (.47–71) demonstrated strong relationships between items and their scales, supporting internal consistency. Composite reliabilities exceeded .70 (metacognitive CQ = .71, cognitive CQ = .85, motivational CQ = .75, and behavioral CQ = .83; Fornell & Larcker, 1981). The appendix lists the twenty items in the cultural intelligence scale.

STUDY 2: GENERALIZABILITY ACROSS SAMPLES

A second, non-overlapping sample of 447 undergraduates in Singapore (70% female; mean age 20; 2 years of work experience) voluntarily completed the 20-item CQS for partial fulfillment of course requirements. CFA analysis demonstrated a good fit of the data to the hypothesized four-factor model: χ^2 (164*df*) = 381.28, CFI = .96, and RMSEA = .05 (*p* < .05). Standardized loadings (.50–.79) were significantly different from zero (*t*-values: 8.32–12.90, *p* < .05), with moderate correlations between factors (.23–.37) and acceptable variances (.87–1.05). Corrected item-to-total correlations for each subscale (.46–.66) demonstrated strong relationships between items and their scales, supporting internal consistency.

Results of Study 2 extend the results in Study 1 and provide additional support for the four factors of CQ as measured by four items for metacognitive CQ (α = .77), six for cognitive CQ (α = .84), five for motivational CQ (α = .77), and five for behavioral CQ (α = .84). Table 18.3 (page 242) reports descriptive statistics and correlations for the four factors of cultural intelligence in Study 2, and Figure 18.1 (page 243) reports completely standardized parameter estimates for the four-factor model.

APPENDIX: Cultural Intelligence Scale (CQS)

Read each statement and select the response that best describes your capabilities.
Select the answer that BEST describes you AS YOU REALLY ARE (1 = strongly disagree;
7 = strongly agree)

CQ Factor	Questionnaire Items
Metacognitive CQ:	
MC1	I am conscious of the cultural knowledge I use when interacting with people with different cultural backgrounds.
MC2	I adjust my cultural knowledge as I interact with people from a culture that is unfamiliar to me.
MC3	I am conscious of the cultural knowledge I apply to cross-cultural interactions.
MC4	I check the accuracy of my cultural knowledge as I interact with people from different cultures.
Cognitive CQ:	
COG1	I know the legal and economic systems of other cultures.
COG2	I know the rules (e.g., vocabulary, grammar) of other languages.
COG3	I know the cultural values and religious beliefs of other cultures.
COG4	I know the marriage systems of other cultures.
COG5	I know the arts and crafts of other cultures.
COG6	I know the rules for expressing nonverbal behaviors in other cultures.
Motivational CQ:	
MOT1	I enjoy interacting with people from different cultures.
MOT2	I am confident that I can socialize with locals in a culture that is unfamiliar to me.
MOT3	I am sure I can deal with the stresses of adjusting to a culture that is new to me.
MOT4	I enjoy living in cultures that are unfamiliar to me.
MOT5	I am confident that I can get accustomed to the shopping conditions in a different culture.
Behavioral CQ:	
BEH1	I change my verbal behavior (e.g., accent, tone) when a cross-cultural interaction requires it.
BEH2	I use pause and silence differently to suit different cross-cultural situations.
BEH3	I vary the rate of my speaking when a cross-cultural situation requires it.
BEH4	I change my non-verbal behavior when a cross-cultural situation requires it.
BEH5	I alter my facial expressions when a cross-cultural interaction requires it.

SOURCE: © Cultural Intelligence Center 2005. Used by permission of Cultural Intelligence Center.

NOTE: Use of this scale granted to academic researchers for research purposes only. For information on using the scale for purposes other than academic research (e.g., consultants and nonacademic organizations), please send an email to cquery@culturalq.com.

Table 18.1 Comparing the Fit of Alternative Nested Models With CFA (Study 1)[a]

	Model	χ^2	Df	NNFI	CFI	SRMR	RMSEA	$\Delta\chi^2$	p-value
A	20-item four-factor model	822.26	164	.91	.92	.06	.08		
	Alternate nested models:[b]								
B	(a) Four-factor orthogonal model	1199.76	170	.87	.88	.17	.11	377.50	p < .001
C	(b) Three-factor model (metacognitive CQ and cognitive CQ combined versus motivational CQ versus behavioral CQ)	1234.17	167	.86	.88	.08	.11	411.91	p < .001
D	(c) Two-factor model (metacognitive CQ and cognitive CQ combined versus motivational CQ and behavioral CQ)	2137.25	169	.79	.81	.12	.15	1314.99	p < .001
E	(d) Two-factor model (metacognitive CQ versus the other three factors combined)	2453.43	169	.75	.77	.12	.16	1631.17	p < .001
F	(e) One-factor model with all items loading on a single factor	2753.78	170	.72	.75	.12	.17	1931.52	p < .001

a. $n = 576$

b. Compared to the hypothesized four-factor model

STUDY 3: GENERALIZABILITY ACROSS TIME

A subset of respondents ($n = 204$, 76% female, mean age 20) from Study 2, Singapore cross-validation sample, completed the CQS again 4 months later (at the start of the next semester) in exchange for partial fulfillment of course requirements. We used these responses to analyze temporal stability of the CQS.

We used procedure suggested by Vandenberg and Lance (2000) to examine longitudinal measurement invariance of the

Table 18.2 Means, Standard Deviations, Scale Reliabilities, and Intercorrelations (Study 1)[a]

	MN	SD	1	2	3	4
1. Metacognitive CQ	4.71	.75	(.71)			
2. Cognitive CQ	3.03	.84	.39[b]	(.85)		
3. Motivational CQ	4.72	.80	.45[b]	.33[b]	(.75)	
4. Behavioral CQ	4.10	.03	.28[b]	.36[b]	.21[b]	(.83)

a. $n = 576$. Reliability coefficients are in parentheses along the diagonal.
b. $p < .01$

Table 18.3 Means, Standard Deviations, Scale Reliabilities, and Intercorrelations (Study 2)[a]

	MN	SD	1	2	3	4
1. Metacognitive CQ	4.89	0.87	(.77)			
2. Cognitive CQ	3.16	0.89	.23[b]	(.84)		
3. Motivational CQ	4.74	0.92	.32[b]	.25[b]	(.77)	
4. Behavioral CQ	4.22	1.05	.37[b]	.34[b]	.31[b]	(.84)

a. $n = 447$. Reliability coefficients are in parentheses along the diagonal.
b. $p < .01$

CQS, using CFA and an augmented covariance matrix as input (rather than a multi-sample approach) to account for time-wise correlated errors. We used a 20-item/two-measurement occasion matrix and specified eight latent variables (four T1 CQ factors and four T2 CQ factors), with unique variances of identical items correlated across time (Jöreskog & Sorbom, 2003).

We began with a correlated four-factor model with no constraints (parameters at T1 and T2 freely estimated). Results demonstrated an acceptable fit (Model A: χ^2 [692df] = 981.18, CFI = .95, RMSEA = .04), indicating that the four-factor model held across the two time periods (see Table 18.4, page 244). We then developed two alternative models: Model B (factor loadings constrained to be invariant) and Model C (item intercepts constrained to be invariant). The chi-square difference between Model A and B (nested factorial invariance model) failed to reach significance ($\Delta\chi^2$ [16df] = 22.79, p = ns), providing strong support for invariance in factor loadings across T1 and T2. The chi-square difference between Model B and C (item intercepts constrained to be invariant) also failed to reach significance ($\Delta\chi^2$ [14df] = 17.59, p = ns), providing support for item intercept invariance.

Finally, we assessed the means for the four factors across time. Unlike personality characteristics that are relatively stable traits, Earley and Ang (2003) conceptualized CQ as a

Figure 18.1   Confirmatory Factor Analysis of 20-Item CQ Model (Study 2)

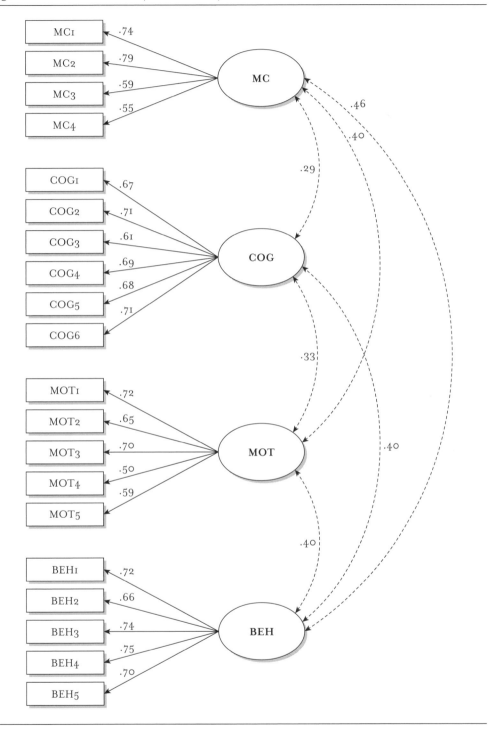

Table 18.4 Multiple Group CFA Across Time: Comparing the Fit of Alternative Models (Study 2)*

	Model	χ^2	df	NNFI	CFI	SRMR	RMSEA	$\Delta\chi^2$	p-value
A	Four-factor model with factor loadings freely estimated across time	981.18	692	.94	.95	.06	.04		
B	Four-factor model with invariant factor loadings across time	1003.97	708	.94	.95	.07	.05	22.79	p > .05
C	Four-factor model with invariant item intercepts across time	1021.56	722	.94	.95	.07	.05	17.59	p > .05
D	Four-factor model with invariant means across time	1045.35	726	.94	.94	.07	.05	23.79	p < .05

* n = 204

malleable capability that may change based on cultural exposure, training, modeling, mentoring, socialization, and other experiences. Thus, we anticipated that some means for the four CQ factors could change across time, depending on experience and/or education. We compared Model C (item intercept invariance) with Model D (means invariance) that constrained means of the four factors to be invariant across time. Results showed a significant decrease in fit: Model C (χ^2 [722*df*] = 1021.56) versus Model D (χ^2 [726*df*] = 1045.35), with a significant change in χ^2 ($\Delta\chi^2$ [4*df*] = 23.79, p < .05). Closer examination of the individual means demonstrated significant changes in factor means for cognitive CQ, which increased .33 (t = 4.87, p < .001) and behavioral CQ which increased .21 (t = 2.87, p < .01). This makes sense because respondents studied cultural values and participated in experiential activities including role-play

exercises during the time interval that separated T1 and T2 assessment of CQ. Neither metacognitive CQ nor motivational CQ changed significantly. Thus, the results provide evidence of malleability as well as test–retest reliability.

STUDY 4: GENERALIZABILITY ACROSS COUNTRIES

A fourth sample of undergraduates (n = 337; 55% female; mean age 22; 1 year of work experience) at a large Midwestern school in the United States voluntarily completed the 20-item CQS for partial fulfilment of course requirements. Table 18.5 reports descriptive statistics, correlations, and reliabilities for this sample.

We assessed equivalence of the CQS across countries (Kirkman & Law, 2005) and compared the U.S. sample with the Singapore sample in Study 2 (n = 447),

Table 18.5 Means, Standard Deviations, Scale Reliabilities, and Intercorrelations (Study 4)[a]

	MN	SD	1	2	3	4
1. Metacognitive CQ	4.98	0.95	(.78)			
2. Cognitive CQ	3.66	0.98	.38[b]	(.81)		
3. Motivational CQ	5.34	0.94	.50[b]	.36[b]	(.80)	
4. Behavioral CQ	4.20	1.14	.37[b]	.43[b]	.31[b]	(.81)

a. $n = 337$. Reliability coefficients are in parentheses along the diagonal.
b. $p < .01$

using sequential tests of model invariance (Byrne, 1998). Model A (four-factors with loadings freely estimated across samples) demonstrated a good fit: χ^2 ($328df$) = 723.23, CFI = .97, RMSEA = .05, indicating equivalence in number of factors.

We tested two alternative models: Model B (four-factors with loadings forced to be invariant) to test if items were interpreted equivalently across settings and Model C (four-factors with factor covariances forced to be invariant) to test if covariances among factors were equivalent across settings. The chi-square difference between Model A and B (nested factorial invariance model) failed to reach significance ($\Delta\chi^2$ [$16df$] = 13.74, $p = ns$), providing strong support for invariance in factor loadings across settings. The chi-square difference between Model B and C (nested covariance invariance model) failed to reach significance ($\Delta\chi^2$ [$10d$] = 17.96, $p = ns$), supporting invariance in factor covariances. These multiple group tests of invariance demonstrated that the same four factor structure holds across the two countries (Singapore and U.S.).

STUDY 5: DISCRIMINANT AND INCREMENTAL VALIDITY

Extending the results of Studies 1–4, which assessed psychometric characteristics of the CQS and measurement invariance of the four

factors across time and across two countries, Study 5 focuses on discriminant and incremental validity of the CQS. To do this, we had respondents in Study 2 and Study 4 complete a second questionnaire, including measures of cognitive ability, emotional intelligence, cultural judgment and decision making (CJDM), interactional adjustment, and mental well-being. We obtained matched data for 251 respondents in Study 2 and 249 respondents in Study 4 (56% and 74% response rates, respectively). Using this data, we first examined the discriminant validity of the four factors of CQ relative to cognitive ability, emotional intelligence, CJDM, interactional adjustment, and mental well-being. Second, we assessed incremental validity of CQ over and above demographic characteristics, cognitive ability, and emotional intelligence in predicting CJDM, interactional adjustment, and mental well-being.

MEASURES

For CJDM, we adapted five scenarios from Cushner and Brislin (1996). Participants read scenarios describing cross-cultural interactions and indicated which response best explained the situation. We summed each participant's correct responses (range 0–5).

We measured *interactional adjustment* with three items from Black and Stephens

(1989): Rate how well you have adjusted to your current situation in terms of "socializing with people, interacting with people on a day-to-day basis, getting along with people" (1 = extremely unadjusted, 7 = extremely adjusted; $\alpha = .93$).

We measured mental *well-being* with four items (Goldberg & Williams, 1988): Rate your general well-being at this time in terms of "[being] able to concentrate on whatever you have been doing, feel[ing] that you are playing a useful part, feel[ing] capable of making decisions, and [being] able to face up to your responsibilities" (1 = not at all, 7 = to a very great extent; $\alpha = .82$).

We measured *cognitive ability* with the Wonderlic Personnel Test (1999) of problem-solving ability. This test has support in the literature as a reliable and valid measure of cognitive ability (e.g., see LePine, 2003). We assessed *emotional intelligence* with eight items from the Schutte et al. (1998) scale that is based on Salovey and Mayer's (1990) model of emotional intelligence. Items include "I seek out activities that make me happy" and "I arrange events that others enjoy" ($\alpha = .80$).

Participants reported their age (years) and sex (0 = female, 1 = male), and we created dummy codes for each sample (0 = U.S., 1 = Singapore).

Since we previously demonstrated equivalence in number of factors, factor loadings, and structural relationships across countries (U.S. and Singapore), we combined Sample 2 ($n = 251$) and Sample 4 ($n = 249$) for these analyses ($n = 500$). Table 18.6 reports descriptive statistics, correlations, and reliabilities for the combined samples.

DISCRIMINANT VALIDITY

We assessed discriminant validity of the four factors of CQ relative to cognitive ability, emotional intelligence, CJDM, interactional adjustment, and mental well-being

using confirmatory factor analysis with Study 5 data. Results demonstrated a good fit for the nine-factor model (c^2 [595df] = 1303.47, CFI = .96, RMSEA = .05), supporting the distinctiveness of the four CQ factors, cognitive ability, emotional intelligence, CJDM, interactional adjustment, and mental well-being. All factor loadings were significant, with t-values ranging from 8.96 to 33.07.

INCREMENTAL VALIDITY

We tested the incremental validity of CQ with hierarchical regression. For controls, we entered age, sex (0 = female, 1 = male), and sample (0 = U.S., 1 = Singapore) in Step 1 and cognitive ability and emotional intelligence in Step 2. In Step 3, we added the four factors of CQ (metacognitive CQ, cognitive CQ, motivational CQ, and behavioral CQ). We used Change-F statistics to assess each regression step and t-values to assess significance of individual beta values. Table 18.7 reports results of the regression analyses for CJDM, interactional adjustment, and mental well-being.

PREDICTIVE VALIDITY

Results showed that age, sex, and sample explained 4% of the variance in CJDM, 4% in interactional adjustment, and 14% in mental well-being. The addition of cognitive ability and emotional intelligence in Step 2 increased the explained variance significantly for CJDM ($DF = 12.20$, $p < .001$), interactional adjustment ($DF = 13.67$, $p < .001$), and mental well-being ($DF = 41.83$, $p < .001$). Results in Step 3 demonstrate the incremental validity of the four factors of CQ, over and above demographic characteristics, cognitive ability, and emotional intelligence in predicting CJDM ($DF = 4.97$ $p < .01$), interactional adjustment ($DF = 3.73$, $p < .01$), and

Table 18.6 Means, Standard Deviations, Scale Reliabilities, and Intercorrelations (Study 5)[a]

	MN	SD	1	2	3	4	5	6	7	8	9	10	11	12
1. Cultural Decision Making	3.23	1.11	—											
2. Interactional Adjustment	5.63	1.16	.03	(.93)										
3. Mental Well-Being	4.98	0.97	.01	.49[e]	(.82)									
4. Metacognitive CQ	4.94	0.88	.17[e]	.17[e]	.24[e]	(.74)								
5. Cognitive CQ	3.41	0.96	.11[d]	.10[d]	.26[e]	.27[e]	(.83)							
6. Motivational CQ	5.00	0.98	.03	.23[e]	.41[e]	.43[e]	.34[e]	(.81)						
7. Behavioral CQ	4.21	1.09	.09[d]	.17[e]	.25[e]	.39[e]	.39[e]	.32[e]	(.82)					
8. Cognitive Ability	27.59	5.58	.24[e]	-.05	-.12[e]	.06	-.05	-.10[d]	.03	—				
9. Emotional Intelligence	5.27	0.78	-.03	.26[e]	.42[e]	.33[e]	.24[e]	.33[e]	.28[e]	-.05	(.80)			
10. Age	21.14	2.88	.10[d]	.07	.17[e]	.05	.11[d]	.14[e]	.10[d]	-.14[e]	.05	—		
11. Sex[b]	0.46	0.50	.08	.02	.09[d]	.02	.10[d]	.15[e]	.10[d]	-.01	.03	.24[e]	—	
12. Sample[c]	0.50	0.50	.11[d]	-.19[e]	-.37[e]	-.01	-.25[e]	-.29[e]	.02	.42[e]	-.19[e]	-.29[e]	-.22[e]	—

a. $n = 500$. Reliability coefficients are in parentheses along the diagonal.
b. 0 = female, 1 = male
c. 0 = U.S., 1 = Singapore
d. $p < .05$
e. $p < .01$

Table 18.7 Hierarchical Regression Analysis (Study 5)[a]

Variable	Cultural Decision Making			Interactional Adjustment			Mental Well-Being		
	Step 1	Step 2	Step 3	Step 1	Step 2	Step 3	Step 1	Step 2	Step 3
Age	$.12^e$	$.13^e$	$.12^e$	.02	.03	.01	.06	.07	.05
Sex[b]	.09	.07	.07	−.03	−.04	−.05	.00	.00	−.03
Sample[c]	$.16^e$	.06	.07	$−.19^f$	$−.17^e$	$−.17^e$	$−.35^f$	$−.30^f$	$−.26^f$
Cognitive Ability		$.24^f$	$.22^f$		.04	.04		.04	.03
Emotional Intelligence		−.02	−.08		$.23^f$	$.16^e$		$.36^f$	$.26^f$
Metacognitive CQ			$.16^e$			.05			.01
Cognitive CQ			$.11^d$			−.06			.02
Motivational CQ			−.04			$.11^d$			$.21^f$
Behavioral CQ			−.01			$.10^d$			$.10^d$
F	6.43^f	8.91^f	7.32^f	6.63^f	9.65^f	7.14^f	27.04^f	35.63^f	26.306^f
ΔF		12.20^f	4.97^e		13.67^f	3.73^e		41.83^f	10.64^f
R^2	.04	.08	.12	.04	.09	.12	.14	.26	.32
ΔR^2		.04	.04		.05	.03		.12	.06
Adjusted R^2	.03	.07	.10	.03	.08	.10	.14	.26	.31

a. $n = 500$
b. 0 = female, 1 = male
c. 0 = U.S., 1 = Singapore
d. $p < .05$
e. $p < .01$
f. $p < .001$

well-being (DF = 10.64, p < .001). Overall, the adjusted R^2 statistics explained 10% of the variance in CJDM, 10% of the variance in interactional adjustment, and 31% of the variance in mental well-being.

For CJDM, results demonstrate that metacognitive CQ (β = .16, p < .01) and cognitive CQ (β = .11, p < .05) increased explained variance, over and above the effects of demographic characteristics, cognitive ability, and emotional intelligence. Together, metacognitive CQ and cognitive CQ increased explained variance in CJDM by 4%. Overall, the adjusted R^2 was 10%. For interactional adjustment, results demonstrate that motivational CQ (β = .11, p < .05) and behavioral CQ (β = .10, p < .05) increased explained variance, above and beyond demographic characteristics, cognitive ability, and emotional intelligence by 3%. Overall, the adjusted R^2 was 10%. For mental well-being, motivational CQ (β = .21, p < .001) and behavioral CQ (β = .10, p < .05) increased explained variance, above and beyond demographic characteristics, cognitive ability, and emotional intelligence by 6%. Overall, the adjusted R^2 was 31%.

DISCUSSION

This chapter highlights the importance of using a theoretical approach to conceptualizing and measuring intercultural competencies. In addition, the chapter provides a detailed description of the rigorous process used to develop and validate the CQS: the Cultural Intelligence Scale. Early research results suggest that managers can apply the CQS with a high level of confidence based on empirical evidence, that the scale measures what it was designed to measure, and that results are stable across samples, across time, and across cultures. In addition, results demonstrate that the CQS has discriminant validity compared to other constructs

such as cognitive ability and emotional intelligence. Results also demonstrate that CQ increased explained variance in cultural judgment and decision making as well as mental well-being, over and above the effects of demographic characteristics, cognitive ability, and emotional intelligence.

Analysis of results from these five studies allows us to draw several important conclusions. First, the sequential and systematic scale development process described in the five studies provides strong evidence that the CQS has a clear, robust, and meaningful four-factor structure. In addition, results demonstrate that this structure is stable across samples (Study 2), across time (Study 3), and across countries (Study 4). More important, results in Study 5 support the discriminant validity of the CQS compared to cognitive ability, emotional intelligence, CJDM, interactional adjustment, and mental well-being.

Study 5 also demonstrates that the CQS has incremental validity in predicting CJDM, interactional adjustment, and mental well-being. Specifically, metacognitive CQ and cognitive CQ increased explained variance in cultural judgment and decision making by 4%. This makes sense since metacognitive CQ and cognitive CQ represent mental capabilities and since CJDM emphasizes analytic abilities such as deliberate reasoning and evaluation of alternatives. In addition, results demonstrate that motivational CQ and behavioral CQ increased explained variance in interactional adjustment by 3%, and motivational CQ and behavioral CQ increased explained variance in mental well-being by 6%. Since motivational CQ and behavioral CQ focus on drive and flexibility in culturally diverse situations, it also makes sense that they predicted both interactional adjustment and well-being.

From a theoretical perspective, the findings of these five studies (n > 1,350 respondents) indicate that the 20-item CQS holds promise as a reliable and valid measure of cultural intelligence. Potential uses of the scale in substantive research include further exploration of the nature and dimensionality of cultural intelligence. For example, future research could examine subdimensions for each factor of CQ. Additional theoretical work is also needed on the nomological network of CQ, including predictors, consequences, mediators, and moderators. Future research should also assess additional outcomes as indicators of predictive validity. For example, it would be interesting and useful to examine cultural intelligence as a predictor of expatriate and global leader adjustment and well-being as well as different aspects of work performance. It also would be beneficial to examine CQ as a predictor of adjustment, well-being, and performance for those in domestic jobs who work in multicultural groups.

Cultural intelligence and the CQS also have promising practical application. For example, it can provide important insights and personal information to individuals on their own cultural intelligence. According to Paige and Martin (1996), feedback and self-awareness are key to enhancing intercultural effectiveness. Thus, the 20-item CQS can provide insights about specific personal capabilities for functioning effectively in situations characterized by cultural diversity. Knowledge of cultural intelligence could also provide a foundation for personal self-development.

Also, organizations could use the CQS to identify employees who would be particularly well suited for overseas assignments. It also could be used to screen out those who are proficient in domestic settings but unlikely to succeed in cross-cultural settings or in jobs that require frequent and ongoing interaction with those who have other cultural backgrounds. It also could be useful to predict reputations of global leaders (Van Dyne & Ang, 2006). Finally, CQ could be used to develop corporate training and self-awareness

programs or to identify employees who could serve as supportive mentors to those starting overseas assignments.

In conclusion, these five studies suggest both theoretical and practical implications for cultural intelligence and the CQS. We encourage others to use the CQS to enhance our understanding of ways in which the individual capability to function effectively in culturally diverse settings predicts important personal and work outcomes. For example, future research could consider ways in which use of the CQS enhances self-awareness and has application to corporate selection, training and development, and promotion decisions. Generally, we suggest that the CQS has exciting implications for domestic and international managers and leaders.

◆ Discussion Questions

1. Using your own words, how would you define cultural intelligence?

2. How is the development of the CQS (Cultural Intelligence Scale) different from prior work on other intercultural competency measures?

3. Why is it important to assess the construct validity of measures like the 20-item CQS before using scales in applied settings?

4. What is the difference between cultural intelligence and other constructs such as cognitive ability and emotional intelligence?

5. Explain the meaning of the following: "CQ increased explained variance in cultural judgment and decision making as well as mental well-being, over and above the effects of demographic characteristics, cognitive ability, and emotional intelligence." Why is it important to assess these relationships?

6. Rate your own cultural intelligence using the 20-item CQS. Then ask five people who know you well to answer the same questions about you, describing their views of your cultural intelligence. Reflect on this feedback and then prepare a personal development plan in which you set specific goals to enhance your metacognitive CQ, cognitive CQ, motivational CQ, and behavioral CQ.

7. How can you use your new knowledge of cultural intelligence as applied to your own life? Be sure to consider personal relationships you have with people who differ from you in age, sex, functional background, and ethnic/national culture.

8. Assume that you are planning a trip to a part of the world that you have never visited before. How could you use the four aspects of cultural intelligence to help prepare for that trip? What could you do before the trip to enhance your metacognitive CQ, cognitive CQ, motivational CQ, and behavioral CQ? What could you do during the trip to enhance each of the four aspects of CQ?

9. Think about two specific people who you know with contrasting levels of cultural intelligence. Describe these people and explain why you view one as low in CQ and the other as high in CQ. Based on your analysis, what action steps would you recommend that the person with lower cultural intelligence take to improve his/her cultural intelligence?

◆ References

Adler, N. J. (2002). *International dimensions of organizational behavior* (4th ed.). Cincinnati, OH: South-Western.

Aguinis, H., & Henle, C. A. (2003). The search for universals in cross-cultural organizational behavior. In Greenberg, J. (Ed.). *Organizational behavior: The state of the science* (2nd ed., pp. 373–414). Mahwah, NJ: Erlbaum.

Ang, S., Van Dyne, L., Koh, C. K. S., Ng, K. Y., Templer, K. J., Tay, C., & Chandrasekar, N. A. (2007). Cultural intelligence: Its measurement and effects on cultural judgment and decision making, cultural adaptation, and task performance. *Management and Organization Review, 3,* 335–371.

Bandura, A. (1986). *Social foundations of thoughts and actions: A social cognitive theory.* Englewood Cliffs, NJ: Prentice Hall.

Bandura, A. (2002). Social cognitive theory in cultural context. *Applied Psychology: An International Review, 51,* 269–290.

Bhaskar-Shrinivas, P., Harrison, D. A., Shaffer, M. A., & Luk, D. M. (2005). Input-based and time-based models of international adjustment: Meta-analytic evidence and theoretical extensions. *Academy of Management Journal, 48,* 257–281.

Bhawuk, D. P. S., & Brislin, R. W. (2000). Cross-cultural training: A review. *Applied Psychology: An International Review, 49,* 162–191.

Black, J. S., Gregersen, H. B., Mendenhall, M. E., & Stroh, L. K. (1999). *Globalizing people through international assignments.* New York: Addison-Wesley Longman.

Black, J. S., & Mendenhall, M. E. (1990). Cross-cultural training effectiveness: A review and a theoretical framework for future research. *Academy of Management Review, 15,* 113–136.

Black, J. S., Mendenhall, M. E., & Oddou, G. (1991). Toward a comprehensive model of international adjustment: An integration of multiple theoretical perspectives. *Academy of Management Review, 16,* 291–317.

Black, J. S., & Stephens, G. K. (1989). The influence of the spouse on American expatriate adjustment and intent to stay in Pacific Rim overseas assignments. *Journal of Management, 15,* 529–544.

Byrne, B. M. (1998). *Structural equation modelling with LISREL, PRELIS, and SIMPLIS: Basic concepts, applications, and programming.* Mahwah, NJ: Erlbaum.

Caligiuri, P. M. (2000). The Big Five personality characteristics as predictors of expatriate's desire to terminate the assignment and supervisor-rated performance. *Personnel Psychology, 53,* 67–88.

Caligiuri, P. M., Hyland, M. A. M., Joshi, A., & Bross, A. S. (1998). Testing a theoretical model for examining the relationship of family adjustment and expatriate's work adjustment. *Journal of Applied Psychology, 53,* 67–88.

Cantor, N., & Kihlstrom, J. F. (1985). Social intelligence: The cognitive basis of personality. *Review of Personality and Social Psychology, 6,* 15–33.

Cushner, K., & Brislin, R. W. (1996). *Intercultural relations: A practical guide* (2nd ed.). Thousand Oaks, CA: Sage.

Deci, E. L., & Ryan, R. M. (1985). *Intrinsic motivation and self-determination in human behavior.* New York: Plenum.

Earley, P.C., & Ang, S. (2003). *Cultural intelligence: Individual interactions across cultures.* Palo Alto, CA: Stanford University Press.

Earley, P. C., & Gibson, C. B. (2002). *Multinational work teams: A new perspective.* Hillsdale, NJ: Erlbaum.

Eccles, J. S., & Wigfield, A. (2002). Motivational beliefs, values, and goals. In S. T. Fiske, D. L. Schacter, C. Zahn-Waxler (Eds.), *Annual review of psychology* (Vol. 53, pp. 109–132). Palo Alto, CA: Annual Reviews.

Erez, M., & Earley, P. C. (1993). *Culture, self-identity, and work.* New York: Oxford University Press.

Ford, M., & Tisak, M. (1983). A further search for social intelligence. *Journal of Educational Psychology, 75,* 196–206.

Fornell, C., & Larcker, D. R. (1981). Evaluating structural equation models with unobservable variables and measurement error. *Journal of Marketing Research, 18,* 39–50.

Gardner, H. (1993). *Multiple intelligence: The theory in practice.* New York: Basic Books.

Gelfand, M. J., Erez, M. E., & Aycan, Z. (2007). Cross-cultural organizational behavior. *Annual Review of Psychology, 58,* 479–514.

Goldberg, D. P., & Williams, P. (1988). *A user's guide to the General Health Questionnaire.* Basingstoke, UK: NFER-Nelson.

Goleman, D. (1995). *Emotional intelligence.* New York: Bantam Books.

Gudykunst, W. B., & Kim, Y. Y. (1984). *Communicating with strangers.* Beverly Hills, CA: Sage.

Gudykunst, W. B., & Ting-Toomey, S. (1988). *Culture and interpersonal communication.* Newbury Park, CA: Sage.

Gumperz, J. J. (1982). *Discourse strategies.* Cambridge, UK: Cambridge University Press.

Hall, E. T. (1959). *The silent language.* New York: Doubleday.

Hechanova, R., Beehr, T. A., & Christiansen, N. D. (2003). Antecedents and consequences of employees' adjustment to overseas assignment: A meta-analytic review. *Applied Psychology: An International Review, 52,* 213–236.

Hedlund, J., & Sternberg, R. J. (2000). Practical intelligence: Implications for human resources research. In G. R. Ferris (Ed.), *Research in personnel and human resources management* (Vol. 19, pp. 1–52). New York: Elsevier Science.

Hinkin, T. R. (1998). A brief tutorial on the development of measures for use in survey questionnaires. *Organizational Research Methods, 1,* 104–121.

Hinkin, T. R., & Schriesheim, C. A. (1989). Development and application of new scales to measure the French and Raven (1959) bases of social power. *Journal of Applied Psychology, 74,* 561–567.

Hofstede, G. (1991). *Culture and organizations: Software of the mind.* London: McGraw-Hill.

House, R. J., Hanges, P. J., Javidan, M., Dorfman, P. W., & Gupta, V. (2004). *Culture, leadership, and organizations: A GLOBE study of 62 societies.* Thousand Oaks, CA: Sage.

Jöreskog, K. G., & Sorbom, D. (2003). *Windows LISREL 8.54.* Chicago: Scientific Software.

Kanfer, R. (1990). Motivation theory and industrial/organizational psychology. In M. D. Dunnette & L. Hough (Eds.), *Handbook of industrial and organizational psychology. Volume 1: Theory in industrial and organizational psychology* (pp. 75–170). Palo Alto, CA: Consulting Psychologists Press.

Kirkman, B. L., Gibson, C. B., & Shapiro, D. L. (2001). "Exporting" teams: Enhancing the implementation and effectiveness of work teams in global affiliates. *Organizational Dynamics, 30*(1), 12–29.

Kirkman, B. L., & Law, K. S. (2005). International management research in AMJ: Our past, present, and future. *Academy of Management Journal, 48,* 377–386.

Kraimer, M. L., Wayne, S. J., & Jaworski, R. A. (2001). Sources of support and expatriate performance: The mediating role of expatriate adjustment. *Personnel Psychology, 54,* 71–99

Landis, D., Bennett, J. M., & Bennett, M. J. (Eds.). (2004). *Handbook of intercultural training.* Thousand Oaks, CA: Sage.

LePine, J. A. (2003). Team adaptation and postchange performance: Effects of team composition in terms of members' cognitive ability and personality. *Journal of Applied Psychology, 88*(1), 27–39.

Lievens, F., Harris, M. M., Van Keer, E., & Bisqueret, C. (2003). Predicting cross-cultural training performance: The validity of personality, cognitive ability, and dimensions measured by an assessment center and a behavior description interview. *Journal of Applied Psychology, 88,* 476–489.

Lustig, M. W., & Koester, J. (1999). *Intercultural competence: Interpersonal communication across cultures* (3rd ed.). New York: Addison-Wesley Longman.

Marsh, H. W. (1996). Positive and negative global self-esteem: A substantively meaningful distinction or artifacts? *Journal of Personality and Social Psychology, 70,* 810–819.

Mayer, J. D., & Salovey, P. (1993). The intelligence of emotional intelligence. *Intelligence, 17,* 433–442.

Mendenhall, M., & Oddou, G. (1985). The dimensions of expatriate acculturation: A review. *Academy of Management Review, 10,* 39–47.

Murdock, G. P. (1987). *Outline of cultural materials* (5th rev. ed.). New Haven, CT: HRAF Press.

Nisbett, R. (2003). *The geography of thought: How Asians and Westerners think different . . . and why.* New York: Free Press.

O'Neil, H. E., & Abedi, J. (1996). Reliability and validity of a state metacognitive inventory: Potential for alternative assessment. *Journal of Educational Research, 89,* 234–245.

Ones, D. S., & Viswesvaran, C. (1997). Personality determinants in the prediction of aspects of expatriate job success. In D. M. Sauder & Z. Aycan (Eds.), *New approaches to employee management, Volume 4: Expatriate management: Theory and research,* 63–92. Greenwich, CT: JAI Press.

Paige, R. M. (2004). Instrumentation in intercultural training. In D. Landis, J. M. Bennett, & M. J. Bennett (Eds.), *Handbook of intercultural training* (3rd ed., pp. 85–128). Thousand Oaks, CA: Sage.

Paige, R. M., & Martin, J. N. (1996). Ethics in intercultural training. In D. Landis & R. S. Bhagat (Eds.), *Handbook of intercultural training* (2nd ed., pp. 35–60). Thousand Oaks, CA: Sage.

Pintrich, P. R., & DeGroot, E. V. (1990). Motivational and self-regulated learning components of classroom academic performance. *Journal of Educational Psychology, 82,* 33–40.

Salovey, P., & Mayer, J. D. (1990). Emotional intelligence. *Imagination, Cognition and Personality, 9,* 185–211.

Schmitt, N. W., & Stults, D. M. (1985). Factors defined by negatively keyed items: The results of careless respondents? *Applied Psychological Measurement, 9*(4), 367–373.

Schutte, N. S., Malouff, J. M., Hall, L. E., Haggerty, D. J., Cooper, J. T., Golden, C. J., & Dornheim, L. (1998). Development and validation of a measure of emotional intelligence. *Personality and Individual Differences, 25,* 167–177.

Scollon, R., & Scollon, S. W. (1995). *Intercultural communication.* Oxford, UK: Blackwell.

Shaffer, M. A., Harrison, D. A., Gregersen, H., Black, J. S., & Ferzandi, L. A. (2006). You can take it with you: Individual differences and expatriate effectiveness. *Journal of Applied Psychology, 91,* 109–125.

Spreitzer, G. M., McCall, M. W., & Mahoney, J. D. (1997). Early identification of international executives. *Journal of Applied Psychology, 82,* 6–29.

Sternberg, J. R. (1986). A framework for understanding conceptions of intelligence. In R. J. Sternberg & D. J. Detterman (Eds.),

What is intelligences? Contemporary viewpoints on its nature and definition (pp. 3–15). Norwood, NJ: Ablex.

Sternberg, R. J. (1988). *The triarchic mind: A new theory of human intelligence.* New York: Viking.

Sternberg, R. J. (Ed.). (2000). *Handbook of intelligence.* New York: Cambridge University Press.

Sternberg, R. J., & Detterman, D. J. (Eds.). (1986). *What is intelligence? Contemporary viewpoints on its nature and definition.* Norwood, NJ: Ablex.

Takeuchi, R., Tesluk, P. E., Yun, S., & Lepak, D. P. (2005). An integrative view of international experiences. *Academy of Management Journal, 48,* 85–100.

Takeuchi, R., Yun, S., & Tesluk, P. E. (2002). An examination of crossover and spillover effects of spouse and expatriate adjustment on expatriate outcomes. *Journal of Applied Psychology, 87,* 655–666.

Ting-Toomey, S. (1999). *Communicating across cultures.* New York: Guilford Press.

Triandis, H. C. (1994). *Culture and social behavior.* New York: McGraw Hill.

Tsui, A. S., & Gutek, B. (1999). *Demographic differences in organizations: Current research and future directions.* New York: Lexington Books/Macmillan.

Tung, R. (1988). *The new expatriates.* Cambridge, MA: Ballinger.

Vandenberg, R. J., & Lance, C. E. (2000). A review and synthesis of the measurement invariance literature: Suggestions, practices, and recommendations for organizational research. *Organization Research Methods, 3*(1), 4–69.

Van Dyne, L., & Ang, S. (2006). Getting more than you expect: Global leader initiative to span structural holes and reputational effectiveness. In W. H. Mobley & E. W. Weldon (Eds.), *Advances in global leadership* (Vol. 4, pp. 101–122). New York: JAI Press.

Ward, C., & Kennedy, A. (1999). The measurement of sociocultural adaptation. *International Journal of Intercultural Relations, 23,* 659–677.

Williams, K., & O'Reilly, C. (1998). The complexity of diversity: A review of forty years of research. In L. L. Cummings & B. M. Staw (Eds.), *Research in organizational behavior* (Vol. 20, pp. 77–140). Greenwich, CT: JAI Press.

Wiseman, R. L. (1995). *Intercultural communication theory.* Thousand Oaks, CA: Sage.

Wonderlic, E. F. (1999). *Wonderlic Personnel Test user's manual.* Libertyville, IL: Wonderlic, Inc.

INTERCULTURAL SENSITIVITY FOR GLOBAL MANAGERS

◆ Dharm P. S. Bhawuk
and Keith H. Sakuda

◆ *Initial Questions for Discussion*

INSTRUCTIONS

Please reflect on the following questions, fill out the intercultural sensitivity survey, and then read the chapter. Following these steps should help maximize your learning.

1. Why is it important for managers to be interculturally sensitive?

2. Reflect on your past experience and describe three incidents in which you acted sensitively in intercultural contexts.

3. Reflect on your past experience and describe three incidents in which you DID NOT act sensitively in intercultural contexts.

4. What are the situations in which you find it difficult to be interculturally sensitive? Why is it so? How can you change to be interculturally sensitive in these contexts?

5. Why is becoming interculturally sensitive a challenge?

6. If you had unlimited resources, how would you prepare yourself to become an interculturally sophisticated global manager?

7. With the limited resource that you have, how would you prepare yourself to become an interculturally sophisticated global manager?

Prior to globalization, most international business was conducted between countries that shared similar cultural perspectives. Transatlantic trade with Europe was the driver of U.S. foreign investment, and the majority of international commerce in Asia remained west of the Pacific. The demands of the global economy have forced the business community to look beyond the familiar to confront an expanding world of cultural differences. As a greater diversity of cultures has been added to the world of commerce, the cultural gap between the familiar and unfamiliar has grown. International business has evolved beyond trade between a handful of countries and nations to become a global phenomenon encompassing a world teeming with different cultures.

Too often only the visible manifestations of culture receive attention from managers, as if managing them were the essence of cross-cultural understanding. International business travelers often assume that by familiarizing themselves with the daily routines and activities of a culture, they can absorb enough cultural knowledge to achieve their companies' objectives in that country. However, culture and cultural differences manifest themselves in more than just surface-level activities. Visible facets of culture, such as language, music, and food, also capture differences in core values and beliefs that are not as apparent. These internal, or deep-level, differences drive peoples' behaviors in all cultures. Recognizing and managing cultural differences is not enough for international success. One must learn to understand, respect, and appreciate both surface- and deep-level cultural differences to develop the sensitivity needed for global success.

Intercultural sensitivity has long been recognized as a necessary skill for effective intercultural relations (Bhawuk, 1989; Bhawuk & Brislin, 1992; Cushner, 1989). We begin by presenting an incident that we believe exemplifies the highest level of intercultural sensitivity one can acquire. We use this incident to illustrate the key elements of intercultural sensitivity. Then aspects of intercultural sensitivity in the three domains of cognition, affect, and behavior are discussed, and we suggest how individuals can apply them in their daily and professional lives by following a four-step process. Finally, an intercultural sensitivity scale (Bhawuk, 1989; Bhawuk & Brislin, 1992) is provided to help readers explore their own intercultural sensitivity.

It is sincerely hoped that this chapter will motivate readers to further explore intercultural sensitivity. Unlike many concepts taught to business managers, intercultural sensitivity is not solely concerned with organizational performance and assessment. Rather, it seeks to expand beyond business toward all human relations. Its reward is not just international success but self-development leading to compassionate humanism and appreciation for culture's complexities.

◆ A Benchmark for Intercultural Sensitivity

Gangadhar Shastri was an Indian scholar visiting England, and during his sojourn he was invited to tea at the home of a genteel woman. The two discussed the usual pleasantries as Gangadhar described his first few days in England. Tea was served in a beautiful porcelain cup and saucer, and Gangadhar, ever the gracious guest, complimented his host on the exquisite tea set. Then, with elegant grace, he poured tea from his cup into the saucer, inhaled the aroma gently, and quietly savored his Earl Grey. It was, he told his host, the finest tea he had ever enjoyed.

As Gangadhar sipped tea from his saucer, the British lady responded by mirroring his actions. She poured tea into her saucer and enjoyed her Earl Grey in a similar fashion. The hostess and the guest had a pleasant conversation and exchange of ideas. The hostess was delighted that she had invited Gangadhar for tea and learned much from him about Indian culture, philosophy, and way of life. Gangadhar was grateful to the hostess for her generous hospitality and fine tea. They parted with a promise to meet again to continue their discussion. Both the hostess and the guest were happy with their interaction and that the purpose of their meeting was fulfilled.

Gangadhar's behavior, by Western standards, would easily qualify as odd, amusing, or perhaps even rude. If placed in a similar circumstance, most could probably refrain from giggling, but some would be unable to contain a reflexive facial expression of surprise or even disapproval. Most would simply attempt to carry on, sipping tea from their cups and hoping that Gangadhar would eventually recognize proper tea behavior. Of course, the boldest might even admonish the man for such brutish behavior in the presence of such a refined lady. Regardless of our personal response, it is fairly safe to assume that his peculiar tea drinking manners would be noticed.

Instructing Gangadhar on proper tea etiquette could be a sensitive matter. From his perspective, a lesson on a subject as fundamentally basic as drinking tea could become demeaning. Directly correcting him could lead to an uncomfortable confrontation, while more indirect communication could get lost in nonverbal translation. From the British lady's perspective, watching Gangadhar slurp from the saucer could be an affront to generations of her tea drinking heritage. Most likely Gangadhar's actions would not be interpreted as intentionally offensive, but at a minimum, it would be construed as odd.

Instead, what transpired was a perfect act of intercultural sensitivity, which led to a moment of intercultural harmony. The British lady quickly recognized that Gangadhar's cultural script, or culturally appropriate sequence, of drinking tea was different. Instead of relaying her shock or discontent, she seamlessly altered her behavior to maintain interpersonal harmony. Had she responded differently, she risked embarrassing her guest and disrupting the grace of the moment. Eventually it might be wise to inform Gangadhar of the British tea etiquette, but such lessons could wait till a later time.

It is amazing how a world of cultural differences can emerge from a simple act such as drinking tea. The gap between the cultural practices of sipping from a cup or saucer may seem irrelevant to some but may hold tremendous importance to others. In this situation, the British lady managed to bridge the difference in a respectful manner that flawlessly graced an imperfect moment. Her definition of acceptable drinking manners stretched to accommodate her partner, but like a piece of elastic snapping back into place, it would not render any permanent change in her habits. It was simply a sincere and authentic display of sensitivity for the Indian man. For both Gangadhar and the British lady, the afternoon became part of a journey of personal growth greater than drinking tea. Together, both aware and unaware, they successfully navigated the complexities of cultural difference.

◆ Three Domains and the Four-Step Process of Intercultural Sensitivity

Intercultural sensitivity, unlike many other attempts to gauge intercultural competence, involves the three active domains of learning: cognition, affect, and behavior. Cognition involves recognizing cultural differences and is the first step of intercultural sensitivity. Those with the lowest level of cognitive intercultural sensitivity mindlessly cruise through their intercultural encounters oblivious to cultural differences. Their expectations and interpretations of the world are grounded in a "cultural baseline" comprising the conditioned values and beliefs gained during socialization in their own culture. Differences between themselves and their intercultural counterparts are often attributed to individual personality differences not cultural differences.

Those with high levels of cognitive intercultural sensitivity are able to ascertain the subtle nuances of cultures by looking beyond superficial differences toward differences based on cultural values and beliefs. They recognize that their own cultural baseline may not be sufficient to properly explain intercultural behavior, so they attempt to attribute differences through the cultural perspective of their intercultural counterparts. Recognition of a cultural difference becomes the trigger point for analyzing the world through the cultural baseline of the other person.

Intercultural sensitivity also involves positive affective, or emotional, responses to intercultural differences. Many people express an interest in experiencing other cultures or a desire to expand their cultural existence through international exchanges, but their interest often wanes when confronted with the realities of intercultural adversity. In contrast, interculturally sensitive individuals persist in their interest despite the setbacks and misunderstandings that are inevitable in intercultural encounters. Part of their tenacity includes an emotional component that perceives cultural differences from a positive perspective. Those with low intercultural sensitivity instinctively recoil from cultural differences that challenge their core values and beliefs, while those with high intercultural sensitivity refrain from judgment and seek to learn more about the cultural differences.

Many examples of the affective domain can be found in cultural cuisines. For many Americans, horses symbolize graceful power, beauty, and the prairie frontier, so they may recoil in shock if presented with raw horsemeat as a dinner appetizer. However, in many cultures horsemeat is a delicacy reserved for distinguished guests and special occasions. For local hosts who serve such a dish, their American guests' emotional reaction may be perceived as an affront to their hospitality. A more interculturally sensitive response would be to suppress any signs of shock, show appreciation for the gesture represented by the dish, inquire about the cultural significance of horsemeat, and continue the meal in a pleasant manner. It is okay to decline to eat, but it is inappropriate to show shock or horror at the meal. Even worse, it would be interculturally insensitive to berate the host for barbarically slaughtering horses.

After cognitive recognition and affective acceptance of a cultural difference, one must still be able to formulate a culturally appropriate response. In monocultural settings the mind interprets the world through a three-step process. Step 1 involves scanning the environment to gather information from one's immediate surroundings. In this stage the mind is interested in maximizing the flow of sensory inputs into the brain. Only the simplest cognitive processes are active in deciphering the flow of information into awareness of social phenomena. In Step 2, the mind compares the information collected in Step 1 against its innate operating norms, or cultural baseline, and actions, words, and behaviors are evaluated against its normal expectations of people and the world. Based on these expectations, which are grounded in past experiences and culture, the mind deciphers and interprets the environment to make sense of the situation. In Step 3, the final step, the mind builds on Step 2 to process a set of appropriate strategies for interacting with the environment. From this set of strategies, one will be selected and performed as a situation-appropriate response, which constitutes Step 3. This process is captured in Figure 19.1. These three steps are derived from cybernetics and are referred to as single-loop learning in management literature (Argyris & Schon, 1978; Morgan, 1997).

Intercultural settings are much more complicated because the mind must process an additional cognitive step. Properly responding to an unfamiliar intercultural situation demands a second learned cognitive subcomponent to Step 2. After information about a cultural difference is gathered in Step 1 and processed in Step 2, interculturally sensitive people proactively critique the validity of their perceived information. They recognize that their lack of experience with the other culture may be obscuring their understanding of the situation. To compensate for their inexperience with the other culture, they reassess the actions and behaviors of others through the lens of their respective culture. However, since their cultural baseline is inadequate in deciphering cultural differences, an interculturally sensitive person supplements his or her innate operating norms by attempting to adopt the operating norms of the other culture. From this dual set of operating

Figure 19.1   Intercultural Sensitivity as a Process of Cultural Learning

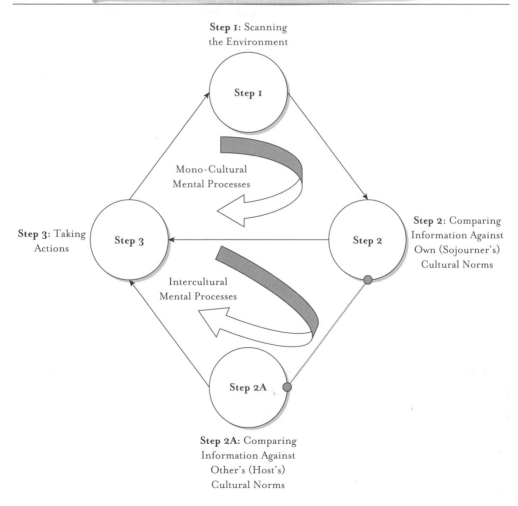

norms, he or she moves to Step 3 and attempts to bridge cultural differences by producing a culturally sensitive set of appropriate interacting strategies. One of these strategies will be selected and performed as a situation-appropriate response. This is captured in the second loop shown in Figure 19.1, which includes Step 2A. The additional step adds a second loop and is referred to as double-loop learning (Argyris & Schon, 1978; Morgan, 1997). We posit that intercultural sensitivity entails double-loop learning and is thus much more complex than monocultural settings. We also hope that managers will find this approach useful since they have to manage change all the time and may find the application of an organizational learning model to intercultural sensitivity interesting and useful.

Let's examine how somebody from the United States may interpret a smile in Thailand. Most people in the United States not only view a smile as a friendly gesture and as a sign of happiness but also may assume that it is so universally. Thus, unfamiliar with the Thai culture, a visitor from the United States may naturally respond to a smiling Thai person with a gesture of friendliness. An interculturally sensitive person may initially assume a smile as friendly, but by questioning their initial interpretations, they may catch subtle clues that may suggest that the smile might not indicate friendliness. Awareness of this possible interpretation may lead the sojourner to formulate a different set of culturally appropriate responses than a person with no intercultural sensitivity.

The performance of culturally appropriate behaviors is the third domain of intercultural sensitivity. After selecting a response from one's set of appropriate strategies, the interculturally sensitive person must be able to carry out the response in a manner that is accepted by the local culture. This behavioral domain of intercultural sensitivity is crucial because one's performance is readily visible and transmits signals to others. Cognitive and affective domains occur in the mind, but behavior is open to public review. Sometimes a poor performance of the right behavior may be more inappropriate than a good performance of the wrong behavior. In some situations, such as bowing, behavioral intercultural sensitivity is measured by the effectiveness in which one can mirror the nuances of the cultural behavior. In other situations, such as the horsemeat example, the challenge may simply be a matter of doing what needs to be done.

Intercultural sensitivity is more than just the ability to psychologically switch into the mindset of one's intercultural partner. It is also the ability to switch quickly and seamlessly back to one's home culture. A person who lives in another country for 3 years is likely to become competent in the local culture, but that does not mean that he or she is interculturally sensitive. An expatriate who has "gone native" becomes so immersed in the new culture that he or she abandons the home culture in favor of the native cultural baseline. While such a person may feel interculturally competent, his or her inability to switch back to the home culture makes him or her incapable of navigating cultural differences. Change and adaptability compose the core of intercultural competence, but it is flexibility and elasticity to return to one's home culture that marks the true essence of intercultural sensitivity.

◆ Measuring Intercultural Sensitivity

The Intercultural Sensitivity Inventory (ICSI) (see Form 19.1, pages 262–264) determines whether a person can successfully modify his or her behavior in a culturally appropriate manner when moving from one culture to another. Those who can perform such alterations demonstrate greater intercultural sensitivity and are believed to have greater potential for successful overseas assignments. Based on the theory of individualism and collectivism, one of the core foundations of cross-cultural psychology, the ICSI has been validated in conjunction with intercultural experts at the East-West Center using a sample (n = 93) of international subjects.

The theory of individualism and collectivism is used in the ICSI as a means for distilling cultural differences into more readily understandable categories. Creating an instrument that fully captures the nuances of every possible pairing of intercultural interactions would be an ambitious yet extremely impractical project, so cultural theory is used to organize and account for cultural variation. The theory of individualism and collectivism (Hofstede, 2001; Triandis, 1995) is one of the most widely accepted theories in cross-cultural studies. It suggests that people in a culture either conceive themselves as individuals or as interconnected members of a larger collective based on extended family or kinship relationships. Research has determined that American culture is strongly individualistic, implying that children are raised to view themselves as singular entities responsible to themselves and their immediate families. Most Asian, African, and Latin American cultures are considered strongly collectivist, implying that children are raised to view themselves as members of larger interconnected social networks. By using the theory of individualism and collectivism, the ICSI can be expanded to a greater combination of cultures.

The ICSI is administered by asking respondents to react to a set of intercultural situations. By using scenario-based assessments, it is possible to determine if people naturally (a) identify differences between culturally expected behaviors, (b) empathize with members of other cultures, and (c) are willing to modify their behaviors to match a culturally appropriate response. Unlike most existing instruments, which measure potential for intercultural success based on personality factors, this instrument moves beyond cognitive abilities to involve affective and behavior dimensions. In the ICSI, the willingness of respondents to modify behaviors and beliefs, both current and future, is weighed against past intercultural experiences to measure intercultural sensitivity.

The ICSI consists of three sections. The first section, referred to as the US section, requires respondents to answer 16 items by imagining that they were living and working in the United States. In the second section, called the JPN section, people are required to respond to the same set of 16 items while imagining that they are living and working in Japan. The United States and Japan were chosen because the United States ranks as one of the most individualistic countries, while Japan ranks as one of the most collectivist countries. Both countries are also key contributors to international affairs and business. Although it is likely that many respondents will not have experienced living and working in both the United States and Japan, even those with a low level of intercultural sensitivity should recognize a degree of cultural difference between these countries.

The third section, referred to as the Flex/Open section, consists of items to measure flexibility and open-mindedness. Research has consistently shown that these two personality traits help facilitate intercultural success, and those who demonstrate them are believed to encounter less stress during intercultural experiences. Flexibility and open-mindedness are believed to enhance intercultural sensitivity by helping individuals recognize cultural differences as unthreatening and by encouraging them to perform unfamiliar cultural behaviors.

Form 19.1

Intercultural Sensitivity Inventory

There is no right or wrong answer. Please follow the instructions carefully.

PART ONE

IMAGINE YOU ARE LIVING IN THE U.S. AND YOU WANT TO DEVELOP YOUR CAREER IN THE UNITED STATES. INDICATE YOUR RESPONSE TO THE FOLLOWING STATEMENTS ON THE SEVEN-POINT SCALE OF "STRONGLY DISAGREE" TO "STRONGLY AGREE."

1	2	3	4	5	6	7
Strongly Disagree			Neutral			Strongly Agree

1) _____ When I disagree with a group, I would allow a conflict in the group to remain, rather than change my own stance on important issues.

2) _____ I would offer my seat in a bus to my supervisor.

3) _____ I prefer to be direct and forthright when dealing with people with whom I work.

4) _____ I enjoy developing long-term relationships among the people with whom I work.

5) _____ I am very modest when talking about my own accomplishments.

6) _____ When I give gifts to people whose cooperation I need in my work, I feel I am indulging in questionable behavior.

7) _____ If I want a subordinate to perform a task, I tell the person that my superiors want me to get that task done.

8) _____ I prefer to give opinions that will help people save face rather than give a statement of the truth.

9) _____ I say no directly when I have to.

10) _____ I define the other person's status by paying attention to name, gender, age, and other demographic attributes.

11) _____ To increase sales I would announce that the individual salesperson with the highest sales would be given the "Distinguished Salesperson" award.

12) _____ I enjoy being emotionally close to the people with whom I work.

13) _____ It is important to develop a network of people in my community who can help me out when I have tasks to accomplish.

14) _____ I enjoy feeling that I am looked upon as equal in worth to my superiors.

15) _____ I have respect for the authority figures with whom I interact.

16) _____ If I want a person to perform a certain task I try to show how the task will benefit others in the person's group.

PART TWO

IMAGINE YOU ARE LIVING IN JAPAN AND YOU WANT TO DEVELOP YOUR CAREER IN JAPAN. INDICATE YOUR RESPONSE TO THE FOLLOWING STATEMENTS ON THE SEVEN-POINT SCALE OF "STRONGLY DISAGREE" TO "STRONGLY AGREE."

I	2	3	4	5	6	7
Strongly Disagree			Neutral			Strongly Agree

1) _____ When I disagree with a group, I would allow a conflict in the group to remain, rather than change my own stance on important issues.

2) _____ I would offer my seat in a bus to my supervisor.

3) _____ I prefer to be direct and forthright when dealing with people with whom I work.

4) _____ I enjoy developing long-term relationships among the people with whom I work.

5) _____ I am very modest when talking about my own accomplishments.

6) _____ When I give gifts to people whose cooperation I need in my work, I feel I am indulging in questionable behavior.

7) _____ If I want a subordinate to perform a task, I tell the person that my superiors want me to get that task done.

8) _____ I prefer to give opinions that will help people save face rather than give a statement of the truth.

9) _____ I say no directly when I have to.

10) _____ I define the other person's status by paying attention to name, gender, age, and other demographic attributes.

11) _____ To increase sales I would announce that the individual salesperson with the highest sales would be given the "Distinguished Salesperson" award.

12) _____ I enjoy being emotionally close to the people with whom I work.

13) _____ It is important to develop a network of people in my community who can help me out when I have tasks to accomplish.

14) _____ I enjoy feeling that I am looked upon as equal in worth to my superiors.

15) _____ I have respect for the authority figures with whom I interact.

16) _____ If I want a person to perform a certain task I try to show how the task will benefit others in the person's group.

(Continued)

Form 19.1 (Continued)

PART THREE

INDICATE YOUR RESPONSE TO THE FOLLOWING STATEMENTS ON THE SEVEN-POINT SCALE OF "STRONGLY DISAGREE" TO "STRONGLY AGREE."

1	2	3	4	5	6	7
Strongly Disagree			Neutral			Strongly Agree

1) _____ When I am living abroad, I assess situations as quickly as I do when I am living in my own country.

2) _____ I get upset when I do not get a letter or call from my close friend(s) for more than a month, when I am living abroad.

3) _____ Given acceptable hygienic conditions, I would not mind if my children ate local food at school, when I am living in another country.

4) _____ I do not like to receive unannounced visitors at home.

5) _____ I do not like custom officers meddling with my baggage at the airport.

6) _____ We all have a right to hold different beliefs about God and religion.

7) _____ I do not like to meet foreigners.

8) _____ It is unusual for people to eat dogs.

9) _____ I decorate my home or office with artifacts from other countries.

10) _____ Culturally mixed marriages are wrong.

11) _____ A woman's place, truly, is at home.

12) _____ I would not allow my subordinate to promote his nephew if there is someone marginally better than him. The person who is better must be promoted at all costs.

13) _____ Chinese influence is threatening the national identity of many Asian countries.

14) _____ While living abroad I spend most of my personal time with people from my own country.

◆ *Scoring the ICSI*

While Section 3 is scored like most self-assessment instruments, the scoring of Sections 1 and 2 is different from standard procedures. The score for any one item is based on whether the behavior is appropriate in either an individualist or a collectivist society. An item related to individualistic behavior is expected to be scored high in the US section and low in the JPN section, while items related to collectivism are expected to be scored high in the JPN section and low in the US section. For the US section, individualism items (#1, #3, #6, #9, #11, #13, and #14) are scored normally, while collectivism items (#2, #4, #5, #7, #8, #10, #12, #15, and #16) are reverse scored. For the JPN section, scoring and reverse scoring are opposite. For example, when answering the item concerning being direct and forthright with people (#3), an interculturally sensitive person would recognize each culture requires a contrasting approach to directness and forthrightness. As a result, they would score the item high in the US section and low in the JPN section (reverse scored in JPN section). The total scores from both sections (score range: 32–224) should be divided by 32 to give an average composite score.

Section 3 is designed to measure flexibility and open-mindedness. Except for reverse-scored items (#3, #6, and #9), higher scores reflect lower levels of flexibility or open-mindedness. The Flex/Open section can be broken down into specific components. Flexibility indicates a willingness to engage in new behaviors and discuss challenging topics with local hosts. Section 3 items #1, #2, #4, #5, #12, #13, and #14 address flexibility. Open-mindedness indicates a general orientation toward dealing with issues that may cause cross-cultural stress. Section 3 items #3, #6, #7, #8, #9, #10, and #11 address open-mindedness.

Surprisingly, foreign language ability has not been shown to be related to intercultural sensitivity (Bhawuk & Brislin, 1992), indicating that language learning and sensitivity are different concepts. Fluency in the language of a country is an undeniable asset to international business, but it does not necessarily lead to greater sensitivity to cultural differences. There is a natural inclination to think that if people could speak more than one language, they would experience a greater frequency of social relationships with

those from other cultures and would establish deeper interpersonal relationships across cultures. However, in developing deeper interpersonal relationships, individuals encounter differences in personal values and beliefs that may have gone unnoticed in less intense relationships. These deep-level differences may strain personal relationships and lead to more arguments.

Studies of intercultural marriage (Romano, 1988) reveal a similar pattern, as greater intimacy leads to greater potency in conflicts. These problems challenge and negatively affect interpersonal relations across cultures. Intercultural sensitivity also involves aspects such as respect, graciousness, and enjoyment when interacting with those who are culturally different. This level of sensitivity may be different from the deep emotional interrelatedness that marks real friendships. Research on interactions between expatriates and their local hosts have consistently shown that initially amiable ties often erode as social pleasantries are overcome by more intense daily work responsibilities.

A very strong relationship exists between intercultural sensitivity and the number of ethnic foods a person has experienced. To enjoy foods from different cultures, one must be open-minded, flexible, and willing to try new things. Also, those who experience a wide variety of ethnic foods are likely to have taken personal initiative to arrange such experiences. It is possible that the number of ethnic foods tried may be related to environmental factors. For example, large cosmopolitan cities will have a greater selection of ethnic foods. Also, those who travel abroad extensively are more likely to experience the cuisines of foreign destinations. Individuals in such environments will naturally experience a greater number of intercultural encounters than those in more homogenous environments.

♦ Summary

It takes 3 or more years of cross-cultural experiences to become interculturally sophisticated (Bhawuk & Brislin, 1992), so multinational corporations should consider posting first-time expatriates to countries that are not critical to their operations. As expatriates develop their intercultural sensitivity, they may be sent on more critical postings and may assume more responsibilities. Factoring in such experiences when selecting candidates for overseas assignments, while considering the technical requirements of each job, is likely to lead to greater chances for success.

It is also important to recognize that intercultural sensitivity is a skill that needs to be cultivated by individuals and their organizations. The ICSI is not intended to be a screening tool for hiring or firing; rather, it is best used as an assessment device to assist in intercultural training and to track a person's skill development over time. Successful international organizations, or organizations that desire to increase their international presence, need to make a commitment to train their members for intercultural encounters. Assessment through the ICSI should be just the first step in preparing an organization's human resources for overseas assignments. Additional resources should be commitment by both the organization and the individual to enhance and develop intercultural sensitivity.

By stimulating the three domains of learning, cognition, affect, and behavior, intercultural sensitivity moves beyond traditional means of preparing global leaders. It is impossible to train or prepare international business professionals for the full range of cultural diversity in the global marketplace, so the focus must change from learning about cultures to learning how to learn about cultures. Only then can one be prepared for transnational business beyond political borders.

The development of intercultural competence through intercultural sensitivity can best be summarized by an analogy to bridges. Cultural differences exist as gaps between cultures. Some gaps, such as differences in fundamental values and beliefs, are insurmountable without a bridge of intercultural sensitivity. Building the bridge can be done from one's own cultural baseline, but it is faster and wiser for the bridge to be built from the opposite shores to meet halfway. Traffic on the bridge should flow both ways, allowing travelers the opportunity to quickly and easily return to their own side. Last, while a bridge serves the immediate function of traversing a gap, the bridge itself is not the essence of the journey. Building a bridge is hard work, but it merely grants access to the opposite shore. Once across, it remains the individual's responsibility to seize the opportunities of an increasingly international world.

The ICSI aims to help people cultivate their own intercultural sensitivity. It is not intended to label or define a fixed destination, categorize individuals as sensitive or insensitive, or to evaluate prospective talent. Instead, it measures how much one has achieved in their pursuit of intercultural competence. Unlike business skills or professional tools that seek to make one more marketable or functional, it is about personal growth and intrapersonal development. Intercultural sensitivity has no finite goal and no measurable point of excellence. It is simply an endless pursuit of a lifelong voyage of personal development.

♦ References

Argyris, C., & Schon, D. A. (1978). *Organizational learning: A theory of action perspective.* Reading, MA: Addison-Wesley.

Bhawuk, D. P. S. (1989). *Measurement of cross-cultural sensitivity developed by living abroad.* Unpublished master's thesis, University of Hawai'i at Manoa.

Bhawuk, D. P. S., & Brislin, R. W. (1992). The measurement of intercultural sensitivity using the concepts of individualism and collectivism. *International Journal of Intercultural Relations, 16,* 413–436.

Cushner, K. (1989). Assessing the impact of a culture-general assimilator. *International Journal of Intercultural Relations, 13,* 125–146.

Hofstede, G. (2001). *Culture's consequence: Comparing values, behaviors, institutions, and organizations across nations* (2nd ed.). Thousand Oaks, CA: Sage.

Morgan, G. (1997). *Images of organization.* Thousand Oaks, CA: Sage.

Romano, D. (1988). *Intercultural marriage: Promises and pitfalls.* Yarmouth, ME: Intercultural Press.

Triandis, H. C. (1995). *Individualism and collectivism.* Boulder, CO: Westview Press.

PART V

CONCLUDING
THOUGHTS

20

ANALYZING ORGANIZATIONS THROUGH THE SPELIT METHODOLOGY

◆ June Schmieder-Ramirez
and Leo A. Mallette

O ne way of analyzing the evolving role of cultural diversity in companies is to evaluate specific intercultural drivers in the context of how they intersect with other aspects of the organization. The previous section detailed specific assessments that measure inter-cultural competence and cross-cultural adaptability. An alternative method of measuring or evaluating intercultural relations within an organization may be to analyze the intercultural environment in comparison with various other environments that exist. Thus, we are introducing the SPELIT analysis methodology, which is a framework for students and leaders to determine and formulate the answer to the organizational question, "What is?" It is used to systematically analyze the social, political, economic, legal, intercultural, and technological environments of an organization (Figure 20.1). SPELIT is a leadership tool that is intended for use by practitioners doing a market analysis or diagnosis prior to implementing transitions or benchmarking in antic-ipation of an intervention. This methodology aligns with established and more current theories and is a new environmental analysis tech-nique. This chapter will address what the SPELIT model is, provide examples, and define how the model can be used in organizations.

Figure 20.1   The Environments of the SPELIT Interdisciplinary Analysis Methodology

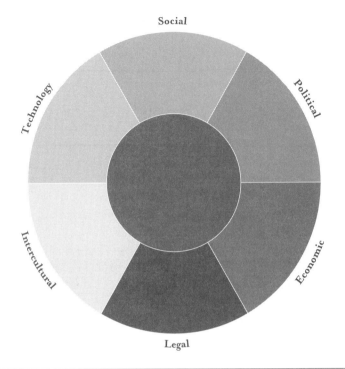

CASE STUDY

The following scenario (by Jacqueline B. Pritchett, in Schmieder-Ramirez & Mallette [2007, pp. 19–23]) reflects how the methodology can guide adult learners, business leaders, and educators in gaining a clear picture of where they are currently and how to systematically create solutions toward planned change for the future.

Samantha is a seasoned human resource (HR) recruiter at a nonprofit organization for young women's leadership development. She is a single mother of two wonderfully energetic children: Kate, 5 years old, and Sam, 10 years old. Recently, Samantha heard that there will be changes in upper management soon and that many employees will be newly assigned and/or laid off throughout the entire organization. Samantha has a great professional record. She has scored high on all her 360° reviews throughout her 7-year tenure at the organization. Although a superb and dedicated worker, Samantha has concerns about how the change in management will affect her. Therefore, Samantha schedules a conference with her manager, Ken, who has always supported Samantha and who has been with the organization for 12 years and completely understands what changes to expect from the new senior managers.

Samantha and Ken begin their conference by outlining initial concerns she may have about her recruiting position. Ken reassures Samantha that the new senior managers know of her excellent record and invaluable contribution to the department as well as to the entire organization. Samantha is relieved at the positive feedback; however, the new managers will require all senior HR recruiters to go back to school for further training, and Samantha hasn't been to school in 10 years and has two kids in school—not to mention a heavy load of responsibility at work.

Samantha has many different aspects of her personal and professional environments to think about to come to a suitable solution about whether to keep her current position as senior HR recruiter. If Samantha utilizes SPELIT to help guide her decision-making process, it could be described by Table 20.1. The methodology can clarify the present environment by bringing forth negative and positive effects, strengths and weakness, or pros and cons that will assist Samantha in making an informed decision about her career in her new organizational climate.

◆ Background

Many authors of change theories stipulate benchmarking or diagnosing the current condition as a first step in the change process (Christiansen, 1997; Cummings & Worley, 2005; Holcomb, 2001; Kaufman, 2000). This first step may be specific as in Holcomb's book *Asking the Right Questions*. Her first question is, "Where are we now?" (p. 17) This first step can also be implied in Lewin (1947), who has a three-phase process for implementing a transition. His first step, *unfreezing*, requires being able to show differences between the existing condition of the organization and to understand what is being unfrozen (and by how much). This requires knowledge of the organization in its current environment. This is a model that derives from the force-field analysis of Lewin and adds a new tool to the toolbox of organization analysis instruments.

There is a need to analyze the existing or potential environment in many aspects of an organization's life. People in organizations perform an environmental analysis when contemplating a merger, acquisition, or a reorganization. It is always beneficial for one to enter a new organizational structure by knowing what one is leaving. Mathematicians call the existing environment when they start to look at a problem the *initial conditions* or

initial state. SPELIT helps define the initial state of the organization.

There are many works compatible with the SPELIT analysis methodology. Most change theories have an early step dedicated to existing conditions or diagnosing the current environment. In the article "Environmental Scanning: Radar for Success," Albright (2004) defines environmental scanning as "a method for identifying, collecting, and translating information about external influences into useful plans and decisions" (p. 40). Similarly, Thompson, Strickland, and Gamble's (2005) book *Crafting and Executing Strategy* discusses analyzing a company's external environment, including the macroenvironment. Bolman and Deal (2003) identify four frames of reference: (1) structural, (2) human resource, (3) political, and (4) symbolic (p. 16). Each of these frames is a point of view and can be useful for evaluating the environment of an organization. A key step in the "general model of planned change" is the diagnosis of organizations, diagnosing groups within organizations, and diagnosing individuals prior to designing interventions. SPELIT performs environmental scanning or diagnosis of different frames or environments of an organization.

Lao-Tzu has stated, "Knowing others is intelligence; knowing yourself is true wisdom; mastering others is strength; mastering yourself is true power." Similarly, one

Table 20. 1   Utilizing the SPELIT Analysis Methodology in Decision Making

SPELIT MATRIX	Negative Effects	Positive Effects
Social Drivers	(–) Learning to become a graduate student and dealing with new college peers and professors' expectations (–) Less quality time with the children (–) Risking the loss of key relationships in HR department (–) Risking the loss of seniority status in organization and HR department. (–) Resistance from new upper management regarding reassignment	(+) Opportunity to learn more in the field of HR (+) Opportunity to keep seniority status (+) Building new relationships with new upper management in current position (+) Becoming a key player in the current change process (+) Opportunity to network at the graduate level with other like-minded HR professionals (+) Less responsibility in new assigned position, which may mean more free time with the children and time for other social endeavors
Political Drivers	(–) Resistance and backlash from HR staff and colleagues (–) Starting from the beginning politically in another department or organization	(+) Maintaining key relationships throughout the HR department and organization
Economic Drivers	(–) Cost for paying for graduate classes and support materials (–) Additional childcare costs (–) Possible pay reduction in new position	(+) Organization reimburses for half of the cost of attendance (+) Salary will remain the same in current position
Legal Drivers	(–) New contractual agreement with childcare agencies (–) Filing more complicated tax returns with student status (–) Confronting new HR legal policies and changing the current legality structure in the entire HR department	(+) Tax benefits from being a student (+) A more sophisticated legal structure for the HR department.
Intercultural Drivers	(–) Resistance in developing new diversity program implemented by new upper management (–) Time and effort implementing new diversity program throughout entire organization	(+) Opportunity to create a new culturally aware work environment (+) Opportunity to learn new information about cultures and organizational diversity
Technological Drivers	(–) Upgrades to personal computer equipment to handle coursework requirements (–) Possible costly upgrades to departmental equipment	(+) Opportunity to create more efficient methods of working

must know oneself as well as one's environment to achieve effectiveness in leadership. SPELIT can be used to assess one's own strengths and to assess the organization. In contrast to a SWOT (strengths, weaknesses, opportunities, and threats) analysis of an organization, SPELIT takes a laser beam and analyzes the organization. In a SWOT analysis, the assessment is fairly rote and does not take into consideration human strengths and weaknesses to the extent of SPELIT.

It should be noted that the SPELIT model differs from a SWOT analysis in that it specifically analyzes the intercultural component of an organization. This is the result of the increasing impact of globalization and the factors that influence organizations as a result of the global environment.

◆ Driving Forces From the Environment

An early political observer wrote that one could form an accurate opinion of a leader based on observing the people that support that leader (Machiavelli, 1515/1947). A variation of this could be that an organization can be evaluated by observing its environment. As stated earlier, this technique is intended for practitioners doing a market analysis or diagnosis prior to implementing transitions or interventions or as a method of benchmarking an organization. These six

environments constitute the six major facets (Figure 20.2) for the analysis of an organization.

There are different ways to describe perspectives about the environment. Bolman & Deal (2003, p. 19) listed terms such as *schemata* or *schema, representations, cognitive maps, paradigms, social categorization, implicit theories, mental models, root metaphors*, and *frames*. Christiansen (1997) used the terms *mapping* and *factors*. We use the term *environments* to describe the elements of the SPELIT analysis model. Many theorists systematically evaluate the environment of an organization, if for no other reason than to have a baseline to measure if change occurred after an intervention.

All the theories mentioned above include (or infer) a step for analysis or diagnosis of the current environment that *defines the way things are now*. SPELIT is used to systematically analyze the environment of an organization such as a family, a company such as General Mills or Boeing, a physical community such as a homeowners association, or a symbolic community such as a professional society—for example, the Society for Intercultural Education, Training, and Research. The first step in many change or transition theories is to quantify the existing environment of an organization. This can be analyzed using the six-environment SPELIT analysis tool. All six perspectives or environments may not be needed, and some of the topics can be eliminated or weighted differently. Figure 20.3 shows the six environments equally weighted.

Figure 20.2   The Six Major Environments of an Organization That Can Be Analyzed by SPELIT

Social   Political   Economic   Legal   Intercultural   Technology

Figure 20.3   Some SPELIT Environments May Not Be Needed, and Some of the Topics Can Be Eliminated or Weighted Differently

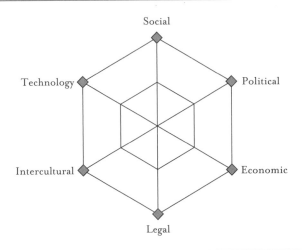

◆ *Practical Presentation Methods of the SPELIT Model*

The SPELIT model can be used in any learning situation where it is important to define the environment. In Clayton Christensen's (1997) analysis of the Butterfield Fabric Company, he notes that Butterfield had never formalized a strategy to meet the demands of change and was being bested by more focused competitors. The company used the "driving forces technique" outlined below and divided these forces into competitive, technological, demographic, and economic forces that constituted threats or created opportunities. If the company had used the SPELIT model in combination with the driving forces, then the implications for strategy would have become obvious to the entire employee workforce.

DRIVING FORCES FORMAT

There are many ways to present the results of a SPELIT analysis. One popular method is the driving forces format, in which individual driving forces are listed.

These driving forces can be bulleted in one box or itemized for each SPELIT topic. This scenario (by James R. DellaNeve, in Schmieder-Ramirez & Mallette [2007, p. 142]) describes how the interdisciplinary analysis methodology can be formatted to address driving forces in a research project to consider and analyze organizational change and learning factors for large information technology projects. The process consisted of using external references as a source of information for the analysis. A modified version of the model was used (Table 20.2), which included the Social/Political, Economic, and Legal/Ethical elements.

Examples of major intercultural driving forces are culture, gender, age, religious, management/union, and minority/majority differences. Minor intercultural driving forces could be differences between fans of the USC and UCLA football teams.

FORMAT FOR DESCRIBING POSITIVE AND NEGATIVE EFFECTS

Alternatively, opposing driving forces can be juxtaposed for each SPELIT topic where

Table 20.2	SPELIT Analysis Tool Showing the Conditions That Are Present in the Firm That the Information Technology Project Leader Will Need to Account For
Environment	*Analysis*
Social/Political	Defense-related business is highly regulated and dependent on congressional funding as well as geopolitical factors. Intelligence-related deficiencies uncovered in post-9/11 analysis require improved intelligence capabilities. U.S. defense strategy movement from large-scale engagements to smaller, more limited wars.
Economic	The commercial satellite market experienced a dramatic downturn in sales from the boom years in the 1990s to 2002 resulting in general industry overcapacity. Drastic cost-cutting measures lead to reductions in personnel, which resulted in disruptions and quality problems.
Legal/Ethical	The Federal Trade Commission ruled that the firm was in violation of the Clayton Act, which forces restrictions on the firm. In addition, the State Department ruled against the firm in disclosing satellite technology information to China, which resulted in further restrictions on the firm's handling of technical data as well as monitoring of ethics training and International Arms Regulations and Trafficking (ITAR) awareness.

drivers can be organized into strengths and weaknesses, pluses and minuses, pro and con, right and wrong, good and bad, or credits and debits. We chose the words *negative* and *positive* for the example in Table 20.1. The next example, by David Silverberg (in Schmieder-Ramirez & Mallette [2007]), describes how he came back from a trip to Africa determined to create an educational nonprofit organization to import teacher training and used the interdisciplinary analysis methodology (Table 20.3) to assess his progress.

My process included interviews with Tanzanian civilians, educators, and businesspeople as well as American nonprofits, fund raisers, educators, and students. The results were overwhelming: This was a needed service, but there would be significant administrative challenges. Social considerations included the ability to account for cultural differences, language differences, and varying educational needs, both between the United States and Tanzania as well as between different parts of Tanzania

itself. Political considerations involved the receptivity, efficacy, and reliability of regional and national governmental bodies as well as the desire to enlist passive or active support of the United States, United Nations, and UNESCO. Economic considerations focused mostly on how to fund this startup nonprofit through grants and gifts. Legal considerations emphasized the acquisition of appropriate nonprofit status, thereby clearing the way for donations. Intercultural considerations focused on the need to attune teacher training modules to real-world needs. Technological considerations included the development of a Web identity for the project (www.teachtheworld.org) as well as the prospect of Web-based instruction modules. (pp. 145–146)

Several real examples of the use of the SPELIT analysis and different formats that can be adapted to any particular organization were presented above. The user might consider weighting the criteria or arranging particularly difficult problems within an

Table 20.3 Table Format for SPELIT Analysis Tool Showing Negative and Positive Effects

SPELIT MATRIX	Negative Considerations	Positive Considerations
Social Drivers	(–) Challenge of attunement to local needs	(+) Need for teacher training
Political Drivers	(–) Acquisition of practical endorsement	(+) Philosophical support
Economic Drivers	(–) Time needed to garner funding	(+) Funding potential
Legal Drivers	(–) Learning curve regarding taxes	(+) Nonprofit status
Intercultural Drivers	(–) Reticence of American funding sources	(+) Attunement to local needs
Technology Drivers	(–) Technological divide between the United States and Tanzania	(+) Development of Web identity for project (www.teachtheworld.org)

environment in a Pareto diagram. The SPELIT analysis methodology lays out each step and involves the thinking of all those affected in any planned change.

◆ Conclusion

We showed how perceptive leaders can analyze environments in preparation for possible future action. In examining the intercultural drivers within an organization, SPELIT enables a researcher to evaluate such issues in comparison to the other environments that exist. Doing so will ensure that a thorough analysis is completed in preparation for leadership initiatives. Ultimately, the tool can be used to assist leaders in effectively incorporating change initiatives.

◆ Discussion Questions

1. Should the intercultural environment be considered as part of an environmental scan of every organization? Give examples of situations where it

would not be required or weighted less (or more) than other environments (see Figure 20.3).

2. Two people meet while on vacation in Hawaii. Song is from South Korea, Bill is from Massachusetts, and neither speaks very much of the other's language. They become engaged to be married. What would a SPELIT analysis of their new organization (their marriage) look like?

3. Make the assumption that Song is male in the above question. How does that change the legal and intercultural environments?

4. Is the ethical environment wholly contained within the intercultural environment? Why or why not?

5. Your company has a novel idea and a special team has been formed to develop a new product (hardware, software, service, or process) and bring it to market. Patent applications have not been submitted. Define the product, perform a SPELIT analysis of the special team's environment, and add the security environment to the analysis.

◆ References

Albright, K. S. (2004). Environmental scanning: Radar for success. *Information Management Journal, 38*(3), 38–45.

Bolman, L., & Deal, T. (2003). *Reframing organizations, artistry, choice, and leadership.* San Francisco: Jossey-Bass.

Christensen, C. M. (1997, November–December). Making strategy: Learning by doing. *Harvard Business Review, 75*(6), 3–12.

Cummings, T., & Worley, C. (2005). *Organization development & change* (8th ed.). Cincinnati, OH: South-Western.

Holcomb, E. (2001). *Asking the right questions: Techniques for collaboration and school change.* Thousand Oaks, CA: Corwin.

Kaufman, J. (2000). *Mega planning: Practical tools for organizational success.* Thousand Oaks, CA: Sage.

Lewin, K. (1947). Frontiers in group dynamics. *Human Relations, 1,* 5–41.

Machiavelli, N. (1947). *The prince* (T. G. Bergin, Trans.). New York: Appleton-Century-Crofts. (Original work published in 1515)

Schmieder-Ramirez, J., & Mallette, L. (2007). *The SPELIT power matrix: Untangling the organizational environment with the SPELIT leadership tool.* North Charleston, SC: BookSurge.

Thompson, A., Strickland, A., & Gamble, J. (2005). *Crafting and executing strategy: The quest for competitive advantage* (14th ed.). New York: McGraw-Hill.

CLOSING COMMENTARY

The Future of Intercultural
Competence in an Era of Globalization

◆ Marc Lamont Hill

As we near the end of the 21st century's first decade, organizational leaders face a unique set of circumstances. The expansion of global capitalism has changed the very structure and scope of many organizations, transforming them from local to transnational, monocultural to multicultural. In addition to the changing economic landscape, globalization has effected profound shifts in the way that culture is imagined, transmitted, and consumed within the global landscape. As the contributors to this fine volume have demonstrated, the ability to recognize and respond to this new cultural milieu stands as one of the primary challenges of organizational leaders. To respond to these conditions in ways that yield more safe, humane, and productive organizations, several challenges lay before us.

First, we must *acknowledge the intrinsic value of multiculturalism.* Although legal mandates and public invocations of "political correctness" create the conditions for compulsory forms of diversity, authentic intercultural competence hinges on a deeper investment in diversity, one that extends beyond the instrumental and the pragmatic. Simply put, organizational leaders must recognize the fundamental advantage of appealing to the vast range of histories, perspectives, traditions, and practices that inevitably constitute contemporary organizations. Absent this stance, organizational diversity and intercultural engagement become superficial and perfunctory responses to political exigency, rather than a signpost of deepening humanistic principles. Such principles are vital to the development of thicker forms of multiculturalism within and outside of organizational structures.

To fully appreciate the fundamental value of multiculturalism, organizational leaders must also *move beyond ethnocentric approaches* to intercultural competence. Although extreme forms of ethnocentrism such as White supremacy and anti-Semitism are becoming considerably less permissible (in overt fashion) within mainstream contexts—although no doubt coterminous with rising tides of xenophobia and sustained levels of sexism and homophobia—more subtle and nuanced forms of cultural chauvinism continue to countervail institutional attempts at increased intercultural competence.

As a result, forms of cultural difference are often recognized within institutions but nonetheless rendered marginal. A classic example of this is the schoolteacher who decides to teach students about Hanukkah and Ramadan in addition to Christmas. Rather than teaching students about these holidays on their own terms, the teacher devotes all of class time to explaining how these holidays are similar to and different than Christmas. In response to such well-meaning but narrow-minded approaches, organizational leaders must resist the urge to view the world strictly through the lens of their own experiences, values, and worldviews. Instead, we must begin to understand and engage various cultures on their own terms. Such a shift requires organizational leaders to reposition themselves at varying moments as both leaders and followers, teachers and students, mainstream and "other."

In our attempts to create institutional spaces that promote forms of pluralism without hierarchy, we are forced to *expand dominant conceptions of difference*. Although

the current body of theory and research on intercultural competence within organizations appropriately spotlights race, gender, and geographic origin as predicates of difference, this preoccupation has frequently undervalued or obscured other forms of difference. This focus is problematic for two reasons. First, it relies on static notions of identity that ignore the ways in which racialized, gendered, and national identities are constantly transformed within the contemporary global context. Also, by privileging the aforementioned forms of difference, we ignore the ways in which subject categories such as disability, age, and class position, to name a few, are linked to globally mediated cultural practices that must be taken seriously within organizational settings.

Finally, we must *consider the broader contexts* within which contemporary organizations and cultures are situated. As discussed throughout this brief essay, organizations, as well as the individuals that operate within them, are shaped by myriad social, cultural, political, and economic forces. Thus, our ability to engender more culturally diverse and responsive organizational environments rests on our understanding of these forces within the current historical moment. This requires organizational leaders to transform themselves from insulated technocrats to worldly cultural workers who take seriously the public and its problems. Furthermore, in practical terms, this means that organizational leaders must eschew one-size-fits-all models of leadership in favor of dynamic, engaged, and contextually specific approaches.

Although the future of organizational leadership and intercultural competence is by no means certain, this book provides us with tangible reasons to be encouraged. The insights offered throughout this text, and hopefully this essay, better enable us to craft spaces that positively respond to an increasingly multicultural world. From these spaces, we are able to radically transform both our organizations and the world.

INDEX

ABOUT THE EDITOR

 **Michael A. Moodian** (www.moodian
.com) is an assistant professor of
social science and sociology at
Chapman University. He holds an
EdD in organizational leadership
from Pepperdine University and an
MA in communications from
California State University,
Fullerton. His doctoral dissertation
research focused on the intercultural competence levels of
postgraduate students throughout various stages of study.

Dr. Moodian has contributed to numerous books, academic
journals, and other publications. *Contemporary Leadership and
Intercultural Competence* is his first edited volume. In addition to
his scholarly endeavors, Dr. Moodian serves as a consultant in a
variety of areas, including leadership development and communication skills. He is a certified administrator of the Intercultural
Development Inventory and Intercultural Conflict Style Inventory.
His memberships include the International Academy for
Intercultural Research and the World Affairs Council of Orange
County.

A native of Southern California, Dr. Moodian lives in the city
of Rancho Santa Margarita.

ABOUT THE CONTRIBUTORS

Soon Ang is Goh Tjoei Kok Chair Professor in Management at the Nanyang Business School, Nanyang Technological University, in Singapore. She is the executive director for the Center for Global Leadership and Cultural Intelligence. She specializes in cultural intelligence, global leadership, and outsourcing. She has published extensively in *Academy of Management Journal, Journal of Applied Psychology, Management Science, Information Systems Research, Journal of Organizational Behavior, MIS Quarterly, Organization Science,* and *Social Forces,* among others. She co-authored two pioneering books on cultural intelligence (Stanford University Press) and co-edited the *Handbook on Cultural Intelligence* (ME Sharpe). She won Best Paper awards at the Academy of Management, Association of Computing Machinery, and HICSS; Best Reviewer Award from *Human Relations*; and the Distinguished Leadership Award for International Alumni from the University of Minnesota. She is senior editor of *Information Systems Research,* associate editor of *Management Science* and *Decision Sciences,* and on editorial boards of other management and applied psychology journals. She holds a PhD from the University of Minnesota.

LaRay M. Barna, Associate Professor Emerita, is well-known as a pioneer in the field of intercultural communication. She developed one of the first courses in intercultural communication in 1967, which was used as a model for other universities. One of her articles, "Stumbling Blocks in Intercultural Communication," has appeared in many anthologies, which, along with her numerous presentations for professional conferences in the United States and seven foreign countries, helped initiate international interest in the field. Professor

Barna originated and directed the intercultural communication program at Portland State University, where she was a faculty member for 32 years, and served as assistant dean for the College of Arts and Letters from 1978 to 1980. Currently she is teaching in the intercultural relations program of the University of the Pacific and the Intercultural Communication Institute. She is also on the faculty of the Summer Institute for Intercultural Communication.

Janet M. Bennett is the executive director and co-founder of the Intercultural Communication Institute (ICI) and the ICI director of the master of arts in intercultural relations program. For 12 years, Dr. Bennett was the chair of the Liberal Arts Division at Marylhurst College, where she developed innovative academic programs for adult degree students. As a trainer and consultant, Dr. Bennett designs and conducts intercultural and diversity training for colleges and universities, corporations, social service agencies, healthcare organizations, and international aid agencies. She teaches in the training and development program at Portland State University and has published numerous articles on the subjects of intercultural training and adjustment processes. Most recently she co-edited the third edition of the *Handbook of Intercultural Training*.

Martin F. Bennett, a principal in Bennett Consulting, consults on the diversity implications of nationality, ethnicity, and spirituality in organizations. Founder of the Hong Kong Institute of Human Relations, co-founder of Bennett Associates, a former vice president in Cendant Intercultural, and a clergyman, Mr. Bennett has over 35 years' experience in the application of intercultural theory, training, consulting, and business and organization development for companies such as Nokia, Motorola, P&G, General Motors, and Capital One. He authored *Hong Kong Update* and co-authored *Global Diversity Desk Reference: Managing an International Workforce*. He is currently writing *God's in the Boardroom—Managing Religious and Spiritual Workplace Diversity*.

Dharm P. S. Bhawuk is a professor of management and culture and community psychology at the University of Hawaii at Manoa. He received his PhD in organizational behavior and human resource management from the University of Illinois at Urbana–Champaign and also holds an MBA from the University of Hawaii at Manoa and a degree in mechanical engineering from the Indian Institute of Technology, Kharagp ur. His research interests include cross-cultural training, intercultural sensitivity, diversity in the workplace, individualism and collectivism, culture and quality, culture and entrepreneurship, culture and creativity, indigenous psychology and management, and political behavior in the workplace. He has published several papers in the *Journal of Cross-Cultural Psychology, International Journal of Intercultural Relations, International Journal of Psychology, Cross-Cultural Research, Applied Psychology: Inter-national Review, Indian Psychological Review, Delhi Business Review,* and *Journal of Management*. Dr. Bhawuk is a citizen of Nepal.

Carlos E. Cortés is Professor Emeritus of history at the University of California, Riverside, and recipient of the American Society for Training and Development's National Multicultural Trainer of the Year Award. With Dr. Louise C. Wilkinson, he teaches an annual course, Developing and

Implementing a Multicultural Vision, at the Summer Institute for Intercultural Communication. The author of such books as *The Making—and Remaking—of a Multiculturalist*, he has facilitated multicultural vision development for corporations, educational institutions, government entities, communities, and the mass media. Dr. Cortés lectures throughout the world, serves on the faculties of the Harvard Institutes for Higher Education and the Federal Executive Institute, is creative/cultural advisor for Nickelodeon's *Dora the Explorer* and *Go, Diego, Go!*, co-authors a social studies textbook series, and performs his one-person autobiographical play, "A Conversation With Alana: One Boy's Multicultural Rite of Passage."

Michael S. Dukakis was the longest serving governor in the history of the Commonwealth of Massachusetts and the Democratic Party's nomination for president of the United States in 1988. In 1986, his colleagues in the National Governors Association voted him the most effective governor in the United States. He has served in the Massachusetts state legislature and on the board of directors for Amtrak. Today, Governor Dukakis is a Distinguished Professor of political science at Northeastern University and a visiting professor of public policy at UCLA. He holds a JD from the Harvard Law School.

Leslie A. Evans holds an EdD in organizational leadership and an MBA with a double emphasis in leading organizational change and global business from Pepperdine University. With over 20 years of leadership experience, Dr. Evans has consulted for both large corporations—including Amgen, BP, and First American Title—and small nonprofit

organizations. Dr. Evans has published many peer-reviewed articles and is a frequent presenter on such topics as global business strategy, cross-cultural capability, leadership, women in business, and ethics in the workplace. She was the co-recipient of the Best Theoretical Paper Award from the Western Business and Management Conference in 2004. Dr. Evans is currently an adjunct professor of management at California State University, Fullerton, coauthor of a book on writing, and an active board member of the Society of Educators and Scholars.

Charles M. Fischer is an associate professor at the University of California, San Francisco, teaching health services management. He is also the president of Profiles Pacific, Inc., a company that provides psychological assessments and training for organizations and businesses. For the past 25 years, Dr. Fischer has been a health services management and communications consultant. His company, Health Industry Management, specializes in program design and implementation plus strategic planning. Dr. Fischer has a BS in public health from UCLA, a DDS and MS in psychopharmacology and toxicology from the University of California, San Francisco, and a EdD in organizational leadership from Pepperdine University. Dr. Fischer has lived and traveled extensively throughout Europe, Asia, and Latin America and has been a cross-cultural business communication consultant.

Lee Gardenswartz, partner in Gardenswartz & Rowe, has been consulting with organizations regarding diversity since 1977, including Sempra Energy, Shell Oil, British Telecommunication, Kaiser Permanente, Boeing, Home Depot, Walt Disney World, Starbucks, Harvard Medical School, the National Oceanographic and Atmospheric Administration, and the Train-the-Trainer certificate program of SHRM. Dr. Gardenswartz and her partner, Dr. Anita Rowe, co-authored the award-winning *Managing Diversity: A Complete Desk Reference and Planning Guide* in addition to *The Managing Diversity Survival Guide, The Diversity Tool Kit, Divers e Teams at Work, Managing Diversity in Health Care, Managing Diversity in Health Care Manual*, and *The Global Diversity Desk Reference: Managing an International Workforce* with Patricia Digh and Martin Bennett. Their newest book, *Emotional Intelligence for Managing Results in a Diverse World: The Hard Truth About Soft Skills*, will be out in early 2009.

Sangeeta R. Gupta is a management and organizational development consultant and a specialist in diversity and intercultural consulting, facilitation, and training. Dr. Gupta is an expert in non-Western history and cultures and speaks several languages. She has conducted research and published extensively in the fields of gender, ethnicity, and immigrant studies. Dr. Gupta is the co-founder and a partner in Gupta Consulting Group. She is also the founder and director of the South Asian Women's Conference (SAWC), an interactive international forum for the discussion of issues relating to South Asian women globally. By combining her academic background and her business experience, Dr. Gupta works with her clients to improve their overall performance while targeting bottom-line results. She won UCLA's coveted Cary McWilliams Award for her honors thesis on the Asian Indian immigrant community. She is the editor of and a contributor to *Emerging Voices: South Asian American Women Redefine Self, Family, and Community.*

Mitchell R. Hammer has an international reputation as a social innovator, developing powerful ideas and innovative practices that improve people's lives by addressing some of our most difficult human problems. He is president of several organizations and in 2006 was awarded Professor Emeritus from the American University in Washington, DC. Dr. Hammer has developed (a) the Intercultural Conflict Style Inventory, (b) the Intercultural Development Inventory, and (c) the S.A.F.E. model of crisis negotiation for de-escalating hostage/crisis situations. His work focuses on intercultural communication, cross-cultural adaptation, cultural diversity, cultural considerations in crisis (e.g., hostage) negotiations, and conflict resolution. His new book, *Saving Lives* (2007), presents a comprehensive explanation of the innovative S.A.F.E. approach for resolving crisis situations. His earlier book, *Dynamic Processes of Crisis Negotiation* (1997), was honored with the Outstanding Book Award in 1998 by the International Association of Conflict Management. In 1992, Dr. Hammer was given the Senior Interculturalist Award of Achievement by the Society of Intercultural Education, Training, and Research. He holds a PhD from the University of Minnesota.

Md Mahbubul Haque is a third-year doctoral student in organizational leadership at the Graduate School of Education and Psychology at Pepperdine University. Mr. Haque has more than 8 years of work experience in financial, technical, and management industries, including with HSBC and ANZ Grindlays Bank, two leading financial services organizations. Mr. Haque holds a master's degree in public administration. In addition, he earned a master's degree in business administration (MBA) from Maastricht School of Management, Netherlands, and a master's degree in business technologies (MBT) from Marymount University and Virginia Commonwealth University. He has presented and published in several refereed conferences, including the fourth Hawaii International Conference, the International Academy of Business and Public Administration Disciplines (IABPAD) Conference, Society of Educators and Scholars (SES) Conference, International Academy of Business and Economics (IABE) Conference, and OD Network Conference.

Marc Lamont Hill is assistant professor of urban education and American studies and affiliated assistant professor of anthropology at Temple University. His primary research examines the relationships between neoliberal globalization, pedagogy, and youth identities. His work has appeared in numerous books, journals, and anthologies. He is the co-editor of *Media Learning and Sites of Possibility* and the author of the forthcoming books *Beats, Rhymes and Classroom Life: Hip-Hop, Pedagogy, and Youth Identities* and *You Ain't Heard It From Me: The Politics of Other People's Business in Hip-Hop's Public Sphere.*

L. Hyatt is an associate professor in the organizational leadership doctoral program at the University of La Verne. She earned an MBA and a doctorate degree at Pepperdine University with research leading to the development of a model for the new paradigm of sustainable leaders. Her other scholarly endeavors include writing numerous articles, presenting at conferences, serving as associate managing editor for a peer-reviewed journal and on several editorial boards, and authoring two books for McGraw-Hill. Her research interests include leadership, learning and change, and the powerful climates created by our convergent stories as individuals, organizations, and communities.

Christine Koh is assistant professor at Nanyang Technological University. Her research interests include cultural intelligence, cross-cultural issues in managing foreign talent, and outsourcing management. Her papers have been published in *Group and Organization Management, Management and Organization Review, Information Systems Research, MIS Quarterly, Journal of IT Cases and Applications,* and *Journal of Global IT Management.* She is the director of technology and psychometrics at the Center for Leadership and Cultural Intelligence. Dr. Koh earned her PhD from Nanyang Technological University.

Dan Landis is an affiliate professor of psychology at the University of Hawaii at Hilo. He holds a similar appointment at the Manoa campus of the same university. Previously he was professor of psychology, director of the Center for Applied Research and Evaluation, and dean of the Liberal Arts College at the University of Mississippi. He is the editor of all three editions of *The Handbook of Intercultural Training* (1983, 1996, and 2004) and author and co-author of over 120 books, chapters, and articles in referred publications. He is also the founding and continuing editor of the *International Journal of Intercultural Relations* and the founding president of the International Academy for Intercultural Research, which, in 2007, honored him with a Lifetime Achievement Award.

Leo A. Mallette is an engineering manager, has worked in the aerospace industry since 1974, and is currently managing high-technology subcontracts for space systems. He received his MSE degree from the University of Central Florida and MBA and EdD degrees from Pepperdine University. He has co-authored the book *The SPELIT Power Matrix* (BookSurge, 2007) and is co-authoring the book *Writing for Conferences* (expected 2008). He has published over 50 conference and journal articles on atomic frequency standards, satellite systems, optical detectors, circuits, genealogy, and organizational leadership. Dr. Mallette is a senior member of the Institute of Electrical and Electronics Engineers, a member of the advisory board for the Precise Time and Time Interval Conference, and a board member of the Society of Educators and Scholars. He and his wife, Kathy, live in Irvine and Rancho Mirage, California. He enjoys playing with his granddaughters, gardening projects, traveling, and writing.

Vijayan P. Munusamy is a senior research associate at the Center for Creative Leadership-Asia. He started his career as a mechanical engineer in Malaysia and made his first "cultural crossing" after observing that many of the conflicts in the workplace and in society are due to cultural misunderstandings. Recognizing cultural education as a powerful tool to advance multicultural understanding, he founded a social enterprise to promote the sharing of children's stories from different cultures in Malaysia, Singapore, and Indonesia. The lessons he learned from this experience and the need to develop theoretical, methodological, and experiential expertise in cross-cultural issues led him to make his second "cultural crossing" toward becoming a Degree Fellow at the East-West Center, Hawaii, and a PhD student at the University of Hawaii. His recent publication includes a book chapter in

Teaching About Asian Pacific Islanders: Effective Activities, Strategies, and Assignments for Classrooms and Workshops (AltaMira Press, 2006). An Asian Development Bank Scholar and a recipient of the Wall Street Journal Student Achievement Award, he has been recognized numerous times for his achievement in academic, work, and community service.

Jennifer Palthe is associate professor of management at Western Michigan University and a PhD and MLIR graduate from Michigan State University. She teaches graduate MBA classes in managing change and international human resource management, and undergraduate classes in multinational management and organization development at the Haworth College of Business. Prior to commencing her doctoral studies, Dr. Palthe was senior change management consultant for Andersen Consulting (now Accenture). She has change management consulting experience in Europe, Africa, and the United States. Dr. Palthe has publications in the *International Journal of Intercultural Relations, Journal of Asia Business Studies, California Management Review, Competitiveness Review, Health Care Manager, Consulting Psychology Journal,* and *Journal of Organizational Change Management.* She is also co-author of the book *Knowledge-Driven Work: Unexpected Lessons From Japanese and U.S. Work Practices* (Oxford University Press, 1998) and author of "Globally Managing Human Resources" in *Managing Human Resources in the 21st Century* (South-Western Publishing, 1999).

Sheila J. Ramsey is founder of the Crestone Institute, a Washington, DC–based consulting firm, specializing in the interface between global leadership, change, and creativity. Since 1975, she has worked with global leaders in the corporate sector, in government, and in international development. Clients have included the U.S. Department of State, the United Nations World Food Program and UNAIDS, the Smithsonian Institution, the U.S. Peace Corps, the National Albanian American Council, the Environmental Protection Agency, Jakarta International School, Intel Corporation, Apple Computer–Japan, Proctor and Gamble, Fuji–Xerox, Kodak–Japan, and Motorola–Japan. She is a visual artist, worked for several years as a professional photographer, and has studied as a potter's apprentice in Japan. Dr. Ramsey is one of the three founding directors of Personal Leadership Seminars, LLC, and a co-author of the book *Making a World of Difference. Personal Leadership: A Methodology of Two Principles and Six Practices.*

Anita Rowe is a partner in Gardenswartz & Rowe, where, for over 20 years, she has helped a variety of regional and national clients manage change, handle stress, build productive and cohesive work teams, and create intercultural understanding and harmony in the workplace. She has helped clients such as Cox Communications, Starbucks, Shell, Boeing, and the IRS manage diversity and create cultures of inclusion. Together with Dr. Lee Gardenswartz, Dr. Rowe has co-authored a series of books on diversity themes, including *Managing Diversity: A Complete Desk Reference and Planning Guide, The Managing Diversity Survival Guide, The Diversity Tool Kit*, and *Diverse Teams at Work.* She is also co-author of *The Global Diversity Desk Reference: Managing an International Workforce.* Their newest book, *Emotional Intelligence for Managing Results in a Diverse World: The Hard Truth About Soft Skills*, will be out in early 2009.

Keith H. Sakuda is a third-year doctoral student in international management specializing in international organization and strategy at the Shilder College of Business at the University of Hawaii at Manoa. His research interests include cross-cultural training and intercultural group dynamics. Prior to joining the PhD program, he was an instructor at TransPacific Hawaii College. He currently holds a master's degree in business administration (MBA) from the University of Hawaii and a graduate certificate from Fujitsu's Japan America Institute of Management Science (JAIMS). His work experience includes education, education administration, and business in both the United States and Japan. He is also involved in several social entrepreneurial ventures. Mr. Sakuda has presented at conferences for the Academy of Management (AOM) and the Society for the Advancement of Management (SAM).

Barbara F. Schaetti is one of the three founding directors of Personal Leadership Seminars, LLC, principal consultant of Transition Dynamics, and a member of the faculty of the Intercultural Communication Institute. She has a particular passion for helping people access their core creative capacity and works worldwide to help her clients engage the transformative potential inherent in a life lived across cultures. Dr. Schaetti consults primarily in the academic and civil sectors and with organizations working in the field of international cooperation. She specializes in multicultural team development, building inclusive communities, providing expatriate family services, and developing a personal practice to leverage intercultural competence. Dr. Schaetti is lead author of the book *Making a World of Difference. Personal Leadership: A Methodology of Two Principles and Six Practices.* She holds dual nationality (U.S. and Swiss), was raised in ten countries on five continents, and is currently based in Seattle, Washington.

June Schmieder-Ramirez is the interim associate dean of education of the Education

Division of the Graduate School of Education and Psychology of Pepperdine University. She has co-authored numerous texts on school finance, personnel, and law. She has published over 50 articles on leadership, environmental forces, and the political nature of governance groups. She received her MBA from Saint Mary's College of California and her PhD from Stanford University in administration and policy analysis. She and her husband, Ramon, live in Quail Valley, California.

Douglas Stuart, director of intercultural training at IOR Global Services, is an authority on intercultural competency tools. He is licensed to deliver and interpret a variety of intercultural assessment instruments, and he writes and presents on the selection and use of such tools at conferences and seminars, including the 2005 SHRM Global Forum in Chicago and a 2007 white paper for the SHRM Web site. Dr. Stuart also develops intercultural competence curricula, delivers workshops, and conducts executive coaching. Prior to joining IOR, he served as an educational specialist in Andersen Worldwide's Performance Consulting group. His background in international education includes faculty positions at Chicago's Illinois Institute of Technology (IIT) and the Economics Institute, University of Colorado, as well as training management positions in Algeria, the U.A.E., and Vietnam and teaching positions in Germany and Egypt. Dr. Stuart earned his PhD in linguistics at IIT and pursued postgraduate studies at the Illinois School of Professional Psychology and Naropa University, earning a certification in client-centered therapy from the Chicago Counseling and Psychotherapy Center.

John C. Tobin is an adjunct professor who holds dual appointments at Pepperdine University's Graduate School of Education and Psychology and the Graziadio School of Business and Management. He has lectured on negotiation theory, business law, and bankruptcy law. He has been involved with legal research and writing at Pepperdine University, the College of Law at the University of La Verne, and the University of California, Riverside, since 1995. When not at the lectern, Professor Tobin is a United States administrative law judge, as well as a colonel in the judge advocate general's corps of the U.S. Army Reserve. He is a 1981 graduate of the Judge Advocate General's School at the University of Virginia and a 1980 Juris Doctor graduate of School of Law of the University of Louisville. He completed the certification in mediation at the Straus Institute at Pepperdine University in 1995 and was designated a mediator for the bankruptcy courts of the Central District of California and the Superior Court, Riverside County, California, in 1996.

Fons Trompenaars is CEO of Trompenaars Hampden-Turner Consulting, an innovative center of excellence on intercultural management. He is the world's foremost authority on cross-cultural management and is author of many books and related articles, including the bestseller *Riding the Waves of Culture, Understanding Cultural Diversity in Business* (McGraw-Hill, 1993). This book sold over 120,000 copies and was translated into French, German, Dutch, Kore an, Danish, Turkish, Chinese, Hungarian, and Portuguese. Dr. Trompenaars is the co-author of *Seven Cultures of Capitalism* (Doubleday, 1993) and *Mastering the Infinite Game* with Dr. Charles Hampden-Turner. In 1999, he was listed as a top five management consultant alongside Michael Porter, Tom Peters, and Edward de Bono, in a leading business magazine.

Linn Van Dyne, professor at Michigan State University, has two primary research programs: proactive employee behaviors and cultural intelligence. She is associate editor of

Organizational Behavior and Human Decision Processes and is on the editorial boards of *Academy of Management Journal, Journal of Applied Psychology, Academy of Management Perspectives, Personnel Psychology, Human Relations, Management and Organization Review,* and *Journal of Organizational Behavior.* She is a fellow in the Society of Organizational Behavior and has published in the *Academy of Management Journal, Academy of Management Review, Journal of Applied Psychology, Organizational Behavior and Human Decision Processes, Research in Personnel and Human Resources Management, Research in Organizational Behavior,* and other outlets. Prior to becoming an academic, she was director of worldwide human resources and director of compensation, benefits, and international personnel for a global manufacturing firm. Dr. Van Dyne earned her PhD at the University of Minnesota.

Gordon C. Watanabe is Professor Emeritus of education and former special assistant to the president for intercultural relations at Whitworth University in Spokane, Washington. Dr. Watanabe is one of the three founding directors of Personal Leadership Seminars, LLC, and is co-author of the book *Making a World of Difference. Personal Leadership: A Methodology of Two Principles and Six Practices.* Dr. Watanabe is a member of the faculty of the Intercultural Communication Institute and consults with corporate, community, and educational institutions. His work focus, whether in the United States, Europe, or Asia, is on the critical role of deep self-understanding in intercultural teaching, learning, and team building. Informed by his background as a third-generation Japanese American, and his years counseling international and American ethnic-minority

students, Dr. Watanabe is often called upon to be a cultural bridge between individuals and groups. He is a qualified facilitator of the Intercultural Development Inventory.

Louise C. Wilkinson is on the faculty of the Summer Institute for Intercultural Communication where she teaches Developing and Implementing a Multicultural Vision with Dr. Carlos Cortés. She brings to it her work empowering teams and leaders to develop themselves and the cultures around them. She helps design programs to increase inclusion in the corporate environment and develops and facilitates sessions on diversity, leadership, globalization, mentoring, privilege, and intercultural competence for the Boeing Company and other companies and universities. She has shared her vision as a global multicultural leader at national and international conferences. An award-winning video writer/producer/director, her doctoral research focused on the use of film for intercultural education. This research is summarized in her recent article, "A Developmental Approach to Uses of Moving Pictures in Intercultural Education," in the *International Journal of Intercultural Relations.* Dr. Wilkinson uses her certificate in developmental coaching to support intercultural development.

Peter Woolliams is Emeritus Professor of international management at Anglia Ruskin University (UK) and is an owner/partner in Trompenaars Hampden-Turner Consulting with Dr. Fons Trompenaars. He has collaborated and published jointly with Dr. Trompenaars for over 18 years. Dr. Woolliams is co-author of *Business Across Cultures* (available in several languages) and *Marketing Across Cultures* (Capstone-Wiley, 2004).